Creative teaching

in the

elementary school

ABRAHAM SHUMSKY
Brooklyn College

Creative teaching

in the

elementary school

APPLETON-CENTURY-CROFTS

Educational Division

New York   MEREDITH CORPORATION   69552

PRINTED IN THE UNITED STATES OF AMERICA
390–80625–0

Rabban Johanan Ben Zakkai had . . . disciples . . .
He used to list their outstanding virtues:
Rabbi Eliezer Ben Hyrcanus—a plastered cistern which
loses not a drop . . .
Rabbi Eleazar Ben Arak—Ever flowing stream . . .
Plastered cistern: He never forgot a thing he learned.
Ever flowing stream: In his learning he could even add
to the traditions he received and knew how to deduce one
thing from another . . .
He used to say: If all the sages of Israel were in one
scale of the balance and Eliezer Ben Hyrcanus were in the
other scale, he would outweigh them all . . .
Abba Saul says in his name: If all the sages of Israel
were in one scale of the balance, and even if Rabbi Eliezer
Ben Hyrcanus were with them, and Rabbi Eleazar were in
the other scale, he would outweigh them all. (*The Living
Talmud*, selected and translated by Judah Goldin.)

To my children *Alina* and *Ron*
With the hope that
The Ever Flowing Stream
Will be your teacher.

PREFACE

This book draws on my experience in teaching courses in elementary education and educational research, and in supervising student teachers. I want to express my appreciation to the many teachers who shared with me their understanding of, and attitudes toward, the "repetitive-creative conflict."

Whereas the responsibility for the development of the position stressed in this work is mine, the project was supported by the Department of Education of Brooklyn College by provisions for "release time."

Dr. Rose Mukerji contributed the chapter entitled "Art: Repetitive or Creative?" Dr. Don Watkins conducted the study of teachers' perceptions of the ethnic child. Dr. Helen Wood helped by suggesting her observations on science teaching. Dr. Walter Murray shared in the study of the impact of discipline on the novice teacher.

And finally, I would like to acknowledge the help of my wife, Dr. Adaia Shumsky, who shared in the development of this project from its inception. In many respects she is a coauthor.

A.S.

CONTENTS

II. THE SUBJECT AREAS: AN APPROACH

CONTENTS

III. THE EDUCATING AGENTS

Introduction

1

The teacher and educational change

There is ferment in the field of education today. More than ever before the goals, structure, and content of education are under reexamination. Powerful pressure and interest groups are attempting to mold the educational system in their own image. Giant foundations are supporting research, demonstrations, and action programs which attempt to affect, and in some cases even dictate, change. There is a sense of urgency in the air as the technological era of automation calls for an educational revolution.

Even a cursory survey of popular and professional magazines reveals the pervasiveness of educational innovations, such as educational television, programmed instruction, teaching machines, team teaching, nongraded classrooms, and language laboratories. Leading television networks discovered the great appeal of the education issue to the public, and in the prime evening hours began to transmit programs on such problems as the teaching of reading, the dropouts, and the gifted.

The training of teachers has developed into a national issue. Alternate programs stressing the role of liberal arts and professional education are in severe competition. The Conant report entitled "The Education of American Teachers," which questions the present state certification system and calls for more autonomy for the individual university, is a best-selling book.[C2]

College professors in the academic disciplines, who traditionally viewed public education and teacher training as primarily the domain of education professors, rediscovered education and began to take a lead in teacher training. They join in committees and workshops to establish new goals, revise courses of study, and rewrite textbooks. Experimental programs are in progress, introducing such innovations as set theory and the teaching of foreign languages in the elementary school, or the lowering of the age for beginning reading to kindergarten. The new slogans are: "quality," "upgrading of education," or "the pursuit of excellence."

 ⚡ Perhaps for the first time in its history is this nation united in the realization that education is the major avenue to national survival—that it may hold the key to leadership in the international arena, technological progress, adaptation to the severe social problems and to automation, or the resolution of the Negro revolution. Perhaps for the first time in the nation's history do the citizens of this country realize that education is their major guarantee for personal security and progress in the automation era.

THE TEACHER: THE MOST IMPORTANT EDUCATIONAL AGENT

It is difficult not to respect the great surge of interest in education, nor to admire the great scholars of the subject disciplines who are ready to redirect their basic orientation and ask: "how can my discipline be taught to toddlers?" It is difficult not to appreciate the dedication of the giant foundations and their attempt to develop programs for the gifted, or open higher horizons for the culturally deprived. It is difficult not to recognize the inventiveness of the school superintendents and their staffs in reorganizing century-old administrative policies.

However, with all this, one must question whether the position of one educational agent has been forgotten, or at least somewhat neglected? Perhaps in the turmoil and the rush to introduce or force educational change, led by the "giants" (scholars, foundations, publishers, superintendents), one tends to forget to examine the conceptions and attitudes of the most important educational agent—*the classroom teacher.*

The teacher's conception of the learning experiences which should operate in the school is the most important single factor which determines the direction and quality of the educational program. The improvement of education is more subtle than the revision of courses of study led by subject matter specialists. Real improvement calls for understanding of the teacher's conception of the learning experiences, examining and improving the teacher's relatedness to knowledge, his sense of realization and security in more creative ways of teaching. The teacher is the key to curriculum improvement.[M14]

The improvement of education is more than a sequence of additions, revisions, production of new materials, and new administrative organizations. An "additive" conception of change is too often ineffective unless based on a change in the conception of education in the *mind and the heart* of the classroom teacher.

Criticism of teachers, not atypical of sentiments commonly expressed by laymen, is voiced by an educational editor of a newspaper.

Why are teachers indifferent to educational television?
Why don't they use televised programs as they use books?
It is time to leave the horse and buggy era and join the automation age!

What this well-meaning editor fails to realize is the basic difference between the relatedness of teachers to a book and to a televised program. A teacher can choose the book he prefers to use, read it before the lesson, think about it, select the parts he wants to emphasize, and interpret or introduce variations. In other words, in using a book the teacher experiences a creative professional role!

In contrast, a televised program is not selected by the teacher. He too often views it for the first time together with his pupils, with no previous opportunity for reflection and preparation. The program in many cases relegates the teacher to the unfortunate role of a student teacher whose cooperating teacher says to him in the middle of the lesson: "Take over and continue my work, I have to see the principal." Many teachers resent the noncreative role of a technician allocated to them by television. They tend to resolve this conflict by perceiving television as a stopgap device and entertainment, which is a nonintegral part of the curriculum.

Many educational leaders run into difficulty in initiating change, not because of their lack of vision or sound programs, but rather because they fail to take into consideration the perceptions, feelings and attitudes of the classroom teacher. They plan primarily in terms of the *goals* of curriculum change, and do not take into account the intricate *process* of change.

Educational change cannot be brought by remote control, nor by administrative decree. What would happen if a principal came to a traditional school and demanded that teachers introduce committee work? In many cases teachers might comply formally by organizing committees, but might not change their teacher-centeredness in the guidance of children. They would be quicker to comply with the form of the change rather than with the spirit.[86]

Classroom teachers themselves too often tend to perceive the improvement of education as a sequence of additions, revisions, and production of new material. They do not realize that curriculum revisions without an understanding of the theoretical considerations and of the deeper meaning underlying them are of little value.

Within the past several decades the American educational system has gone through colorful eras. (Some disillusioned teachers call them "fads.") There was the what-do-you-want-to-do-and-talk-about-today period; the "self-expression" and let's-do-it-in-a-group era; and so on. Each of these approaches to educational change had *depth of value* which tended to be run into the ground as the result of the attempts of teachers to use them as formulas to cushion their teaching. Under pressure of the educational culture to "change and grow," some teachers learned the new phrases early and went through the motions in a literal fashion, without attempting to delve into the meaning of the suggested innovation; without developing conviction and insight.

There is an unfortunate dichotomy in education between theory and practice. We speak about the educational practitioner as distinct from the educational theorist. In teacher training institutions the courses are departmentalized into the theoretical and the practical. In the theoretical courses the tendency of many college professors is to get too far away from the realities of field situations. In practical courses the instructor, under pressure to teach "how to do it," may overlook the more far-reaching aspects of the classroom problems.

The result of a lack of integration between theory and practice is a tendency on the part of teachers to look for a gimmick, a prescription, or a rule of thumb as an answer to curricular problems. These are the teachers who (in the language of some illustrations) go through the motions of introducing committee work without changing their autocratic attitudes; teachers who claim to teach science by experimentation but in reality dictate the experiment to children step by step; teachers who shift from discrete subject matter to a core curriculum with the result that the only "progress" that can be observed is a change in the length of the session. In other words, these are teachers who change the external form rather than the content and the spirit.

I am not trying to portray a pessimistic picture, nor to label the classroom teacher as resistant to change. I am trying, rather, to develop the basis and the need for the discussion in this book. The improvement of education calls not only for setting of new goals, but also for a careful study of what is involved in the process of change—the conceptions and attitudes of the classroom teacher. Any attempt to initiate curriculum improvement should emphasize the exploration of three basic questions which face the teacher-learner: What is my understanding of the educational innovation? How do I feel about it? What are the behavioral adaptations called for by this innovation?

The purpose

It is this observation of the role of the personal experience of the teacher in the process of his learning to improve his work and adapt to curriculum change, and not the nature of the goals of education alone, which led to the writing of this book. The emphasis of this project is both on the stating of goals for improved teaching behavior and on analyzing the process of achieving these goals. More specifically, the purpose of this book is to both conceptualize the meaning of creativity as a teaching behavior, and examine carefully the factors which tend to block or facilitate the progress of the teacher toward this goal.

Within the last several years creativity became a subject of wide interdisciplinary interest. Attempts were made to suggest criteria for recognizing the process of creativity as seen in the social and natural sciences. In the broad area of education original contributions were made to the analysis of the meaning of creativity and its measurement by Guilford, Getzels, Torrance, and others.[G8, G3, T1] This book will not attempt to undertake further study of the creative child, nor of the creative adult—the Shakespeares, Newtons, or Einsteins. The interest is focused rather on the potential for creative teaching in the average teacher.

The theorist of education is opposed to that teaching which is a process of sheer acquisition of knowledge. He speaks about productive thinking, the stimulation of intellectual curiosity, and about creative thinking. A basic interest underlying this work is to contribute toward a better understanding of creativity as a way of teaching—as a teaching behavior.

As stressed earlier, however, the stating of goals and the descriptions of programs which facilitate creativity is not sufficient. There is need for a study which explores the meaning, the challenge, and the threat of creative teaching to teachers.

An intensive analysis of the meaning of one's own teaching behavior is a potentially rich experience. One book on the preparation of teachers suggests that[81:118]

. . . a major reason so many teachers are dissatisfied with themselves in their work is that their training did not illuminate the nature of their learning process and how this relates to and affects the learning process of their pupils . . . As a result, the teacher does tend to function as a *technician* who applies rules which are contradicted both by her own learning experiences and her pupils' unproductive learning.

This book aims at promoting the goal of helping the teacher engage in teaching as a creator and not merely as a technician. It focuses on the teacher's self-understanding as a learner and a teacher as he promotes the achievement of the goal of creative teaching.

The structure

The book is composed of three parts which attempt to examine sequentially three aspects of creative teaching: (1) The repetitive-creative conflict, (2) the meaning of repetitive and creative teaching in the main subject matter areas, (3) the impact of the major "educating agents" on the novice teacher in terms of the repetitive-creative conflict.

Part I describes a demonstration of three ways of teaching, ranging on a continuum from repetitive to creative behavior. The discussion attempts to (1) explain the rationale underlying these three "models," and to evaluate their role in elementary education, (2) understand the intellectual and emotional connotation of the repetitive-creative conflict to a group of novice teachers.

Part II further develops the concept of creative teaching. It goes into a systematic analysis of the major issues involved in teaching the various subject areas, and identifies the factors which promote either a repetitive or a creative program.

The position to be developed is that since at the present time the school's curriculum and the quality of the teacher's behavior is skewed in the repetitive direction, there is a need for an increased emphasis, both in teaching and in curriculum construction, on the creative orientation.

Part III examines the relationship of the teacher in training and the beginning teacher to the three "educational agents" most crucial in his education: (1) children, (2) the field practicum, and (3) the education department of his college. It stresses primarily the impact of these factors on the novice teacher himself in terms of his search for a more creative teaching behavior.

(1) Is it possible that the expectations of teachers and the way they perceive different types of children—the bright and the slow, the aggressive and the shy—affect their teaching behavior? What is the relationship between the problem of discipline (the problem foremost on beginning teachers' minds) and the conflict of repetitive-creative teaching?

(2) As reported by student teachers, the field practicum is the most valuable influence in their training. What are the experiences of student teachers in the various stages of the practicum—observation, assisting, and independent teaching? What is the impact of the most forceful model of teaching behavior—the cooperating teacher—on the novice? Does this model encourage primarily imitative or creative teaching behavior?

(3) The main function of the Education Department is to

train teachers. In some respects the role of this department differs from the function of most other college divisions. In contrast to the others, the success of the Education Department is determined not only by its ability to communicate concepts on the intellectual level, but also by its impact on the *operational* values of teachers. The intellectual and operational learning of values is not identical, with the latter being much more difficult to achieve. The question is: What is the impact of the Education Department on both the intellectual understanding and the teaching behavior of novice teachers? What are the processes of education which either promote or deter the novice's search for creativity as a way of teaching?

In an attempt to answer the question raised in *Part III*, data was collected by means of responses to incomplete sentences, interviews, logs written by beginning teachers, and observations.

The challenge

This book is an exploration into the dynamics of teaching, with emphasis on the search for creative teaching. The discussion is not eclectic in nature, but rather a statement of a position critical of the repetitively skewed curriculum. It promulgates movement toward creativity in teaching behavior.

As stated by Fischer, our era is characterized by the "revolution of rising expectations:" [P4:5]

Caught up in this new wave of the future, men and women who once had no other thought than to live out their tragic and depressed lives in quiet desperation, are now discovering that it is reasonable and possible to reach for self fulfillment and attain it."

The school is the most promising means of giving the masses of people what they want. Education all over the world is becoming a talisman of hope and the symbol of striving toward success.

To meet this striving for a better education, the too common tendency of the educational administrator is to resort to the "additive and quantitative" approach: more teachers, more services, more materials, an extended school day, an extended school week, a longer school year. Although these proposals merit serious consideration, the additive formula of "let's have more of the same" is quantitative rather than qualitative in nature. In practice, quantity cannot compensate for lack of quality.

The difficult problem is not of getting more teachers or extending the school day. The main issue is, rather, that of having better teachers and making better use of the present time allotment. The resoultion of the problem of cultural deprivation does not lie in merely increasing school services, but rather in raising the professional competencies of the present teachers in coping with the cultural and social disadvantages. The education for effective and productive thinking does not merely call for more hours at school, but rather movement from a repetitive toward a creative curriculum.

It is tempting and relatively easy to perceive curriculum progress as an act of an administrative decree of change.

The Great Brook school system inaugurated a televised education program.

The new principal announced that within one year his school is going to change from the traditional practice of group reading to the modern individualized approach.

Televised education, if not properly used, can become a device which has a numbing effect on both learner and teacher. Or individualized reading originally intended to offer intensive contact between a mentor and his pupil can also become merely an administrative device. Where the program may have been a setup to promote and examine the personal meaning of reading to the reader, in practice it may become another technique. Under the banner of individualizing, an "efficiency expert" is able to establish smooth working conditions and by this organizational pattern detach himself from the learner. "You are expected to work on your own; don't bother me."

One of the main needs underlying the planning of educational change is to be less preoccupied with quantitative, additive, and administrative solutions, and to focus more intensively on the *quality* of the teaching experience. It is the qualitative examination of the *teaching behavior* of the elementary school teacher, which is the center of discussion in this book.

1

The repetitive—creative conflict

2

Model A: The repetitive teacher

What would be the reactions of beginning teachers to a teaching behavior characterized by emphasis on recall, identification and specificity of facts? Would they recognize the teacher centeredness, controlling behavior, or lack of emphasis on productive thinking in this way of teaching? Or would they perceive this teaching orientation as democratic, stimulating, and creative? If the last question is answered in the affirmative, what are the factors responsible for the subversion of the good judgment of the novice teacher, causing him to confuse repetitive and controlling instruction with democratic teaching behavior?

To answer the above questions, a group of novice teachers were advised:

I am going to role-play a lesson illustrating a way of teaching. To avoid any value judgment on my part, I'll call this teaching behavior teacher A.

On the completion of the demonstration, please write your reactions to teacher A, emphasizing his characteristics, the way he would be expected to teach other subject areas, and the motivation underlying his teaching behavior.

The subject matter taught was a reading lesson based on a simple story taken from a second grade basal reader, *The New Friends and Neighbors*[21], Scott, Foresman & Company. The story is called "Long-Tail." It describes Dick, Jane, and Sally finding a baby squirrel and thinking that it is a long-tailed kitten.[G7]

The following is a brief summary of the role-playing of teacher *A*.

Motivation: A brief discussion of children's experiences with pets.

New Words: Puts the new words, such as *mewing, bigger,* and *long-tail,* on the blackboard. The class discusses the meaning and structure of the new words.

Objective: Announces the objective—reading "Long-Tail."

Reading and Discussion: A brief paragraph is orally read by a pupil. The teacher tests comprehension by asking questions emphasizing specificity: What did Dick hear? (Funny noise.) Where? (In the playhouse.) What did he open? (The door.) A second brief paragraph is read by another child and the testing of comprehension continues in the same pattern: What was the cat's color? How many kittens? Children take turns in reading aloud brief paragraphs. The teacher continues to test the comprehension of the specific and detailed facts. From time to time she emphasizes the spelling and structure of words.

Analysis of Picture: The teacher sensitizes the children to the detailed elements of the pictures: Who is in the picture? What does the boy wear? What does the girl wear?

Dramatization: Children are assigned roles. (Dick, Sally, Father, etc.) Each child reads his part from the text. The teacher pays special attention to correct pronunciation.

Seat Work: The teacher distributes mimeographed work and instructs the children to draw a line under the correct word:

Father saw Long-Tail (during, before, after) dinner.

(Mother, Father, Dick) said: "Well, well."

Dick found (a squirrel, a kitten, a duck).

Draw a picture of Puff and the kittens.

In their reaction to the role-playing, the observers felt that the demonstration was a portrayal of a teacher familiar to them in their experience as pupils and as student teachers. They differed, however, in their evaluation of teacher *A*, assessing the behavior as varying from democratic and modern to authoritarian and traditional. A substantial majority of the group had a positive evaluation of model *A*.

THE IMPARTER OF KNOWLEDGE

Both positive and negative responses viewed teacher *A* as an imparter of knowledge. They differed, however, in their evaluation of the quality of this behavior.

The positive group

As perceived by the "positive group," model A is a portrayal of a teacher who stresses knowledge. To them this is the fundamental and most important function of the teacher. Teacher *A* is seen as one who is thorough, comprehensive, and systematic. He covers the subject matter of the story, as well as the rest of the course of study prescribed by the Board of Education. Whether teaching reading, arithmetic or science, he is going to pay attention to the facts, develop the basic skills, and establish a sound foundation for future education.

Bloom states in the *Taxonomy of Educational Objectives*[B6] that the most common educational objective in American education is the acquisition of "knowledge." For the taxonomy purposes, he defines "knowledge" mainly as remembering the idea or phenomenon in a form very close to the way in which it was originally encountered. Or to use Guilford's terminology,[G8] this type of objective emphasizes primarily the psychological processes of cognition and memory, as distinguished from a broader conception of knowledge which includes processes of convergent thinking, divergent thinking, and evaluation.

Those young teachers favorably inclined toward model *A* do not sense the narrowness of his conception of knowledge, but rather, perceive his behavior as one which promotes thinking, culture, and the necessary fundamentals of a sound education. For example:

Children are young. They have little experience. They know so little about the world. You have to give them facts and information. This is especially correct with regard to the children we new teachers work with—lower-class children. They come from deprived homes. Their parents do not tell them much. We have to start from the beginning to teach them about the world, so that they will know something.

Remember that the emphasis of teacher A on specific skills and facts is basic to all the other ends of education. The broader objectives of problem-solving and thinking cannot be carried on in a vacuum. The teaching of the specifics is a prerequisite to any other learning. You should have your groundwork before you are ready to spread your wings.

Model A is perceived as an energetic teacher who works relentlessly to sensitize his pupils to facts and information. He is dedicated to the promotion of the reverence for knowledge. The data collected in this study shows that this knowledge is justified not only because of its importance to children, but also because of the important emotional role it plays in the life of the teachers themselves.

Teacher A is me and my friends studying in your class. We grew up in middle-class families where it was so important to gather information and know things. I see how my older sister treats her children. She wants the young one to look at a book and to name the animals. "This is not a horse, this is a giraffe. Say *giraffe*." She wants the older one to watch the informative educational programs on television. The children watch a trip to the Treasury Department and then are asked questions: "Do you know what counterfeit money means?" "What do they call the police who track counterfeiters?" This type of information is important in my family.

I remember I took many sightseeing tours with my parents. They felt it was very important for my education. And when we would come home, my father would say: "Do you remember the number of bridges we passed? What were the names of the islands that we saw on the Hudson and on the East River?"

Level A of knowledge may often express the fundamental dynamics of a parent-child relationship. Many of the hopes, aspirations and sense of fulfillment of parents is expressed in their involvement with their child's learning. Much anxiety, guilt, and even sense of defeat is aroused when the child is slow or fails to learn. Subtle or even direct pressure is applied in order that the child will make progress in absorbing knowledge and in being *interested* in knowledge.

OK, tell me, what did you have at school today?
Nothing.
What do you mean nothing? Didn't you have a pretest in spelling?

Yes, here is the paper.
I see you had a mistake in spelling "piece." How do you spell it?
P-e-i-c-e.
No, here is a rule to remember: "*I* before *e* except after *c*."
For the middle-class child groping for knowledge, knowing

how to read and spell, learning the meaning of words, etc., has a definite emotional connotation. It must be seen as an integral part of the deepest possible matrix, namely reaching for parental approval.

In reacting to the demonstration of model *A*, many teachers spoke about the nature of knowledge emphasized in their own schooling and its resemblance to the knowledge communicated by teacher *A*. Their reactions reveal the tremendous weight which factual information played in their own education. It was the basic way by which they knew how to succeed at school. Much of their respect for model *A* can be explained in terms of this identification and sense of continuation. Some teachers feel that teacher *A* is an extension of their identity.

I belong to a group of people who were always successful in school. We knew the answers on the short-answer tests, or multiple-choice quizzes. We had status with our peers and our teachers. Many of us graduated with honors and were admitted to the college with very high grades in high school. May I put it this way; I believe this teacher *A* went to school together with us. She got the same education and had the same success. I guess most of us are going to teach like her.

The negative group

The negative reactions to model *A* criticized his conception of knowledge as narrow and limited. They questioned the intellectual level on which teacher *A* functioned.

I found it both dull and meaningless to stop and evaluate each short sentence. The questions were of a rote nature. How unexciting for young children this person would be, with his emphasis on repetition and mechanical questions. He provoked no thought in the minds of pupils.

He is interested in comprehension but this to him ends with noticing the specific elements and details in the story or the pictures. His questions require mere identification, rather than any thinking or creativity on the part of children. . . .

Teacher A does not sift the needed facts for the development of a generalization, or a basic idea. As one reaction puts it, "He makes his pupils slaves to the details." The assumption underlying the A way of teaching is that the mere summation of details will, by itself, create the total idea—the gestalt. Aware that a total idea is greater than the composite of its parts, this group suggested that pupils exposed to model A may master the detailed information but miss the basic message. They may learn the importance of memorization, but might fail to learn the importance of productive thinking.

Any appraisal of the quality of the educational process must start with the fundamental question of whether the intellectual development of children is facilitated or hindered by the teacher's behavior. With this question in mind, examine the following not atypical illustrations of classroom practices. The first is an assignment given to an average third grade.

The answers to these questions are on the blackboard. You must think and look carefully in order to find them.

1. Who were the first settlers in the "new land?"
2. What does their name mean?
3. Where did they first go before coming to America?
4. What boat did they come to America on?
5. What ocean did they cross?
6. Where was the very first place they settled?
7. Who was their leader?
8. Who were the Indians that made peace with them?
9. What did the Indians teach them to grow?
10. Who brought about the first Thanksgiving day?

All these questions can be answered with a one-word factual response. The mental process required is exclusively that of memory and identification. No opportunity is offered to explore, to put facts together, or to elaborate an idea. No attempt is made, for instance, to ask children to state the main problems with which the Pilgrims were faced.

Social studies, a discipline whose main function is to develop critical thinking and social awareness, has too often become methodology which merely attempts to cover subject matter and impart an aggregation of factual information. For instance, in studying the export-import balance of a given country the main emphasis often becomes the naming of the export items, instead of opening this study to the relationship between import and export, or its impact on the way the people make their living.

This narrow conception of knowledge, with its emphasis on specificity and recall, is a central and dominant feature of the reading comprehension test.

Two scientists "camped" for a week on the bottom of the sea. Their underwater home was a cabin shaped like a barrel. The shelter was anchored to the sea floor.

1. For how long did the scientists camp?
2. Where did the scientists "camp" for a week?
3. What kept the shelter from floating away?

To answer such questions, children do not have to think, to ask why, or to create a generalization. They were not asked to demonstrate *comprehension* by stating, for example, why the scientists were "camped" on the bottom of the sea, or why their shelter was anchored to the sea floor. They were asked only to *repeat*.

The common equation of comprehension with the identification of specific details does not characterize only the achievement test. It is rather a dominant feature of the total curriculum. The reader is urged to examine the climate of the classroom by raising questions like the following:

What is the nature of the verbal interchange between the teacher and the pupils? Do the teacher's questions elicit primarily recall type of responses or foster productive thinking?

In discussing subject matter, is the emphasis primarily on "covering" the content, or rather on the understanding of the major issues? To what extent are children encouraged to come forward with their own ideas or react to divergent questions? ("What do you think may happen because of the St. Lawrence Seaway?" "What do you think should be done?" Or, "How would you feel if you were there?").

In reading children's compositions, is the emphasis merely on the "correction" of the specifics of spelling mistakes, or does the teacher attempt to react to the main thoughts the writer wanted to convey?

To conclude, model A was developed as a "stereotype" to illustrate an extreme accentuation of specificity and recall. It is correct to suggest that very few teachers are as extreme as he is. However, it is also correct to observe that the "acts" of his teaching behavior play a too prevalent role in the present elementary school curriculum. The traditional conception of the teacher's role as being predominantly a purveyor of information and a checker of learned facts is a major deterrent to the intellectual development of children.[H5]

FRIENDLY OR CONTROLLING?

The positive reactions viewed model A as friendly, supportive, warm, nice and a rewarding teacher. The negative responses perceived him as controlling and constricting. Is teacher A friendly or controlling? The attempt to answer this question will lead us to an analysis of the meaning of *control*, a characteristic of teaching behavior seen by some observers[H12] as a dominant and destructive educational factor.

Positive reactions state:

Teacher A is not punitive. He is nice, friendly and rewarding. I remember his expressions: "How smart this class is today!" Or, "Oh, this class has all the answers."

The atmosphere was lots of fun. Children enjoyed answering the questions. You saw on their faces the satisfaction of giving the right answer . . . The teacher showed interest in what they had to say.

Teachers live in a culture which is other-directed. As stressed by Riesman,[R2] the concern is less with the *quality* of production than with smooth group relationships. What matters is not so much depth of learning but rather "participation" and external manifestations of satisfaction. When asked why they want to be teachers, the major answer was "I like children." As a group, they come from child-centered homes where parents always sacrificed and gave. As college students, they live in an educational culture which idealizes the child, his needs, and interests, and speaks more than on anything else about the dynamics of human relations. They live in an educational culture which believes that there are three levels of "nastiness"—nasty, very nasty, and authoritarian. Therefore, is it possible to call a seemingly friendly, praising, and smiling teacher by the terrible name "controlling and authoritarian?"

In the fairy tales there is a sharp polarization into "good" and "bad." It would have been easy to do the same with model A. It would have been possible to portray a teacher who is hostile and punitive. This path was not followed deliberately. On the contrary, every effort was made to present a teacher who moves through the motions of being friendly and "nice."

The equation of authoritarian and constricting with punitive and harsh is an extreme oversimplification of the problem. The majority of teachers are friendly rather than hostile. The overwhelming majority of their "acts" toward children are pleasant and supportive rather than punitive. Nevertheless, the majority of elementary school teachers tend to be at least somewhat overcontrolling in their teaching behavior.

The major means of *control* in the classroom is not the threat of punishment, but rather the way the teacher *structures* the learning process. Model A overstructures the learning process and therefore he is an overcontrolling teacher.

Observing model A, one of my colleagues had a picturesque reaction: "A mother hen controls the peeping of the chicks through her feathers." What are the elements in the behavior of teacher A which engender control? Again and again, teachers say:

In following teacher A's behavior, I know what to ask, I follow the text and I don't have to worry what will come next.

The following of the text means *structure*. It alleviates a major problem of the novice teacher—what to say, what to do, or where to go next. As new teachers say: "There is something to hang on to." The end result is security in following the text—the authority.

A second element which contributes to control and security is the *fixed answer problem-solving*. The problems teacher A asks have fixed answers. The exact answer to be regurgitated by the student can be found in the text. One has only to parrot back the text's words. For instance:

1. The first settlers in the "new land" were (the Pilgrims).
2. Before coming to America they went to (Holland).
3. The boat they came to America on was (the Mayflower).

Whether the child responds orally or in writing, it is very easy to control and direct this kind of learning behavior. Teaching becomes so routinized that hardly anything unexpected happens. The learner's responses are fixed and predetermined. The degree of routinization of learning is well illustrated by Dewey's story in which he asked a class "What would you find if you dug a hole in the earth?" Getting no response, he repeated the question with no results. The teacher chided Dewey, "You are asking the wrong questions." Turning to the class, she asked, "What is the state of the center of the earth?" The class replied in unison, "Igneous fusion."[B6]

A third element in teacher A's behavior which enhances the sense of control and security is the impression of *success*. So-called success is easy to achieve under teacher A's pattern of leadership. The easy questions which call for reproduction rather than production, mean quick response and almost complete "participation" on the part of children. Participation is equated with "interest;" if everyone participates, then everyone is interested.

Immediate and predetermined responses to narrow stimuli (questions) give the impression of quick and smooth movement from one question to another. The reason is simple. What can one say in response to the question: "Where did Dick see the cat?" The text says: "Dick saw the cat in the playhouse." There is not much that the learner can add to this point of information. The only thing to do is to progress to the next question: "How many kittens did the cat have?" Smooth progress from one point or part to another gives the illusion of success. And the feeling of success in turn enhances the sense of security and achievement which the teacher is craving for. He feels he is in complete *control*.

The reader may ask: "What is wrong with this control? Do you want children to run wild in the classroom? Do you advocate a theory of teaching behavior of the nature of 'children what do you want to do today?'"

These are real and down-to-earth questions. This book is not written from a child-centered point of view; it definitely believes that the teacher has to play a directive and even controlling function. It is a controlling behavior which is *constricting* that is criticized here, rather than the control itself. Young teachers who perceived the *A* model negatively wrote:

It is one-way communication . . . Preconceived ideas of what should be said or done.

She does not hear unless it is an answer to something she is posing. She stifles and blocks.

It is education for obedience, important in robot training. The predetermined response does not provide freedom for children to think and create. If you are exposed to this teacher, it affects your own sense of being a person.

The last sentence stresses that the *A* climate "affects your own sense of being a person." An attitude is conveyed by the overcontrolling teacher that the child himself lacks power and strength. The only thing the child can do is move when the teacher tells him how, where, and when to move. The pupil is not supposed to make a movement on his own. The following are some illustrations of *A*-oriented classroom practices which convey the attitude that the learner is powerless and little, and therefore must be directed on each step.

A second grade is discussing the safety problem in crossing the street.

Teacher: Let's play it. Who has something red? (A child raises her red pen.) O.K. Come and stand here. You are the red light. Who has something green? (A girl points to her scarf.) Very good, stand near the "red." You are . . . (The girl completes: "green light.") Now, who wants to be a person who crosses the street? (Children raise their hands with excitement.) Sue, you were very nice today, come and join the play. What are you? (Sue: "I'll try to cross the street.") Oh, I forgot—we need a truck. Who wants to be a truck? (Children raise their hands with excitement.) Come Harry, you will be the truck. (Takes a piece of chalk and makes a line.) What is this? (Looks playfully at the children and waits until everyone raises his hand. A child answers: "A street.") Yes, you are very smart today. Now, we are ready. Show red light! Show green light! Sue, quick, cross the street. Red light! Now, Harry the truck, it is your turn to pass.

The children are happy. The teacher is happy. Everyone is happy. They had "lots of fun," and what can be a greater achievement in our culture, which is fun-oriented? Despite the overt enjoyment, psychologically speaking, the example illustrates a process of diminution conducted with disarming sweetness. Without verbalizing it the child learns, as one of the negative reactions states, that: "Only what the teacher has in mind is important. I have no power to think on my own." If the teacher were harsh then the children could rebel, or at least hate. The *A* model is "nice and sweet." It is difficult to reject or resist her.

It is possible in trying to demonstrate the scene of crossing the street, to ask: "Children, how are we going to play it?" It is possible to appoint a small group to play and demonstrate the scene. An approach of this nature means that the learner has to mobilize his resources, think through the needs of the situation, and come out with a plan of his own.

The following is an illustration from the methodology of arithmetic, demonstrating the contention that the constricting behavior of the *A* model does not provide children with *freedom* to think. A first grade is studying numbers.

The teacher puts on the blackboard $1 + 4 =$. The children raise their hands. The teacher calls on a boy to go to the blackboard and write the answer. The boy looks for a piece of chalk and climbs on a chair to reach the correct spot. He finds it difficult to write with chalk, but finally he has it—number 5. The class waits patiently. The teacher puts on the blackboard $2 + 3 =$ and again a child writes 5. The same procedure is repeated with $3 + 2 =$, $4 + 1 =$. No one makes a mistake. Everyone has the correct answer. The class is very orderly. The teacher is satisfied and happy with the achievement.

In situations like this, I am very tempted to walk to the blackboard and write $2 + 4 =$; $1 + 5 =$. My guess is that at least some children, operating on the assumption that the expected answer is 5, will "give" out of habit the expected answer.

It is possible in teaching number 5 to call on several children and ask them to go to the blackboard and put down all the combinations of two groups which make number 5. Let them have *freedom* to figure out a *variety* of combinations, rather than limiting their role to repeating the correct response. Let several people work on the blackboard simultaneously so that the classroom climate will not be dominated by waiting for one's turn. It may be pretty deadly to wait. . . .

In reacting to curricular proposals of this nature, some teachers feel that the end result will be confusion or even failure: "The children would not know what to do. You must give them step-by-step instructions." In addition to an underestimation of the ability of children to think and organize on their own, there is in these comments a misconception of the role of confusion and failure in learning. It often seems that teaching in the elementary school is on a level which is too easy for children. Teachers deliberately try to present the learning content in small chewable portions so that children will not get confused.

What is wrong with running into difficulty, experiencing confusion, or even failing? It is wrong when (1) the confusion does not lead to increased efforts and mastery, and (2) when failure is looked down upon and is punished by a poor grade. With these exceptions, a certain level of confusion and even some failure is a very educative experience for children. As Chapter 5 will demonstrate, a prerequisite to the development of creative thinking is tolerance for ambiguity and confusion.

The overprotective teacher tends to underestimate both the child's ability to take frustration, and the importance of this characteristic for growing into maturity. As suggested by Heil in a research study on the characteristics of teacher behavior,[H7] many teachers tend to feel most secure when things run smoothly. It seems that the internal need for control and smooth functioning interferes with a sound estimation of the pupil's ability and their level of frustration.

The reader is urged to observe the classroom in terms of the overcontrolling problem. How do teachers give instructions? How do they regulate the learner's responses and behavior? What is the degree of *freedom to think* that pupils have? How can it be increased?

CONCLUSION

This chapter does not suggest that the mastery of facts is not important, nor that the teacher should not play a directive role. The criticism is, to use Huxley's language, "that those who refuse to go beyond facts rarely get as far as facts." The criticism is that the overcontrolling behavior of model A is *constricting* in nature.

The present-day elementary school teacher tends to be friendly and warm. His means of control is not punitive action, but rather overstructuring of the learning climate through overemphasis of memory and recall of specifics to the detriment of the processes of productive thinking.

Havighurst and Neugarten say:[H5:390]

It is in the role of mediator of learning that the teacher tends to be most sure of himself. What is to be taught and how it is to be taught are the teacher's main stock in the trade . . . It is also within this role, as contrasted with others, that the teacher's behavior is the most *highly ritualized* and *formalized.*

Marie Hughes concludes an intensive investigation into the behavior of the elementary school teacher by saying:[H12:186]

The furniture in the classroom, the color on the walls, the illustration in books . . . have all changed, as has the appearance and grooming of the teacher. But the basic pattern of teacher-child relation [control] has not changed.

Although this conclusion is perhaps somewhat extreme, it would seem that a major function of the elementary school teacher is to break away from a repetitive and controlling way of teaching, toward a behavior which aims at *productive thinking.* Toward this direction models B and C are going to move in the next two chapters.

SELECTED BIBLIOGRAPHY

BURTON, H. William, *The Guidance of Learning Activities*. New York: Appleton-Century-Crofts, 1962. Chapter 5 criticizes the overemphasis on memorizing of isolated facts.

HEIL, M. Louis, POWELL, Marion, and FEIFER, Irwin, *Characteristics of Teacher Behavior Related to the Achievement of Children in Several Elementary Grades*. New York: Brooklyn College, 1960. An investigation into the relationship between teacher personality, teacher behavior, and pupils' achievement. Teacher *B* has important implications to my discussion of model *A*.

HUGHES, Marie, *Assessment of the Quality of Teaching in Elementary Schools*. Salt Lake City, Utah: The University of Utah Press, 1959. Chapter 5 is a discussion of the controlling teacher.

3

Model B: The main–idea teacher

In another class session, a demonstration was presented before the same group of novice teachers, illustrating how the *same lesson* (the story called "Long-Tail") could be taught emphasizing the *B* orientation. It was followed by written reactions and interviews. The following is a sketch of the role-playing of teacher B.

Motivation: Discussion of children's experiences with identifying animals.

Objective: The main idea in the story.

Reading: The class is asked to read the story silently from the beginning to the end.

Discussion and Reading: The teacher raises questions attempting to tap and develop the pupil's comprehension of the basic theme of the total story: What happened? What are the main points? What is the main idea? *Why* did they make a mistake in calling a squirrel a long-tailed kitten? Would you make a mistake like this? Much of the emphasis is on the *why*. Pupils read orally the parts they like best, explain these parts, and speak about favorite words and expressions.

Picture Analysis: Emphasis is placed on the basic message of the pictures: What does the picture say? What else? How does it help to understand the story?

Dramatization: The group decides on the major scenes in the story, (work which calls for organizing the major parts). They select one scene for dramatization. Children volunteer for roles. The children play one scene spontaneously, sticking to the content of the story but without reading from the book. The teacher emphasizes spontaneous and logical oral expression.

Seat work: Draw a picture of the part that you like best and write the story in your own words.

Whereas the group's perception of model A was polarized, the perceptions of model B were very favorable. While there were some teachers who perceived weaknesses in the B approach, or predicted some dangers in its application, the overall response was—"I want to be like teacher B."

The following are some illustrations of the favorable written reactions to model B.

Teacher B strives to teach the child to look for the general meaning. What is the main idea? The child reads with meaning and pleasure. . .

What does the picture say? This emphasis on a central meaningful question gives the student a chance to think for himself, rather than being almost told the answer in teacher A's way of questioning—Is the cat big or small?

I would like to be a child in the class of teacher B because he allowed more room for freedom and encouraged children to think for themselves.

It was the feeling of the group that the emphasis of teacher B on the meaning of basic ideas, his encouragement of productive thinking, and his provisions for freedom constituted a higher level of teaching than the stress of model A on specificity and overstructured behavior. The following discussion will attempt to elaborate the interrelated concepts of basic ideas, productive thinking, and provisions for freedom, inherent in the B orientation, and develop their educational implications.

LEVEL B OF KNOWLEDGE

The group realized that the major characteristics underlying the B approach was the emphasis on the main idea—the Gestalt. Perhaps all the other characteristics are a product of this emphasis. The search for the development of a main idea, the producing of a generalization, and a structure permeates the various steps taken by teacher B, such as reading, discussion, and picture analysis.

This teacher continuously asks himself: "What are the key concepts which are central? What are the principles to be developed?"

There has been within the last several years a renewed interest in American education in the meaning of knowledge. The study of the structure of the various disciplines of subject matter is becoming a major endeavor of the postprogressive education era. Bruner's book, *The Process of Education,* is a landmark signifying the great interest in the meaning of *structure,* that is, the learning of how things are related and the understanding of the fundamental principles "ordering" a discipline. Bruner says:[B13:31-32]

Teaching specific topics . . . without making clear their context in the broader fundamental structure of a field of knowledge is uneconomical . . . such teaching makes it exceedingly difficult for the student to generalize from what he has learned to what he will encounter later . . . learning that has fallen short of a grasp of general principles has little reward in terms of intellectual excitement. The best way to create interest in a subject is to render it worth knowing, which means to make the knowledge gained usable in one's thinking beyond the situation in which the learning has occurred . . . An unconnected set of facts has a pitiably short half-life in memory. Organizing facts in terms of principles and ideas from which they may be inferred is the only known way of reducing the quick rate of loss of human memory.

The objective of teacher *B* is to help the learner distinguish between data and structure, and to move as quickly as possible from the first to the second. In contrast to *A,* he is a *constructionist,* who attempts to organize the encountered data in a manner which is conductive to discovery of regularity and relatedness. To quote from the reactions of teachers:

In teaching about housing she will stress major concepts. For example, the relationship between types of housing and climate, or the relations between housing and safety . . . A typical question will be: "Why are the houses in the European farms arranged in villages, whereas the farms in America are far from each other?"

I see teacher *B,* teaching science and arithmetic. In teaching science, she will try to show what various scientific facts and observations mean in terms of a major principle, such as, "air takes space." She will always ask for the why, the reason and explanation. In teaching arithmetic, she will not be satisfied with drill, or the knowledge of accurate computation. Teacher B will rather emphasize arithmetical relationship and the main concepts.

To the extent that the learner is less mature in terms of his thought processes, or less versed in the specific discipline which he is studying, he will tend to have difficulty in grasping the uniting structure. His thinking will be characterized by *empiricism* rather than *constructionism.*

In playing the game of Twenty Questions, the immature child tends to ask specific questions: "Is it an apple, an orange, a banana?" He is concrete and empirical in his thinking. The mature child attempts to identify constraints in the problem: "Do we eat it? Is it fruit? Is it round?" This child is a constructionist. In contrast to the first, he is able to organize and utilize the learned information and therefore will tend to be faster in finding the solution.[B11]

Model B attempts to develop the capacity of children to move from empiricism to constructionism. For him it is not sufficient that the child knows the correct answer to an arithmetical computation. The pupil must, rather, understand the rationale underlying the principle. For teacher B, arithmetic is a system of ideas rather than merely an aggregation of correct responses. Likewise, he is not satisfied with the child's knowing the correct answers to level A questions on a reading comprehension test. To him, real comprehension calls for the grasp of the main ideas communicated by the reading matter. In brief, in contrast to A, B is not interested in *covering* the subject matter; his interest is, rather, in the uniting structure emerging from the factual data.

To develop theory and structure means to grasp the relatedness of knowledge. Without structure, arithmetic becomes an aggregation of computation skills, history becomes merely reporting of events, and science is identical with the observation of discrete facts. The emphasis on structure means the potential to apply knowledge. As Bruner says: "It bestows the gift of intellectual travel beyond the information given."[B12:109]

As the role of research is to deepen man's understanding of the structure of knowledge, that is, increase his intellectual mobility, education which helps the child think in terms of constructs and grasp of the structure stimulates growth toward intellectual mobility.

Main ideas—difficulties

The tendency of many teachers is to select concepts that are too easy in terms of children's comprehension and too trivial in terms of social significance. Stendler[818] makes the point that knowing that Bolivian women wear many petticoats may be an interesting fact, but is hardly socially significant; knowing that firemen slide down a pole from their upstairs quarters to answer an alarm is insignificant in relation to the concept that fire departments are maintained by local taxes. In a study of dairying it is more important for children to know that the quantity of milk can be improved by providing proper grazing and food for cows, than to know that the four breeds of cows most commonly found in the U.S.A. are Jerseys, Holsteins, Guernseys, and Swiss.

What are the factors that stop teachers from following the *B* orientation, which emphasizes significant concepts and generalizations? A partial answer to this question was given in the discussion of model *A*. The factors include a limited conception of knowledge, home and school experience, and the need for security and control. Additional answers are found in an analysis of the reactions to teacher *B*. These include confusion with regard to the role of formulating objectives and its impact on the reality of teaching. An interviewee says:

Teacher B is the one who emphasizes the main ideas. I think in my teaching, I resemble teacher B. When I plan a unit or a lesson, I decide on my objectives. These objectives are the major concepts I want children to learn.

In planning a unit or a lesson, the teacher is expected to think first about her objectives, that is, the key concepts she wants to communicate. In doing this, the teacher follows one aspect of the *B* orientation. It seems, however, that a continuity between the objectives (key concepts), and the specific subject matter is too often lacking. To put it in extreme terms, one often has the feeling that the objectives were written by one person and the subject matter by another. Teachers revealed, during our interviews, that planning of objectives was not sufficiently meaningful when it came to actual teaching behavior. For instance

Statement of objectives is found only in the Board of Education materials, or in the lesson plans presented to the college professor who supervises student teachers. The classroom teacher, who has to teach the whole day, does not bother with "objectives." Perhaps she puts some in the planbook to be inspected by the assistant principal. But anyhow, she does not follow her planbook.

These critical remarks are honest. The formulation of key concepts expressed in the language of objectives is often perceived as dictated by an authority—an assignment by the college instructor or an expectation of the principal. The teacher is not always convinced of the educational value of this step and its helpfulness to him as a practitioner. He often tends to emphasize specific elements of subject matter, questions, materials, and activities, rather than the totality (so central in the *B* orientation) that has to emerge.

What one witnesses here is not an uncommon phenomenon. The basic idea which is the primary reason for the development of an educational activity loses its central role and is pushed to the periphery, to a secondary position. A major reason is the preoccupation of an anxious practitioner with the minutes of teaching. In an interview one of my colleagues said:

Many of our education majors are pragmatists. That is, details come before the whole. They are more interested in things (Pragmata) than in the ideas (Gestalt). This type of teacher works *minutely* on school jobs and can often be interrupted by messages and office calls without being frustrated. It does not interfere with the development of the whole. (Being in their perception of secondary importance).

In a research study on the characteristics of teachers, Heil and his associates[H7] describe a profile of a teacher whose greatest academic achievement is the acquisition of detailed information. As a teacher, he has difficulty making his own integration of such information and applying such integrated information to new situations. The profile of this teacher illustrates the difficulty under discussion here. The emphasis is on a smooth and organized presentation of minute subject matter and activities, without sufficient thinking through of the final concepts to emerge.

Another difficulty which some teachers mention is a conflict between the desire to develop the major idea and the sense of obligation to "cover" the subject matter. An interviewee says:

I wanted to teach a poem which conveyed a feeling of loneliness. The plan was to ask children to describe the mood and explain the clues which give the empression of loneliness. As the lesson proceeded, however, the center of discussion became the analysis of the difficult words and the attempt to put them in sentences.

The above teacher cuts her emphasis on the B orientation with a lengthy discussion of word study. In this process the B orientation is undermined and the emergence of the key concept—the mood of loneliness—is lost. The A orientation is so strong and ingrained that in too many cases it permits mainly the coverage of factual information. Observations of curricular practices show that this is especially true in the areas of language arts and social studies. It appears to a lesser extent in the areas of science and arithmetic.

In the area of language arts, the skills of reading and writing (in the narrow sense of the word "skill") often become dominant. In this process, the ideas and values communicated in the reading and writing matter often become irrelevant, or at least secondary. In social studies the factual information of dates, names, events, and numbers, receives a dominant role. In this process the development of the Gestalt, so central in the B orientation, is relogated to secondary position. The development of significant key concepts is often not reached, and sometimes not even attempted.

Interestingly enough, it is in two disciplines of the curriculum, considered difficult to teach by so many teachers, where the B orientation proved to be most successful. These areas are arithmetic and science. In arithmetic the emphasis is on developmental and gradual emergence of concepts through the use of firsthand experiences and representative materials. The emphasis is on logic and relationships rather than solely on the mechanics of accurate computation. Many teachers are working hard on following the teaching of developmental arithmetic with its emphasis on structure and Gestalt—the major characteristics of the B orientation.

The major factor responsible for the relatively successful implementation of the B approach in the teaching of science is the emphasis on experimentation. The method of scientific investigation with its emphasis on the one hand on experimentation and observation, and on the other hand on inductive and deductive thinking, is a common approach which many teachers take in teaching science. The end result is often the emergence of a Gestalt—the basic concept.

It seems that the science of education has progressed in the subject areas considered difficult by teachers (science and arithmetic), but has been neglected in the subjects in which traditionally the teacher is considered secure. The criticism of language arts and social studies in terms of lack of sufficient emphasis on the B orientation raises the question of whether the assumed security is misleading. Perhaps it too often constitutes a cover-up for routine and acceptance of unimaginative teaching.

PRODUCTIVE THINKING

The teaching behavior of model B is composed of two basic elements: (1) the level of knowledge he wants to communicate, and (2) the process by which he wants to reach this level of knowledge. These two factors are interrelated. Teaching often centers on the conclusion of an intellectual inquiry without giving equal emphasis to the process of inquiry itself. On many occasions I have heard first graders argue about Columbus.

He said that the world is flat.
No, he said that the world is round. The teacher said so.

A generalization which is transmitted by the teacher rather than developed by the learner himself may lead to verbal glibness and superficiality. This danger requires further examination of the B orientation in terms of the *process of arriving* at a major idea and its educational implications.

A teacher writes:

I call teacher B creative because she does not stick to the information in the text. She asks children to look at facts and create a new idea . . . The idea is not stated explicitly in the subject matter and therefore I call it newly produced and created.

The full-blown term—"creative," for teacher B, will be questioned in the next chapter; however, in terms of the discussion here, the above reaction stresses the aspect of production and creation in the *B* orientation. In other words, the *A* approach is denoted by reproductive and the *B* by productive thinking.

Perhaps it is extreme to call the process of reproductive thinking a passive way of learning. There is some degree of activity on the part of the learner, in the *A* emphasis on identification and recall. However, productive thinking calls for a much higher degree of activity, participation, and creation on the part of the learner. He has to put much more of himself into the productive thinking process. He has to perceive the essential in a specific phenomenon or constellation, to limit and organize the infinite variety of reality phenomena, and finally to form a new concept, or reach a conclusion.

Psychologists are unanimous in ascribing paramount importance to the process of productive thinking in that complex which is called "intelligence." The ability to think productively and abstractly is a primary factor for the higher levels of intelligence. Typical illustrations of the interest of the test builder in this primary factor of intelligence, are test items such as: "How are a plum and a peach alike?"

One child may answer: "They are fruits." Another child may answer: "They have pits." The first child is able to see relationships on a higher level than the second and abstract a new concept—fruits. The latter has a low-level response. He reacts to one characteristic (the pit) rather than to the whole concept.

Another typical illustration of the interest of the testologist in productive thinking is the following test item taken from the revised Stanford-Binet Form *L:*

My neighbor has been having queer visitors. First a doctor came to the house, then a lawyer, then a minister. What happened there?

Nowhere in the story is the word "death" mentioned. The subject has to put together not only the basic facts in the story, but also some of the information about customs in our culture that are known to him, and reach the conclusion—"someone was dying." Some subjects may think this way: "The facts are that the doctor came first, the lawyer second, and the minister last. What is the work of these people? In my knowledge, when do they come in this order to visit a family? The answer is—"someone was dying."

The process of productive thinking which is described here in a somewhat logical and sequential way may be too orderly. Perhaps what takes place during the process of productive thinking is what the Gestaltists call "insight." The intelligent individual toys with the factors presented in the problem situation, and with the factors known to him in his previous experience, and suddenly "sees the relationships" and "arrives at closure" as if, metaphorically speaking, the discrete elements in the problem situation are isolated and are therefore "open." Only by the act of "insight" does the learner "unite" the important parts and reach "closure."

As said earlier, forming concepts is more than just receiving information. The learner must be able to organize his information into major generalizations. For instance, in reading, the pupil looks for the major idea conveyed by the data; in science, for the explanation of the observed phenomenon, or in arithmetic for the reasoning underlying the specific algorithm. Forming concepts and generalizations must be viewed as an *active process of search* on the part of the learner. Some of the typical questions he may be thinking about during this process of search are: What is the main idea? How can it be explained? Why? What does it mean? What is the conclusion or solution? What are the similarities or differences? In brief, productive thinking is a process of discovery which culminates in a structure of a generalization or an answer.

The underestimation of the importance of the *process* of productive thinking generally results in two forms of teaching behavior. One is the teacher who "gives" children the "answers," or transmits the main idea to pupils rather than allowing them to discover it. A typical illustration is the memorization of a rule of grammar or of arithmetic without an inductive process which leads to the formulation of the rule. Two, teachers who are anxious to get the "expected answer" may tend to rush prematurely toward structuring of the discovery process.

Observation of classroom practices demonstrates that the second is a more common practice. For example, a teacher wants to develop the concept that vibration causes sound. She utilizes a tuning fork but the children do not feel that it vibrates. They look with dismay at the teacher. A girl who sits near the teacher says,

"The fork vibrates." The teacher immediately *approves* the correct answer by putting it on the blackboard, and the class repeats, "Sound is vibration." Most of these second graders learned the new word "vibration," but its relation to sound is still not clear. The teacher had to wait with the final structuring of the generalization, and let more children touch and feel the vibrating fork. Most of them would not express their discovery by the scientific word "vibration," but would instead say: "I feel it is shaking," or "It is moving and moving." Then other instruments should have been used to illustrate vibration, such as drums. The vibration of an instrument should be slowed down or stopped to show its impact on sound. The end result of an inductive process of this nature is not a glib repetition of the word "vibration," but rather a meaningful conceptualization.

The emphasis on the importance of the process of thinking which leads to the structuring of a new generalization underlies the *programmed instruction* approach. The limitations of these materials will be presented in other chapters. Here the interest is only in the extent to which they illustrate the process of conceptualization under discussion. Programmed instruction reflects two central interests in modern educational thinking. One is the organization of subject matter, and the other, the process of learning. The concept, or generalization to be mastered, is reduced into small steps generally called "frames." These frames are arranged in sequential order moving gradually from the simple to the complex and from the concrete to the abstract. In terms of teacher education, a major contribution of programming is sensitizing the teacher to the importance of the relationships between the part and the whole. The position is that teaching is not the transmission of discrete facts but rather a planned and developmental approach to concept formation.

In terms of the process of learning, the programmer believes that optimum learning occurs when the learner progresses on his own without having to slow down or speed up because of group norms. The responses of the learner are immediately reinforced. He knows whether he is right or wrong and can correct his mistakes. In brief, programmed instruction is based on the assumption that the *process* of conceptualization is of crucial importance, and not only the final concept itself.

Productive thinking: difficulties

The process of productive thinking, denoting the B orientation, is more demanding and energy consuming than the process of reproductive thinking characteristic to the A approach. When teacher B asks "Why did the children call the squirrel a long-tailed kitten?", the pupils have to work on putting together facts presented in the subject matter and facts known to them in their previous experience, and reach insight. This is much more difficult than responding to the question of teacher A, "Who said, 'Well, well,'" which calls only for identification and recall.

Questionnaire data show that the level of difficulty of the productive thinking required by the B approach troubles many teachers. A typical reaction is

The emphasis of teacher A on thinking is very good for bright students. But I work with Puerto Rican children. They are practical and concrete-minded. I wouldn't try teacher B's approach with them. They will not understand.

On the one hand the teachers under discussion identify with teacher B as a professional ego ideal, but on the other hand, at least one-half of the group questions whether this approach "will work with ethnic and lower-class children." As some say:

It is better to start teaching on the primary grades like teacher A, and only when they have the foundations of facts and information, to move to the thinking emphasis of teacher B.

The difficulty which these teachers are speaking about is very real. There is a higher incidence of concrete thinking and low ability to abstract and generalize among certain segments of the population. More children in a lower-class than in a middle-class community react to a test, which calls for generalizing and conceptualizing, in a concrete way.[P5]

However, the fact that a child, or a group of children has difficulty in thinking productively on the ideational level, does not mean that this process has to be dispensed with. In our western civilization the individual whose ability to think productively and abstractly is weak would tend to lag behind those in whom this ability is more developed. Therefore, the problem is not that of postponing the *B* emphasis on thinking in working with the relatively concrete-minded lower-class and ethnic child. The problem is rather that of discovering more efficient ways of helping him look at firsthand experience and factual information, and see their essential interrelations and key concepts.

The interview data show that in addition to the perception of the *B* emphasis on productive thinking as being "too difficult for many children to comprehend," many teachers feel that the *B* approach is not conducive to good control. The stress on productive thinking in contrast to the emphasis on specificity permits much more *freedom* to the learner. It seems that this freedom constitutes a threat to some novice teachers.

When model *B* asks children to read the whole story, or to look at a picture and suggest the main idea, the pupils are free to work on their own until they develop the answer. When teacher *B* asks children to observe a series of scientific facts and produce a generalization, or to explain the logic of a division computation in arithmetic, the students must take time to work on their own and think. The search for the answer is not so intensely structured as it is in the *A* emphasis on detailed information.

We witness here two different patterns of leadership. Teacher *A* employs short-range objectives, and teacher *B* more long-range goals. Teacher *A* must continuously ask more and more questions, or give more and more instructions in order to move the children from the accomplishment of one goal to another. Teacher *B* can limit his instructions to a few basic questions. The children are much more on their own.

The power that drives and continuously moves class *A* is the teacher. If he stops, there is no movement. The pattern of discussion is teacher-centered. The teacher asks a question; a child gives an answer; teacher questions, child answers, etc. There is very little room for interaction among pupils. The reason is simple— there is no content and process of thinking which calls for give-and-take among the learners.

These patterns are much less typical of class *B*. The teacher is less dominant and the children more active. The pattern of discussion is less teacher-centered. There is more room for pupils' interaction, pooling ideas together, reacting to each other, and arguing with the positions others take.

The essence of productive thinking, denoting the process of work of the *B* model, makes him much less authoritarian and controlling than the *A* teacher. It seems, however, that this lack of controlling structure threatens some novice teachers. As one of them said in an interview:

My cooperating teacher asked them (the children) a stimulating question. There was silence, no answer. He waited and waited. A few minutes passed and he sat waiting. I would not be able to take it, and would ask a simpler question. Finally the children figured it out and had interesting answers. I have a lot of respect for him.

This student teacher is able to recognize a sound and educative approach; however, she admits that this approach threatens her need for control. Or, as another beginning teacher puts it:

In spite of everything said in favor of teacher *B*, let's admit it, teacher *A* knows exactly what her children are doing every minute of the day. I would not say the same thing about teacher B.

The need for control is very acute in the educational orientation of many anxious beginners. This factor tends to contribute towards an idealization of *B*, but an acceptance of the reality and practicality of *A*.

CONCLUSION

The last interview question was: "What do you think teacher *C* will be?" The replies were interesting. The overwhelming majority felt that teacher *C* was going to be a merger between patterns *A* and *B*. They looked for a balance between the secure but rigid emphasis on specificity, identification, and recall, and the potentially richer but less safe stress on the totality of the basic idea and its corollary—productive thinking.

With almost no exceptions, the teachers failed to sense the need for a more creative model, one whose conception of knowledge and way of teaching emphasize interaction between the individual and the subject matter, and encourage divergency and creativity. These ideas will be elaborated in the next chapter.

SELECTED BIBLIOGRAPHY

BRUNER, S. Jerome, *The Process of Education*. Cambridge: Harvard University Press, 1961. Emphasis on the importance of understanding the structure of the discipline.

FLEMING, S. Robert, *Curriculum for Today's Boys and Girls*. Columbus, Ohio: Charles E. Merrill Books, Inc., 1963. Chapters 8 and 9 deal with the problem of thinking in terms of its curricular applications.

4

Model C: The creative teacher

When the collection of the reactions to the *B* orientation was completed, the *C* model was presented before the same group of teachers. It was followed by written reactions and interviews. The following is a sketch of the role-playing.

Motivation: A discussion of a popular television program, Lassie, leads to the observation that Timmie's (the child hero) parents sometimes don't believe his stories, such as his seeing a wild horse. The discussion attempts to explore the feelings of both Timmie and his parents in situations like this.

Objective: To read a story where parents don't believe what their children see and to understand the feelings of the people involved.

Reading and Discussion: Silent reading of the whole story. Discussion of the main ideas with emphasis on the misunderstanding in calling a squirrel a long-tailed kitten. Selection of parts best liked by children. Reading and discussion of these parts in terms of content and style. An attempt to encourage children to read between the lines and analyze the feelings of Dick and his sisters when father is sarcastic and does not believe their observation of a long-tailed kitten. These feelings are not reported in the story and call for putting one's own feelings into the story. Some children suggest that Dick felt angry and bitter; others suggest that he was not sure of himself anymore, and so on. All interpretations of possible reactions are accepted and encouraged. The point is emphasized that one cannot judge these different reactions by the criterion of correct or incorrect. All of them are logically possible.

Dramatization: Rather than repeating and sticking to the notes of the story in dramatization, the class creates a scene where Dick is going to Long-Tail to complain about his nontrusting parents. This scene is not presented by the text and constitutes a product of the children's imagination. The children are encouraged to develop the new scene by a discussion of Dick's possible reaction to his parents' disbelief, the impact of his feelings on his behavior, his way of speaking, gestures, etc., and a detailed description of the scenery.

A scene where Dick speaks with Long-Tail is played by several pairs of students. Each team has an opportunity to plan its own presentation in terms of its own interpretation. Each scene is followed by class discussion and an analysis of the character which the team attempted to portray.

Picture Analysis: An attempt to develop empathy and imagination. Typical questions are: How do the characters in the pictures feel? What happened before? What will happen later? The teacher encourages different and even opposing interpretations of the situation. Some children disagree and discuss their disagreement.

Seat Work: In contrast to teachers A and B, the assignment does not include a review of the story, but rather moves a step ahead. Children are asked to suggest topics for writing different endings to the story. For instance, one suggestion is: "One day the cat felt that Long-tail acted strangely. What happened?" The children write stories of different endings and illustrate with pictures.

On the continuum of repetitive versus creative teaching, the majority of the teachers perceived the A and B orientations as representing the opposing extremes. They expected model C to represent the middle point on the continuum; that is, an integration of the educative and practical qualities in the two so-called extreme teachers.

The presentation of teacher C as one who extends the continuum, rather than constitutes a balance point, and as one who pushes the horizons of teaching even further than the B orientation, was a genuine surprise to the group. The impact on the majority of the teachers was a change in the professional ego ideal: from B to C. Typical written reactions were:

If I hadn't seen teacher C, I might want to be like teacher B. But after seeing teacher C, I know that my vision was limited.

Teacher C is the ideal teacher . . . He believes in children and he believes in education . . . As young teachers, we now have a new goal.

The demonstration of teacher C also served as a strong emotional stimulus. Many teachers looked at the new professional ego ideal and asked themselves the searching question—what does it mean in terms of me as a teacher, and most important, as a person.*

The C demonstration was a stimulus to the teachers to speak about their unfulfilled hopes and aspirations, and especially about their struggle to reach others, and in this process to reach their own self. It encouraged the young teachers to speak about their desire of reaching their potentialities, give of themselves, and in this process grow professionally.

In the group's perception, the major characteristics of the C model were emphasis on: (1) the teacher's subjective meaning of subject matter; (2) movement from the known to the unknown; (3) divergent thinking; (4) democratic teaching.

THE SUBJECTIVE MEANING OF SUBJECT MATTER TO THE TEACHER

Perhaps the most important single characteristic of the C approach to the promotion of creativity is the fact that he himself is a creative person. In contrast to teacher A who approaches the teaching matter with the question "What are the specifics?", and in contrast to teacher B who looks for the main ideas inherent in the subject matter, model C approaches knowledge with the question "What does the subject matter mean to me as a person?" The emphasis is on the teacher himself experiencing his own interpretation of the subject matter—in this case, a story. Teachers write:

The story, "Long-Tail," is simple and somewhat dull, like most stories in the primary readers. Even in a story like this, teacher C is able to read between the lines and get insight into the dynamics of family relations.

Teacher A starts by asking factual questions and teacher B by asking children to read the story as a whole. They themselves are not in the

* The data analysis shows that the C presentation was strongest in terms of its *personal* impact, A was second, and B was last. The reason may be that the A and C orientations constitute two extremes, while the B model has some elements of both.

story. Teacher *C* is involved. He relates the story to his own personal life. He sees in it something new.

A teacher can communicate a rich experience to children only if he experiences it himself as an adult person. How do teachers feel about the subject matter or experience to be taught? What is the message it communicates to them as people? An answer to this question will give us better insight into the dynamics of creative teaching. A teacher writes:

I wanted to teach about inventions. I read about it and then I started to think about how to introduce it to children. I knew that if I would ask them, "What are you going to invent?" their imaginations would run wild and the end result would be a household (especially the kitchen) where Mama had to do nothing but push a button. However, for me inventions are much more than kitchen gadgets. It is satisfying man's more basic needs, such as food and health.

This teacher is able to look at the subject matter of "inventions" and ask herself, "What does it mean to *me?*" She is afraid that the limited experiences of children and their concrete thinking will result in a "gadget-centered" lesson. Therefore, she decides to move in the direction of inventions in the area of food and medicine. The involvement with subject matter, the experiencing of one's individual interpretation of an idea, is a rewarding experience for the teacher who can reach it. To quote from an interview:

The rewards in developing your own ideas and approach to the problem are thrilling. And you know all the time that the children will get "charged-up" and excited about learning. I felt "gung-ho." I did not feel fatigue that night. I could stay and work.

The impact on the teacher's behavior

The following discussion is reported here to demonstrate the impact of the ability to experience the subjective meaning of subject matter on the teacher's behavior in the classroom.

On Columbus Day, another group of teachers was asked to react in writing to three questions. The second question was announced only after the reactions to the first were completed. The third question was announced only after the reactions to the second were completed.

1. Suppose a group of Japanese teachers comes to our room and asks, "What is Columbus Day?" Jot down a brief speech answering this question.
2. How would you teach children about Columbus? Illustrate by one brief lesson plan.
3. What does Columbus Day mean to you?

The analysis of the responses to the first question (the "speech") revealed that most answers were factual and prosaic. The emphasis was on the historical facts of Columbus' birth, port of embarkation, names of the queen and the three boats, the year of the discovery of America, and on the statement that the world was round rather than flat. The writing of the speeches was trite. They did not convey a sense of emotion and drama, but were rather matter-of-fact. In brief, emphasis was primarily on level A of knowledge.

The same can be said about the majority of the responses to the second question—the lesson plans. In essence, they were a digest of the previous factual speech with some additions of arts and crafts activities. It is interesting to note that while working on the speech and on the lesson plan, some participants said to the instructor: "I don't think I can do it. I am not up-to-date on the facts."

A *minority* of the group members, however, both in the writing of the speech and the planning of the lesson, attempted to identify with the struggle experienced by Columbus, struggle against man, convention, and nature. They looked for the symbolic meaning of the life of the explorer, that is—level C of knowledge. For instance, one teacher wanted to ask children to describe Columbus' childhood. Another wanted to put on a debate of the merit of the trip to be presented in the Queen's council. One lesson plan suggested focusing on Columbus' experiences in prison. (Interestingly enough, this is the only point of information omitted by most teachers, despite its significance in the understanding of the conflicts underlying Columbus' mission. It seems that the intention is to present a stereotyped sugarcoated portrait and to avoid struggle and controversy.)

The responses to the third question ("What does Columbus Day mean to you?") suggest an explanation for the two types of reactions to it. The teachers who were factual in their speech and lesson planning tended to answer that Columbus Day had no meaning to them as adults.

It is only for children. For teachers—a day of vacation.

We learned one thing about him in public school and then it proved to be wrong when we studied history in college. We feel skeptical.

There was laughter in the group when the third question was read. The laughter expressed the skepticism of the participants. However, the teachers who searched for the personal struggle in Columbus' life tended to answer the third question by saying:

He stands for one of the great misunderstood people. Whether he was really great or not does not bother me. The important thing is the symbol.

We are a unique country composed of immigrants from almost all over the world. Our history is one long story of the struggle and courage of the immigrants. Columbus' importance is that he was the first immigrant (in America).

These comments suggest: (1) positive correlation between the teacher's own responding to subject matter and a C-oriented way of teaching, and (2) a positive correlation between lack of the teacher's responding to subject matter and an A oriented way of teaching.

That the nature of knowledge communicated to children is related to the personal meaning the teacher experiences, came out in some of the interviews. The following is a hardworking novice teacher speaking about a lesson she had given:

I taught my third grade about transportation. They are pretty bright and eager to learn. We spoke about ways different people go to work, and then we put it on a chart. (Opens the rolled chart.) It reads:

> People go to work by car.
> People go to work by bus.
> People go to work by train.

They enjoyed the lesson, but I don't think that they learned much. They learned to read and write. They enjoyed participating. But con-

tent-wise, it was not much . . . Planning the lesson on transportation.
I thought about an interesting central theme—*the world is small,* but
my mother (a teacher) said it would be too difficult for the children
to grasp. They are not *ready* . . .

What a person prizes, he does. What the teacher values, she
teaches. The problem of the young teacher is to understand the
diversions which undermine her ability to experience rich value
in subject matter. In the case under discussion, the teacher
stopped listening to her own sound judgment of what is central
and valuable, and when she had guilt feelings about a certain
depth that was not achieved and meaning that was not tapped,
she quieted her conscience. "The children are not ready." With
this rationalization, too many novice teachers commit the elementary school child to six years of "readiness."

In this case the young teacher does not develop her own
interpretation of the subject matter because she trusts the judgment of another more experienced teacher, rather than her own.
The insecurities of a beginner make her dependent rather than
independent. This dependency, which interferes with the teacher's
ability to look at subject matter creatively, is seen in many interviews. Typical comments are

The expectation is that we will follow the course syllabus. There is no
place and time for the new teacher to develop her own ideas.

How can you be like teacher *C*? I spoke about it with my cooperating
teacher. She says that the Board of Education is dogmatic. Democracy
in education is only for the children. Little free thinking is allowed to
teachers.

Teacher *C* is an independent thinker. She follows her own ideas, not
only those of others. But look at the way most of us plan our work.
We are dependent on the teacher's manual. (Opens a teacher's guide
to a primer and shows it to the instructor.) The author tells you the
exact words to be used. Now, they have guides with an arrangement
where you can take the instruction page out. You can read it while
you teach. I am often tempted to read the instructions aloud rather
than use my own words. It is exactly the opposite of teacher *C*.

This interview data illustrate the novice's feeling that not
only internal insecurities, but also external pressures, interfere
with her freedom to develop her own ideas. The objective observer

of the school life may claim that the teacher is freer than she thinks herself to be. However, the perception of the beginning teacher is that she is supposed to follow the *notes* developed by others. She feels that she is expected to be dependent.

In the book *Zen Buddhism*, the Japanese philosopher Suzuki relates a story relevant to the discussion of the teacher's difficulties in developing his own meaning of subject matter, difficulties stemming mainly from his dependence on the notes developed by others.

Kyogen (a student monk who wanted to become a master) assiduously studied his notes which he had taken during the sermons given by his late master. He failed to come across a suitable passage which he might present as his own view. He returned to Yisan (a master) and implored him to teach him the faith of Zen. But Yisan said: "I really have nothing to impart to you. Whatever I can instruct you is my own, and will never be yours." Finally Kyogen decided to burn up all his notes and memoranda, which were of no help to his spiritual welfare. When he did, he reached the "satori" (enlightenment) and knew that he could be a master.[823:94]

A common difficulty of many of the teachers under discussion was the development of their own "notes," their own meaning of what is important in the knowledge to be taught. They depended to a great extent on the notes of others—the authority figures and the textbook. The teacher is the most important factor determining the quality of the classroom experience. The teacher who applies notes mechanically will tend to emphasize repetitive teaching. The teacher who learns to develop and experience his own meaning will move in the direction of interaction between the learner and the subject matter—in the direction of creativity.

The study of child development points out that a basic way a child learns is through identification with the significant people in his life—his parents. The child is influenced not only by the attitudes and behavior of his parents towards him, but also by his experiencing of *what his parents are* as people. The same can also be said about learning from the parent-surrogate—the teacher.

The pupils experience the various types (somewhat stereotypes) of teachers portrayed here, identify with them, and learn the essence of their being. From teacher *A* they learn the rigid search for specificity; and from teacher B, the importance of basic understanding. It is only in experiencing the involvement of teacher C that they learn the importance of the active search for subjective interpretation, that is, putting one's own personal meaning into the subject matter. Recognizing this challenge of the creative model, interviewees say:

I would like to be a child in teacher C's class because I would have to approach the story in terms of my own experience . . . I would understand my environment better and have more knowledge about my own reactions and personality. It is this kind of teaching which helps people like me develop new ideas in terms of their potentialities.

Teachers A and B stand for two different schools of thought. However, for both of them the center is the subject matter rather than the child. It is only teacher C whose emphasis is on the interaction between the child and the content of the lesson. Out of this interaction, a new meaning is created. It is most rewarding to the class and the teacher.

The philosopher Maimonides, in his book *Guide for the Perplexed*,[M2] discusses a hierarchy of four levels of perfection that men might seek. The lowest level is the possession of riches and goods. The second is a strong body. The third is moral perfection. The fourth and highest is the true perfection of man—his intellectual capacities. In reacting to the above formulation of Maimondies, Bruner says:[B12:82]

For if man's intellectual excellence is the most his own among his perfections, it is also the case that the most personal of all that he knows is that which he has discovered for himself . . . Does it, as Maimonides would say, create a unique relation between knowledge and its possessor? And what may such a relation do for a man—or, for our purposes, a child?

Suzuki, the Japanese philosopher,[S23] emphasizes that unless it grows out of oneself, no knowledge is really of value to the individual. A borrowed plumage never grows . . .

FROM THE KNOWN TO THE UNKNOWN

While the subjective meaning of the subject matter to the teacher is one condition of creative teaching, another characteristic denoting the C orientation is the movement from the known to the unknown. Teachers who perceive this element in the behavior of teacher C say:

Teacher C illustrates in her teaching a simple attempt to help children to create new ideas based on the known subject matter of the story. The teacher encourages discussion and role-playing of possible feelings and behavior of the characters. The analyses and scenes developed by the children are not reported in the story. The pictures are discussed in terms of what happened before and what will happen later.

The difference between teachers B and C is clear. Teacher B wants children to think and understand the subject matter. Teacher C wants children to think and interpret the subject matter. In teacher B's class, all the good thinkers will come out with the same answer. In teacher C's class, all the good thinkers will come out with different answers, as if each child rewrites the story in his own way.

⨯ Creative thinking involves the production of new ideas— movement from the known to the unknown. Progress depends upon new solutions; that is, upon the creative thinking that children are able to do.

In an article dealing with some aspects of creativity,[L1] it is suggested that college students who are successful in mathematics tend to be characterized by turbulence, both in feelings and thoughts. They tolerate and even prefer disorder. They find thought, fantasy, and creativity ways of making order out of disorder. In contrast, the article suggests that the *best* elementary school teacher personality is a person who has a great deal of self-control and has things well organized and running smoothly.

Reading these findings, one gets the impression that the successful mathematician is a *creator* of new knowledge and is able to move toward the unknown, while the successful elementary school teacher is a transmitter of predigested knowledge and is able only to impart the known.

These findings have validity if the criteria of "teacher success" are of smooth and orderly discipline, repetition of specifics (level A), and some emphasis on the development of basic ideas inherent in the subject matter (level B). As measured by these criteria, the "successful teacher" is a technician rather than a creator—a transmitter of predigested knowledge.

However, the discussion of teacher C by the novice teachers reveals that, at least in terms of their professional ego ideal, they want to move ahead from a sole preoccupation with transmission of subject matter to the developing of knowledge. They are not satisfied with being technicians only, but they wish to experience the rewards of creating and developing this ability in children. They do not perceive their role as merely emphasizing the ready-made and neat package presented by the book, but want to expand their professional role in the direction of ordering a new knowledge and fostering in their pupils the readiness to move from the known to the unknown.

Toward the unknown: difficulties

If a young teacher develops her own subjective interpretation of a certain subject matter, and if, in terms of the teacher's professional orientation, she wants to encourage in children the creative ability to move from the known to the unknown, what are the factors which interfere with the teacher's progress in this direction? Interviewees say:

Teacher A is oriented toward security. It is so much easier to present a lesson and get all your facts across. You know what you want to do, you plan on it, and you do it. Unless you have undergone the experience many times, it is difficult to structure your work along C lines.

Remember the experiment on rubber? I wanted to ask them (refers to a fifth grade class) to find some of the qualities of this material, without giving them any further instructions. But I changed my mind. You will get stuck and fail to come out with what you had in mind. If things don't work out as you structured them, then you are horrified . . . While the children are working, you look at them and think: "What are they doing? Where are they going? What will they ask?" A sense of timing is important in teaching. You see how time flies, and you don't know exactly where your class is.

Teacher C's movement from the known to the unknown is characterized by a phase of disorder. The learner starts with the known, such as a problem, a story, or a picture, and then experiences a phase of disorder where he moves in divergent directions. He reacts to the stimulus (the known) in his own individualistic way. Not being clear about the direction, he tries different ideas.

He may pass an incubation period. Finally, the learner reaches his own insight and orders a new knowledge.

Barron attempted to determine how creative people respond to order and disorder. He says that the way in which the common human need for order is related to the constructive possibilities and fruitful challenges which may be found in apparent disorder provided the focus for an early series of his experimental studies.[B2:151-155]

There is little doubt that most people dislike being confronted with disorder. In individuals who turn out original work in science or in art, however, a reversal of the usual attitude may be observed . . . Behind the inclination to like and to construct what is not too simply ordered, there appears to be a very strong need to achieve the most difficult and far-reaching ordering.

In other words, the creative response to disorder is to find a new order more satisfying than any that could be evoked by a simpler configuration.

Barron's subjects are highly creative individuals. They are tolerant of disorder and ambiguity. Their response is a search for a new and more satisfying order. The teachers under discussion here were not selected in terms of the creativity variable, and as the above interview points out, their reaction to this phase of disorder is a feeling of threat and loss of power.

In some respects, the task of the teachers in coping with disorder is more difficult than the task which confronted Barron's subjects—the scientists. The latter reacted to the "disorder test situation" working individually. The former have to cope with the phase of disorder while they are teaching a group of youngsters; that is, while they are in a leadership role. To quote from an interview:

I was working on remedial reading exercises. The group read several paragraphs about a class reporter and then answered comprehension questions of the *A* type, such as the name of the reporter and where he went. I had a very small group, so I decided to try some of the *C* approach. I decided to ask a general question based on the story, but one which did not have only one correct answer. I asked: "What would you do if you were a reporter?" The first two responses were: "Who wants this junk?", and, "I'll make money."

You see, this approach is threatening to the teacher, because you don't know what you are going to get. If I had a full class I would feel lost. The class would laugh and they would start fooling around.

To repeat, the normal human difficulty of coping with the phase of disorder is accentuated by the teacher's role of leadership and control. In the perception of many teachers, guidance of the class in movement from the known to the unknown, and good discipline are too often incompatible roles.

These young educational practitioners operate in terms of their role expectation of what a teacher is. The idealism, the giving of one's self and the sense of fulfillment that the teacher's image calls for, enhance the novice's desire to try to guide children toward the *C* orientation of ordering new knowledge. However, other dimensions of the teacher's image deter this type of experimentation.

My problem is that I look too young. Perhaps I should wear my hair differently—then the children will accept me as an authority.

Today I saw my girlfriend (another novice teacher) teaching. I never saw her in this light. She was so serious and full of authority.

The role expectation of the teacher is that he should be an all-knowing authority, definite and creative. In daily life, adults sometimes say: "Don't be a teacher." They mean: "Don't tell me what to do." These dimensions of the teacher's image undermine the teacher's ability to tackle the phase of disorder, denoting the movement from the known to the unknown.

The role expectation of teachers is that they will be able to make quick decisions. Tolerance for ambiguity and disorder, inherent in the creative process, calls for some postponement of decision-making. It warns against premature structuring. The traditional role expectation of the teacher and the tolerance for some disorder are in conflict. As stressed by Heil,[H7] intolerance of uncertainty and the need for a smooth-functioning operation is a major characteristic of many teachers.

The problem becomes even more difficult when the teacher, examining his teaching behavior, must distinguish between tolerance for ambiguity and irresolution, between the ability to delay a choice of direction and indecisiveness.[G3] The basic difference between these two seemingly similar manifestations of teaching behavior is not the external manifestation itself but rather, the sense of strength which the teacher experiences. If one waits patiently for the ripe moment of creating structure, he has tolerance for uncertainty. It is only when one waits because he feels lost and hopes that "the situation will take care of itself," that he is indecisive.

The movement from the known to the unknown is central in the process of creativity. The young teacher who settles solely for the A and B orientation because of the threats of the unknown and the security of the known, is deterring both his professional and personal growth.

In his book *Metamorphosis,* Schachtel discusses the conflict of human development and the psychology of creativity. In contrast to Freud, who believed that the newborn, in complete helplessness, strives only for reduction of tension, Schachtel believes that man lives throughout his life in a conflict between emergence and embeddedness.[82:6]

The movement of life is toward increasing mobility, relative separateness of the organisms from their immediate environment, and individuation. In man this means separation, first from the womb, then from maternal care and progression to a position of relative independence.

The relative strength of the conflict between the force of growth and the anxiety of separation from embeddedness differ at different stages of development. But both forces are present in all men and in all times.

The conflict described in this section, between emphasis on the A and B orientation denoted by the security of the known, and emphasis on the C way of teaching characterized by the challenge of the unknown, is an integral part of the human problem of emergence from embeddedness.

DIVERGENT THINKING

Many of the interviewees pointed out that in contrast to models A and B, teacher C did not respond to or judge his students in terms of right or wrong. For example:

I was impressed with teacher C's way of evaluating children's answers. In answering the questions of teachers A and B, the children know that they are right or wrong. In answering the questions of teacher C, the students know that it is accepted as the individual's interpretation, by the teacher and by the class.

An important function of the teacher is to be a transmitter of organized knowledge, called here levels A and B. Inherent in this concept is the teacher's role of reacting to the pupil in terms of reinforcing correct responses and discouraging false answers.

The pupil is usually aware that his teacher, his parents, his friends, or he himself, can find out whether he knows or does not know a computation skill, a generalization in science, the spelling of a word, the rules of a game, a norm of behavior. The realization of right or wrong is essential in developing consciousness of checking reality, and setting goals for the learner's aspiration. It structures learning by giving the child a way of evaluating whether he objectively knows.

The process of social learning achieved by judging in terms of right or wrong is well-recognized and does not need further elaboration at this point. There is a need, however, to discuss the dangers inherent in *overemphasis* on this process of learning. A teacher says:

It is not difficult to see that in teacher C's class children are freer and therefore more creative (than in the A and B classes). An important factor is the way teacher C responds to them. In the A and B classes, what counts is the ideas of the teacher and the book. There is not much room for the child's own ideas. In teacher C's class, the child is free to react in his own way. He is more independent. The end result is the creation of variety of additions to the story.

In the group's perception, the C approach to evaluation encourages divergent rather than convergent responses and, therefore, places a high premium on the *subjective and independent* thinking of the learner. In doing so it promotes creativity. The relationship between divergency and creativity needs elaboration. Two kinds of productive thinking operations generate new knowledge from known and remembered information: convergent and divergent thinking.

In convergent thinking, the information leads to one correct answer, or to a recognized best answer. This type of thinking is inherent in the B orientation. The B teacher channels or controls the thinking of the learners in the direction of the correct answer or conclusion.

In divergent thinking operations, denoting the C orientation, the learner thinks in different directions, sometimes searching (the phase of disorder), sometimes seeking variety. In Guilford's language:[G8:9]

It is less goal-bound. There is freedom to go off in different directions . . . Rejecting the old solutions and striking out in some new direction is necessary, and the resourceful organism will probably succeed.

The B orientation encourages a convergent thinker who focuses on the stimulus (the story, picture, etc.), since he seeks objectivity which others will recognize as correct. He conforms to the standards and expectations of others, mainly the elders.

The C orientation encourages a divergent thinker who personalizes the stimulus and reacts to it in terms of his own subjective perception. He is tuned to himself and not only to the crowd and its norms. The stimulus is still very important and has to be understood, but the response draws primarily on the resourcefulness of the individual.

A study comparing the highly creative and the highly intelligent adolescent concludes that:[G2:17]

The high I.Q.'s tended to converge upon stereotyped meaning, to perceive personal success by conventional standards, to move toward the model provided by teachers, to seek out careers that conform to what is expected of them.

The high-creatives tended to diverge from stereotyped meanings, to move away from the model provided by teachers, to seek out careers that do not conform to what is expected of them.

The emphasis of the A and B orientations on judging children's knowledge in terms of correct and incorrect, presupposes an orderly, rational, and conscious approach to learning. In the evolutionary sense, the most advanced adaptation of the human organism is the ability to learn through conscious attention. However, working toward the strengthening of consciousness, of true and false, should not subvert the educator from tapping the other rich source of reaching knowledge—the inner self or even the unconscious. The latter is perhaps more primitive than consciousness, but it is also more original.

The emphasis on judging in terms of right or wrong is an attempt to teach the child to be rational and face reality. However, it is also a way of fostering the dependence on, and subservience to, reality, rationality, and external norms.

From birth, the child is put into a constricting maze of rearing practices which accentuate his adaptation to the realities of the external world. He learns that his source of strength, his way of fulfillment, and his means of being accepted can be reached by looking at the external, objective, and uniform norms of right and wrong.

The parent-surrogate (the teacher), the school culture, and the peer group only accentuate the dependence on the external objective of truism. Through a continuous, comprehensive, and deliberate system of formal education, the child conforms to the realities of knowledge, taste, and behavior required by the rational society. He is right or wrong, good or bad, A or F, 100% or zero, popular or rejected, depending on whether he is rational and conforming.

In this process of learning the *overconsciousness* of the external world of right and wrong, a rich potential is lost. The development of the individual's ability to reach knowledge through listening to his inward and maybe even irrational self, is pushed to the background.

The creative individual is the one who reaches for knowledge not only by developing his conscious faculty, but also by turning to the dimly realized life of his inward self. Reaching the latter means having contact with the life of the unconscious, with fantasy, reverie, and the world of imagination. This knowledge gained by inner orientation cannot be classified into the rigidity of true and false.

The learner who is channeled toward thinking solely in terms of external norms of right and wrong may become intelligent, informed and productive. However, he would not become creative. His opportunity to be enriched by the primitiveness and originality of his inward life may be lost. By encouraging different interpretations and by emphasizing that not all knowledge can be classified as right or wrong, model *C* illustrates a search for balance between objectivity and subjectivity.

Divergency: difficulties

As suggested earlier, the novice teachers realized that the acceptance and encouragement of a variety of interpretations was conducive to a learning climate of divergency and creativity. In the interviews, the question was raised whether they followed this approach in their own teaching, and if not—why not?

The answers reveal that one of the major areas where divergency rather than convergency is encouraged is creative writing.

I start a story and ask them to write an end. I show them a picture and ask them to tell a story. I stress not to stick to the facts, but rather to be imaginative. Then we read their writings and enjoy it.

It is interesting to note that in *creative* writing, where the goal of creativity is explicitly stated, the emphasis is on divergency rather than judgment in terms of right or wrong. However, this educational objective is not perceived as central in the *major* subject areas.

When I think about creativity, I think about music, writing, dance, and art. I play music to my class and let them express their feelings in movements they develop. I don't show them what to do . . . But when it comes to our main work—reading, arithmetic, and science, there we have to teach the subject matter and see that the children comprehend.

In the perception of many teachers, the elementary school curriculum consists of the *major* subjects which are the province of the *A* and *B* orientations, and the *minor* subjects, where the *C* approach is dominant. Creativity is "extra." Divergency can be encouraged only if "time permits," that is, only if "the important subject matter is covered." A student teacher says:

I was impressed with teacher *C* and decided to adopt his approach. I had to teach my fifth grade the story of Dr. Doolittle. It deals with a doctor who gave up his flourishing medical practice, filled his house with animals, and took care of them.

I encouraged the children to read between the lines and discuss Dr. Doolittle's personality, his sense of values and his fight against public pressure. I encouraged them to disagree in their evaluation of the man. Some saw him as queer and others as a man of principles.

My cooperating teacher was very complimentary, saying it was original, and then added, "But with these children we don't have time to do it. It will be impossible to cover the subject matter. They need to learn the language first". . . I don't know where I stand now.

The notion expressed above is that the development of divergency and creativity are "extra-curricular," to be worked on only if the essentials of the A and B levels of knowledge are accomplished.

The beginning teacher, harassed by a tradition of a primarily A oriented school, and by his own anxiety over control and direction, starts to confuse the reading of many pages with getting meaning out of reading. Under external and internal pressure to achieve, the novice stops listening to his own sense of values and joins the rush toward false production—covering subject matter.

Gradually the correctness of the specifics of the subject matter itself becomes crucial and even sacred, and the divergent responses of the learner become secondary, or are even omitted. The following extreme illustration demonstrates under a magnifying glass the dynamics involved.

A slow first grade class of Puerto Rican origin was studying a story describing a child who walked through the forest and asked various animals for a gift for his mother. The children dramatized the story.

One boy was a "goat" and asked: "May I have a gift for my mother?" The "goat" answered: "Glon, glon, I don't have a gift for your mother." The teacher interrupted: "What did the goat say?" The "goat" repeated: "Glon, glon, I don't have a gift for your mother." The teacher interrupted again: "Class, how is it written in the book?" The class answered: "Glan, glan, I don't have a gift for your mother."

In this lesson, no effort was made to encourage *divergent* responses to the experience of walking in the forest and speaking to animals. Despite their limited vocabulary and articulation ability, the children could express their feelings of fear, threat, joy, and discovery in the way they walked in the "forest," or in their voices when they spoke to the "animals."

No attempt was made to develop divergent interpretations. The emphasis was, rather, on reinforcing a correct response to a trivial detail. The above observation illustrates the *sclerosis* of knowledge which too often interferes with the novice's ability to move in the direction of divergence and creativity.

Divergent thinking and the achievement test

An important factor contributing to the emphasis on the correct response and discouraging divergent thinking is the achievement test. Its relationship to the teaching practices of the novice is often mentioned in the interviews.

A new teacher is very impatient to see definite results quickly: teach a lesson, give a test. With teacher *A* it is on the table. You give a lesson, you quiz them and that's it. With teacher *C* it is drawn out over a longer period, and you don't know whether they absorbed.

This reaction illustrates a need for closure and evaluation. The *A* teacher can satisfy this need by testing. The *A* teaching and the testing program are interwoven into one logical and coherent unit. The test has a direct impact on the teaching behavior of teachers. Bothered by the problem of what to teach, they look for a guide in the course syllabi, teacher's manual, and the achievement tests.

Last week the principal said that my class was going to have a reading test. I am responsible for the reading program this week. I was not sure that I had taught them the right things, so I took out a test from the library. We prepared for the test by practicing similar questions . . . I don't have to invent these questions; I find them in the workbook.

As early as the elementary school level the program is often test-oriented. Sometimes it is a deliberate plan of a teacher threatened by the exposure of the class achievement and the comparison with other classes. However, even in the class of the secure teacher, the test is an important factor. A similar educational philosophy often permeates the curriculum and the test. Both are primarily level *A*-centered. It is difficult to expect the promotion of divergency under these pressures.

To support the contention that the testing program stresses the *A* and overlooks the *C* orientation, the discussion will examine one typical item, from one of the best-known reading comprehension tests.

The following item is taken from a test widely used in many schools.[L6:8]

When my brother Ted and I were sick, a man from the Health Department came to our house. He put a sign with the words "Mumps—Keep Out" on our door. When the other boys saw that red sign, they knew they could not play with us. We had to stay at home until the man came back and took down the sign.

I. Who is telling this story?
    (1) Ted's mother.
    (2) Ted's brother.
    (3) One of Ted's playmates.
    (4) A man from the Health Department.

II. What was the matter with Ted?
    (1) He did not want to play with the other boys.
    (2) He did not like to go to school.
    (3) He was angry with his sister.
    (4) He was sick.

III. Why was the sign put on the door?
    (1) To scare the people in the neighborhood.
    (2) To let the doctor know someone was sick.
    (3) To help keep other children from catching the mumps.
    (4) To tell the attendance officer why the children were not in school.

IV. Who took the sign down?
    (1) The man who put it up.
    (2) Another man from the Health Department.
    (3) Ted's doctor.
    (4) Ted.

V. What does this story show?
    (1) That boys are more likely to catch mumps than girls.
    (2) That children will get sick if they play outdoors.
    (3) That the Health Department tries to protect children from diseases that are catching.
    (4) That sick children get very lonesome.

Do these test items, in terms of their impact on the reading program, encourage specificity, convergent thinking, or divergent thinking? Do they encourage a level *A*, *B*, or *C* curriculum?

Out of the five questions of reading comprehension, three tap level *A* of knowledge (I, II, and IV), two level *B* (III, and V), and *none* level *C*.

One does not have to read and comprehend the whole story, but rather, repeat one phrase in order to know the correct answer to the *A*-oriented questions. For instance, it is sufficient to read four words ("When my brother Ted") to answer question I ("Who is telling the story?"), to read the first line ("When my brother Ted and I were sick") to answer question II ("What was the matter with Ted?"). The answer is given in one phrase or sentence. One does not have to put things together to produce, or to think.

The answers to questions III and V call for productive thinking of the convergent type. For instance, to answer question III ("Why was the sign put on the door?"), it is not sufficient to read: "When the other boys saw that red sign, they knew they could not play with us." The subject must add his own understanding that the children could not play with the sick boys because mumps are contagious. This is not stated explicitly in the text. Then the subject produces the conclusion: "To help keep other children from catching the mumps."

To repeat, out of five questions, three are level *A*, two are level *B*, and none are level *C*-centered. However, when one examines *teacher*-made tests, the ratio is even less balanced. An examination of tests developed by the novice teachers under discussion, shows that around 80% of the items are *A*-, 20% are *B*-, and none are *C*-oriented. The emphasis is on recall of specifics, a "touch" of convergent thinking, and no attention to divergence.

The test is one of the most formulated expressions of the teacher's philosophy and objectives. It expresses an attempt to spell out in detail the nature of knowledge that, in the teacher's understanding, has to be learned. School testing permeates the practitioner's methodology. It is often a philosophy which leaves little room for creativity, divergence, or intuitive thinking.

Speak with professional people—a scientist, a medical doctor, or a teacher. What most of them prize in their colleagues is intuition and the ability to come out with fresh ideas. The testing philosophy, with its preoccupation—almost obsession—with recall and the correctness of the end result, discourages the development of intuitiveness, divergence, and originality. It discourages the learner from making an intelligent guess, or from developing an intuitive feeling into a confusing problem.

Within the last several years the whole movement that is called "objective testing" has come under severe criticism. For instance, Bruner, in his book *The Process of Education,* says:[B12:66]

The assignment of grades in school typically emphasizes the acquisition of factual knowledge, primarily because that is what is most easily evaluated; moreover, it tends to emphasize the correct answer, since it is the correct answer on the straightforward exam that can be graded as correct.

The present testing philosophy teaches the learner to rely primarily on his memory and to be overconscious of specific facts. The child quickly learns that he is penalized for being interested in the *process,* for questioning the surface truth, or for searching for a divergent response. The present testing philosophy teaches the novice teacher not only to stress level A of knowledge out of all proportion, but also to overemphasize the end result and pay little attention to the process. In an interview, a teacher said in a definite and authoritative voice: "I give them a test and I want to know whether they know or don't know. That's all."

"Does he know, or doesn't he know?" becomes the central question, rather than the way the child arrives at knowledge. The process of learning, that is, the way the learner thinks, his attitude toward discovery and inquiry, are pushed to the background by a so-called objective test which measures only true or false *final* answers.

The test is surrounded by such an aura of scientific infallibility that the novice teacher fails to recognize its limitations in terms of validity (what it measures) and objectivity. However, some writers on this topic are very critical. For instance, in an article entitled "The Tyranny of Multiple Choice Tests,"[H11] Hoffman calls for a reexamination of the major assumptions underlying the construction and use of tests. The test constructor should look for ways of evaluating not only the acquisition of information, but also divergency and creativity. In terms of the science of testing, it may mean movement from the present overemphasis on multiple choice in the direction of projective materials, rating techniques, and interviews.

The search for balance in the testing program is an integral part of a search for balance in the meaning of knowledge. A more balanced philosophy of education and curriculum organization are interrelated with a more balanced testing program.

It is interesting to note that one of the most important tests in the literature, the Stanford-Binet Test of Intelligence, in one phase of its work (Responses to Pictures, 3½ Years Old) attempted to develop a scoring system based on differentiation of three levels of difficulty comparable to levels *A, B,* and *C,* under discussion here.

In the author's words:[T3:204]

> The test was originally intended to differentiate the three difficulty levels represented by *enumeration, description* and *interpretation.* However, levels II and III did not prove to be entirely satisfactory and only difficulty I has been retained in the present form.

The significance of this illustration is in the fact that the test builders recognized that description (*B*) is a higher level than enumeration (*A*), and interpretation (*C*) is higher than description. They recognized, also, the need for a scoring system to tap these levels of difficulty.

Pioneering work in developing tests which measure creativity in children is reported by Getzels and Jackson in their book, *Creativity and Intelligence,*[G3] and by Torrance in his book, *Guiding Creative Talent.*[T5] The realization is growing among educators that intelligence and creativity, convergent and divergent thinking, are not identical, or even highly related abilities. Torrance reports[T4:7] that in one study:

> The highly creative group ranked in the upper twenty percent of their classes on creativity but not on intelligence. The highly intelligent group ranked in the upper twenty percent on intelligence but not on creativity . . . About seventy percent of the top twenty percent on creativity would have been excluded from gifted groups selected on the basis of I.Q. alone.

Getzels and Jackson identify two major intellective modes. The first mode focuses on the understanding of the known by learning the predetermined. The second mode moves toward the revision of the known, the exploration of the undetermined, and the new creation.

A person for whom the first mode or process is primary tends toward the *usual* and *expected*. A person for whom the second mode is primary tends toward the *novel* and *speculative*. The one favors certainty, the other risk . . .

Psychologists use different terms in discussing these two modes. Guilford speaks about "convergent and divergent thinking"; Maslow, about "defense" and "growth"; Rogers, about "defensiveness" and "openness"; Schachtel, about "embeddedness" and "independence." Whatever formulation is used, the position is that one mode stands for "intellectual acquisitiveness and conformity, the other intellectual inventiveness and innovation."[G3:14]

Whereas both modes are *equally* important, it is primarily the first one which is stressed by the present intelligence test. There is an urgent need for enlarging our limited concept of intelligence and intelligence testing to encompass the creative and innovating orientation.

DEMOCRATIC TEACHING

The written reactions and the interview data show that the role-playing demonstration of teacher *C* intensified and solidified the rejection of *A* as a constricting teacher, aroused doubts as to whether the democratic leadership of *B* was sufficiently deep and comprehensive, and focused the group's attention primarily on the role of the learner in the process of learning. The teachers were impressed with the attempt of teacher *C* to bring pupils into the *planning* of some aspects of the lesson. They felt that they were sensitized to a deeper understanding of *democratic teaching*.

My understanding of democratic teaching changed. I called teacher *A* democratic because he was friendly. I equated democratic behavior with being nice. I called teacher *B* democratic because he gave children a view of the total project. He set a goal so that they would know where they were going. I respect his emphasis on thinking.

Now comes teacher *C* who believes in the individuality of the learner and who encourages children to participate in planning. In the *B* class, children work toward goals set by the teacher. They learn subject matter decided on only by the teacher. The outcome is known. In the *C* class, children participate in developing the goal and the content.

The democratic process in learning, with its emphasis on pupil-teacher interaction, is one of the most valued ideals of modern education. It is also one of the most elusive concepts. The depth and meaning of the cooperative process of teacher-student participation is often misunderstood by both theorist and practitioner of education. No wonder it is confused by the novice teachers.

Many teachers called teacher *A* democratic, emphasizing primarily his being "nice," his use of praise, and the amount of participation in his class. At the beginning, they failed to recognize his manipulative and constricting approach.

The majority of the group perceived *B* as democratic primarily because he raised long-range objectives and because of his respect for the children's ability to think. They started to question the *A* orientation and recognized its authoritarian and controlling qualities.

Under the impact of the *C* demonstration, the teachers came to realize that even the *B* approach lacked democratic emphasis to some extent. The children have to work toward goals set only by the teacher. The subject matter, outcomes, and process of learning are predetermined. They identified with the *C* orientation and its richer provisions for the expressions of the individuality of the learner. They perceived it as a step ahead on the road toward democratic teaching.

Teacher- or child-centeredness?

Despite the potential promise inherent in the *B* approach of unifying subject matter and creating basic Gestalt, this approach still suffers from a major limitation. As Snygg points out,[S14: Part 2] the attempt is to change the behavior of the learner by manipulating the environment *outside* the perceived self. The *B* orientation attempts to change the course of study, to manipulate the organization of content and materials with the hope that it will affect the learner. Unless educators are prepared to go beyond the external steps of subject matter integration and stress the interaction between the learner and the subject matter, the goal of curriculum improvement may not be fully attained.

The *C* orientation is an attempt to move in this direction by emphasizing not only the integration of subject matter and its uniting structure, but rather by developing a curriculum pattern based on continuous interaction between the learner and learning. The emphasis is on a somewhat emerging curriculum, a curriculum which is neither child-, nor teacher-centered. A child-centered curriculum tends to be laissez-faire. A teacher-centered curriculum tends to be authoritarian in nature. Both of these approaches have their strengths and limitations.

The child-centered curriculum stems from an idealistic belief in the resourcefulness of children. The belief is that there is richness and uniqueness in every individual, but that these qualities are sometimes latent, or covered by a shell. The function of education is primarily to help children realize what *they* want, what potential *they* have, and where *they* want to go, and then to help them get there.

The teacher-centered curriculum is a belief that the child is molded by the values and the norms of the culture surrounding him. It is the function of organized education to see that learning the modes of the culture will not be a trial-and-error process. The teacher, being an authority, has to select the knowledge and values that have to be learned. The teacher has a responsibility to direct the immature child and lead him toward maturity.

The child-centered approach suffers from a naive conception of the meaning of growth. Growth is not only a process of "unfolding the child's potentialities." Growth is a result of the experiences which impinge on the child. It is the function of the teacher to select the right experiences to help the child grow in a healthy direction.

The teacher-centered approach underestimates the power of children and the importance of self-direction. In some cases, at least, it develops a teacher authority who is preoccupied with his own conception of the knowledge to be taught and is not *open* to the needs and perceptions of children.

The C orientation is an attempt to look for a balance between the child- and the teacher-centered positions and to build on the strength in both of them. The C teacher in the role-playing demonstration initiates the activity in an authority-centered way. He develops his own interpretation of the subject matter. He directs and structures. However, as the activity proceeds, he permits children, individually and in groups, to come into the planning and develop the lesson in their own divergent ways. He encourages children to move from the known to the unknown; unknown even to the teacher. The teacher is not laissez-faire; he does not follow a "do-anything-you-want-to-do" approach. The C teacher creates a setup and structure for systematic and serious study, which encourages children to learn by identifying with an adult authority and also by developing their own sense of self-direction.

The teacher who is A-oriented reveals to his pupils a short-range objective; the one who is B-oriented reveals to his followers a long-range objective. Whereas the difference between these two approaches is fundamental, the similarity is fundamental, too. In both ways of teaching, it is the teacher who presents an objective which the pupils had almost no part in planning.

Observing the teachers under discussion here, one finds that in performing lessons they often conceal the next topic from their pupils, and hide the new posters, records, and other materials. This behavior is significant and revealing in terms of the democratic quality or criterion of the teacher-pupil relations.

The teacher wants to arouse class interest by surprising and fascinating the pupils with the richness of the materials which she prepared and preplanned. In the A and B classes, children are going to be surprised by the goal and by the presentation. The pupils' function is primarily to absorb and accept rather than initiate and plan.

In following the A and B orientations, the teacher tends to stress primarily the technique of explanation. Facing the class is a dynamic, sometimes even overpowering, young teacher who "monopolizes the stage." He attempts to be interesting by asking questions (sometimes bombarding them with questions), demonstrating, planning, and acting. The children's role expectation is to be "motivated" to move where the leader wants them to go, and be interested in doing what the leader wants them to do.

It is not difficult to recognize in this description the attributes of leadership which is skewed in the authoritarian direction. It is the teacher alone who determines the goal and plans the program of the group. To use Lewin's terminology, it is the leader's "field of power" which keeps the pupils going. Children's initiative, self-direction, and involvement in learning are often insufficiently promoted under such conditions of teacher-pupil cooperation. As one interviewee puts it:

Teacher C makes provisions for children to work on a common interest. In the role-playing they plan for a few minutes before presenting their idea. In C as a way of teaching, it may mean getting involved in a long-range project. They (the children) will develop independence and responsibility in working on their own ideas, without the teacher stopping them every few minutes and telling them to work on another task.

Task involvement or reinforcement?

A basic attribute of democratic teaching is the encouragement of *task* involvement. The pupil learns subject matter because the knowledge is intrinsically meaningful to him. A basic attribute of teacher-centered teaching is the use of extrinsic motivation, even coercion or manipulation. An interviewee says:

I always thought it is good to compliment children and praise them. I believed that reward is better than punishment. Now I see that the use of reward may be a manipulative technique, to make children do what the teacher wants them to do.

The excessive use of praise is, at least in some cases, the major tool of a benevolent autocracy.

Teacher A is a master of praise and reward. She asks many questions, gives many assignments, and gets immediate results. Each "result" is rewarded. It gave us a feeling of artificial behavior, but we decided she is a friendly and warm person. I guess we took it for granted this is the way one should behave at school.

The artificiality of A's rewarding behavior was recognized; however, it was compatible with the group's image of a "nice" school teacher. Teacher *B*'s rewarding behavior is less extreme and, therefore, is not manipulative in nature. An interviewee says:

Teacher *B* raises few thought questions which tap the children's understanding of the main ideas. The children work hard to reach the correct answer. My feeling is that when they were praised, they deserved it. It was a praise well-earned.

The difference between the "rewarding behavior" of *A* and *B* is fundamental. However, one should recognize that both of them use praise for the same goal—approving behavior which agrees with the specific objectives and values of the leader. The rewarded children are those who please the leader.

Rewards are not limited to marks, promotions, or stars; nor is punishment limited to nonpromotion or expulsion from the group. A nod of approval, a reassuring smile, a frown, and criticism, are subtle ways in which the teacher rewards or promotes a particular act of behavior.

Through a system of punishment and rewards the child often learns to work not for his own goals, but for the adult's (teacher's) objectives. The positive impact of this process is fully recognized. It is a major channel of socialization. Generally, children learn to accept the rewarded goal and it becomes their own. However, the overuse of reward has, in many cases, negative effects.

The intrinsic relationship between the learner and the subject matter is sometimes supplemented by the relationship between the learner and the reward. In the language of learning theorists,[H10] the learner aims for the reward, an indication that a task had been completed, rather than for the *success* inherent in the mastering of the task itself. A common illustration is the pupil who is encouraged to learn to read in order to get a high grade (reward) rather than to satisfy his own quest for knowledge (success).

The direct personal relations between the learner and the subject matter often disappear. One learns for the culminating symbol of graduation. Of course, graduation satisfies a personal need too. In satisfying it, however, the subject matter learned becomes secondary.

In contrast to the *A* and *B*, the *C* orientation illustrates a teaching behavior which is not based primarily on the law of effect, or the reinforcement theory. Teacher C limits his use of reward or punishment. He centers his educational approach on Lewin's belief in the power of the intrinsic motivation of task involvement.

In a discussion of "Field Theory and Learning,"[L3] Lewin points out some of the difficulties in applying the law of effect drawn from "maze experiments" to *classroom* situations. Psychologists have tended to perform their experiments in confining runways or with subjects strapped to the apparatus. They overlooked the importance of the factor of the maze barrier on the results of their experiments. The animal is compelled to learn an intrinsically disliked task not only because of the fear of punishment, but also because the maze barrier does not permit it to run away and "leave the field." In terms of classroom practices, it means that the teacher who wants to resort to punitive motivation in the learning process must not only employ punishment but also erect authoritarian and "police" barriers around the learner; or, using Lewin's example, put him in a maze.

Teachers A and B can be rewarding or punitive in nature. When they are rewarding, the reward is *externally* related to the task of learning. In an attempt to obtain such rewards, children tend to develop a variety of shortcuts. For example, copying on an examination is an attempt to get reward without working on the learning task.

One of the greatest challenges for the educator is to make knowledge a part of the lives of students and to make subject matter personally meaningful. The C demonstration illustrates a beginning of movement in this direction. Each child is encouraged to try to be successful in working on a task he sets for himself; to experience progress toward his own level of aspiration. The pupil works not because of the approval or disapproval of his elders (teachers), but because he is ego-involved in the task. Underlying the ideal of democracy in education is task involvement in learning.

Individual worth

Observing at work the overwhelming majority of teachers who follow the A and B patterns of rewarding behavior, one finds that the signs of approval and disapproval are not distributed equally among all pupils. Already in the first grade the class is sorted into two groups: the approved and the disapproved. The approved pupils are those who obey the teacher's request for attention; they follow the directions, do neat, clean work, keep obviously busy, and finish their work on time. The disapproved pupils are those who, for various reasons, cannot keep up with the others and cannot measure up to the same standards, or those who want to assert their independence and do it their own way.

Those who belong to the disapproved group introject the teacher's evaluation of them. They tend to lose their security and initiative and stop investing effort in mastering the subject matter. They tend to develop a defeatist approach toward the school and the teacher, which in turn brings about more disapproval from the teacher and, consequently, further passivity toward the educating agent. A look at a typical class discussion illustrates this point.

In order to arouse interest and keep the discussion going, the teacher tends to raise many questions. It is not a discussion where everyone contributes from his experiences, hopes, and uncertainties. It is an aggressive search for the correct answer which often only a few pupils can provide immediately.

The teacher, being interested in a "good discussion," tends to prefer those who can produce the right answer and sometimes tends to ignore the other pupils. A discussion pattern is established where the class is divided into an active group, which has something to contribute, and a passive group which, in some cases at least, is considered by the teacher and by itself as lacking in ability to contribute; it is considered, to put it somewhat extremely, as worthless.

Democracy in education means the belief in the worth of an individual. If this last sentence should become an item on a scale testing the educational beliefs of teachers, the response of all of them would be "strongly agree." However, the above observations of teachers in action suggest that a wide gap exists between one's professed ideals and his teaching behavior.

Teacher C illustrates an attempt to implement the democratic belief in the work of every individual.

Teacher *C* looks at the child's answer or work from the point of view of the child. He tries to understand what the child wanted to say and where he wanted to go. He respects children.

To conclude, democratic teaching does not mean only nice and friendly human relations, nor the sole emphasis on unity of subject matter and productive thinking. Democratic teaching means primarily cooperative planning, task involvement, and respect for the worth of the individual student. These three are interrelated.

Movement from repetitive toward creative teaching cannot be realized without an understanding of the deeper dynamics of democratic teaching.

Democratic teaching: difficulties

Democratic teaching was perceived by the novice teachers as a major characteristic denoting the *C* orientation. Some of the difficulties experienced by teachers in translating the ideal of democracy into the language of teaching behavior will be discussed in this section.

A major problem is the difficulty in understanding the nature of freedom inherent in democratic teaching, and its confusion with an atmosphere of laissez-faire. This difficulty can be observed both on the *conceptual* and *behavioral* levels. The following experiment illustrates cognitive confusions involved.

In a college class, three staff meetings were demonstrated through role-playing before a group of teachers. In the first "staff meeting" the "principal" played a *laissez-faire* role. One could not distinguish his role from those of the other group members. The nature of his participation in terms of its quality and quantity resembled the participation of the other members. There was no attempt on his part to move the discussion ahead, reach conclusions, etc. After the first demonstration was over, the group was instructed to indicate whether the principal played a laissez-faire, democratic, or authoritarian role. The majority answered, "democratic;" the minority—"laissez-faire," and none "authoritarian."

A second "staff meeting" was demonstrated where the "principal" played a *democratic* role. He identified the problems and developed an agenda cooperatively with the staff. He was attentive to human relations, attempted to clarify and synthesize positions, and moved the discussion ahead.

The group of teachers was again instructed to decide whether the principal played a laissez-faire, democratic, or authoritarian role. The responses were almost equally divided between "democratic" and "authoritarian."

In the third "staff meeting" the "principal" played an *authoritarian* role. He dictated a preplanned agenda, made decisions, and assigned tasks without encouraging the group to present their ideas. Without exception, the teachers decided that the last "principal" portrayed an authoritarian leader.

On the perceptual level, the teachers are in some agreement with regard to the operation of authoritarian leadership, but in disagreement with regard to the nature of laissez-faire and democratic behavior. Their misconceptions show a very definite trend which has significant educational implications: it is the laissez-faire teacher who is perceived as democratic, and not vice-versa; it is the democratic teacher who is often perceived as authoritarian and not vice-versa.

To put it in other words, it is the laissez-faire teacher, the one who does not *assert* leadership, direction, and power, who is perceived as meeting the *ideal* of democratic behavior. It is the democratic individual, the one who asserts some degree of leadership, who is often perceived negatively as authoritarian. On the professed verbal level, democratic leadership is equated with lack of assertion of direct power.

Traditionally, the role of the teacher is seen in an assertive light. The dictionary defines the term "teach" as, "to make to know how; show how; hence, to train or accustom to some action." In many languages the teacher is called "instructor," that is, the one who gives instructions or orders. The professed belief that democratic leadership means lack of assertion is a reversal of the traditional image of the teacher. How does this reversal affect the teacher's behavior?

One expression of the translation of the teacher's conception of democratic leadership to the language of teaching behavior is withdrawal, nondirection, and delegation of complete responsibility to children; a teaching behavior which is more laissez-faire than democratic. This pattern is especially prevalent when the subject matter is *art*, the area that traditionally is considered the province of creativity. In many instances, observing coloring activities, "cut-and-glue" projects, the novice teacher would come to me and say:

I let them have free time to express their own ideas. I don't want to impose mine and stifle their creativity. Don't you think it is a workshop atmosphere?

Free time for children to do what they want, and nondirection on the part of the leader, is equated in this typical illustration with democratic teaching and with the process of promoting creativity.

It is relatively easy to surrender the traditional role of the teacher—the one who structures and directs—in the general area of art. This area is conventionally seen as one where norms of production are not established, definite achievement is not expected; an area with relatively no pressure of standards. It is also relatively easy to resign the role of directiveness in the arts because the tendency is to perceive them as secondary in status in the hierarchy of school subjects. To put it somewhat radically, it is not really seen as serious business, but rather as extracurricular, or even as frills. Let the children express their creativity by doing what they want, by drawing pictures, or by putting on a skit. This will be lots of fun.

The role of directiveness is diminished primarily when the activity is denoted by lack of norms of achievement and an atmosphere of fun rather than systematic and hard work. This is a sad commentary on one frequent approach to democratic teaching and creativity.

A second area known to be the domain of democratic teaching is *social studies*. The teacher is aware that the teaching of social studies calls for the application of the principles of the democratic process. Should the teacher, whose professed value of democratic leadership is characterized by withdrawal, apply nondirectiveness to the teaching of social studies?

The answer to this question is negative. Social studies is perceived as a fundamental area of the curriculum. It has subject matter to be covered and achievement to be reached. It is a serious business. The teacher cannot afford to abdicate the responsibility of leadership and invest complete authority in the children. On the contrary, the obstacle to democratic teaching in the area of social studies is a high degree of teacher-centered teaching, or "pseudo-democracy." The last term refers to the known practice of moving through the external motions of democratic teaching, but, in reality, manipulating children to do what the teacher wants them to do. An example might be "guiding" the child to decide on a topic, or on committees that the teacher "had in mind." In cases of this nature, the teacher realizes that his teaching behavior is pseudo-democratic; that he only pays lip service to the ideal.

To conclude, both on the conceptual and behavioral levels, many teachers have difficulty with the principles of democratic teaching. The major issue is the definition of the nature of freedom for children, as opposed to direction on the part of teachers.

Some proponents of an extreme atmosphere of freedom in the elementary school claim that the end result will be a higher level of creativity. The function of the teacher, according to this freedom-centered position, is to provide a permissive atmosphere and to supply tools and materials for the development of self-expression. Any attempt in direction or setting standards is seen as a danger stiffling the innate talents of children. Direction is seen as imposing the teacher's own set of values and channeling children into the prevalent pattern of production. The Rogerian psychology of nondirective therapy was adopted by some educational theorists and practitioners[46] and contributed toward the building of the image of the "ideal teacher": permissive, nondirective, and objective.

The impact of these educational and psychological theories on the beginning teacher was a mixed blessing. On the one hand, the novice was sensitized to the importance of identifying children's interests and following the child. Teachers realized, at least on the verbal level, that autocratic and overstructured teaching is a deterrent to the growth of children's creativity. On the other hand, the emphasis on the relationship between freedom, child-centeredness and creativity sometimes led many young teachers to the equation of democratic leadership and the creative process with laissez-faire oriented behavior, or to "pseudo-democratic" behavior.

The *C* orientation is based on the belief that creativity means neither child- nor teacher-centeredness. Teacher *C* starts the lesson with a definite structure and sense of direction. He does not abdicate the teacher's responsibility, but rather, leads. However, in the middle of the lesson children are encouraged to come into the preplanned structure and develop their own orientation. They are expected to work seriously and systematically, and present their accomplishment—that is, the structure they reached. They are expected to work hard on achieving the task.

Democratic teaching, as an element of the creative process, means the initiation of a flexible structure and direction by the teacher that accommodates the direction and structure suggested by children. It is an attempt to reach a synthesis between the child- and teacher-centered schools of thought.

THE REPETITIVE-CREATIVE CONTINUUM: QUESTIONS

The theoretical formulation of the repetitive-creative continuum was presented to various groups of educators and was read by some of my colleagues. I find that since several questions recur, despite the fact that to some extent they are touched on in the previous chapters, it would be worthwhile to discuss some of these questions as a conclusion to Part I of this study.

Question: In the example utilized to demonstrate the creative teacher you assume a preselected topic for discussion and I am wondering whether this is consistent with your discussion of "open and closed systems." It would seem to me that creative teaching would begin at an earlier step which would provide the opportunity for children to participate in the organization of their learning activities.

This question, raised by the head of a department of elementary education, implies a criticism of the *C* model as too structured in its "earlier steps." The topic is preselected by the teacher. The first part of the lesson is relatively teacher-centered. It is only as the lesson proceeds that teacher *C* "opens" it for children to exert their sense of direction and participate in planning the activity.

I am in agreement with my colleague that it is possible to

formulate a creative model which is even more "open" than the one under discussion. For instance, in the chapter on the methodology of science, illustrations of learning based on children's questions will be brought out, and the chapter on social studies will examine the problem of cooperative planning.

There are several reasons for building model C as one who starts with his own structure and only later on opens it for the emergence of a new structure.

(1) The discussion in this chapter fully illustrates that a major difficulty which teachers observe in the C model is its phase of "disorder." Any attempt to create a model which starts in a nonstructured and nonteacher-directed way, may have very little impact on the novice's behavior. Burton[B16] criticizes the proponents of the creative orientation in teaching for "sentimentalizing" about the goal and the product, and not doing enough work on describing the procedure of reaching the goal of creativity. An attempt is made here to present a process, a *flexible model*, of working towards creative thinking.

(2) The discussion here is not child-centered in its orientation. It does not believe in the oversimplification of "let the child express himself" or "let him unfold his inner talent." As following chapters will demonstrate, the prerequisite to a creative product is an *immersion* with an experience. To the extent that the immersion is deeper, the divergent product will tend to be of a higher quality. To illustrate, a fruitful approach to creative writing does not mean complete freedom to write on anything the child wishes. It is, rather, a matter of reacting to an experience or a stimulating discussion, out of which the child may move in divergent directions. In brief, the formulation of model C assumes that the meaningful and rich experience is the father of the creative idea!

Question: Your position is to encourage your teachers to give creative lessons. When would they learn to give *regular* lessons, such as teaching social studies, or reading?

The implication of this question is that creativity is "play which lacks meat." To some extent, proponents of the creative orientation are responsible for this misconception. I have recently heard a lecture at a P.T.A. meeting where creativity was presented as "self-expression in playing with mud pies," and the advice to teachers was to teach three lessons: "Silence No. 1, No. 2, and No. 3." Whereas, "playing in the mud" for a certain age group, and provisions of quiet time for the pursuit of individual and group interests, merit serious consideration, the major approach to creativity should be serious involvement with the *depth* of *subject matter*. For instance, the chapter on reading will stress that teaching reading creatively does not mean "play" but rather, a search for the development of the personal meaning of the reading matter to the reader.

Creative thinking was presented here as a mode of behavior which should become an integral part of the *regular* lesson in social studies, reading, etc. Regular teaching calls for a balance between specificity, convergent, and divergent thinking. At present, the balance is very far from being reached.

Question: How are the A, B, and C models related to modern theories of creative thinking?

The formulation of the repetitive-creative continuum is based on the modern findings concerning modes of thinking. Whereas the leading researchers in this area stress primarily the *measurement* of creative abilities, the contribution of the present study is the conceptualization of creativity as a *teaching behavior*.

The emphasis on specificity, convergent, and divergent thinking, does not only mean the emphasis on a different mode of thinking, but rather, constitutes a different *total climate of teaching*. For instance, the climate of specificity is characterized by recall, teacher-centeredness, short questions, repetition, and constricting behavior; the climate of divergency is characterized by the teacher's subjective interpretation, movement toward the unknown, de-emphasis of evaluation in terms of right or wrong, and democratic teaching.

The conceptualization of the process of creative teaching as a total climate of behavior rather than as a single act has implications relevant to the work of the teacher. The main approach to the promotion of creativity is not the initiation of piecemeal lessons and artificial stimulants of creative nature, such as practicing exercises resembling the new tests in creativity. What is rather needed is a change in the *total intellectual atmosphere* of the school. What is needed is a reexamination of the basic methodology of the major disciplines in the light of the search for a creative mode of thinking. This examination is to be the objective of Part II of this book. To quote from *Creativity and Intelligence:*[G3:127]

Are there certain areas of instruction in which opportunities are promoted for "discovering" as well as for "remembering?" Is there provision in the curriculum for playing with facts and ideas as well as for repeating them? Can we teach students to be more sensitive to the nature of problems? Can we teach them that a problem may have several different interpretations and solutions? Even if there is only one right answer, as in mathematics problems, can the student solve the problem in a number of different ways?

SELECTED BIBLIOGRAPHY

BRUNER, S. Jerome, *On Knowing: Essays for the Left Hand.* Cambridge: Harvard University Press, 1962. A most stimulating discussion on learning and the meaning of knowledge.

BURTON, H. William, *The Guidance of Learning Activities.* New York: Appleton-Century-Crofts, 1962. Chapter 16 is an excellent formulation of the process of creative teaching written from a curriculum point of view.

GETZELS, Jacob, and JACKSON, Philip, *Creativity and Intelligence.* New York: John Wiley & Sons, Inc., 1962. A pioneering study into the nature of giftedness. Of special interest are Chapters 1 and 2 and the last section of Chapter 3.

TORRANCE, Paul, *Guiding Creative Talent.* Englewood Cliffs, N.J.: Prentice-Hall, Inc., 1962. A comprehensive and original discussion of creativity.

II

The subject areas:
An approach

5

Reading: Repetitive or creative?

There are few problems in education which arouse more controversy and heated discussion than the problem of teaching reading on the elementary school level. The discussion of the "reading problem" is found not only in educational literature, but has even reached the popular magazines and daily newspapers.

Both educators and laymen are fully aware of the fundamental role of reading ability. In the life of a nation it means literacy —a prerequisite to social progress and political democracy. In the life of the adult it means competence for the competitive market of labor, and a source of personal growth. In the life of the student, reading disability can lead to failure in school and emotional maladjustment. The ability to read is a foundation for success and growth.

The purpose

The function of this chapter is to describe the types of experiences and problems which the novice teacher encounters in teaching reading. An attempt will be made to identify the creative as well as the repetitive aspects of the process as *both are needed* in the successful teaching of reading. One central question which will be raised throughout the discussion is whether the reading methodology is extremely skewed in the direction of specificity to the detriment of the healthy development of creative reading ability.

Perhaps out of zeal to make reading a science of specific skills, or in the rush for shortcuts for the development of speedy and correct reading, the most important aspect is neglected—namely, the personal relationship of the reader to the reading matter. Is it possible that we have overlooked, in the excitement over the painful issue of "why Johnny can't read" the equally fundamental issue of why many of those "Johnnys" who are able to read are not *interested* in reading? Is it possible that reading methodology has become too narrowly geared to the teaching of the reading skills, excluding the values of the intellectual, emotional, and aesthetic aspects inherent in reading?

With these questions in mind the discussion will proceed to examine some of the main practices and issues in the teaching of reading: reading readiness, word recognition, individualized reading, reading skills, creative reading, the literary quality of the basal reader, and implications to the total language arts program.

READING READINESS

In the past, the reading of words and letters was introduced immediately on the first day of the first graders at school. Today it is common practice to postpone the formal teaching of reading to such time when the child is *ready* to learn. Reading readiness calls for a positive attitude toward reading, certain visual and auditory skills, ability to concentrate on formal learning, and a certain level of comprehension. To achieve these goals, the modern school has inaugurated the phase of reading readiness, which precedes the direct instruction of learning to read.

There are two distinct approaches to the development of readiness: (1) centeredness on reading readiness workbooks, and (2) an experiential approach based on a broad language arts program. Generally speaking, the first tends to be repetitive and highly structured, while the second is potentially more creative in orientation.

The reading readiness workbook

To understand the workbook-centered approach it might be enlightening to examine the position and the suggested practices of one of its supporters. One writer of a book on reading [M8] and of a reading readiness series [M9] identifies six instructional skills to be developed as a basis for a reading readiness program.[M8:145]

1. Providing training in visual discrimination.
2. Providing training in auditory discrimination.
3. Developing the understanding that reading matter is to be observed from left to right.
4. Providing training in listening.
5. Creating a desire to learn to read.
6. Constructing concepts and developing listening vocabulary needed for beginning reading.

The workbook, entitled *Getting Ready*,[M9] is devoted exclusively to the development of the skills, mentioned above, needed for reading readiness. Following are some illustrations.

In order to read the child has to develop his visual discrimination,—that is, he must be able to differentiate between the forms of words and letters. In the workbook the child may find pairs of letters arranged in boxes, such as *AA BR HH CO KK*. He is asked to decide which pairs include letters that are alike, and which include different letters. The same procedure may be repeated with words. The child is not taught to read the words or the letters. He only receives practice in visual discrimination of forms.

In order to read the child has to develop his auditory discrimination. In the workbook the child may find a series of five pictures —man, mitten, money, coat, moon—and is asked to indicate which of them begins with the same sound.

As the English language is read from left to right, this skill is practiced in the workbook through following instructions dealing with pictures arranged in a left to right sequence.

To read, the child has to know how to listen and to comprehend. The pupil is thus given practice in listening and comprehension by being asked to follow instructions dealing with pictures presented in the workbook, or by discussing the ideas "told" in pictures.

A somewhat different approach to the development of the reading readiness is suggested by the workbook *Before We Read*.[G6] It is different from the previous workbook in two respects. (1) It does not have any exercises in visual discrimination of words and letters. The practice of this skill is limited entirely to discrimination between pictures. This approach holds that exercises with forms of words, which do not convey any meaning to the child, are not particularly beneficial. (2) In contrast to the former workbook, which is organized around skills, the *Before We Read* approach is divided into units of content. The unit divisions deal with topics like "Fun With Pets," "Fun With Toys," "Fun With The Family" (it is always "fun") which, in the authors judgment, are meaningful to the child.

The difference between the two workbooks is fundamental. The teacher is not expected to move directly to drill the class in exercises of auditory and visual discrimination, but is rather encouraged to start with a *discussion* of a topic. The discussion is an opportunity for stimulating children to relate experiences and hear stories and poems. In other words, the *Before We Read* type of workbook stems from a potentially broad language arts program which eventually culminates in exercise of specific reading readiness skills.

Reading readiness workbooks: evaluation

As reported by the group of novice teachers under discussion, reading readiness workbooks are generally used in the classrooms where they practice. They recognize the fact that the formal act of entering first grade does not necessarily mean being ready to read, and they therefore tend to be positively impressed with the workbook approach. In their search for structure, a sense of direction, and a seemingly realistic preparation for the needed reading skills, they find in workbooks the answer to many of the educational needs of children during their initiation to school. They provide practice in concentrating on a book task and give children ample activities for independent work, freeing the teacher to work with an individual or a small group of children.

As time proceeds the novice finds that his initial excitement over the reading readiness workbook gradually diminishes, and in some cases even changes into an outspoken rejection. What had once been seen as a systematic and structured development of skills is later perceived as a repetitive program. What had once been considered as rich activities are later evaluated as "busy work." What had once been perceived as an individualized approach tends to be perceived later as a standard and uniform treatment of children.

The workbook-centered readiness program suffers from basic limitations, some of which are inherent in the nature of the workbook itself, and others in the nature of its use by the teacher. The major limitation of this readiness may be said to be in its exaggerated emphasis on the drill of narrow skills, and its failure to focus on a curriculum of intellectual stimulation which aims at building the child's broad language powers.

Historically, the reading readiness workbook was originally to be used as supplementary material in the stage which preceded the preprimer. As supplementary materials, workbooks are still useful. They are a good source for independent work when used in conjunction with literature, poetry, experience charts, dictation by children, discussion, or records.

However, under the impact of an educational philosophy focused on specificity, and under the harassment of its corollary—a narrow testing program—a strange thing happened. The supplementary exercises of the workbook become the *center* of the curriculum in too many first grades. The literature, poetry, records, children's experience, or discussion became the *supplementary* materials! For instance, the teacher's edition of the workbook *Before We Read* suggests that *Time For Poetry* (an unusually rich anthology of poems for children), and *Poetry Time and Sounds Around Us* (excellent albums of children's records) will serve as supplementary materials to accompany the reading readiness exercises. The poetry has become supplementary to the drill—the exercise.

A similar situation is reflected in the actual teaching behavior of many teachers. A typical reading readiness lesson is composed of a brief "motivating discussion," which leads to the major and basic part of the lesson, namely "covering" one page of the workbook which stresses one of the "skills." If time permits, a quick supplementary activity of reading a story or a poem is added. This type of activity centering on drill and specificity is repeated every day.

The level A-oriented school, almost obsessed with the need to transmit specific skills and detailed facts, has lost its sense of balance. It has relegated poetry, literature, and exploration to the service of narrow skills of visual and auditory discrimination.

The experiential and functional approach

Milner's study [M19] on the relationship between readiness and the pattern of parent-child interaction, suggests that children who rarely participate in a two-way type of conversation at home, who are subject to orders or instructions, and who make little contribution to family discussion, also tend to be the slow readers.

Almy's study [A1] on the relation between children's experiences prior to first grade and their success in beginning reading, points out that children who have had much experience in listening to stories and poetry and who have been encouraged to ask questions about reading materials, are also more successful in reading.

The emphasis on experiences, discussion, children's literature, and exploration are major contributing factors to readiness to read. Reading readiness should be equated with a rich program aiming at promoting language facility and intellectual curiosity—curiosity about books and their message. A program of this nature will include discussion, trips, films, listening to literature and poetry books read by the teacher, accompanied by open discussion about them, children's own "reading" of stories by looking at the pictures, children's dictation of stories and poems, science experiments, and experience charts which illustrate to the child the process of transforming ideas into reading matter.

The activities mentioned above are only a few illustrations which stress a main position: The elements of visual and auditory discrimination, left to right sequence, and the desire to read, should not be perceived as discrete and independent skills. They are rather a product and a manifestation of a rich experiental background and a satisfactory maturational level. Therefore, the major approach to reading readiness is not to work on the discrete "symptoms"—the skills, but rather to enrich the child's experiences, with emphasis on his language development.

Readiness and the deprived

Most of the novice teachers with whom I work do their practice teaching in lower-class communities, and are going to be teachers of lower-class children. It is unfortunate that in these impoverished environments, where the need for enrichment is so great, too many teachers are looking for a shortcut to the goal of reading. They are impatient with the slow progress. They too often tend to perceive experiences, oral discussion, exploration, and literature as "dressing up" and "extras" to be cut out when the going is rough and tedious.

As suggested by Deutsch,[D5] the cultural and material deprivation of the lower-class child has effects on both the formal (the process by which stimuli are perceived and reacted to) and the contentual (actual content of knowledge) aspects of his cognition. An illustration of the "formal equipment" is the ability to use the adult as a source of information, and as one who encourages and rewards intellectual curiosity. Examples of "contentual equipment" would be information and verbal facility. The lower-class child tends to be farther away from his maturational ceiling in academic learning as a result of his *experiential* poverty.

The main implication of these findings to the readiness program for the culturally deprived is the inauguration of a broad and wide language arts program to perceive and accompany the stage of formal reading. Working in an impoverished environment, the teacher should realize that a readiness program centered on exercises is not a balanced program. It is rather a starvation diet offered to culturally starved children!

The novice teacher often argues that a reading readiness workbook gives her a sense of direction. Some young teachers say that as newcomers to the school community they are not in position of creating "revolutions." They must adjust to the atmosphere and the teaching pattern of the school. In other words, they believe they cannot initiate a functional reading readiness program, but must follow the workbook.

These arguments are sometimes valid and realistic. To these novice teachers, I would like to suggest a possible way of resolving their conflict. Distinguish between your experiential-functional program and the workbook-centered approach. Do not substitute the first for the second. Teach the workbook as an entity by itself. See it as an exercise. Concurrently develop an experience- and literature-centered readiness program. Gradually, with increased experience and security, you will find that the workbook assumes a secondary position as the role of the functional program expands.

The problem of developing reading readiness was discussed in some detail for the following reasons:

(1) It is a typical illustration of how a psychologically and educationally sound idea can turn into a level A-oriented practice.

(2) Many student teachers start their field practicum on the first grade level. They want to be creative and give of themselves. They want to learn. The school culture often "welcomes" these dedicated young people by exposing them to, and asking them to follow, a constricted reading readiness program. It is sad that some future educators are being molded in the direction of the repetitive pattern of teaching so early in their career.

(3) The criticism of the workbook-centeredness in reading readiness illustrates my main criticism of reading methodology in general. Both the theorist and especially the practitioner tend to overemphasize the mechanical and skill aspects of reading. There is a lack of at least equal attention to the fact that reading should be primarily a *thinking* process, where the reader comprehends and reflects on the reading matter.

The repetitive orientation in reading leads to an emphasis on the mechanical aspects, while the creative orientation means emphasis on interpretation and critical reading. Both aspects are needed for growth in reading. However, the former is overaccentuated and the latter neglected to a very great extent.

WORD RECOGNITION

Reading readiness is a stage of preparation during which emphasis should be put on language experiences, including extensive contact with reading matter. The phase of beginning to read continues with stress on language art experiences, but also moves further into the actual teaching of reading.

Phonics and reading difficulty

There is no aspect in reading methodology which received more attention, both from educators and laymen, than this phase of beginning reading. The value system communicated by the basal readers, the problem of teaching literature to children, or the meaning of reading to the child, are seldom discussed by the public. Whether beginning reading should be taught by the phonic or sight vocabulary method is the controversy that has turned almost into a national issue. At least in one state this issue has become a problem for state legislation and in several communities a topic for school board regulations. (Imagine the reaction of medical doctors if the legislator attempted to formalize into law the specific technique of administering their services.)

Several months ago the educational section of *The New York Times* had a leading article on The New Society for the Reform of Education, whose main platform was the teaching of beginning reading through phonics. In a best-seller published a decade ago— *Why Johnny Can't Read*—by Flesch,[F2] the elementary school is criticized for allegedly teaching reading by the sight method (teaching words as a whole), and neglecting the phonic approach. Flesch suggests that we begin the teaching of reading with letters and syllables to help the child build up the sound of words from the symbol and its pronunciation.

Despite the fact that Flesch's criticism concerning the lack of phonic teaching is unfounded and despite the fact that his approach to reading methodology stresses rote learning, his book became a best seller. In a powerful and most readable way he was able to arouse the anxiety of an already anxious public.

Why Johnny can't read is a very painful and complicated question. There are many partial answers to this question: cultural deprivation, physiological and constitutional disruptions, emotional problems which interfere with learning, and teaching techniques which fail to create rapport with the child and encourage him to pursue academic tasks. To equate reading difficulties with the phonic problem is an extremely unsound position.

Experimentation is currently taking place in England and in this country in teaching beginning reading by the use of the Initial Training Alphabet,[P6] which corresponds to the forty-three sounds in the English language. Even though these techniques show promise, and even if English had changed and become an entirely phonetic language, or phonics had become the sole approach to the teaching of word recognition, reading difficulties would not have been alleviated very significantly. Research on the frequency of reading difficulties in countries where the language is phonetic and therefore permits the development of sound phonic generalization, supports this contention.[87]

The need for an integrated approach

The present controversy among educators is not whether phonics has to be used, but rather on the extent to which, and the manner in which, it should be used. The majority of reading specialists view phonics as one of the several techniques of word recognition. If the child is to develop independence in reading, he must learn to attack unfamiliar words on his own. There is a variety of techniques for the development of independent reading skills: (1) being aware of the general configuration of a word, or other distinctive features; (2) the comprehension of the context in which the unfamiliar word appears; (3) analyzing the structure of the new word, such as compound words, prefixes, and suffixes; (4) sounding of new words—phonics.

Most basal reading programs do not stress formal instruction in phonics until a child has acquired a sight vocabulary of around seventy-five words. At the preprimer level most of the instruction in phonics is incidental. The child is sensitized to the relationship between speech sounds and written words wherever there is occasion to do so. As the pupil progresses in reading usually by the end of the first and continuing into the second and third grade levels, a systematic program of teaching phonics is initiated.

A minority position concerning the development of word recognition holds that phonics is the only skill needed in beginning reading. This position can best be illustrated by a quote from an introduction to a reader stressing phonic instruction.[M6:12]

Reading is first of all and essentially the mechanical skill of decoding, of turning the printed symbols into the sounds which are language . . . In the earliest stages of learning to read, there is very little need for thinking or reasoning on the part of the child. What he needs is practice in decoding skill, and the thinking will come along some time later.

In addition to its extreme overemphasis of the carry-over of the development of phonetic rules to reading ability, this position greatly underestimates the function of understanding the content both as a word recognition skill and as a source of motivation to read.

The fact that beginning readers tend to "guess" in reading often illustrates that they are trying to utilize the meaning of the context as a clue to deciphering a new and unknown word. Good reading calls not only for the utilization of the discrete word attack skills, but also for facility in using such skills in conjunction with each other. The independence of the reader develops through the promotion of an integrated approach to word recognition.

Diagnostic teaching

The following are some observations concerning some common misinterpretations of the novice in developing word recognition.

Some novice teachers tend to teach the new words of a story before the child has had an opportunity to meet the unfamiliar word in the context of the story. This procedure if followed consistently may protect the pupil from making mistakes, but it may also "overprotect" him by interfering with the child's development of independence in word attack. The same limitation can be observed when the novice consistently "corrects" the mistakes of the child who reads orally, rather than guides him to figure out the difficult word on his own.

The novice lacks sufficient diagnostic ability to sense the pattern of mistakes made by a specific child or by a group of children. Remediation or correction is thus often uniform and disregards the specific difficulties of an individual or a group. Although diagnosis should lead to remedial help dealing with the nature of a child's particular need, the common practice is often one of assigning workbook exercises (especially of the phonics type) to the class as a whole with no attempt to distinguish between those pupils who have a mastery of the skill and those who are deficient. To the good readers this procedure means monotonous and unnecessary practice which interferes with progress.

In addition to the definite need for some reinforcements the function of the word recognition exercises in the workbook should be primarily *remedial*. The exercises should be used *selectively* with children in terms of the learner's specific deficiencies. Rather than looking at the material in the workbook as something that the teacher is expected "to cover," it would be beneficial to think in terms of the individualized use of the workbook.

Two levels of knowing rules

Contrary to the allegation that the school does not teach phonics, perhaps too much time is being spent on this task at the expense of other aspects of reading instruction, such as the actual time spent on reading simple stories.

Tediously and laboriously the novice spends too much of the reading sessions on the inductive development of phonic rules. He feels that in doing so he "puts his teeth in something concrete to help children." There is a scientific aura about the importance of rule development. It is difficult for many teachers to accept the observation that the carry-over from generalizing rules to reading facility is somewhat *limited*.

Examine the following phonics rules about the sounds of *a* suggested in a typical workbook. Is it possible to think and draw on these rules when one reads?

1. Usually *a* is short, as in *apple*.
2. Sometimes *a* is long, as in *cane*.
3. If *a* is followed by *l*, it usually sounds as it does in *all*.
4. If *a* is followed by *w*, it usually sounds as it does in *saw*.
5. If *a* is followed by *r*, it usually sounds as it does in *farm*.

There are nine rules of this nature, but they still do not cover the long *ea* in one syllable words, the long *ea* team in accented syllables, and the short *ea* team. Now, which one of the above rules helped you in pronouncing the letter *a* in the following words: *target, lawyer, salt, speak*?

The main fallacy underlying the above typical exercises is a superficial understanding of the meaning implied by the *knowledge of rules*. There are two levels of "rules knowledge." The first is the development of verbal generalizations. In the elementary school this level generally means looking at a series of examples and by this inductive process formalizing a precise generalization. The school believes that children really form concepts and discover relationships mainly when they express their findings in the language of a definition.

There is lack of sufficient attention, however, to the fact that there is a second level of knowing rules. For lack of a better expression, we'll call it "the experience of discovery." On this level the child is not even aware of his knowledge and cannot always verbalize his findings. He nevertheless experiences it, and therefore makes use of it.

An understanding of the concept implied by the experience of discovery of a rule, and its relation to language and reading development, can be gleaned from the following observation.

A nursery school boy is playing in the sand on the beach. His sister, wearing a bathing suit, is excited and as she says, "You know, I am an excellent swimmer." He looks at her, and with the same excitement replies, "And I am an excellent sander!"

The nursery school boy gave new meaning to the word *sander,* and in this sense created a new word. He did it because he experienced and discovered the structure of the word swimmer used by his sister, and because he had previously discovered on the subverbalized level the structure of words like painter, owner, or reader.

Implications for word recognition

The methodology of teaching word recognition should be redirected to come closer and borrow from the natural process of language growth in children. A child does not learn to speak by learning rules *about* the language structure (phonics, syntax, etc.), but rather by experiencing the discovery of the rules of the language on a subverbalized level. The child says "I played with the car" partly because he repeats an expression he heard, and mainly because he has a functional awareness of the structure of the language. We recognize the child's insight when he uses expressions like "I shooted him." The child does not repeat in this case a pattern he has heard, but rather creates a verb according to his feeling for the structure of the language. He is not yet aware that there are exceptions to the basic structure of the English language.

The discussion of the two levels of "knowing rules" calls for a revision in reading methodology and its word recognition techniques. It calls for less emphasis on formulating verbal generalizations *about* the structure of oral and written language (phonics, structural analysis) and much more emphasis on providing children with time, space, and books to *read.*

The average child, the one who does not suffer from physiological defects interfering with reading, needs minimum help in developing verbalized rules about word recognition. However, he needs maximum provisions for actual reading experiences of very simple but interesting reading matter. Through the process of ample reading the child will get insight into the rules of word recognition on the subverbalized level. This level is sufficient for reading facility.

This proposal does not suggest the elimination of instruction in phonics, but rather suggests reducing it to the necessary fundamentals. Especially for the reader on the third grade level and on, the teaching of phonics has a limited effect on his reading facility. Therefore, mainly those relatively few rules helpful in the improvement of spelling should be stressed.

The implication of this proposal is a balanced school curriculum where children are engaged less in "filling in spaces" of the repetitive type, and more in a library atmosphere of reading fiction and nonfiction. The potential for creative reading can be deadened by the too common overemphasis on the first, and flourish under maximum provisions for the second approach of reading and discussing books.

INDIVIDUALIZED READING

An approach to reading which potentially provides maximum provisions for reading experiences is "individualized reading." If fully understood and practiced, it may become one of the most significant recent developments in reading methodology. It is important to understand the potential contribution of individualized reading and how it contributes to creative reading, as well as to recognize the blocks hindering progress toward this objective.

The basal reader

Individualized reading stems from a questioning of the basal-reader monopoly on the reading program. The reader commonly used in schools is used in an attempt to teach reading *systematically*. It is based on careful readability and controlled vocabulary formulas. For instance, one typical preprimer[M9] consists of only 20 new words which are gradually introduced in 62 pages; each word is generally repeated at least 20 times. Each of the 20 words used in the first preprimer is repeated at least 14 times in the second preprimer. Each new word appears in the context of previously taught words. As the child progresses from one book to another the number and complexity of words, sentence structure, and ideas is increased.

The basal reader is more than a book. It is rather a comprehensive system. It provides children with workbooks for skill practice and with supplementary reading materials. It provides teachers with guides which include detailed suggestions on ways to motivate a given lesson, guiding silent and oral reading, developing word recognition and comprehension skills, and enrichment activities.

A major criticism of the basal reader is that it does little to insure that individual differences will be respected. Far too often it is the practice of teachers to instruct the whole class from the same page at the same time, giving little consideration to the learner's level of reading ability. This practice often results from, as well as reinforces, the belief that all children must be kept on the same achievement level. "This is the material the fourth grade has to cover, no more and no less."

Vertical and horizontal criteria

On the surface it may seem that individualized reading is primarily an attempt to adapt instruction to the various reading levels of children in one classroom. It helps the bright child to remain unhampered by the slow one, and lets the slow pupil move according to his ability and without having to compete with the bright; he thus avoids the experience of defeat.

The most widely accepted rationale of individualized reading is the attempt to adjust the reading instruction to the child's *pace* of learning. This objective is undoubtedly very important, but may be somewhat limited in emphasis. It assumes a *vertical* approach to learning, namely that all children have to climb a well defined and delineated "ladder of learning," and differ primarily in their pace of climbing.

Traditionally this has been the most prevalent conception of individualization. The Dalton Plan was an attempt to organize the course of study into "contract units," through which the child had to move at his own pace. Another illustration of the vertical criterion of individualization is the grouping practice in reading: the class is divided into three groups, each expected to move through the same reading matter at a different rate of progress.

The S.R.A. programmed materials, one of the most recent developments in reading, also illustrate the vertical approach. The reading matter is organized into many booklets according to carefully graded levels of difficulty, each level represented by a different color. The child is motivated to "climb" from one "color" (level) to another at his own pace. He can move to a higher level of reading matter only after he has received a satisfactory score on exercises presented at the end of each booklet.[P3]

At one time children used to ask their friends: "Do you read the first or the second grade reader?" At a later time the question was changed to: "Do you read the book with one star or two stars?" Today in some classrooms they ask: "Do you read the orange or green booklet?" Despite these changes, the basic assumption did not change—namely, that all children are expected to read the same materials.

The conventional emphasis on the vertical concept of individualization ignores the fact that in addition to the rate of progress, children differ in their interests and tastes; they have a desire to explore on their own. Individualization is a *horizontal* as well as a vertical concept. To become a creative person, children do not necessarily have to climb the same ladder, but rather explore and work on the uniqueness of their potentialities.

The motto of the individualized reading movement is seeking, self-selection, and pacing.[M16] In the past, attention was given primarily to "pacing." Now the problem is that of giving equal stress to the values inherent in "seeking" (the importance of the child's desire to look for a book), and in "self-selection" (the importance of the child choosing a book in terms of his interest).

An important aspect of creativity is the attitude of search, curiosity, and preference. People who do not care, who are lukewarm about things, are not creative. A basal reading program concentrating on a diet of one book is not conducive to the development of the curious reader. The individualized reading program attempts to provide opportunities for the learner to explore a variety of reading matter, choose books which appeal to him, and in this process develop the reader's preferences and taste.

The library-centered reading program

To achieve the goal of "seeking," "self-selection," and "pacing," the pupils must have direct access to an adequate supply of a wide range of books, varied in terms of difficulty and content.

That a major approach to reading is a library-centered classroom may seem a simple idea taken for granted. However, strangely enough this approach is still underestimated both in theory and in practice. The basal reader system looks at library books as "supplementary" materials, the extra rather than the center. Observing a classroom, one often hears: "O.K. children, any one who has finished his work may take a book and read." The reading of a book is not seen as the real work. It tends to be pushed out when there is pressing "work" to be done.

Observing classrooms, one notes that under these provisions, the bright child, the one who tends to finish his "work" early, usually finds some time to read. The slow child, however, continues to labor on his work and cannot reach the activity of reading a book of his own choice.

Individualized reading tends to be more an accepted practice in classes of bright rather than slow learners. Teacher's behavior and even their verbalized attitudes seem to express the underlying belief that the slow learner needs more time to cover the prescribed course of study which he must complete, even if it means eliminating all extras, including reading for pleasure. There is a lack of sufficient awareness that these practices undermine rather than promote reading.

It is correct that the slow reader tends to have a shorter attention span, lacks a strong motivation, and needs more direction. It is correct that there is a great shortage of high interest-low readability books for slow readers. However, the recognition of this reality does not imply the elimination of a library-centered reading program; it rather suggests the need for more imaginative efforts in this direction.

The problem of insufficient stress on a library-centered program, especially when it comes to the slow reader, is accentuated when one examines the social class ramifications of the reading problem.

Allison Davis says that the middle-class child learns to read at home, rather than at school.[D2] While this statement may be somewhat extreme, it serves to remind the teacher that even if the reading curriculum is extremely skewed in the direction of phonics, word study, and low-level comprehension skills, the middle-class child still gets the needed balance by spending much time reading library books at home. The growing use of the public library by children is one of the most encouraging developments within the last decade.

Library reading is not a common practice in the homes of the culturally deprived child, the one whose main academic difficulty is manifested through limited reading ability. If both school and home fail to provide this child with ample experiences of choosing books and reading a variety of materials, where is he to learn that reading is a rich human experience? How can reading become his cultural need and where is he going to learn to read?

Individualized reading: dangers

Despite the positive rationale of individualized reading as expressed in "seeking, self-selection, and pacing," one should be aware of certain limitations inherent in this approach, and mainly some of the dangers involved in misusing it.

One limitation has already been discussed in the context of the narrow interpretation of individualization which stresses "pacing" and deemphasizes the horizontal aspects of learning, "seeking," and "self-selection."

Another danger becomes apparent when individualized reading which was originally conceived as an attempt to give individual attention to children, becomes an administrative disguise under which some teachers detach themselves from children. In some cases the result is an organizational pattern where a detached or noninterested teacher is able to create smooth and efficient working relations without really getting involved in the guidance of children. In this setup, the children always read on their own, and the teacher always keeps herself busy taking care of administrative chores. Individualized reading becomes not a way of coming close to the reader, but rather a means of dismissing him.

In some cases, lack of organizational ability on the part of the teacher may also result in lack of guidance and consequently loss of contact with the individual reader. Speaking with school administrators one finds that this is one of their major objections to individualized reading. "Both teacher and child may get lost." Many school administrators feel that it is easier for teachers to supervise children under the basal reader system where every one reads the same story, or works on the same skill, than under a library-centered program.

The proponents of individualized reading are fully aware of these problems and make very definite suggestions for strengthening the guidance of the readers. Illustrations are: careful record-keeping both by the child and by the teacher, sharing sessions where children report to the class on aspects of their reading, and most important, individual reading conferences.

The belief of modern education in the individualization of instruction and in guidance could reach its optimum implementation in the *"reading conference."* This is an opportunity to look at the child not as a number in a mass production mill, but rather as a person with interests, values, achievements, and failures. Of course, to give personal attention to a child is much more than the physical setup of an individual conference; it is, rather, a psychological atmosphere of listening.

Too often, however, the potentially rich opportunity for conferring is misused. The reasons for this are many, the most prevalent being the teacher's preoccupation with the relatively mechanistic aspects of word-calling skills, and the lack of equal emphasis on the subjective meaning of the reading message to the reader. What is kept as a record by the teacher are mainly notations concerning the child's trouble with prefixes or suffixes, while little attention is paid to the reader's understanding of the meaning of the story. The child as a creative reader is too often pushed to the periphery, and the center of interest becomes the determination of whether he reads correctly and speedily. It cannot be overemphasized that in terms of the dynamics of teaching, it is relatively easy to work on the mechanistic aspect, and difficult to be sensitive to the creative goal.

Similar observations can be made about the aspect of individualized reading which is generally called *sharing* or *selling* books. The positive element of this practice is the opportunity to the child to present his thoughts and reactions to a book before the class. Research shows that peers' evaluations of books is a most prevalent factor in choosing reading material.[S11] The excitement of one's own friends is a motivating factor instrumental in creating a new group norm. Reading becomes a cultural need.

The negative aspect of the "sharing session" is that the interest is too often in the process of selling, rather than in stressing the main idea of the book and its evaluation. In the same way as the advertiser tries to sell a car by the extrinsic appeal of a beautiful girl sitting in it, rather than by stressing the car's inherent qualities, many pupils tend to outshine their friends with extemporaneous audio-visual effects which often do not communicate the essence of the book. The teacher, recognizing this problem, can help children understand that the main function of sharing is dealing with the message of the book.

The last misconception of individualized reading to be dealt with here is the belief that this practice should become the only approach to reading instruction. Reading instruction, as well as instruction in all other subject matter, should be developed on three levels: the class as a whole, group work, and complete individualization. There are values in class and group work which cannot be reached in an individual setup. A long session which permits going into the depth of the subject matter, give-and-take among group members, and the opportunity for each child to listen and react critically and constructively to his friends are experiences which could not be obtained outside of the group.

The future of individualized reading

The findings of the Harvard report on reading[44] reveal that individualized reading is not favored by the majority of the school administrators. They stress the following main factors as causes for their caution: lack of familiarity with the method on the part of teachers, lack of supplies, and class size. On the other hand, the majority of the novice teachers under discussion strongly believe in individualized reading, and at least on the professed verbal level indicate their readiness to move in this direction. They feel it is an opportunity to work on their own search for creative teaching.

The Harvard report on reading[44] found that schools in which individualized reading was implemented were well equipped with library books, while the "basal reader schools" had a very limited supply. One interpretation of this finding is that only the well-equipped schools can initiate individualized reading. Another interpretation might be that the schools eager to implement individualized reading tend to recognize the need for a rich library, and tend to be resourceful in getting it.

In my visit to the Middle East I saw a group of children seated around a table, reading from a single book placed in the middle. The fact that this group had only one book can be explained in terms of the poverty of the community. However, it can also be explained in terms of the conception of education of both teachers and laymen in this community.

The conception of education held by a teacher plays a major role in creating the physical setup for teaching as expressed in the school's equipment, library, class size, etc. The conception of education affects the definition of the task of the teacher. If the educator believes in teaching centered on educational television, the physical setup of the future school would be large halls where programs could be projected on huge screens and the teacher's role definition will become primarily a traffic policeman who directs children to the television hall. However, if the teacher's conception of education is based on individualized reading, the future setup of the school would be small classes and rich libraries, and the teacher's role definition would come closer to the one of the mentor.

Despite all the difficulties described here, the observer of the educational scene can notice a slow but steady growth in the direction of individualized reading. Well-equipped libraries are built in schools, and librarians are added to the staff. There is an enormous growth in the area of children's literature, especially "beginning reading" type of books. The recognition that reading can be learned primarily by the process of reading an abundance of high quality books is making slow but steady progress.

The future of individualized reading depends on the teacher's understanding of this practice. If the practice is perceived primarily as an administrative pattern, then its values are limited and its future is questionable. However, if the depth of the rationale underlying individualized reading can be recognized and practiced, it would become a most significant contribution to the improvement of education.

THE TYRANNY OF THE READING SKILLS

Research on reading deals primarily with word perception, phonics, and ways of developing certain types of comprehension. There is a dearth of research on the intellectual, emotional, and aesthetic reactions of the reader to the author's presentation; there is a dearth of discussion about creative reading. The following anonymous poem written by an anonymous writer may convey the meaning of creative reading better than any definition could.[S12:9]

Adventure

Here's an adventure! What awaits
Beyond these closed, mysterious gates?
Whom shall I meet, Where shall I go?
Beyond the lovely land I know?
Above the sky, across the sea,
What shall I learn and feel and be?
Open, strange doors, to good or ill!
I hold my breath a moment still
Before the magic of your look
What shall you do to me, O Book?

What shall you do to me, O Book? The way the repetitively oriented reading curriculum answers this question is by building a program based on the "tyranny of reading skills," namely, the stress on low-level comprehension, word learning, and study skills, without equal stress on creative reading.

To understand this criticism, it would be enlightening to examine the major parts of a typical reading test for sixth grade pupils.[01] This examination is based on the assumption that the test is not an isolated aspect of the reading program, but rather an accurate reflection of the kind of questions stressed in the classroom, and the exercises found in workbooks. The test is a reflection of the focuses of the reading program.

Low-level comprehension skills

Part I of the test consists of a series of graded paragraphs which, according to the test-makers, measures "comprehension"—namely, the ability to understand words and sentences, to gather information, to read for specific details, to select the central thought in a paragraph.

In order to illustrate the limited definition of comprehension suggested in this typical test, let us try an experiment. The following is the first comprehension paragraph presented by the above test.[01:31] Read it only *once* at your normal rate.

When Hugh Lofting was a soldier in the British army during the First World War, his children at home begged for letters. As he watched the army horses working so faithfully, he had an idea. Why not write letters about a country doctor who loved animals so much that he gave up doctoring people to take care of animals? His letters delighted the children so much that he decided to put them into book form. This was the beginning of the famous Dr. Dolittle books.

Now, *without* consulting the above paragraph again, answer the following "comprehension" questions presented by the test.

1. What country was Hugh Lofting fighting for? France, U.S.A., England, Germany.

2. What word tells best how the army horses worked? willingly, loyally, carefully, continually.

3. The best title for this paragraph is:

A Famous Animal Doctor   Army Horses

The Origin of the Dr. Dolittle Books   Hugh Lofting

Despite the fact that this is the easiest paragraph in the test, most readers would tend to encounter difficulties in answering the "comprehension" questions. The reasons children are successful in checking the correct answers are (1) They read the paragraph very slowly, rather than at their normal rate of reading a book and (2) they reread the paragraph once or twice in terms of the specific questions raised by the test.

Reading of this nature is not an accurate representation of the way an adult or a child generally reads. It is correct that when one looks for very specific information, or is interested in digesting every fact as in reading a manual, his reading would be characterized by very slow movements, rereading paragraphs, and paying attention to specifics. In general reading of this nature is the exception rather than the rule, and is applied to specialized material.

Think about the last book you have read. Would you be able to answer "comprehension questions" of the kind presented by tests and workbooks? For most people the answer is in the negative. One's comprehension of a book is generally in terms of the main message, the mood, or the nature of the characters. The creative reader generally attempts to *"review"* the book, to think of how he feels about it. Does he agree or not? Where does it lead him as a person? The conventional concept of "comprehension" does not recognize these components at all; it is limited mainly to a photographic reading of paragraphs.

A case reported by Nila Smith will be brought here to illustrate the negative impact of the limited conception of comprehension on the thinking of teachers[8][11:286]

A boy was sent to Dr. Smith for diagnosis. He was considered at school *a good reader* but was failing in other subjects. The boy was asked by the examiner to read the story of Johnny Appleseed and then was asked questions which could be answered by restating what had been said directly in the text. He was asked such questions as: "How long ago did Johnny Appleseed live?" "What was his real name?" "How did he spend his time?" The boy answered all these questions correctly.

The consensus of the Education students who observed the testing of the boy had been that his comprehension was perfect. However, when the boy was asked a question calling for the interpretation of meaning, conveyed but not stated directly in the text, his lack of real comprehension was discovered.

Why did Johnny choose to plant his trees deep in the wilderness when the settlers had not yet come?
He wanted to be alone while he was working.

The boy missed the main implication that the motivation for planting the trees was to prepare the ground for the future settlers.

This case was presented in some detail to illustrate how a limited conception of comprehension subverts the good judgment of teachers. It interferes with their ability to recognize difficulties children may have in comprehension, and furthermore it teaches them to develop a reading curriculum which aims primarily at these low-level comprehension skills.

The pervasiveness of this type of "literal comprehension" of the paragraph can be found in every reading workbook. In too many classrooms reading becomes a process of reaction to "easy to score" objective type questions, factual items, true-false statements, or multiple choice sentences.

The foregoing discussion does not suggest that there is no room for some practice of the low-level comprehension skills. They are definitely needed, especially in the lower grades and with certain types of subject matter. However, when the total reading program becomes geared to low-level comprehension, I cannot but agree with those discerning teachers who call this emphasis, "busy work," or "filling in spaces."

Even some children's magazines were almost overtaken by the zeal to join the bandwagon of "building comprehension skills." The main function of these magazines is to present current events on the child's level, to arouse curiosity and foster critical thinking. However, as a member of an editorial staff of one of the magazines told me in a conference, "We are forced into the busy work business." The end result is seen in the following example, which illustrates a typical feature in many magazines.

A magazine for fifth graders presents a half-page story about a new Mississippi channel and then a full page called "how-to-study guide" with eight multiple choice questions of the repetitive type that almost no one can answer without searching for the fact dealing with each item. For instance

> The channel will not be completed for three
> a) weeks   b) months   c) years

This "study guide," dealing solely with literal comprehension, puts teachers under pressure; the subject matter has to be covered and "comprehension" must be achieved. What suffers in devoting too much time to the pursuit of this limited goal is the development of the pupil's understanding of the problems of building a channel, and the need for a channel in other communities.

To conclude, comprehension is the heart of the reading program, because reading is a thinking process. There is, however, overemphasis on the low-level literal comprehension, without at least equal stress on the higher dimensions of reading comprehension—namely, creative reading. This criticism does not question the need for literal comprehension, but rather the lack of balance. A team of researchers has remarked [44:40]

It was rare indeed that members of the study staff heard teachers trying to help children draw conclusions from what they had read, make inferences or comparisons, evaluate the facts, or participate in other activities that would develop critical reading skills. Indeed it was not uncommon for teachers to ask their pupils what one story book character said to another when the only words on the page were "Oh, Oh, Oh!"

Word learning

Part II of the test under discussion deals with *vocabulary*. It taps the understanding of the meaning of fifty words. The assumption underlying the vocabulary part is that knowing words is a good measure of language facility. The typical intelligence test also tends to have a vocabulary section because it is assumed that the ability of the individual to think symbolically, his alertness to experiences, images, and ideas is channeled into vocabulary development. The limited individual in terms of the intelligence constellation tends to have a low vocabulary. The bright learner who thinks abstractly tends to have a rich vocabulary. Words are man's attempt to "name ideas."

The rationale underlying the test-maker's interest in vocabulary as an index of intelligence, or language facility, is valid. Perhaps the only serious limitation of this rationale is that some intelligent individuals tend to channel their thinking in directions other than words, such as form and melody.

There is, however, a "hidden danger" in the test-maker's interest in the knowledge of words. It may be generally correct to assume that the mastery of vocabulary is a valid indication of reading ability; however, it is not equally correct to assume that learning vocabulary is a main avenue to the improvement of reading. It may be generally correct to assume that vocabulary is a valid indication of verbal intelligence, however, it is a fallacy to think that learning words will *raise* one's intelligence.

As this section will illustrate, the reading curriculum falls into this trap of circular thinking and thus in addition to the overabundance of phonics and literal comprehension exercises, the program burdens itself with an overemphasis on direct word learning. In this process a main avenue to language facility and vocabulary enrichment is neglected. The experiencing of the intellectual, emotional, and aesthetic ramifications of the reading content, namely creative reading, assumes a secondary place while words rather than ideas become a central focus. The following observations may illustrate this point.

A teacher often starts a reading activity by putting the new words on the blackboard and devoting a significant part of the lesson to the study of the "new words." In essence, this type of teaching behavior implies that what counts is word knowledge, rather than the adventure of ideas. Too many children read to study words, rather than to be nourished by ideas.

In oral reading the child is corrected or helped when he mispronounces a word or does not know the meaning of a word. Lacking is an equal emphasis on oral reading which expresses the child's identification with the characters, or his understanding of the mood.

Similarly, the most dominant aspect of the teaching of writing is the "spelling program," emphasizing the correct spelling of dis-

crete words. There is lacking an equal emphasis on the communication of ideas and feelings through the media of writing.

In discussing stories or poems, the teacher often tends to rush
into the analysis of the particulars, the difficult words, rather than
delve into the message or meaning of the content. Two examples
will illustrate this aspect of word-centeredness.

"The Star Spangled Banner" is taught to a group of sixth
graders. The novice teacher tells the group the story of Frances
Scott Key, who was inspired to write the poem by the sight of the
American flag flying over Fort McHenry during its bombardment
by the British frigate *Surprise*. She tells them that he, himself, was
a captive on the boat. When the story is finished the children read
the poem orally. The lesson is culminated by looking for the meaning of the difficult words with the help of a dictionary.

What is the impact of the experience of the poet on the message of the poem? Why was the poem selected to become the
national anthem? How do the children feel when they sing it? No
attempt was made to delve into questions of this nature. The novice rather rushed to find refuge in the safety of vocabulary development and dictionary skills.

The second illustration is an "observation lesson" dealing with
a poem by Robert Frost—"Stopping by Woods on a Snowy Evening." The lesson consists of biographical information about the
poet, oral reading with no emphasis on mood, questions of literal
comprehension, discussion of the poem's rhythm, and seat work
on the picture words. There was no attempt to discuss the message to children of this classic in American poetry.

In a college session the problem of teaching the above poem
was presented before a group of novice teachers. They were asked
to read the poem and discuss the following question: What does
the poem mean to me? They spoke about loneliness, about rushing toward false glittering goals. They spoke about lack of time to
meditate, and about feeling the beauty of life in the simple things
they daily encountered.

When the discussion was over the teachers were asked to try
to teach the poem to a sixth grade, with emphasis on the meaning
of the poem to the children. Difficult words were to be taken primarily at the end of the discussion, and were to be explained in
terms of their contribution to the symbolism of the poem. The

children's assignment would consist of reactions to the question: What does the poem mean to me? These words could be expressed through any form of communication chosen by the child.

The impact of a poetry lesson centered on interpretation rather than on word learning is illustrated by the following two poems, written by a boy and a girl from two different schools. They are quoted here without corrections.

Stopping by Woods on a
Snowy Evening

A Poem by Robert Frost I've
   read,
And this to me is what he
   said
One snowy dark and wintery night,
An old man comes into sight
He stops by the woods to
   admire its beauty,
But is pressed onward by
   his unfulfilled duty.
His eyes drink in the wonderous scene,
As though he was in an enchanted dream.
I think he feels he
   will see this no more
For life will soon close its door.
Reading this poem, time I've not lost
This beautiful poem written
   by Robert Frost.

What Beauty Means to Me.

What Beauty means to me
I know you cannot buy or sell
What beauty means to me I know
   is a small sea shell,
like apples falling off the trees
or flowers turning yellow
like fish that swim in blue
seas
or man that play the cello
When I spot beauty, I feel
real fine

Because I think that its divine
Yes what Beauty means
to me you cannot
buy or sell.

I was told that the Eskimos have twenty different words for "snow." It is not difficult to explain why they have so many "names," as snow is to them a central element in life. Their success and failure, their very survival, depend to a great extent on their understanding and use of the snow. The end result of this immense experience is a multitude of words for what to us seems a limited term.

People, equally facile in language, will vary in the wealth of their verbal expression depending on the extent of their contact and familiarity with the life situation they are describing. The intellectual, emotional, and aesthetic experience of an idea is the *father of the word,* and is the most productive source for language development. Therefore the major approach to the process of developing a reading vocabulary is the emphasis on the learner experiencing personal meaning in the subject matter read.

However, it should be noticed that a novice teacher may be somewhat blocked in recognizing the rich potentials of this approach. His experience as a student tells him that the way to pass some of the examinations he has to take is to cram from a book on "increasing your word vocabulary." Before some examinations he does not read a novel or become immersed in an intellectual endeavor, but rather memorizes a dictionary list.

The novice was told by his friends that the recent Board of Education examination for teachers asked for the definition of *tachistoscope.* Therefore, he is not interested in the impact of this "reading machine" on children, or the rationale underlying its use; his primary interest is only to learn the *word.*

The novice opens a textbook on the English language written for third graders.[819] He finds a chapter entitled "Enjoying Poetry" to be full of exciting poems. Then he looks at the end of the chapter and finds that the *only* suggestions for testing are "word-centered": (1) The child is asked to choose a word from a list of sound and picture words, and write a sentence using the word. (2) The text presents a list of poem titles and the child is asked to use capital letters where they belong. (3) Two lists of words are presented, and the child is asked to match the words which rhyme.

When the novice is introduced to the basal reader (the book dominating the reading program) he finds out that the major rationale underlying the construction of this book is the science of words as expressed in formulas of controlled vocabulary. He hears much about the science of words, but hears little about the science of ideas, or the literary quality of the reader.

To conclude, the experience of the student teacher tells him that academic success calls for focus on words. He communicates the way he learned to be successful to children by overstressing the learning of words at the expense of the learning of ideas.

The point cannot be overemphasized that words are man's attempt to name ideas and that the experiencing of the idea is the father of the word. Consequently the most promising way to enrich vocabulary is to enrich the children's experience.

Centeredness on study skills

The last part of the test under discussion evaluates proficiency in certain study skills, such as using a table of contents, an index, and a glossary or a dictionary. The following are some illustrations.[01:39-40]

Directions: Here is a make-believe set of encyclopedias. Use it to answer the questions below.

A-ARS, ART-B, C, D-G, H-L, M-PUL, PUM-R, S, T-V, W-Z

  (1) In which book will you find information about Canada?
  (2) In which book will you look for information about the Puritans?

Directions: Draw a line under the right answer.
  (1) On the first line of a title card in a library card catalogue you will find the: title of the book, author's name, date of publication.

Directions: Number the words in each group in the order in which they would appear in a dictionary.
      late   blazed   wavy   escaping   safety

It is generally stressed in teacher's guides that there can be no rigid separation of technical language, such as is expressed in "study skills," and creative expression in reading, writing, or speaking. Facility in the technical aspects of language training frees the child for creative work.[S19:5-6]

The mastery of skills not only contributes to the development of correctness and clarity in thinking and expression but also helps to develop a feeling of security in the use of language. . . In this series of textbooks the teaching of skills and the stimulation of creative expression are not thought of as separate aspects of the language program, but as related parts of an integrated program.

The position presented in the teacher's guide is sound in that both the mechanics of language and the creative aspects are stressed. Without the ability to write or speak in correct forms, without skill in using the encyclopedia or the dictionary, it would be most difficult for children to be creative.

Modern education is critical of spoon-feeding by teachers. It wants to activate children to study on their own—to help them identify a problem, prepare a plan, search for information by the use of a variety of printed materials. The prevalence of independent research (especially library research) is perhaps one of the most significant differences between the present day elementary school and the school of the past.

However, despite the recognition of study skills as a necessary aspect of a sound language art program, one can raise some questions about the hierarchy of values concerning the above skills, as expressed in the teacher's guide and especially in the actual curriculum practiced by teachers.

The teacher's guide generally claims "an integrated approach." However, when one looks carefully for the explanation of this promising concept, he finds that the technical and mechanical aspects are given priority to creative work and are laid as a foundation for it. With few exceptions the suggested sequence is: the mechanical aspects first, and the creative second. Why should this "integrated approach" not change the order of its sequence and recommend that an equal emphasis be on the creative aspects first and the mechanical second? Just as facility with dictionary skills is an aid to the children reading a poem, so is the involvement in a poem a strong motivational force for mastering dictionary skills. In the same manner that the skill in using the encyclopedia frees the child to search for knowledge and do research, the curiosity about a self-initiated project, or the desire to cultivate an interest, makes the learning or the use of the encyclopedia a meaningful and purposeful activity.

The position stressed or implied by the guidebook has a direct impact on the values and behavior of many teachers. They tend to accept and apply this sequence: the skill first and the creative aspect second. In this process the second is often never reached in many classrooms.

Even though no research exists as to the prevalence of this problem, its nature may be somewhat illuminated by reporting on a number of observations.

A group of novice teachers was asked to write a lesson plan in the area of language arts. An analysis of the topics selected showed that there were three times as many choices of study skills, such as dictionary work and correct forms of letter writing, than of creative aspects. Among the teachers who made plans for creative language art experiences, most of them concentrated on creative writing, while very few aimed at creative reading.

It is evident that study skills have a great appeal for the novice teacher, giving him the sense of quick movement, control, and structured teaching. It gives him a feeling of achievement which can be measured by an objective test and a sense of being able to communicate in very definite terms, building a sound foundation, and planting in the hands of children the key to academic success.

"What our children need is better study skills," is the cry in many schools all over the country. The belief is that the knowing how to use the index, the encyclopedia, the right capitalization in a poem, or the use of quotes, is the secret of making the student a researcher, a writer, or a dedicated reader. What our children need primarily is a more intrinsic relatedness to the learning of subject matter. Study skills cannot serve as a substitute for personal meaning in learning.

That overemphasis on the importance of study skills may constitute an oversimplification of the basic issue of learning is seen in the following checklist taken from a research guide for college students. The checklist is a summary of the "important points" in writing a research paper.[P8]

1) Do you have ample accurate notes?
2) Do you have a bibliographical card for each source?
3) Does your outline reflect a good plan of organization?
4) Have you assimilated your source materials?
5) Have you used quotations with skill and moderation?
6) Is your paper well written?
7) Have you all the footnotes you should have?
8) Are your footnotes in the proper form?
9) Is your bibliography complete and accurate?
10) Is your final draft in the prescribed manuscript form?

Reading this type of guide, one gets the feeling that the conducting of research is primarily the *clerical* ability of following a prescribed form. Know the skills of writing footnotes, use of the index, the right capitalization, and your way to research is assured.

Research is one of the most advanced expressions of man's thinking; it is his attempt to move from one level of theory to a higher level of theory. To see the mastery of research as a process of learning study skills and correct forms is very misleading, and is detrimental to the understanding of what is central and what is secondary in education.

In conferences, the college instructor often hears both undergraduate and graduate students complain about their lack of ability to identify a research problem, or develop a project.

My problem is that I don't have the right study skills.
I would like the librarian to show us how to locate information, perhaps this will help.
If I knew the expected format, perhaps I could get started.

These future teachers see the solution of their learning problem in an additional dose of study skills and correct format. As classroom teachers they will tend to communicate the same emphasis to children. These may be the students who later, as teachers, will come to emphasize syntax in the study of poetry, who will react to a child's composition describing the death of his cat with the one word comment, "skip!" (meaning write double space), or who will equate research in the classroom with skill in using the encyclopedia.

What many of these future teachers did not learn both as pupils and college students is that their major difficulty in starting a project is not the relative lack of "study skills," but rather their lack of emotional and intellectual involvement in subject matter. Despite many years of formal education, they did not find themselves as people. They never reached the stage of knowing in what they are *interested*. They were so busy with the external knowledge of mastering facts, skills, words, and correct forms that they failed to concentrate on the creative aspect—their own interest.

The personal meaning of problem identification to some teachers is described in my article "The Personal Signifiance of a Research Problem to Teachers." [88] Following is one excerpt from an interview.[86:72-73]

College instructor: I am interested in knowing how you got the idea to work on the project, "humor in my classroom."

Teacher: I guess it is much deeper than I thought. You see, all my life I was a bookworm. I was a very good student. Everyone liked me, but no one was excited about me. I was always in the right, but I was never "right"—I mean having something original. I went into teaching. I guess this is the only thing I was prepared to do. But perhaps there was another reason involved: working with children puts you at ease—you let yourself go.

The teacher who has the room next to mine often yells at her children, a thing that I seldom do. Actually I have the better reputation as a good teacher. But from time to time you hear roars of laughter coming from her room, a thing that seldom happens in mine. Now you understand, I am working on humor.

To conclude, the greatest challenge for educators is to make knowledge a part of the lives of students and to make subject matter personally meaningful. In essence, this is the starting point for creative learning. The repetitively skewed school curriculum, overemphasizing study skills, word learning, and literary comprehension, undermines the ability of the novice to realize himself as a person and as a teacher.

CREATIVE READING

Underlying the need to develop creative reading in the schools is the belief, as Emerson wrote, that "it is the good reader who makes the good book." Or, as one author puts it,[R7:422]

A writer only begins a book, it is the reader who completes it; for the reader takes up where the writer left off as new thoughts stir within him. Whether that reader be child or man, the book is as good as its effect on him.

An approach

Creative reading is an integral part of the creative orientation in learning. Emphasis is placed not only on the objective comprehension of the message of the book, but also on the subjective reaction of the reader.

The literature [R7, S12] generally mentions two categories of creative reading: interpretation and critical reading. Both aspects involve the reader's reaction, the production of original ideas not explicitly stated in the reading matter, and the reading between the lines. The basic difference between the two categories is that interpretation tends to be colored by emotions and calls for imagery, whereas critical reading tends to be logical and judgemental. In contrast to the first, the latter is interested in accuracy and in the validity of the message conveyed.

The distinction between interpretive and critical reading is helpful for the clarification of objectives, or the development of a taxonomy. However, in the reality of teaching it is difficult in many cases to distinguish between emotional and logical reactions. When one writes a critique of a book, such as *The Waste Makers*,[P1] and speaks about the role of education in a society plagued by conspicuous consumption and waste of resources, it is often difficult to decide whether the review is based on critical, or interpretive reading. Therefore, the concept of creative reading in its entity is the most useful guide.

There is no specific technique for the development of creative reading ability in children. There are, however, some principles and suggestions which may serve as a guide for action. These principles were discussed to some extent in various parts of this book. The section here will attempt only to apply them to reading.

The starting point is the personal meaning of the reading matter to the teacher himself: How does he view the book or the story? What does it arouse in him? The notion that the prerequisite to the fostering of creative reading is a teacher who is a creative reader himself, is controversial. The danger in this position is that the teacher may attempt to impose his own personal interpretation on children, and "guide them" into a constricting track which does not give them freedom to develop their own imagery and evaluation. They will learn mainly to repeat the teacher's sense of creation.

A problem also exists when a teacher is "objective," does not think through his own value judgement, and plans mainly to be open to the feelings and interpretations of children. A teacher who skillfully attempts to develop creative interpretations in others and fails himself to experience his own sense of meaning, tends to move through the motions of asking the right questions, without these questions having real meaning to him. This is the kind of teacher who asks children to think about why they like or dislike a certain character described in a story, without himself exploring the question; he may ask for imagery as a response to a mood poem, while he himself fails to form any imaginative answer.

Children tend to sense a lack of involvement in this teacher; they know that he moves through the correct motions, but somewhere misses the spirit of the activity. To put it in somewhat extreme terms, there are situations where the educator has to learn to withdraw as a teacher and come forth as a person. If the teacher plays only the role of a skilled technician, he tends to withdraw as a person and come forth only as a teacher. In an atmosphere of this nature, creativity becomes an expression of virtuosity rather than an immersion in an intellectual and emotional experience.

The emphasis on the important role played by the teacher's own experience of creative reading does not suggest that he should impose his own sense of creation on children. Here the teacher should utilize his leadership ability in helping children move away *divergently* from his own presentation. This position was developed and illustrated in a previous chapter discussing the characteristics of the creative teacher.

In reading a story or a poem it is important to guide children to understand the characters—their feeling, motivation, and value system. It is desirable to examine the characters, the mood, or the events in the light of the reader's own values and life experiences. It is the tendency of the immature reader to stereotype the characters into good or bad, the liked and the disliked. However, with the exception of the fairy tale, generally the literature is more complicated. It describes the drama and conflict in the life of people. Are children today being helped recognize this drama and understand the conflict in the characters?

In reading *Dr. Dolittle* do they analyze and respect the conflict of values that this doctor, his sister, and their neighbors must have experienced? Do they examine the story in terms of the values they themselves cherish?

In reading *The Fisherman and His Wife*, do they laugh at the seeming stupidity of the old man and his greedy wife, or do they try to understand their motivation or even to develop imaginery scenes which throw further light on the characters and the events?

There is drama behind the headlines in the newspaper. Do children recognize the genuine conflict of interest, or do they instead "pigeon hole" the news into the "right" and the "wrong" side.

To conclude, a major avenue toward reading facility is encouraging the reader to explore the message of the reading matter —to react to it intellectually, emotionally, and aesthetically. The promise of a mature reader, the one who wants to read on his own and the one who searches for literary quality, is mainly in the emphasis on creative reading.

The controversy of literary quality

To read creatively children need to be exposed to stimulating fiction and nonfiction material. What is the literary quality of the typical "basic reading matter"—the main reading diet at school?

The criticism that readers are not tuned to the experiences and problems of deprived children is presented by Burton.[B15:250]

> Books used in beginning reading practically never base content upon the experience known to the whole range of children using the books. The experience of the huge majority is, in fact, usually ignored . . . Not a single series of readers includes the experience of the lower-class children.

However, even the applicability of the typical reader to the middle-class child must be questioned.[D4:31-32]

> One might ask how typical are Dick and Jane, or more important, how meaningful are they and their neat white house in the suburbs to children whose world includes all the blood and thunder as well as the sophisticated reportage of television . . .
> It would be an exciting idea to have primers which deal more directly with people and events which arouse the emotions of sympathy, curiosity and wonder in children . . . Which deal with the "child's world" as reaching from home and family to the moon.

A sharp and well documented critique of the limited literary quality of the readers is presented by Trace. His book, *What Ivan Knows that Johnny Doesn't,* is a comparison of Russian and American textbooks. The first part of his discussion deals with the reading program.[T6:28]

> One basal reader series even says as much: "The selections . . . were written or adapted by authors all of whom have had many years of experience with the vocabularies of the various word lists . . ." It should come as no great surprise then, that the selections in American elementary readers, are almost wholly nonliterary. The reader may imagine, for example, that no small poem by Shakespeare or Wordsworth . . . who knew nothing about the rules of vocabulary control could bear the scrutiny described above.

Jerome Bruner, in his article entitled "Learning and Thinking," identifies two of the main problems as follows:[B10:186]

> The Pablum school readers, stripped of rich imagery in the interest of readability, stripped of passion in the erroneous belief that the deeper human condition will not interest the child—these are no more the vehicles for getting over the barrier to thinking than are the methods of teaching mathematics by a rote parroting at the blackboard.

The two factors underlying the limited literary quality of the typical reader is the preoccupation with controlled vocabulary and the assumption that children should live in a world of their own, protected from "deeper human conditions."

Perhaps both the difficulty and the needed revision can be further understood by the comparison of the modern reader with the *McGuffey's Fifth Eclectic Reader*, which dominated the reading program in the last century. The strength of the latter was that it attempted to communicate to the child the value system and morality of the adult culture. To quote Commager: [M7:12]

They gave to the American of the nineteenth century what he so conspicuously lacks today—a comon body of allusion, a sense of common experience and of common possession.

There is no question that the McGuffey series is obsolete. Its value system stressing the motto of "be good and you will be rewarded" is questionable. Its sense of morality, style, and difficult language did not take into account the needs and interests of the child. The end result was, as Hildreth clearly points out, that the chief goal of instruction had become perfect articulation rather than reading for meaning.[H9]

It seems that in comparing McGuffey readers with the modern basic reading series we are confronted with two extremes. The first stresses the adult morality of a certain era, ignoring readability and children's interest. The second is occupied with controlled vocabulary and the childish aspects of the youngsters life, sacrificing literary quality. Perhaps the solution for the problem of writing reading matter for children is to steer a middle road between these two extremes, to be both *idealistic* and *realistic*.

In *What Ivan Knows That Johnny Doesn't*,[T6] Trace presents an idealistic position about the need for exposing our elementary school children to the classic literature. The title of his book suggests that he does not take into account the realistic criterion. The title of his book implies that the content of the Russian readers is digested and understood by the children. Trace does not bring evidence to support this assertion. His study is limited to a content analysis of textbooks. Is it possible that the Russian child is exposed to a too "academic" literature which only fosters in him repetitive verbalism and platitudes? Therefore, a more accurate title for Trace's book might be *What Ivan Is Taught that Johnny Isn't*. The realist position cannot overemphasize that "taught" and "knows" are not identical!

To be an idealist and demand that our children read high quality literature is not sufficient. The educator must take into consideration the realistic aspect of the child's maturity, his interest, and his level of reading ability. Lack of sufficient attention to the latter criterion will too often lead to a high quality literature which is "jammed down the throats of children."

There is a great need to encourage a creative and mature movement of literature for children, which will be sound in terms of its literary quality and value system, will take into account the needs and interests of children in this era, and will also follow a common sense road with regard to readability.

The need for balance is indicated by Bruner in his critique entitled, "After John Dewey, What?" [B11:117]

It is just as mistaken to sacrifice the adult to the child as to sacrifice the child to the adult. It is sentimentalism to assume that the teaching of life can be fitted always to the child's interests just as it is empty formalism to force the child to parrot the formulas of adult society.

IMPLICATIONS FOR LANGUAGE ARTS

The foregoing discussion has tended to examine the total language arts program, since the development of an approach to reading methodology cannot be limited to the analysis of this subject area itself. The remainder of this chapter will deal at greater length with the language arts aspects of listening, speaking, and writing, in the light of the repetitive—creative conflict.

Listening and speaking

In one of the few discussions on the problem of critical listening, Duker [D10:565] says, in referring to tests of listening, that:

Unfortunately, both these tests disproportionately stress listening for content. A similar criticism, it is true, could also validly be made of most reading tests . . . The important part of the listening and reading process is not the tape recorder type of reception. The real emphasis should be on evaluative or critical listening and reading . . . We need to go on to the teaching of a judgemental type of listening. If we do not do this, the exercise of attentive and even of retentive listening becomes a very sterile activity of little value either to the individual or society.

The repetitively-centered way of teaching tends to promote a tape recorder type of listening. The child listens to Lincoln's Gettysburg Address expecting such questions as: "Where did he give it?" "When did he give it?" "What was the occasion?" What is frequently absent is an equal emphasis on sensitizing the child to expect interpretive questions, such as, "What would you think about if you were at the dedication and heard Lincoln?" Or, "Suppose you have never heard about Lincoln, what would you say about him as a person from just reading his Address?" [B16]

An important factor which affects the pupil's listening and speaking ability is the nature of the teacher's questions. In many respects the classroom climate can be described as a dialogue between a questioning teacher and a group of children who give the answers. Burton points out that: [B16:537]

As long as the aim of education is believed to be the memorization of masses of unrelated fragmentary facts, a barrage of minute fact questions is a natural and legitimate procedure.

Counting the number of questions raised by novice teachers in observation lessons, I sometimes reached close to one hundred. To quote Burton again: [B16:542]

These short choppy questions, invite short choppy answers. Probably as an outcome of the rapid fire fact question there has grown up in schools . . . a thoroughly reprehensible practice, namely, the acceptance from pupils of fragmentary one point answers.

The discussion, a potentially rich opportunity for the development of oral expression and critical listening, has become too often a recitation consisting of an aggregation of short answers to repetitive questions. Under this approach the class interaction is characterized by teacher-child "conversation," without equal emphasis on child-child interaction.

The high prevalence of the "show and tell" period in the primary grades and the reporting of "current events" on the intermediate level points out that teachers recognize the importance of oral intercommunication among children. However, observing these potentially fruitful activities in operation, one finds that in many cases what happens after the report is a brief level A questioning by the teacher rather than a dialogue between the "reporter" and the class.

Dissatisfied with the short answers of their pupils, some teachers tend to say "I want you to give me a full answer." Then the child, in answering the question "What is the capital of England?", rather than giving the short answer "London," gives the "full answer." "The name of the capital of England is London." Some teachers are not sensitive to the notion that to get a really "full answer" from a pupil one has to initiate it with a thoughtful and creative question.

The repetitive orientation in oral expression not only overemphasizes memorization, but also fails to foster in the child the awareness that what he thinks and how he feels counts. Overexposure to the A climate tends to develop a self-image of a pupil who is dependent on the crutch of specific questions, who has to be spoon-fed continuously, and who lacks the power of self-direction.

On the other hand, the child who has many opportunities to think productively and creatively while experiencing such activities as reading, discussion, a trip, or a movie, not only develops his thinking ability, but also a healthy self concept as an *active* learner. He is not a parrot, but rather a creative person.

Examine a teacher's attempt to teach a Puerto Rican group by stressing "patterns of speech." The pattern to be learned is, "I want to buy." The novice brings various "surprises" in a bag and as she takes the object out the group, or an individual, recites, "I want to buy a book," "I want to buy a pen," etc. Another lesson may stress: "Tomorrow I shall go to . . . "This practice of "patterns" has some value for the child who is learning English, but when overemphasized it leads to a trite atmosphere where, with disarming sweetness on the part of the teacher the child is relegated to the role of a repeater. Passivity in learning becomes so entrenched that it is very difficult to uproot or change it.

A more promising approach to oral expression is that of leading a group discussion on a specific topic. The child has freedom to develop ideas on his own and communicate them. It is more typical of the normal way one speaks than is the practice of "patterns." Leading a discussion is an art which calls for insight and skill; it involves on the one hand, the raising of stimulating questions and the ability to synthesize ideas and push the discussion ahead, and on the other, the avoidance of premature structuring which makes the discussion a series of answers to the teacher's questions, rather than a spontaneous attempt to relate experiences.[B4]

The development of oral expression calls for an atmosphere where children feel free to relate their thoughts and feelings. Therefore, the leading of a *small* group discussion where relationships tend to be more intimate, the individual conference, or the dictation of an experience to the teacher, are very valuable.

The teacher's reaction to the child's oral expression should deal primarily with the *meaning* of his ideas. The improvement of grammar and syntax is generally a product of emphasis on the clarity of thoughts. As explained previously, grammar rules are discovered by the child on the subverbalized level through the process of listening, speaking, reading, and writing. The direct teaching of grammar in the elementary school should be limited to the minimum essential principles of language structure. Exactly as a foreign language is taught in the elementary school for its cultural importance rather than as a means to improving the knowledge of English, the goal of teaching grammar is primarily the understanding of the structure of the language, rather than its impact on language facility.

It is difficult to conclude a discussion of an approach to oral expression without touching on the difficult problem of the English usage by the culturally deprived and ethnic child whose speaking habits present a social and economic handicap. There is no question that the function of the teacher is to guide these pupils toward an acceptable substitute. However, there is difficulty in achieving this goal without making children ashamed of their primary group origin. The complexity of the problem is illustrated by the following excerpt from an interview.[86:74]

Very early [in life] I felt the effects of discrimination. I was looked down upon for being Italian. Teachers used to say "you are so nice, you don't look Italian at all." *I changed my Italian accent. I cut myself from the family.* I knew the miserable feeling of being hurt.

Changing a way of speaking is not a mechanistic modification, but rather an integral aspect of the acculturation conflict experienced by the marginal child. As suggested in *The Clash of Cultures in Israel,* in some respects the tension and pain involved in the process of acculturation is inevitable.[87] The teacher should not accentuate these conflicts by a direct attack on the child's speech. On the contrary, a more patient, long-range, and indirect approach may be needed. It may seem paradoxical, but the child who feels that the teacher accepts him for what he is, who is convinced that the teacher does not think that "nice people speak English and not Spanish"; whose teacher does not laugh when he makes mistakes and is not irritated when he hears that "the Puerto Rican flag should be raised higher than the American," will tend to identify with the American way of life and speech faster than the one who is forced to change. The deprived child is looking for a reference group to remodel his behavior. It is mainly a climate characterized by intimate relations and respect which is conducive to cross-cultural contact and its corollary, gradual speech transformation. "Revolutions" in this area are extremely dangerous to the mental health of the marginal child. A gradual evolution will tend to achieve healthier results.

Writing: repetitive or creative?

Educational literature differentiates between practical and creative writing. Reports in social studies and science, business letters, outlines, or instructions, fall into the practical category; creative writing refers to the imaginative development of original stories and poems. A closer scrutiny reveals that this distinction is somewhat artificial. As Stendler points out,[S18] *The Diary of a Young Girl,* by Anne Frank is no less creative because it is not a work of fiction. Therefore, no attempt will be made here to discuss practical versus creative writing. The question to be raised is rather whether the novice's methodology promotes creativity in writing in general. The two stages in writing development to be analyzed are (1) motivating of written expression and (2) reactions to the child's written work. As the discussion will point out, the emphasis of the novice in the first stage is creative in nature, whereas his approach to the second tends to be repetitive.

Teachers tend to recognize that a major factor affecting children's work is the quality of the experience motivating writing. They encourage written expression by discussions of stories, reading a story aloud to the class without completing it, viewing pictures and movies, taking a trip, watching the weather, listening to music, role-playing, puppetry, or art work. They realize that the intellectual, aesthetic, and emotional experience of an idea is the motivating force behind written expression.

There is not sufficient awareness, however, of the implications of this approach to the second stage, namely reacting to the child's written work. This activity may be characterized by two words commonly used by teachers: "mark," or "correct." "Mark" suggests that the main objective in reading a student's communication is to give a grade. "Correct" means that the primary intention is to identify errors and insert correct forms. One may frequently be so accustomed to an expression that he becomes insensitive to its connotation. The real meaning of this type of reaction may become clearer if a teacher were asked to forget his role as a teacher, and to try to view the situation as a person. Would you like a reader to react to you primarily in terms of the number of the specific errors you have made? Or would you like the reader to attempt to understand you and react to your message?

Writing is a way of communicating ideas. The writer wants a response to the essence of the thoughts and feelings presented. Checking of the external aspects such as neatness, spelling, or paragraph arrangement should be secondary in importance to reactions to content.

As students, many young teachers experienced a schooling which taught them that the expected reward for a good composition was a grade of 96, and that their paper was to be returned to the teacher with errors meticulously corrected. In the same manner they tend to treat their own pupils with the same criteria. The following is not an uncommon illustration.

Several fifth graders come to the teacher's desk and read aloud a poem they wrote about friendship. The teacher praises the children and then says, "Now, let us see how we can improve our writing." The discussion which follows deals with margins, spacing, capitalization, and other mechanics of writing.

Teaching of this nature often results in a set formula for operation. Whether children write a sad story or some new funny rhymes, the reaction is the same: "What about the margins?" Or, "Let's check your spelling." It is difficult to believe that this kind of teacher *listens*. He only moves through the motions of correcting. The correct spelling and form are essential aspects of good writing, but they are only secondary to reactions concerning the ideas of the communication.

An integral part of individualized reading is a conference to discuss the pupil's reading. There is a need to promote a similar procedure for the analysis of the child's writing. The following is a report of a novice teacher about her attempt to conduct a *"writing conference."*

Following class reading and discussion of the "Just So" stories by Kipling, Anthony, one of the poorest students on the sixth grade level, wrote:

"How the giraffe got its neck
Because when he was eating grass he hard a nsoe and looked up and his moth opened and the tree fell down and he eat it"

I found Anthony eager to have a conference. I began by telling him that I found his ideas humorous. He enjoyed my remark. Then I asked him to tell me again the story he had in mind. Both of us agreed that his oral version was superior to the written. I raised several questions of clarification, such as, "Where did the tree fall from?" "Where was the giraffe?" Or, "What was the reaction of the other animals?"

I had intended to review several spelling and grammatical errors, but I saw that he was anxious to get his ideas down. I helped him correct these errors after he wrote the second version of his story. I discovered that when I asked him to find the errors himself, he was able to identify some of them. The others I pointed out to him. The final version was as follows:

How The Giraffe Got Its Neck

"A giraffe was eating grass under a cliff. Then a rock fell on his head and he looked up. A tree fell off the cliff and the giraffe looked up. He opened his mouth and swallowed the tree. Then the giraffe started telling the animals that the sky was falling. All the other animals were surprised that the giraffe's neck was so long."

The main function of an editor is to help the writer say better what he, the writer, wanted to say. The teacher playing the role of an editor should encourage the child to speak freely about his ideas, with emphasis on *reliving the experience* which motivated the writing.

As seen in the previous report, the "writing conference" can be most fruitful, but, like any administrative setup, it is no sure road to success. The most common mistake which the novice makes in a conference of this nature is the well-meaning attempt to tell the pupil what to write. This process only discourages the child from expressing personal experiences through writing. Rather than experiencing the creative role of a writer, he becomes almost as passive as if he were taking dictation. Frustrated, confused, and wanting "to get it over with," the pupil does not revise his work, but rather complies with the teacher's corrections.

The position taken here about the need of individualized help for *revising* the child's writing is controversial. There is a school of thought which views attempts of this nature as interference with the spontaneity and the artistic expression of children; as a critique which kills creativity. The child should get criticism and aid only in the practical writing program, whereas creative writing is a personal expression which should not be touched.[B14]

In this chapter the assumption is that both practical and creative writing are personal expressions. The teacher has a definite role in enriching and improving the child's work. Creativity calls for spontaneity, freedom, and inspiration, but also for effort and self-discipline. The "don't touch it" teacher often tends to be detached. His complimentary remarks are too often a coverup for lack of involvement with what the child really feels and thinks.

There is a need in education for less "compliment" and more listening and thinking together. The "writing conference," like the reading conference, is an opportunity for the teacher to come close to the child and help him be more creative. The experience of a novice teacher, reported here, illustrates that both aspects of form, such as syntax and spellings, and the power of expression, can be improved by an emphasis on the teacher's reaction to the essence of the presented message.

A most pertinent concluding remark to the discussion of language arts and reading, with its emphasis on the creative potential of the *experience of the idea,* is a poem written by one of the pioneers in the area of creative teaching—Hughes Mearns.[M12:30]

Grammarian's Child

When looking out I see a car
Of friends come calling from afar,
I cry to mother right away,
"Oh, that is they! Oh, that is they!"

When teacher asks, "Who has, pray speak,
A birthday in the coming week?"
And I have, then I'm mighty spry
To say, "Please Ma'am, it will be I."

But pounding on a bolted door
With bears behind me, three or four,
If I should hear, "Who could that be?"
I'd scream, "It's me! It's me! It's me!"

SELECTED BIBLIOGRAPHY

Austin, Mary, *The First R.* New York: The Macmillan Company, 1963. An interesting survey and evaluation of reading practices.

Russel, David, *Children Learn to Read.* Boston: Ginn & Company, 1961. Chapter 14 discusses the development of creative reading ability.

Smith, Nila, *Reading Instruction For Today's Children.* Englewood Cliffs, N.J.: Prentice-Hall, Inc., 1963. Chapter 9 discusses the different meanings of reading comprehension.

Strickland, Ruth, *The Language Arts in the Elementary School.* Boston: D. C. Heath & Company, 1951. A basic text covering all aspects of language teaching.

Trace, Arthur, *What Ivan Knows That Johnny Doesn't.* New York: Random House, Inc., 1961. A content analysis comparing Russian and American textbooks.

6

Arithmetic: Repetitive or creative?

In examining books on the methodology of arithmetic I was struck by the fact that many writers start their discussion with an observation about the negative attitudes of pupils toward learning this subject. A similar observation can be made with regard to the attitudes of student teachers. They view arithmetic as a narrow operation.

"It's just cut and dry stuff."

"There is one set way of doing it."

"When your method is different from that of the cooperating teacher, the communication between you and the children may be lost."

They see arithmetic as rote learning and a subject matter which is difficult to explain:

"The methods were never explained . . . It is rote and repetitious."

"It is difficult to understand why the child does not grasp the concept of number '4.' I find it difficult to think on his level."

"You cannot predict how children will react to a new concept, or whether they will react at all."

The purpose

It is the purpose of this chapter to suggest a methodology which views arithmetic as a system of ideas rather than merely as a skill; as an experience of creative thinking rather than a process of repetitive learning. With this purpose in mind, the discussion will proceed to examine the basic issues of the methodology of arithmetic: the controversy of the experiential and social versus the scientific and abstract orientations, the movement of mathematizing arithmetic, and the impact of programmed instruction on this subject.

But first a word about the complexity of arithmetical concepts.

The depth of a concept

A seemingly simple concept taught on the first grade level is the understanding that $3 + 2 = 5$. A long process of development leads to the real understanding, not parroting, of this relationship. The beginning of learning starts with the baby's manipulation of objects. This is the basis for his understanding that there are many entities of one. He puts things together, takes things away, asks for more toys, or rejects additional pieces of fruit. This is the basis for his understanding of counting—more or less, small or big, addition or subtraction. The play activity is a source promoting the development of meaningful quantitative concepts.

There are also factors at home promoting rote learning: the prevalent practice of teaching children "to count," or more correctly, to say numbers in order; the memorizing of counting rhymes, such as "one, two, three, four, five / once I caught a fish alive." In the historical development of numbers, man developed number symbols because he had experienced a new concept. He had just finished counting 5 sheep and now he had to count the 6th one. The rote learning of saying numbers precedes the word to its logical prerequisite, namely, the experience of the concept.

As early as the first grade level, the teacher is faced with the problem of rote learning of arithmetic words which do not signify meaningful concepts. When first graders are asked to count, many do it fluently and some make mistakes in the order of numbers, especially above ten. A closer examination reveals that their knowledge *lacks depth*. They often exhibit (1) failure to keep a one-to-one correspondence between objects and names of the numbers, counting, for instance, 9 objects as 10 or 11, (2) lack of comprehension of the cardinal and ordinal meaning of numbers. They may count a row of children and call Alice 7 with no understanding that the number does not stand specifically for Alice. It rather means that Alice, in this arrangement, is the 7th person [the ordinal concept] and that she is the last one in a *group* of 7 [the cardinal concept], (3) despite fluency in counting, children may fail to see the meaning of the order. For instance, 1-2-3 means going up each time by a unit of 1; 21 means 20 and 1.

This lack of depth is partly a result of the shortcuts which parents and teachers take in learning, emphasizing prematurely the *names* of things, rather than experience. However, it should be emphasized also that the above limitations illustrate the normal process of concept formation, namely growth from crude to deeper understanding. The teacher of arithmetic should not be misled by the pupil's ability to name a concept, but should look for its meaning to the learner. To illustrate, the concept of 25 may be understood as: only a number word; comes after 24 and before 26; 1 more than 24; 5 more than 20; 2 tens and 5. Also, the addition of $4 + 5$ may be developed by: counting 9 objects; identifying a group of 4 and then counting 5 objects; doubling 5 and subtracting 1.

The teacher interested not only in the correctness of the end result $(5 + 4 = 9)$ but also in the *process* of thinking which led to the result, will be able to identify many more variations than those mentioned above. He will recognize that to name an arithmetical concept, or to state a rule, is not necessarily identical with satisfactory comprehension. It is the function of the teacher not only to introduce new concepts, but also to help the learner move on the continuum from a crude to a deeper understanding of the known concept. This movement toward depth calls for a two-fold attempt: (1) emphasis on experience and (2) emphasis on logic.

THE EXPERIENTIAL AND SOCIAL ORIGIN OF ARITHMETIC

Looking at the historical development of arithmetic, one can see the role of "experience" as both the *motivating* force underlying the growth of this discipline and the *means* through which it has grown into a science. Historically, arithmetic developed out of man's need to count, measure, build; the origin is man's social experience. Historically too, arithmetic developed through man's manipulation of concrete materials, such as pebbles (the Latin word is *calculus*) or his own fingers (the Latin word is *digitus*).

The same can be said about children. The child's process of learning arithmetic corresponds in many respects to the historical development of the discipline: the origin is mainly his experience and the means is largely his experience.

The social aspect

The social aspect of arithmetic suggests that it is important to introduce a new concept by putting it in a social setting. For instance, in teaching the addition of $4 + 2$ or the multiplication of 3×2, the beginning should be what primary school teachers call a story: "A man planted 4 trees and then planted an additional 2. How many did he plant?"

The social aspect does not imply an incidental methodology. To discuss the issue of incidental versus systematic teaching of arithmetic is to build straw men and then knock them down. With few exceptions, the teaching of arithmetic on an "incidental" basis was not tried, or even advocated. The social-experiential emphasis is an integral aspect of a systematic methodology of arithmetic.

The importance of introducing a new concept in its social setting is not only the motivational aspect of the utilitarian factor (and this factor should not be underestimated), but also is its contribution to the development of *meaning*. It is a common observation that when children enter the first grade they tend to find it easier to solve a concrete problem, such as 3 bottles and 2 bottles, than the more abstract exercise of $3 + 2$. However, when they reach the third or fourth grade the reverse occurs. They tend to find it easier to compute the relatively abstract 8×3 than to figure out the answer to the "social problem"—"A man worked for 8 hours and was paid $3 per hour. How much did he earn?" Faced with the latter problem, some children ask: "Should I multiply or divide?" Tell them, "Multiply!" and they will "give you" the correct answer.

In the process between the first and the fourth grade too many children tend to lose contact with the direct experience of social arithmetic. They start to think in somewhat mechanistic terms of the algorithm: "Put it in a known formula and I'll compute it." They tend to have difficulty in transforming a problem situation to the language of a formula. The reason for this deterioration is, at least partly, the nature of the arithmetic program. The emphasis is on drill of exercises with no equal stress on social problems. Rarely is the learner asked to describe the exercise, such as $7 \times \frac{1}{5}$, in the language of a "story problem."

Observing teachers at work, one finds that on the first grade level there is a relatively good emphasis on the social aspect of arithmetic. For instance, in teaching number 5 the teacher may invite children to group objects on a flannel board and tell a story: "Here are 2 ducks and 3 ducks." "I had 5 apples and I took 3 away." However, as one progresses upwards through the grades there is a continuing decrease of this emphasis, to the detriment of depth in meaning. To test this observation, ask a group of sixth graders to formulate a problem situation for the following exercise: $\frac{1}{3} \div \frac{1}{6}$. In my experience, many cannot compose such a problem at all, and the majority find it difficult. The reason is partly the complexity of the concept and partly the way it is taught to children. It is no wonder that when pupils come to solve the abstract exercise $\frac{1}{3} \div \frac{1}{6}$, they immediately resort to the mechanistic formula of "putting the denominator up and the numerator down" ($\frac{1}{3} \times \frac{6}{1}$). It definitely helps them get "correct" on a test. However, are they really *correct*?

The detrimental effect of the lack of sufficient emphasis on the social aspect of arithmetic can be demonstrated in many areas of arithmetic.

The commutative property of mathematics suggests that $3 + 2 = 2 + 3$, or that $4 \times 8 = 8 \times 4$. Whereas the comprehension of this relationship is fundamental for the understanding of the *structure* of mathematics and is the basis for Algebra, it is in some conflict with meaningfulness as seen by the social emphasis. The latter approaches 4×8 as "I get 4 times $8," where the multiplier (the first factor) is abstract and the multiplicand (the second factor) is concrete. It will be a very different *social* situation if one gets $4 \times \$8$ rather than $8 \times \$4$, despite the fact that the product in both is $32.

The implication of this point is not to diminish the importance of the commutative principle, but rather to give equal emphasis to the social-experiential aspect. When equal emphasis is not given, what suffers is meaningful understanding.

Look at the following exercise: 25 — 9. On the surface it seems that the only issue involved is figuring out the answer. Some of the alternatives may be: "take away 10 and add 1," or "take away 5 and again take away 4." However, from the frame of reference of the social emphasis, the problem is more complicated and calls for additional search for *meaning*. As Clark suggests, [C1] there are three categories of problem situations which may underlie the above exercise of subtraction.

(1) The "how many are left" meaning. The size of the original group is known (25). The size of the group taken away is known (9). How many are left?

(2) The "comparison" or "difference" meaning. The sizes of the two groups are known. What is the difference between the large and the small? For instance, Sam is 25 years old, Rose is only 9. What is the difference in their age?

(3) The "how many more are needed" meaning. For instance, "I have 9 cents and I want to buy a 25-cent object. How much more money do I need?"

A similar observation can be made in the area of division. The problem is not only whether to teach short or long division using the "pyramid" or another approach; the issue is also to understand the meaning of division from the social-experiential frame of reference. Division has two distinct meanings:

(1) Comparison division. Into how many groups of 4 plants can 24 plants be divided? It is a division of a group (24) into groups of a given size (4).

(2) Partitioning division. If there are 24 plants arranged in 4 equal groups, what is the number of plants in each group? It is dividing a group (24) into a given number (4) of equal parts.

When a child experiences a program which develops only one category of subtraction or division, he tends to be limited in the depth of his concept formation. In other words, the lack of depth in meaning experienced by many children is at least partly a product of a program which stresses the development of the abstract algorithm with no equal emphasis on the *variety of social situations* which may underlie the exercise.

Inductive discovery through manipulation

The experiential approach to arithmetic is expressed not only in emphasis on social situations but also on the use of representative materials. To illustrate,

(1) The meaning of 36 is understood by the use of an abacus composed of 10 tens. The child moves 3 tens and an additional 6 beads. He discovers the relationship inherent in 36.

(2) In multiplying 7×5, the learner manipulates the beads and puts together 7 groups of 5. He *sees* that they are equal to 35; composed of 3 groups of 10 and 1 group of 5; or 6×5 and 1×5; of 5×5 and 2×5; or 8×5 less 1×5, etc.

(3) In learning a new concept, such as ½ of ½, the learner draws a rectangle, divides it into two halves and by "taking" or coloring ½ of one of the halves, he discovers that it consists of ¼. In other words ½ of ½ = ¼. Repeating the same graphic manipulation with ½ of ⅓, ½ of ¼, etc., he gradually discovers the relationship involved in this type of multiplication.

The *limitation* of this *empirical* approach will be discussed in the next section. At this point the positive aspects will be explained. In essence, learning through manipulation of representative materials tends to constitute an inductive process of discovery. The child is not told, or drilled on, the final algorithm, but rather discovers it on his own. As Bruner suggests[B12] the search for discovery has several educative benefits.

(1) The increase in intellectual potency. This means that the learner develops the ability to discover the structure of the main organizational principles.

(2) The shift from extrinsic to intrinsic rewards. The learner is rewarded by the task involvement and tends to look less for external reinforcement.

(3) The aid to conserving memory. The learner who organizes the information in terms of his own sense of discovery will tend to have a better chance of "retrieval" than the one who has merely been told about the uniting principles.

The inductive process of learning arithmetic through the learner's own manipulation of materials illustrates the process of discovery. It is one of the most functional and meaningful roads to knowledge.

Premature structuring of the discovery process

Too often, teachers undermine the process of discovery through manipulation by calling for articulation of rules before the learner is ready to structure them. An illustration on the primary grade level is the demand to articulate in precise language that ½ means dividing the unit into two *equal* parts. In the intermediate grades, premature structuring is even more typical, and before getting insight on their own, children may be rushed to recite "the whole number times the numerator of a fraction is the numerator of the product." (On the High School level, premature structuring often tends to be the rule rather than the exception.)

In this process of premature structuring, self-direction in discovery is killed. Rather than relying on their own power to search for structure, the pupils tend to become dependent; they attempt to get their clues from the teacher. The most articulate child tries a generalization. Being sensitive to the teacher's gestures he is able to correct and improve it. The rule is then put on the blackboard. The class follows obediently and repeats the precise statement.

Perhaps the major fallacy of the inductive method is the equation of definition of rules with the advent of discovery itself.[18] Exactly as in language development, in arithmetic conceptualization there are two levels of knowing rules: *articulation* and the *subverbalized level*. Again as in language development, first comes the nonverbalized insight and much later the ability to define.

How does a teacher recognize that the child has discovered the arithmetic principle if the child does not translate it into the language of rules? As suggested in an earlier chapter, the learner expresses his insight into the structure of the language by speaking correctly and by applying the nonverbalized rules to the creation of new forms. The same can be said about arithmetic. To some extent the ability of the child to solve problems, and especially his ability to *apply* the learning to new and unfamiliar tasks, is a good indication that discovery has occurred—at least on the nonverbalized level.

For example, on the first grade level a teacher may deal with the concept of ½. Do children understand that the concept implies division into two *equal* parts, or do they perceive it only as division into 2? "I'll have the big half and you will have the small half," is a common expression used by young children when they divide a piece of chocolate into what they consider to be two halves. It is possible to check the depth of this understanding by observing whether the pupils attempt to divide representative materials into two somewhat equal halves. In the same way it is possible to observe whether the child applies the understanding of "equal" to the learning of new concepts, such as ¼ or ⅛.

On the sixth grade level, the teacher should not press for premature definitions, such as the articulation of the rule regulating the additions of fractions with a noncommon denominator ($⅓ + ¼$). Rather, he should identify the advent of discovery by observing whether the child is able to apply his insight of the nonverbalized rule to an exercise of a higher level of difficulty, such as $⅔ + ¼$. The pupils, who *without being shown,* can apply the knowledge of $⅓ + ¼$ to the solution of $⅔ + ¼$, demonstrate that they have insight into the relationship involved.

This discussion does not deny the importance of verbalized generalizations in arithmetic. The latter, if reached by the learner himself, represents a high level of meaning and indicates the needed ability of the power of abstraction. Rather, it is the premature rushing toward rule formulation, the demand to repeat after a teacher or after one of the "smart boys," which is criticized.

The learner should be encouraged to reach the second stage of the verbalized knowledge of rules, namely the articulation, on his own. Many children cannot develop *precise* definitions. Therefore, the child's own words, even if they constitute a crude generalization, should be the objective. When the teacher approves only the definition of the articulate minority, or overemphasizes his own, the result may be verbalism and formalism.

FROM AN EMPIRICAL TO A LOGICAL RATIONALE

The discussion in this chapter has dealt primarily with the importance of experience and *empirical* learning of arithmetic.

However, the main objective of arithmetic is not *empirical* in nature but rather *abstract* and theoretical. The mathematician searches continuously for the enrichment of his discipline as a system of ideas. It is not only the knowledge of the rules which is important, but mainly the understanding of the logic underlying the relatedness of the ideas.

The need for a rationale

Despite the fundamental importance of the experiential approach to the arithmetic methodology, the approach itself is not sufficient for the understanding of the structure of arithmetic or of the *why* of the system. In some cases, at least, the inductive method of manipulation leads mainly to the discovery of the "how to do it" rules rather than to the development of a conceptualization which explains the rationale of the rules. In order to understand that experience and manipulation do not necessarily lead to insight into the *scientific* explanation of the structure, look at the following illustration.

In a sixth grade the answer to the new concept of ½ of ¼ is found *empirically*. First a rectangle is divided into fourths and one of them is colored. Next the colored fourth is divided into halves and a different color is used to identify one half of the fourth. Finally by counting, each part of the double colored section is found to be ⅛ of the original rectangle. Thus it is concluded that ½ of ¼=⅛. Similar empirical manipulation is conducted with ½ of ⅕, ¼ of ½, and so on.

Through this process of manipulation the child discovers the *rule* that to solve exercises of this nature (½ x ¼), one has to multiply the numerators, multiply the denominators, and divide the product of the first by the product of the second. The learner definitely masters a rule which works. It helps him get an A on a standardized test. Despite this achievement what really is mastered is a skill in arithmetical computation. What may be lacking is the insight into the rationale of the rule. *Why* is ½ of ¼ a multiplication exercise? *Why* does one get a correct answer when he multiplies the numerators, multiplies the denominators and divides the first product by the second?

The discovery of rules and insight into their rationale are not always identical. Children are quick to find out what "has to go up" and what "has to go down" in the computation of fractions, or to discover that "you are supposed to borrow 1 from the second column" in subtraction. They are quick to learn "the way to do it." However, the real goal for the learner is to "think" arithmetic and not merely "do" arithmetic!

To repeat, the mere process of learning arithmetic empirically is not sufficient. Bruner [B12] speaks about two levels of mathematical methodology: one, the level of empirical generalizations, and two, working on the mathematical logic itself. The fostering of productive thinking calls for starting with the first level and moving ahead toward the second.

The discussion in a previous chapter dealing with the "main idea teacher," (the B orientation), stresses that a phenomenon can be explained on two levels: *empirical* and *scientific*. A layman may say, "Anacin is twice as fast as aspirin." The reason for this statement is his empirical evidence. If found to be correct, the implication is merely that the first pain reliever is faster than the other. On the other hand, when the scientist says: "X drug is twice as fast as Y," the reason for his statement is his theoretical understanding of the biochemical processes involved. If found to be correct, this theoretical knowledge can be applied scientifically to the development of new drugs.

If knowledge remains on the empirical level only, then the study of history becomes merely a reporting of events with no uniting movements, and the study of human behavior becomes an observation of diffused actions with no uniting dynamics. Indeed, the whole process of learning becomes identical with the storage of piecemeal information. In the same way, arithmetic learned only on the empirical level may remain a computational skill without insight into the uniting structure.

To move from an empirical to a scientific understanding means to move from "how it works" to "why it works the way it does." The end result is the creation of uniting principles—*structure* of knowledge. To use Bruner's language,[B12:109] "it bestows the gift of intellectual travel beyond the information given." It is the role of education to deepen the learner's comprehension of the variety of principles structuring knowledge. The teacher should help the child apply and thereby become *mobile* intellectually. More specifically, insight into the rationale of arithmetic can be enhanced by the process of emphasis on (1) application, (2) divergent thinking, and (3) mental computation.

The role of application

There is a need for emphasis on application and movement ahead to a higher level of difficulty. This should be done without specific instructions by the teacher and without use of representative materials. For example, the child has learned that $7 \times 5 = 35$. Faced with a new task, 9×5, he says: "I know that this is 2×5 more than 7×5." Or in another example, the pupil knows that $7 + 5 = 12$. Confronted with $17 + 5$, he says: "If $7 + 5 = 12$ then $17 + 5$ is 10 more."

It is good to confront children with a new task and to say for instance: "Here is a new problem we have never discussed. On the basis of your previous learning can you suggest and explain some ways of solving it?" Then let the children move on their own from 32-24 to 322-242 and *explain* to you the logic of their procedure.

One way of fostering insight into the structure of arithmetic is to ask children to develop levels of difficulty of a specific concept. For instance, let them arrange the following exercises in a sequence according to their level of difficulty:

$$
\begin{array}{cccc}
30 & 248 & 28 & 288 \\
-14; & -\ 14; & -14; & -\ 14 \\
\end{array}
$$

Or ask them to add a next level of difficulty to the following exercise:

$$
\begin{array}{ccc}
684 & 684 & ? \\
-123; & -125; & \\
\end{array}
$$

The role of divergent thinking

The methodology of arithmetic is seen too often as a one-track operation. The repetitive teacher is preoccupied with the correctness of the end result and pays little attention to the reasoning underlying the process of arrival. The "main idea" teacher, interested in convergent thinking, may tend to illustrate mainly one method and give one explanation of the logic involved. The *C* teacher, interested in divergent thinking, will not rush prematurely toward the final and efficient algorithm. Rather, he will help to develop a *variety* of ways of solving the problem, each with its own logical explanation.

For instance, faced with the new task of learning to add two-place numbers let the children suggest a variety of approaches:

34+20=54, and 3 are 57
34+3 are 37, and 20 are 57
30+20 are 50; 4+3=7; together they are 57

The following illustrates divergent thinking when the *new* problem of multiplying 7 × 12 is introduced:

$$(A) \quad \begin{array}{r} 10 \\ \times 7 \\ \hline 70 \end{array} \quad \begin{array}{r} 2 \\ \times 7 \\ \hline 14 \end{array} \quad \begin{array}{r} 70 \\ +14 \\ \hline 84 \end{array} \qquad (B) \quad \begin{array}{r} 2 \\ \times 7 \\ \hline 14 \end{array} \quad \begin{array}{r} 10 \\ \times 7 \\ \hline 70 \end{array} \quad \begin{array}{r} 70 \\ +14 \\ \hline 84 \end{array}$$

$$(C) \quad \begin{array}{r} 12 \\ \times 7 \\ \hline 70 \\ 14 \\ \hline 84 \end{array} \qquad (D) \quad \begin{array}{r} 12 \\ \times 7 \\ \hline 14 \\ 70 \\ \hline 84 \end{array} \qquad (E) \quad \begin{array}{r} 12 \\ \times 7 \\ \hline 84 \end{array}$$

The final algorithm (*E*) is a culmination of thinking through the problem in a variety of ways. With this process the meaning of the relationship is stressed. This should not be interpreted as underestimating the need for an efficient algorithm. The latter is definitely needed, and has to be studied and *drilled*. However, when movement toward the ultimate formula is rushed, the end result tends to be a mechanistic adherence to a rule with no insight into the structure.

Divergent thinking in arithmetic should not be developed only in the prealgorithm stage. As children become proficient in the practice of a certain alogorithm, it is desirable to stop from time to time to encourage the learners to reexamine their procedure and to suggest a greater variety of approaches, even "wild ideas." For instance, division is commonly taught by the use of the "pyramid" method. The beginner might figure it out this way:

$$\left.\begin{array}{r} 7 \\ 10 \\ 30 \end{array}\right\} = 47$$

The one who is more proficient might do it this way:

$$\left.\begin{array}{r} 7 \\ 40 \end{array}\right\} = 47$$

```
  2 )94
    60
    --
    34
    20
    --
    14
    14
    --
```

```
  2 )94
    80
    --
    14
    14
    --
```

After the children have mastered this operation, let them survey and study the various methods their parents were taught for solving division computations. Let the children find out some of the other algorithms in this area.

Too often teachers say to children: "Don't ask your parents to explain it to you, we are learning the *new* method." One reason student teachers are hesitant to teach arithmetic is that they are afraid they may explain it "in another way" than the cooperating teacher. The arithmetic methodology is perceived as a rigid operation. The suggestions made here constitute an attempt to change this perception.

Whereas in language arts or social studies divergent thinking is expressed in a variety of *"products,"* in arithmetic it is expressed in intellectual playfulness with the *process*. The cycle of the development of a new algorithm becomes: (a) divergent processes discovered by children; (b) practice and drill on the algorithm; (c) again divergent processes suggested by children.

The role of mental arithmetic and estimation

One approach to the development of insight into the meaning of the arithmetic structure is to stress mental computation and estimation. In mental arithmetic, no longer bound by the use of the conventional algorithm, the learner is able to think through a solution without the distraction of following a prescribed form. The reason for emphasis on mental computation is not only utilitarian, getting the correct change at the store, but rather the ability to *"see arithmetic."* At present, especially in the intermediate grades, there is not sufficient emphasis on this approach. On this level, practice is too often limited to the working out of the computations in written form.

MATHEMATIZING ARITHMETIC

The deepening of the understanding of the structure of arithmetic is the main objective of a new educational movement which calls for "mathematizing arithmetic." The dynamic nature of this school of thought is seen in the fact that it is often referred to as the "revolution in mathematics."

The need for change

There are several factors underlying the drive to mathematize arithmetic:

(1) Means must be found to feed back into our schools the ever-deepening insights which constantly develop on the frontiers of knowledge. Major technological change has required innovation in the field. The automation era too calls for a higher level of mathematical competency.

(2) Progressive education is being criticized for its preoccupation with the child's experience to the neglect of the emphasis on the structure of subject matter. As seen by the mathematician, progressive education has been preoccupied with the social-experiential origin of arithmetic. Such emphasis on the pragmatic aspects brought about a delineation of arithmetic as a skill; emphasis on "do arithmetic" rather than "think arithmetic." Learning failed to move from the experiential to the abstraction.

(3) The present extensive interest in the structure of subject matter has led to the development of the concept of the *spiral curriculum* as a major criterion for curriculum construction. To quote from The Process of Education:[B13:13]

The basic ideas that lie at the heart of all science and mathematics and the basic themes that give form to life and literature are as simple as they are powerful. To be in command of these basic ideas . . . requires a continual deepening of one's understanding of them that comes from learning to use them in progressively more complex forms. . . A curriculum as it develops should revisit these basic ideas repeatedly, building upon them.

In terms of the teaching methodology of arithmetic, the criterion of the "spiral curriculum" calls for: (1) introducing the basic concepts of mathematics in their simplest form as early as the first grade level, and (2) the sequential deepening of such concepts as formal education proceeds.

Mathematizing arithmetic: structure

Whereas the emphasis of the various experimental projects attempting to mathematize arithmetic is somewhat different,[D3] their common denominator is twofold: (1) more attention is given to the thought processes of the structure of arithmetic, and (2) a simplified version of new topics which has been reserved in the past for more advanced study of mathematics on the high school and college level, is now being introduced into the arithmetic curriculum. The following are some illustrations of the greater attention given to the structure of arithmetic.

(1) Emphasis on the commutative law. The order in which two numbers are added does not affect the sum. $4 + 2 = 2 + 4$. The order in which the numbers are used in multiplication does not affect the product. $4 \times 5 = 5 \times 4$.

(2) Emphasis on the associative law. Numbers may be regrouped for adding without changing the sum. $3 + 7 = 3 + (2 + 5) = (3 + 2) + 5$. Numbers may be regrouped for multiplication without changing the product. $2 \times (5 \times 4) = (2 \times 5) \times 4$.

(3) The distributive law combines addition and multiplication. $8 \times 34 = 8 \times (30 + 4) = (8 \times 30) + (8 \times 4) = 240 + 32 = 272$.

It would be a mistake to ask children to memorize the above definitions. The interest should rather be on encouraging the learner to discover and use these properties, and through this process to develop an intellectual playfulness with number relations.

Another illustration of curricular innovations stressing structure is the imaginative work done at the University of Illinois Arithmetic Project under the direction of Dr. Page. Dr. Page's objective is to devise materials to help children view work in arithmetic as a fascinating adventure; to acquire an intuitive understanding of many mathematical ideas which have usually been initiated much later in the child's schooling.[D3] For instance, their publication *Arithmetic With Frames*[P2] includes exercises of the following nature: Find all the numbers which satisfy:

$$■ + ■ = 16 \text{ (ans: 8)}$$
$$▼ \times ▼ \times ▼ = 8 \text{ (ans: 2)}$$
$$■ + 3 = ■ \text{ (ans: no number)}$$

The emphasis on insight into the structure is an attempt to deepen the present scope of the arithmetic program *qualitatively*, and should therefore be welcomed by the classroom teacher.

Mathematizing arithmetic: new content

The second aspect of the *"mathematics revolution,"* the attempt to enlarge the scope of the present elementary program and introduce new topics, such as set theory, modulo systems, point-set geometry, is *controversial.* The educator should recognize the importance of this content in the development of the discipline, the imaginative efforts in simplifying the concepts, the surge of interest on the part of the subject-matter scholars in the education of children, and in working with elementary school teachers. One must remember that these materials are only in their experimental stage and with experience will be improved. Despite this recognition, some limitations must be observed.

The new curricular materials[D3] produced by the various projects attempting to mathematize arithmetic tend to be developed on a high abstract level and ignore, much too often, the social origin of arithmetic. In many cases they stress *precise* mathematical language and are preoccupied with notations and the writing of symbols. Despite statements in the introduction about the importance of discovery, some of the new materials tend to present predigested content and ignore the significance of discovery as a process of learning.

In their rejection of progressive education and its underestimation of the pursuit of excellence, some revisionists threw out the window a whole era of educational progress. Findings in child development and the growth of concept formation, the role of experiential learning, and the most difficult problem of motivation, have been almost completely forgotten. It seems that too often all these have been replaced with *one* principle to guide curriculum construction—the *spiral curriculum*.

The spiral curriculum is a fundamental and an inviting principle. However, it is only one of many to be considered in curriculum construction. An illustration of the lack of clarity in this area is a theory presentation which one project[S22] recommends for the use of first graders, while another writer[S15] develops very similar content as *enrichment* for *fourth* graders. Similar illustrations can be brought from the discussion of geometry.

It is a sad commentary that the theory of Dewey, a leading intellectual of his era, was too often implemented as an activity and child-centered program. In the same way there is a danger that the theory of Bruner, a student of cognitive processes and child development, will be implemented mainly in terms of its "spiral" suggestion, ignoring other aspects of his work. To quote Bruner in *After John Dewey, What?*[B12:121]

Mathematics, like any other subject, must begin with experience; but progress toward abstraction and understanding requires precisely that there be a weaning away from the obviousness of superficial experience.

The new content suggested by the "mathematics revolution" implemented "progress toward abstraction" but has often failed to pay due attention to the springboard—the experience. As a result, some of the new programs, in terms of their new content, communicate a sense of *verbalism and formalism*. Especially today when the education of the ethnic lower-class child is a central issue, excessive return to formalism is highly questionable.

The "mathematics revolution" has managed to arouse a great deal of interest in the teaching profession. In various workshops all over the country teachers are taught the use of the new materials. The learnings gained in these seminars is invaluable both in terms of raising the teachers' depth of knowledge and in stressing the increasing role of mathematical thinking. Despite this positive contribution, discussion with classroom teachers and curriculum workers reveals anxiety over the formalistic nature of the new program:

"They don't want us to speak about lines but rather line segments."
"It is not a circle but a closed curve."
"No more group work; only set work."
"I have to speak in precise legalistic language."

One may view these comments as the resentment of the prac-
tioner over the intellectual articulation of the theorist. The comments also express, however, the lack of meaning which many
teachers experience in the "new content." They have a sense of
being rushed to adopt new terminology without sufficient time to
experience the ideas which led to the new technical terms. There
is the danger that many teachers will, in turn, do the same to their
pupils by rushing them toward logistics.

The danger of formalism can be seen under a magnifying
glass by the portrait in caricature of the school master in Dicken's
story *Hard Times*. The teacher asked the daughter of a horse
trainer to define a horse. Despite the fact that she has lived around
horses all her life, she cannot do so. The bright boy in the class
stands up and recites: "Horse. Quadruped. Graminiverous. Fourty
teeth, twenty-four grinders . . ."

Whereas the "activity curriculum" of the past progressive education era too often remained on the level of the *daughter of
the horse trainer*," some of the "new content" in arithmetic as presented to children today reminds me of the teaching of Dickens'
School Master.

PROGRAMMED ARITHMETIC

Programmed instruction encompasses all subject areas. However, at present, its application in the elementary school is felt especially in the area of arithmetic. In a previous chapter it was suggested that programming reflects two central interests in modern
educational thinking: (1) the organization of subject matter, and
(2) the process of learning.

The first aspect means that the subject matter to be taught is
reduced into small steps generally called frames. These steps are
arranged in sequential order in which the subject matter or skill is
to be learned. A major contribution of this approach may be found
in its sensitizing the teacher to the relationship between the "part"

and the "whole" inherent in subject matter. It demonstrates that subject matter and teaching is not an aggregation of information, but rather a planned and developmental approach to conceptualization.

The second aspect underlying the programming approach, namely learning theory, perceives optimum learning as a situation where the learner progresses independently in small steps, and where his responses are immediately reinforced. The learner is an active rather than a passive recipient.[T8]

The quality of thinking

When one overcomes the scientific aura surrounding programmed instruction, which evolves from being new, experimental, and associated with the automation era, he must question the *thinking processes* underlying this approach. Figuratively speaking, thinking is perceived as if the learner stands in a corner of the room and moves to the other corner in the shortest direct line, always moving forward step by step. This conception is not creative in nature!

Creative thinking does not consist of movements in a linear step-by-step progression. It is rather characterized by "irregular" progress toward the goal: progress, withdrawal, progress, failure and starting from the beginning, insight into one aspect. Figuratively speaking, creative thinking is somewhat like a "spaghetti" kind of movement. To get a taste of this "creative spaghetti" the reader is invited to discover the solution to the following problem, suggested by Bartlett:[B3:51]

This is to be treated as an exercise in simple addition. *Donald + Gerald=Robert.* All that is known is (1) that D=5; (2) that every number from 1–10 has its corresponding letter; (3) that each letter must be assigned a number different from that given for any other letter. The operation required is to find a number for each letter.

Now imagine that this problem is programmed in sequential frames, which lead the learner step by step in a straight line. At each step he is "reinforced" with the knowledge of whether he is right or wrong. Although the learner will undoubtedly master the procedure, in this programmed process of the attainment of knowledge the excitement of discovery and the experience of intellectual playfulness would be lost.

The Skinnerian approach divides programming into carefully graded frames. The position is that at least 90% of the learners should be able to move from one step to another without failure, and be rewarded by positive reinforcement. The programmers are afraid of "confusion" and prefer a smooth progression of correct responses. A certain degree of "confusion" is, however, inherent in the creative emphasis of moving from the known to the unknown. Creativity calls for intolerance to ambiguity and disorder; for struggling toward the structuring of a new order. (It is symbolic that the first creation started with confusion. As stated in Genesis, "In the beginning God created the heaven and the earth. Now the earth was unformed and void . . .")

The questioning potential

Programmed instruction is highly structured. The learner is faced with a beginning point, the steps, and the goal. His only function is to move in a predetermined route. He cannot identify *questions,* nor establish goals to guide his learning. In contrast, a most exciting aspect of creative thinking is the identification of the question. It is possible to suggest that the latter is as important as finding the answer.

The following three arithmetic problems rank from "low" to "high" in terms of their "questioning potentialities":

(1) $8 \times 3 =$
(2) A man worked for 8 hours and earned $3 per hour. How much did he earn?
(3) A man worked for 8 hours and earned $3 per hour. What is the arithmetical question?

In the first, both the question and the type of computation is given. In the second, the question is given but the specific type of the computation needed has to be chosen by the learner. The third is the only problem which calls for the identification of the question and may be considered richest in its potential for creative thinking.

It is possible to make the third question even more "question provoking" by adding information which may or may not be used: For instance,

A man worked for 8 hours and earned $3 per hour of work. Then he rested for 1 hour. What are the various arithmetical questions which could be raised?

The arithmetic curriculum at present stresses primarily the first, and to some extent the second type of problem. There is no emphasis on the intellectual playfulness which the last type of problem may encourage. With the advent of programmed arithmetic there is a danger that even the thinking difficulty inherent in $8 \times 3 =$ will be cut into small, "chewable" portions. Under the banner of self-directed learning, programming may thus make arithmetic into a *"self-service spoon-feeding"* process.

CONCLUSION

There are two main factors which contribute to a repetitively oriented arithmetic program: (1) Emphasis on a mechanistic knowledge of the correct response without equal stress on the process of arrival, (2) Emphasis on verbalistic and formalistic rules. The forces conducive to a creative orientation are also mainly two: (1) Emphasis on the inductive process of discovery through manipulation, (2) Emphasis on intellectual playfulness which promotes insight into the rationale of the *structure* of arithmetic.

SELECTED BIBLIOGRAPHY

BRUNER, Jerome, *On Knowing*. Chambridge: Harvard University Press, 1962. Part II includes three articles: "The Act of Discovery," "On Learning Mathematics," and "After John Dewey, What?" In many respects, my discussion in this chapter is a reaction to these articles.

CLARK, John, *Guiding Arithmetic Learning*. New York: World Book

Company, 1954. A systematic discussion of the methodology of arithmetic.

DEANS, Edwina, *Elementary School Mathematics: New Directions.* Washington, D.C.: U.S. Department of Health, Education and Welfare, 1963. A report about the major experimental projects of the "mathematizing arithmetic" movement.

IONESCO, Eugene, *Rhinoceros.* New York: Grove Press, Inc., 1960. This internationally known play has a penetrating portrayal of the logicians—men who lost direct contact with their experience. It has interesting implications for the experiential formalistic controversy in arithmetic.

TROW, William Clark, *Teacher and Technology.* New York: Appleton-Century-Crofts, 1963. Chapter 4 includes a generally favorable discussion of programmed learning.

7

Science: Repetitive or creative?

The word *science* is derived from the Latin word *scierce*—to know. Whereas the term *scientist* refers both to the specialist in the humanistic and natural sciences, in practice it is used primarily to describe the scholar who specializes in the natural studies. As viewed by many, the natural sciences are the crown of knowledge and the scientist is the most accomplished among learned men. The image of the scientist is of an able and industrious man, objective, creative, and dedicated to the exploration of the unknown.

The assumption is that science learning is important not only for the sale of knowledge, but also because of the secondary characteristics it tends to promote: high level of intellectual functioning, objective thinking, openness, and social responsibility. Science is a "high status" subject. It is seen as providing the potential solution of such major problems as food, health, communication, and defense. The post-Sputnik era further elevated the dominant status of this discipline.

This chapter proposes to examine the work of the elementary school teacher in the light of the great emphasis on the value of science teaching. More specifically, it aims at investigating the factors which promote either a repetitive or a creative approach to science teaching. The discussion will examine both attitudes and the actual teaching behavior of beginning teachers, and will make recommendations for enhancing the creative orientation.

* My appreciation to Dr. Helen Wood for her materials and observations which were used in the preparation of this chapter.

THE STEPCHILD OF THE CURRICULUM

In discussing science methodology, novice teachers tend to stress the potential significance of this discipline in concept formation and intellectual development of children. This is in marked contrast to attitudes concerning other disciplines. In teaching reading, the obvious need of mastering the skill of reading correctly and fluently tends to prevent the teacher from giving equal attention to the intellectual message of the reading matter. In arithmetic the emphasis on the correct stimulus response of computation and the memorization of rules, interferes with paying equal attention to the process of arrival, or the rationale. In social studies, the preoccupation with facts, dates, and names of places and products, interferes with the novice's ability to develop generalizations and critical thinking.

It is mainly in the area of science where the methodology is commonly viewed as experimentation and where movement from the concrete to the abstract and concept formation are viewed as being as significant as the factual subject matter itself.

Beginning teachers report that when they know they are going to be observed, they often select a science lesson.

"It is easier to shine with a science lesson."

"Children are always interested. No problem of motivation."

"The movement from the concrete to the abstract through experimentation is most meaningful to the pupil."

The novice does not think that the approach to science is primarily book learning, but rather the firsthand experience of observation and experimentation. The stress, he believes, should be on concept formation rather than on memorization. In other words, the conception of the young teacher of what science is, and his faith in the potential of the science methodology, are factors conducive to the emphasis on productive thinking and scientific attitudes.

Despite such positive perceptions, the fact is that the *amount of time* spent on science teaching in the elementary school is generally extremely limited. Whereas, on the level of professed values, science is rated as being as important as social studies, in practice the emphasis placed on the first is only secondary in comparison to the second, and is even more limited in comparison to the "major subjects"—reading and arithmetic. It can be said, therefore, that at present science is the stepchild of the elementary curriculum.

Several factors may explain the discrepancy between the teacher's high esteem of the potential of science methodology and his relative lack of emphasis on science teaching in practice. A review of research on creativity and the personality of the scientist suggests that the student majoring in science in college is superior in computational interest and scientific interest, and inferior to other college students in terms of persuasive and social service interest. The scientist is said to prefer individualistic and intellectual activities to interpersonal and emotional interchange; to be immersed in objects rather than in the human realm of personal relations.[N4]

As suggested by a later chapter on relating to children, the strength of the group of teachers under discussion is in the personal relations realm rather than on relationship to objects and tasks. They tend to prefer interpersonal rather than individualistic and pure intellectual activities. Their decision to teach is, by and large, a product of their need to serve children, rather than of a desire to develop ideas or of dedication to a particular discipline.

Most of the elementary school teachers are women, whereas relatively few women select science as a career. Torrance reports, in a study of "The Role of Manipulation in Creative Thinking,[T4]" that in an experiment involving the use of science toys, many girls in the fourth through sixth grades were reluctant to participate in a test called a "Product Improvement Test," in which children were asked to think of all the ideas they could invent for improving common toys. Boys' superiority over girls in this task was already apparent by the second grade, and increased with age. It is generally believed that cultural factors act to discourage girls from *manipulating* objects—a prerequisite to scientific inventiveness and interest.

These factors offer some explanation of why only an extremely small number of elementary school majors select science as a minor or a field of concentration in college. Science ranks low, if not lowest, as a field of specialization. Consequently, a majority of the novice teachers under discussion feel a lack of sufficient proficiency in the subject matter. This insecurity is one of the main factors contributing toward constricting behavior, and a major deterrent to creative teaching in science. The young teacher too often tends to "guide" the lesson in the predetermined direction, and not to allow for unexpected modifications which may call for unfamiliar information.

The traditional objectives of the elementary school, the three R's, do not include science. As the following stanza from a humorous poem illustrates, science is secondary in status.

A Parent's Plea

They teach him physiology
And oh, it chills our hearts
To hear our prattling innocent
Mix up his inward parts.

He also learns astronomy
And names the stars by night,
Of course he's very up to date
But I wish that he could write.

It seems as if this poem is taken from a recent magazine criticizing modern education. But it was actually published in 1907. (The publication is not known.) Today, as in 1907, the conception of the role of the school is too often narrow. It does not recognize that a curriculum centered on the intellectual, emotional and aesthetic experience of science, literature, etc., is the best promise for a high level of skill in reading, writing, and computing.

It is especially in schools serving lower-class children where the pressure of the development of "skills" (in the narrow sense of the word) tends to tempt teachers to look for shortcuts. As reported by novice teachers, a positive correlation exists between economic conditions, academic success, and the amount of time spent on science. In middle-class communities or in above average classes, science plays a larger role than in lower-class or in below average classes. The professed value operating here is that the enrichment of science is extra, since children with ability lower than average need first to learn to read. Under the banner of the need for improved skills, many lower-class children are offered a program stripped of intellectual excitement.

There is a need for a reaffirmation of the central role of science in the elementary school as being of equal importance to the three *r*'s. Despite much progress in the "post Sputnik" era, in the practice of the elementary school curriculum science is still a stepchild.

OVERSTRUCTURED TEACHING

The pursuit of excellence calls for the education of the individual as a *creator*. Bruner says: [B12:116]

For whatever the art, the science, the literature, the history and the geography of a culture, each man must be his own artist, his own scientist, his own historian, his own navigator.

An attempt should be made to examine the contribution of *science methodology* to the development of the scientist in man; to identify its limitations and suggest improvements.

A major contribution of science methodology to the development of the "scientist" in the learner is its emphasis on the process of discovery. In terms of learning, to discover is not mainly to find something new, but to find something for oneself. Inquiry precedes discovery. The teacher who rushes to answer questions rather than guide children to inquire, may be shortcutting the process of discovery.

Examine the following two illustrations reported by Wood: [W9]

In a first grade, a child spills water on the classroom floor. When he returns later to wipe it up, he finds that most of the water has disappeared. The pupil asks: "What happened to the water? Where did it go?" The teacher replies: "It dried up."

In a second grade, a pupil manipulates the bar magnet and exclaims: "Why are there so many paper clips at the two ends?" The teacher responds: "This is because the magnets are strongest at the ends. We call these ends poles. What do we call them, children?"

Both examples demonstrate how a teacher takes the shortest possible route between the question and the answer. In both situations the pupils may have gained information but they did not experience the process of inquiry or discovery on their own. Instead of using the situation to open and enlarge and lead to new learning, the surge of interest was closed prematurely.

As suggested by Wood, in the situation involving the spilled water the teacher may have returned the question by saying: "How can we find out what happened to it?" Typical suggestions may be, "Let's put some water in the sunshine," or "Let's spill more and blow on it." By avoiding a premature closure, this teacher is able to activate the children, enlarge the inquiry, and move toward experimentation.

The same can be said about the question with regard to the magnet. The teacher may say: "This is an interesting observation. How can we find out the answer?" Again the principle involved suggests an extension of the process of inquiry which takes place between the question and the concluding answer.[W9]

Repetitive teaching was described in the chapter on model A as mainly a stress on two interrelated aspects: (1) specificity of subject matter, and (2) overstructured or even constricting behavior. Examination of the teaching behavior of the novice teacher suggests that, with regard to science, specificity of information is not the emphasis. The stress is rather on concept formation. The young teacher is fully aware that even though science is built up of facts, as a house is built of bricks, a mere collection of facts is no more science than a heap of bricks is a house.

A group of novice teachers was asked to record in detail a science lesson they had taught. An examination of these records illustrates the dominant role of the B orientation of concept formation in science teaching. For instance, a lesson on sound, planned for a second grade, aims at developing the following concepts:

(1) A sound is made when something vibrates.
(2) A sound stops when the vibration stops.
(3) There are many ways to set an object into vibration.
(4) The harder the object is struck the louder the sound.
(5) Large objects produce lower tones than small objects made of the same material.
(6) Different materials produce different sounds.

A lesson about the "windy day," taught to a first grade, attempts to make children aware that:

(1) Wind is moving air.
(2) Wind pushes and carries things.
(3) Wind can help dry things.
(4) Wind can be both helpful and damaging.

A comparison of the records of science lessons with the records of language arts or social studies lessons, given by the same group of teachers, shows that the concept formation goal is stronger in science teaching than in any other area of the curriculum. For instance, a typical reading lesson states that an aim is "to understand the story," or a typical social studies lesson may aim at "learning about the problems which confronted Washington." The concepts of social studies or language arts to be developed are *vague* in the teacher's own mind, in comparison to the relative clarity of the science concepts.

The examination of the records of science lessons shows that the typical lesson taught by the novice is a systematic development of the concept through observation and manipulation of materials. Despite this valuable emphasis on productive thinking and level *B* of knowledge, the methodology of the novice tends to be overstructured and often too constricting in nature. It is characterized by a relative lack of *freedom* for exploration as it moves the child step-by-step toward a predetermined goal.

Guiding observations

The expression of the repetitive orientation in science teaching is not in the emphasis on the first aspect of repetitiveness—level *A* of knowledge—but rather on the second aspect of this model—overstructured behavior. To understand this criticism, examine the following observation reported by Wood:[W9]

A teacher places a heap of soil from one sack on the left side of the desk, and a heap of soil from another sack on the right side. The teacher says: "I took the soil on my left from my garden, the other came from the railroad bank. Which one do you think is the good soil and which is the poor?" A child answers and the teacher continues: "Let's see what the good soil has. I am going to choose one child to come up to find the leaves. Everyone else sit still and watch." A child goes to the demonstration desk, pokes in the soil, finds a piece of leaf and shows it to the class. The same procedure continues for the other components of soil that the teacher points out. As a summary the teacher says: "Now we have found what soil is made of. What did we find?" The children summarize the elements that the teacher asked them to find.

In this example, the children's level of activity is limited to finding the specific elements requested in a sequential order by the teacher. Note that no one was asked to find more than one element at the same time. The route to the concept is extremely directed. Perhaps the only level of higher directiveness possible is not to raise questions at all but rather to present the demonstration in a lecture form.

It is possible to replace the lengthy questioning, the controlling behavior of choosing a child to come before the class and "find the leaves," and the time-consuming activity of children coming sequentially to the demonstration table, with one major assignment: "Compare the two types of soil and report your observations." It seems, however, that the young teacher is hesitant to attempt this relatively "open-ended" approach. Perhaps he will not get the right answer. Perhaps the movement will be as smooth as expected.

The following record illustrates how a novice teacher prefers leading children through systematic and specific questioning:

Teacher: What do you see?
Child: Little brown seeds.
Teacher: How are they different?
Child: They are different colors and shapes.
Teacher: (Distributes some lima beans that have been soaked in water) Are the wet beans larger?
Child: They are larger than the dry ones.
Teacher: How is the skin?
Child: Softer.
Teacher: Try to peel it off.
Child: It is easy to do it.
Teacher: What is inside?
Child: A baby plant.

There is no attempt here to underestimate the strength of this approach to observation. It is experiential in nature and leads to meaningful concepts about seeds. It generally arouses the enthusiasm of primary school children. However, despite this positive contribution, the example illustrates the spoon-feeding of step-by-step structuring. In reply to a question, the child's function is limited to one act: "Are the wet beans larger than the dry beans? Are they softer? Where is the baby plant?"

In developing this lesson, it is possible to replace the scores of minute questions with one major task: "Observe the various seeds (apple, dry, and wet lima beans), 'manipulate' them, and be ready to present a report." Under this setup the child has to work *on his own* or in small groups for a certain period, putting things together and creating his own sense of order. The teacher's function is to guide the discussion and further observation on the basis of the presented reports.

Despite the fact that in both approaches children may come out with similar information, in terms of processes of thinking they travel through different routes. In the first route a "powerful person" moves others by his continuous questions. With each question the learner moves a step ahead and waits for the second command to move. His field of vision, his power of aspiration, are limited to one-step movement.

The second route is triggered by the teacher, but from here on the learner is free to go ahead on his own. He takes many steps. Only the sense of his resourcefulness and the nature of the observed objects limit his exploration. He learns to create order on his own, and to prepare himself for the challenge of further questions and information to come from the teacher and from his peers.

Freedom to think does not only mean that a teacher should be nice, accepting, supporting, and interesting. It calls for a teacher to structure learning tasks which provide the learner with a field to stretch, figure out, and play intellectually. The point cannot be overemphasized that present practices too often are denoted by a field limited to one-step distance.

Guiding experiments

In criticizing the bookish approach to the development of experiments, Blough offers the following illustration:[B7:23]

One child reads from the text the directions for performing the experiment; another child performs the experiment accordingly, and a third child reads from the book the results of the experiment.

The analysis of records of the lessons taught by novice teachers suggests that this description is not typical of their teaching behavior. They are experience- rather than book-centered in their presentation. Whereas in high school a common practice is to give students written step-by-step instructions for developing an experiment, this is not the case on the elementary school level. Experimentation through manipulation of materials is the most prevalent type of science activity employed by the novice.

The records of the science lessons taught by the group of teachers under discussion illustrate that what is generally called "doing an experiment with children" is, in practice, mainly a *demonstration* given by the teacher.

Teacher: What do I have in my hand?
Child: A magnet.
Teacher: What does it do?
Child: It picks up nails.
Teacher: What else?
Child: Paper clips and metals.
Teacher: (Puts two boxes on the table; one is marked "yes" and the other "no.") Let's see what are the things that the magnets pick up.

At this point it could have been possible to confront the class with this major question and ask them to suggest ways and materials for proceeding to find the answer. Following this approach means that the learner plays a role in developing the experiment. It calls on the teacher to have a flexible plan which permits the accommodation of the ideas suggested by children. However, as the continuation of the above science lesson illustrates, the novice tends to be teacher-centered in his behavior. He *demonstrates,* rather than encourages children to experiment.

Teacher: Will the magnet lift the ruler?
Child: (Comes to the demonstration table; tries to lift the ruler with a magnet.) No. (He puts the ruler in the "no" box.)
Teacher: Who will come to try the thumb tacks?

Child: (Comes to the desk; tries the object and puts it in the "yes" box.)

The same procedure continues. The teacher selects an object and a child comes to test it. The lesson ends with a summarization of the type of materials attracted by magnets, or unaffected by magnets.

The prerequisite to rich experimentation is freedom to explore. The step-by-step demonstration is limited in its potential for freedom to explore. In too many cases it is even restrictive in nature. Examine the following instructions given by a primary teacher.

We are going to find out what wind does to the sailboat. (Puts the objective on the blackboard.) Take out the bottom of the milk container that I gave you. It has a hole. Put it down on your desk. Now watch carefully that you do not make a mistake. Take your paper first. Take a pencil and draw the sail. (Shows on the blackboard.) Do not make the sail too big because it will not fit on the boat. (Waits until the children finish cutting the sail.) Now, make two holes in the paper, one here and one there. . .

A scientist has to learn both to follow instructions and to *invent* procedures. The conventional approach to demonstration promotes mainly the first aspect—the technician. There is a need for equal emphasis on the second aspect—the creator. For instance, after identifying the problem (what wind does to the sailboat), the pupils should make suggestions on how to find the answer. Let children learn to *plan ahead* an activity.

A novice teacher who tried this approach to the above problem reported that the children made many mistakes. They designed a sail which did not fit the boat. They blew wind on a sail when its wide surface was not opposite the blowing source. The fact that the pupils encountered difficulties only enriched the lesson. They learned to cope with difficulties. They learned that they have to try to predict and plan for possible obstacles.

The overstructured approach to guiding experiments cuts the learning task into small chewable pieces. Observing the process of this Pablum approach to learning, one notices the lack of *confrontation* with a difficult task. Learning becomes smooth movement rather than a struggle for a solution. Examine the following illustration:

In a lesson on sound the concept is developed that when objects made of the same matter are struck, the smaller the object, the higher is the tone, and the larger the object, the lower is the tone. The teacher utilizes a variety of materials, among which are eight bells whose tones represent the scale. However, rather than letting the children have all eight "melody bells" at once, and letting the pupil discover that the bells represent the notes of the scale, the teacher follows a "less difficult" approach. First, the two bells which produce the lowest tones on the scale are presented and compared; then the second pair and so on, until the eight bells are arranged in the scale order.

The activity was enjoyable. The relation between size and tone was stressed. However, the challenge of a difficulty and, therefore, the level of discovery, was limited.

In a conference, this criticism was brought before the young teacher. She decided to try the lesson again with another group. The following is part of her report.

After some discussion and experimentation on the relationship between size and tone, I took out the eight "melody bells" and gave them to a small group of children. I asked them to find the order. They started to ring the bells and put them in order. They made many mistakes and several times had to change the sequence. When finally the group had the eight bells in order, they rang the bells in turn and the class cheered.

I asked them to try it again and find a way of arranging the bells in sequence without use of the tone (melody). They found out that the bells are equal in size, but the inner moving piece of metal is different in size. They measured the length of the metal piece and arranged the bells in order. They rang the bells in turn and saw that they were playing the scale. Again the class cheered.

In both instances the "cheering reaction" was an expression of a sense of triumph over a difficult task. The reader is urged to observe the curriculum in science and other disciplines with these criteria in mind—the extent to which a confrontation with a difficult, but manageable, task is encouraged; the extent to which the capacity to organize experiences is promoted.

Inductive and deductive thinking

The analysis of the records of lessons taught by the group of novice teachers suggests that their teaching promotes both inductive and deductive thinking, with more emphasis on the first rather than the second.

In the inductive method children are given many examples of a concept and are then asked to state the generalization which applies. For instance, the observation which demonstrates the cooling of hot liquids as it is poured into bowls of different sizes leads to the generalization that hot liquid cools faster when more of the liquid is exposed to the air. In the deductive method pupils are told the concept and then asked to give examples of it. For instance, students are asked to give an example to show that heat loss is greater when more of the liquid is exposed to air.

As reported by Stendler,[818:263] "Experimental evidence indicates that when children acquire concepts on their own they use a mixture of both methods." Through an inductive process of trying magnets on various materials, the learner may conceptualize that magnets attract "metals." Then he refines his concept through testing it (a deductive process), and finding out that not all metals are attracted.

There is a need for research on the role of deductive and inductive thinking in the methodology of teaching. In this discussion only few observations will be made. One factor underlying the emphasis on inductiveness is the desire for meaningful learning. The novice teacher does not want the child to be given concepts but rather to discover them through manipulating a variety of materials. A second factor may be that the inductive process tends to be easier to control.

Suggestions to improve the process of learning science inductively will be developed in the next section. With regard to the deductive aspect, it should be treated like a hypothesis. Before moving to testing, the hypothesis should be "debated." The pupils should be encouraged to discuss the reasons why they think the hypothesis is going to be found "correct" or "wrong." To the extent that it is possible, time should be spent in clarifying the meaning of the hypothesis before moving into experimentation.

The potential in questioning

The analysis of the records of the lessons taught by the group of novice teachers suggests that with very few exceptions all questions in the lessons are raised by the teacher. Indeed, the overwhelming majority of records did not include even one question raised by a pupil.

Both Getzels [G3] and Torrance [T4] assess the ability to raise questions and identify problems as one of the indices of creative thinking. One can move through the motions of experience without being touched by it at all. To raise a question may often mean to be open to the experience and the intrinsic desire to know. The ability to raise questions is as important as the ability to find the answer.

Take a young child on a trip and count the number of questions he raises: "Why does the train stop? Why are there pebbles on the rail?" Parents enjoy relating the questions of their young children: "If milk comes from cows, do bananas come from monkeys?" Or, "You always say time is running; why can't time wait?" A main reason parents tend to enjoy their child's questions is because they signify alertness and curiosity. The parents realize that their child is open to his experience and is growing intellectually.

One of the most tragic aspects in the life of many deprived children is that they never learned to raise questions. Very early in life their curiosity was not rewarded by the parents. Seldom did an adult listen to them, enjoy their questions, try to answer, or encourage further questions. The end result was that their intellectual curiosity never blossomed.

The encouraging of children to raise questions is a function to a great extent neglected in the elementary school. An anecdote says that the school is a funny institution where the one who knows, the teacher, raises all the questions and the ones who don't know, the pupils, give all the answers. It seems that a rigid pattern of role expectations is ingrained in the school—the teacher is the only person who takes the lead and directs. As in all areas, the overstructured methodology of teaching science, too, tends to narrow the activity and limit the potential for raising questions.

A major approach to develop the ability of children to identify problems is to balance the overstructured methodology in science with provisions for a more open-ended situation. Brenda Lansdown describes this approach in the article "Orbiting a Science Program." [L2:180] Materials are distributed to the group and their manipulation encouraged. Such manipulation leads the pupils to make discoveries of scientific relations. For instance, to discover the principles of buoyancy, the following materials are suggested:

A dish of water for each group of four children. Things which float, like wood . . . Things which sink, like marbles, a penny . . . Things which sink and float, like plastic sponges.

Small groups are instructed to see what they can find out and to record the questions which they want to raise for general class discussion. After a period of free experimentation the teacher calls on the children to join in a discussion of their questions and findings.

The reader is invited to try this open-ended approach. To illustrate, materials which may lead to the discovery of the principles of electric circuits are:[L2:180-181]

For each pair of children: 2 dry cells, wires, a screw driver, a socket, and light bulb . . . buzzers and bells.

Or, rather than starting a lesson with a directed observation of the various parts of a plant, distribute the object and advise the class to see what they can find out on their own and to decide on questions they want to raise for discussion or further investigation.

The raising of questions by children confronts the teacher with the task of accommodating the pupil's sense of direction. The preplanned route must be modified, or even drastically changed. The teacher is confronted with the task of structuring the questions, deciding on the order of the discussion, and making choices of which questions should be followed by the class as a whole and which should be left for a small group or even individual assignment. In brief, the creative orientation calls on the teacher to experience a stage of disorder before structuring a new order.

Summarizing and testing

The examination of the records of the science lessons taught by the novice teachers shows that a prevalent way of concluding a lesson is by summarizing. When a summary is put on the blackboard, or on an experience chart, it generally includes the following elements: the objective, materials, procedure, and findings. In primary grades simpler language is used, such as, "What did we want to find out?" or, "What did we do?"

The positive contribution of the summary step is the emphasis on the final structure of the thinking process involved. The tendency of many young children is to enjoy the "action" of the activity called experimentation. It is enjoyable, fun, or even resembles a magic show. They may overlook the search to develop a concept. Summarizing is an attempt to stress the rational process and the learned generalization.

The weakness of the summary approach to the culmination of the science lesson is that it is generally limited to the process of convergent thinking, without giving equal emphasis to divergent thinking. There is a need for a summary which not only repeats the known but also encourages the learner to move toward the unknown. Illustrations of the divergent orientation are assignments like the following: What are possible applications of what we have learned today? What are some questions it raises in your mind? Suggest other experiments to test the idea. What are some other things that you would like to know about the topic?

The same tendency toward early closure can be observed in the *testing procedure*. Both teacher-made tests and standardized tests tend to stress levels *A* and *B* of knowledge, neglecting completely the *C* orientation. Illustrations are:

The richest source of vitamin C is:
    1) bananas;   2) grapefruits;   3) pears.
The force of a magnet is strongest in its pole. True or False?
When the speed of fluid increases, ——————— decreases.

Testing of this nature is valuable. It provides the teacher with a measure evaluating the amount of knowledge mastered in a specific lesson or unit. It can serve as a diagnostic technique to identify the specific information that needs further clarification. It can help identify the pupils who need further help.

Despite the value of the above approach to testing, there is a need for equal emphasis on divergency. At present, there is little progress in this area, and any contribution in this direction would be pioneering in nature. In addition to the emphasis on "what we have learned," the test should include items which call for the application of the taught information and generalizations to new situations; items where the information is given and new generalizations have to be discovered; items which call for raising questions about the subject matter; or items which ask for the modification of the experiment taught.

The records of the lessons taught by the group of novice teachers include a section on objectives. The latter are generally stated in terms of the science concepts to be developed, and sometimes also in terms of the "scientific attitudes" to be inculcated. However, the records of the lessons themselves illustrate that the emphasis in testing is only on measuring growth in terms of subject matter mastery. There is a lack of emphasis on the less clearly measurable aspects of learning, such as the understanding of the scientific attitudes and the scientific method.

As suggested by Navarra, a learner who embraces a scientific attitude is sensible to cause and effect relations, examines various points of view, searches for reasons, and weighs evidence. For instance, the ability to weigh evidence can be evaluated by the use of the following points on a rating scale ranging from low to high:[N3:442]

(1) Accepts what he is told
(2) Accepts what he reads
(3) Rejects an idea without giving a reason
(4) Distinguishes the difference between fact and opinion
(5) Challenges and rejects an idea by giving a reason
(6) Holds evidence tentative until he checks authoritative sources
(7) Proposes tests and experiments that will examine the evidence

The quality of the method of scientific thinking utilized by the learner can be observed in his ability to recognize problems, formulate hypotheses, experiment, gather information, and draw conclusions. For instance, "problem recognition" can be evaluated by the use of the following criteria:[N3:443]

(1) The problem is given to the child.

(2) The problem grows out of a concern or interest.

(3) The problem grows out of a conflict of ideas.

(4) The problem grows out of a deep study in an area.

(5) The child limits a broad problem to one which can be attacked and worked on.

(6) The problem is recognized and grows out of an experiment that was in progress.

(7) A problem grows out of the mathematical analysis of accumulated information.

CURRICULUM PROBLEMS

Tools for the teacher

In addition to science equipment for conducting experiments, the teacher generally utilizes textbooks, trade books, television, and films; and the latest addition to the market is programmed materials.

Textbooks. Concerning the often-voiced criticism that the use of textbooks encourages a bookish approach to science education, it is stressed here that books are a fundamental aspect of the learning process when they are utilized constructively. As suggested by Wood,[W9] some elementary school teachers, even though in a minority, are exponents of the "read-the-chapter-and-then-we-will-discuss-it" method, or "answer the questions at the end of the chapter." The dominant activity becomes reading about science. The teaching of science as a process of questioning and a way of behavior is almost nonexistent, or becomes a secondary goal.

Science textbooks and trade books should be used constructively as an integral part of a balanced program including observation and experimentation. Only after the children have had a chance to investigate thoroughly, raise questions, and establish a general direction, may textbooks be utilized for enrichment and depth.

The question is often raised by the novice whether the sequence of activities should always consist of experimentation followed by reading. This sequence is generally recommended for the primary grades, where reading ability is limited. However, on the intermediate level the balance, rather than the sequence, is the important criterion. The modern science textbooks are well-written and illustrated. They invite experimentation and encourage the reader to go beyond the presented subject matter.

The analysis of the records of the lessons taught by the novice teachers illustrates that they emphasize experimentation and observation, and do not misuse the science textbooks for recitation or as a workbook. The data suggest, however, a lack of sufficient emphasis on the integration of science reading materials with firsthand experimentation. It can be said that in comparison to the use of readers or social studies texts, the science textbooks and trade books are relatively neglected in many elementary schools.

Televised Science Programs. Many school systems have embarked on the setting up of television programs. Science activities are among those most frequently used. The contribution of these programs is mainly their use of master teachers and their presentation of operations which are not always possible for the classroom teacher—the operation of a large machine, for example, or the description of a flood.

Despite its rich potential, the practice of televised science programs suffers from some basic limitations. It may encourage passivity, the antithesis of scientific thinking, in both teacher and child. The main criterion of success is the extent to which the program is used by the viewing group.

Reports of novice teachers suggest that in some classes the televised program constitutes an integral part of the science curriculum. It is a basis for discussion and further experimentation, or is a culmination of previous learning. In some classes, however, the televised program constitutes a stopgap and entertainment device which does not feed, or is not fed by, the ongoing science program. Therefore televised education should stress not only the quality of the program, but, equally, its integration into the curriculum.

Programmed Instruction. Despite the fact that this approach is widely discussed in educational literature, as it comes to science at present it is not extensively used on the elementary school level. It is not used at all in the schools where the novice teachers, under discussion, practice.

Whereas the emphasis of programming on self direction, on main concepts, and on the relationship between the elements and the Gestalt is very valuable, it may suffer from a limiting approach to the process of concept formation. It stresses one route to the correct answer and does not encourage the pupil to question, hypothesize, reach a dead-end and try again. Examine the following illustrations: [K9:1]

1) Today we have become used to being told about the _____(a)_____ before it happens. We have not learned to _____(b)_____ it ourselves.

                           (a) weather   (b) predict

2) The "old-timers" like the sea captain . . . depended on the weather to make their living. They needed to understand _____signs. (weather)

In this chapter, which criticizes the overaccentuation of overstructured behavior in science methodology, it must be stressed that the present concept of programming is limited in terms of intellectual playfulness, divergency, and experiential learning.

Curriculum organization

The teaching of science is not incidental in nature. In most schools a structured program is the basis for the course of study. The main approach to the organization of the science curriculum is emphasis on the development of science concepts. This approach is spiral and methodological. To illustrate, the concept that "fire needs air" helps the first grader understand the reason for fanning a fire to get it started; the second grader to observe that the furnace is built with an air door; and the intermediate pupil to learn the function of a carburetor. The attempt is to select the most important science concepts which explain the basic structure of the discipline and deepen the learner's comprehension of these concepts as he climbs the ladder of the school.

A second approach to the organization of the science program, well-known theoretically but little implemented in practice, is the focusing on children's interests. The assumption is that "interest" is an expression of intrinsic relations between the learner and the subject matter. An interest-centered program is most conducive to the development of openness and self-direction in the learner-scientist.

The third approach to the organization of the science curriculum is social. It calls for the integration of science with other areas of the curriculum, mainly health, safety, and social studies. For instance, fire prevention can be developed in terms of its scientific, social, and safety aspects, or nutrition can be studied in terms of its science, health, and social implications.

It should be recognized that each of these three approaches has its contribution to make to the creative process.

(1) A concept-centered curriculum has depth in terms of its potential of learning the basic structure of the science discipline; it is systematic and organized in terms of the level of comprehension of different age groups.

(2) An interest-centered curriculum has an important contribution to make to the development of creative thinking. It builds and promotes curiosity and intrinsic learning. A visit to a science fair may illustrate to the reader the powerful impact of developing a science project based on the interest of a child or of a small group of children.

Carried to extremes, an interest-centered curriculum may lack unity or miss the essence of the discipline. In practice this extreme position is rarely followed. Examination of the work of the novice teacher illustrates that centering on children's interest plays a minor role, rather than being overemphasized.

(3) The third approach emphasizing the integration of science with other subjects is functional in nature. It does not limit the search of the learner to the somewhat artificial boundaries of a discipline. It stresses the interrelationship between social and science problems, and progress. Whereas the scientific law itself is in the realm of "objectivity," the use of scientific inventions may often be the source of, or may be associated with, severe social

problems. The social approach attempts to look at science from a value and moral frame of reference. Science is not presented in a value vacuum. It becomes a social issue!

Observation of the work of the novice illustrates that in contrast to the "interest emphasis," the integrative social approach plays an important role in his teaching. The teacher tends to be alert to the social, safety, or health ramifications of the scientific subject matter taught. To illustrate, a study of the senses on the primary grade will generally be associated with a discussion of services to handicapped people.

Stendler warns that the integrative approach may lead to diminution of science concepts. The emphasis may be on health rules (how to brush teeth), or on safety (how to ride bikes), rather than on the science aspect.[B18] This is perhaps one of the major reasons for the reluctance on the part of many science specialists, including textbook writers, to move toward integration of science with other subjects.

In 1957 the National Council for the Social Studies published a book entitled *Science and the Social Studies*,[C5] which called for reemphasis on the social commitment of science learning. The problem is to explore new ways of presenting science in a social setting, without deemphasizing the structure of the discipline of science.

In brief, all three approaches under discussion have a contribution to make to the creative process. In practice, they supplement rather than negate each other. Therefore, rather than elaborate the conflicting position, one should develop a science curriculum enriched by the three approaches: emphasis on concept development, children's interest, and a social orientation.

CONCLUSION

The analysis of the teaching behavior of young teachers in the area of science identified factors which contribute toward both a repetitive and creative orientation.

The main factors which explain the repetitive aspects of the teacher's behavior are: (1) insufficient mastery of subject matter, and (2) overstructured teaching.

The main factors which explain the creative emphasis in the behavior of the novice are: (1) work toward concept formation, (2) commitment to experiential learning, and (3) attempts to integrate subject matter.

In order to enhance the creative orientation the discussion suggests: (1) Strengthening the subject matter background of the elementary school teacher, (2) A drive by science departments on the college level to "recruit" the prospective elementary school teacher, (3) More provisions for an "open-ended" methodology which encourages children to develop their own experiments, and (4) More emphasis on divergent thinking.

SELECTED BIBLIOGRAPHY

BLOUGH, O. Glenn, and SCHWARTZ, Julius, *Elementary School Science.* New York: Holt, Rinehart & Winston, Inc., 1964. A comprehensive discussion with emphasis on subject matter.

CUMMINGS, Howard H. (Editor), *Science and the Social Studies.* Washington, D.C.: National Council for the Social Studies, 1957. A discussion of curricular practices integrating the two disciplines.

DUNFEE, Maxine, and GREENLEE, Julian, *Elementary School Science: Research, Theory, and Practice.* Washington, D.C.: A.S.C.D., 1957. Of special interest to the reader planning a research project.

LANDSDOWN, Brenda, "Orbiting a Science Program." *Science Education,* March, 1962. Discussion of the discovery approach through use of structured materials.

NAVARRA, J. Gabriel, and ZAFFORONI, Joseph, *Science Today for the Elementary School Teacher.* New York: Harper & Row, Publishers, 1963. An original discussion of methodology. The main emphasis is on subject matter.

8

Social Studies: Repetitive or creative?

A group of novice teachers was asked what subject they found most difficult to teach. Most of them mentioned science and arithmetic, and some art, but only a few said social studies.

A growing number of elementary schools have science, art, or math teachers who serve as consultants or special teachers. Their function is to contribute to the enrichment of the work of the classroom teacher in terms of their field of specialization. Seldom does one meet a social studies "special teacher" on the elementary school level. It seems that many elementary school teachers do not feel fully ready to teach science, arithmetic, or the arts, whereas they consider themselves generally ready to teach social studies.

Several factors explain the contrasting confidence expressed in the ability to teach social studies, as opposed to arithmetic, art and especially science.

First is that social studies, like language arts, is a fundamental subject of the elementary curriculum. It is a core which every child must experience. It can be taught in an integrative fashion with language arts and science. In other words, social studies is not a "specialization" but rather the essence of the curriculum. It is interesting to note that at the height of the progressive education era, a group of distinguished educators developed a design for a secondary education which made social studies the basic "common learning" for "all American youth." [C4:9]

Second, it is assumed that the elementary school teacher, in terms of his own education, academic interest and orientation, is generally a social studies rather than a science or math major. Therefore, he tends to be better prepared to teach social studies.

Third, it is assumed, although this assumption is seldom openly stated, that science and math are very difficult subjects. They have a structure which is hard to master. As one novice put it: "You know or you don't know these subjects; there aren't any in-betweens." In contrast, social studies is perceived as an "easy subject" to master and is, therefore, believed to be easy to teach.

It is interesting to note that both on the college and the elementary school levels the discipline of science is called "science." There are at present attempts to "upgrade" arithmetic and entitle it "elementary mathematics." In contrast, social studies is called a science (social science) only when it is taught on the college level. In the elementary school, it is perceived only as social studies.

THE PURPOSE

This chapter will suggest that the relative assumed security of the teacher in coming to teach social studies is somewhat misleading. This discipline needs clarification in terms of its objectives, scope, and methodology. As stressed by Kenworthy in his article, "Ferment in the Social Studies," [K3] the whole conceptualization structure of this subject area is at present under reevaluation.

This chapter will join the critique, and examine social studies particularly in terms of the main theme of the book—the identification of the factors which contribute toward either a repetitive or a creative orientation.

THE IMPACT OF PROGRESSIVE EDUCATION

I believe that the impact of progressive education on the theoretical conceptualization and curricular applications of social studies, was perhaps of greater magnitude than its impact on any other aspect of the curriculum. It has undoubtedly influenced social studies more than science and arithmetic. To understand social studies in terms of its strength and limitations—its position today and its future direction—one must examine this subject in the light of the progressive education movement and the evolvement of the post-progressive education era.

The impact of progressive education on social studies is expressed in the following trends: (1) Movement toward integration of subject matter, (2) Emphasis on the activation of the learner, (3) Emphasis on group work and social learning, and (4) Emphasis on the present, the immediate, and the functional.

Toward integration of subject matter

A major function of social studies is to introduce children to the study of the human society. A broad conception of this discipline draws not only from geography and history, but incorporates material from virtually all the social sciences, including anthropology, economics, geography, history, political science, social psychology and sociology. As Hanna [H1] points out, the study of Mexico may deal with the country's geographical location, impact of its geographical features on the economic activities of the people, the impact of the Indian and Spanish traditions on the Mexican culture, or examination of the relations between the U.S.A. and Mexico. This example illustrates that social studies attempts to integrate subject matter drawn from various fields, because its essence consists of the study of the development of man into a "social being."

Progressive education called for a unifying concept of subject matter. It held that the "subject matter approach" meant compartmentalized and fragmentary learning, lacked in depth of meaning, and was limited in its potential for creating unity of ideas. It criticized the subject organization which emphasized the exposition of its own logical sequence and failed to pay due attention to the interests and activities of children. It warned that confinement to the subject organization tends to be historical and predetermined in nature, and is therefore too often presented in a social vacuum. It took issue with the overemphasis on the past and the relative inattention to emerging present issues and controversies. It questioned the educational value of an approach which focused on the center of a discipline rather than on moral and value problems of people.

A comprehensive and scholarly critique of the subject matter curriculum, and an analysis of its development, is presented in the book *Fundamentals of Curriculum Development.*[313] In terms of the discussion presented here, it is sufficient to describe the three curricular modifications in the subject matter organization which affected the trend toward unification in social studies.

The first modification toward unity of subject matter was the *correlated curriculum.* In this pattern, two or more subjects are articulated and the relationship between or among them is made a part of instruction. Subject boundaries remain intact. For example, history and geography may be taught so as to reinforce each other. The geography of Egypt taught in a geography lesson may be correlated with the study of the early history of the Egyptians taught in a separate history lesson. The stress on the relationship between the subjects is believed to help reduce compartmentalization.

The second modification in the direction of unity of subject matter was the *broad field curriculum.* Whereas the correlated curriculum follows the separate subject matter organization, the broad field curriculum is, in essence, the first attempt to break away from highly delineated disciplinary structures and organize learning in terms of broader divisions. Typical illustrations are social studies, language arts, or the science-hygiene integrations where longer blocks of time are assigned to each division. The teacher is free to develop a topic, such as a study of a specific country, in terms of the subject matter areas involved in the division.

The third modification, the *core curriculum,* is the most advanced pattern in terms of the process of movement toward integration of subject matter. It is based on a complete breakdown of subject lines. The center of the curriculum is not a broad field, typical of the previous pattern, but rather a central problem. In order to work on a given problem, the learner is guided to draw on whatever needed subject areas pertain to his problem. It is the function of reaching a meaningful understanding of the problem which determines the subject matter, rather than the artificial boundaries of the traditional subject organization.

Examination of the work of the novice suggests that the core pattern of unity of subject matter organization has a strong impact on the work of the teacher, especially in the area of social studies. In essence, the core pattern, or as it is called on the elementary school level—the *unit* organization of subject matter, is the most prevalent approach in social studies. It is common for teachers to equate the social studies methodology with unit teaching.

The unit is an attempt by the teacher to organize learning experiences around a social problem and draw on subject matter from any area which may contribute to a better understanding of the topic. Typical illustrations are: the problems of transportation, shelter, adaptability to various climates, or life in a foreign country.

The unit pattern of planning the social studies program has a definite positive impact on the novice teacher. He is encouraged not to be limited to the piecemeal planning of a discrete lesson, but rather to plan in terms of a long-range objective. The lesson becomes an integral part of a broader conceptualization scheme.

In planning a unit, the teacher should consider the criterion under discussion—*unity of subject matter*. More specifically, he should examine the following questions:

What is the main theme which unites the subject matter into a whole? What are the main concepts which the unit attempts to develop, and how are the concepts related? How would subject matter drawn from various disciplines contribute to an understanding of the main theme? What are the needed activities and materials and how would they contribute to an understanding of the basic idea?

The unity criterion underlying the unit pattern in social studies rejects the traditional conception of aggregation of lessons and attempts to move toward the productive thinking inherent in the integration approach to subject matter. To the extent that the teacher is more aware of his long-range conceputalization goal, to the extent that he sees the relationship between the small part (the lesson or the activity) and the whole (the unit), and to the extent that he views subject matter as an integral part of a broader generalization, the probability is that insight will be communicated to children.

The unit is a promising approach. However, it is only an organizational pattern. It is evident that in some cases the unit is used as a cliché without depth of meaning; as a new word one is expected to use, while traditional practices continue.

In terms of the criterion of unity of subject matter, observation of novice teachers suggests two not uncommon mistakes:

The first mistake is that of giving the unit a "nice title" such as, "Living in Our Community," or, "How Does Man Live in Cold Countries?" without thinking through the main concepts to be developed. Under this "pseudo unit" arrangement, teaching is only an aggregation of lessons with little unity of relations among them.

A second typical mistake is the temptation, or even the sense of obligation, which some novice teachers have to include every subject area in each unit they teach. Rather than thinking in terms of how to study a problem and make it meaningful, the thinking is how to correlate various disciplines with the topic.

The vantage point should be the needs of the problem under study rather than the discipline. The teacher guided by this criterion may often find that some important skills, or important knowledge, cannot be fed into the topic. The implication is that the unit is not all-inclusive. While one unit is in process, some areas of the curriculum, such as arithmetic or some skills, may need a separate and independent treatment.

In brief, whether or not the unit approach achieves its goal of enhancing the integration of subject matter depends on the teacher's perception of this practice. Only if the depth of the rationale of unity of the main idea is pursued does the unit become conducive to curricular organization and productive thinking.

The activation of the learner

The discussion in the previous section dealing with the criterion of integration of subject matter was "teacher-centered" in nature. It is the *teacher* who was encouraged to think through the main objectives and look for the interrelationship between the main idea—the unit and the subparts—the lessons. The following question, however, must be raised. *What is the role of the learner?*

What is the role of the learner? The traditional conception of teaching is that the teacher should be able to command the confidence and respect of his followers and to induce them to accept the presented subject matter. The teacher is the central authority and the children are the followers. They "move" because he "motivates" them to move. The power to decide on the direction, route, and pace is invested in the teacher.

Progressive education raised the ideal of a new conception of teaching: to facilitate the process of learning and to help the child define and achieve his goals. The word "education" derives from the Latin *educere,* which means drawing out of a person something potential or latent. The principle of "activating the learner" is based on the belief in the power of education to bring people out and generate self-direction.

Therefore, the attributes of the modern teacher, as perceived by the progressive education school of thought is in sensitizing the pupil to realize what *he* wants, what potential *he* has, where *he* wants to go, and to help him to go there. The theorist of progressive education does not speak about "teaching," but rather about "helping the child learn." This is not a play on words. It is an expression of a basic philosophy. The main function of the teacher is to activate the learner.

Dewey says that no other aspect in education is more important in progressive education than the participation of the learner in the setting of the goal and the development of the plans for his learning.[D7] As a result of active participation, the pupil tends to assume a greater responsibility for the progress of his own learning than he would under conditions of merely following directions.

It is interesting to note that a similar position about learning is presented by Suzuki in *Zen Buddhism.*[S23:93] Suzuki describes a monk who asks his friend to teach him the mystery of life so that he can become a master. His friend answers:

I am willing to help you in every way, but there are . . . things in which I cannot be of any help to you. These you must look after yourself . . . When you are hungry or thirsty, my eating of food or drinking does not fill your stomach. You must drink and eat yourself . . . And then it will be nobody but yourself that will carry this corpse of yours along this highway.

One must take the responsibility for his own learning. It cannot be done for him by others. The emphasis should be on the learner learning, rather than on the teacher teaching. The ultimate in education is the independence of the learner from his teacher. In Zen the expression of this independence is described as the burning of notes or the monk twisting the nose of his master.[823] Fortunately for we teachers, progressive education does not suggest such symbolic acts. It limits its appeal to stress on intrinsic learning and a higher degree of self-direction.

The impact of progressive education on social studies is expressed not only in the trend toward integration of subject matter, but also in the trend toward a more responsible role for the learner. In social studies more than in any other subject area, the pupil plays a self-directive role of an initiator of activities. He is not merely motivated to move from one lesson to another.

The social studies unit is different from the lesson, not only because it consists of *many* lessons (the duration of a typical unit is four or six weeks), but also because of the role played in it by the learner. The latter criterion of the unit concept is sometimes overlooked. For instance, as discussed in the chapter on reading, some reading readiness books are organized in terms of units: the family, the farm, the school, etc. In other words, *with the exception of social studies,* the typical unit taught at school tends to be based on the first criterion of a long-range theme with some attempt to integrate subjects. It is generally not an attempt to *activate the learner.*

To better understand the process of the activation of the learner, the discussion will compare the way in which novice teachers teach lessons, with the way they tend to implement units.

In teaching a lesson the novice teacher attempts to arouse the class interest by surprising the pupils with the richness of the materials that she has prepared. In some cases the teacher even conceals the next topic or hides the new materials from the pupils. It must be a surprise.

This not uncommon behavior suggests that teachers expect children to wait passively for the new direction to be presented by the teacher in each new lesson. In unit teaching, the teacher attempts to balance the above teacher-centeredness with provisions for cooperative planning and self-direction.

How does the novice move toward a more democratic behavior in unit teaching? A position often advocated in educational literature maintains that the topic of the unit shall be decided cooperatively by the teacher and the class.[m] As reported by novice teachers, they seldom follow this recommendation. In most cases the topic is predetermined by the teacher in accordance with the curriculum guide, the textbook, a significant current event, or an interest which the teacher happens to have.

The first step toward the involvement of children in cooperative planning is children's participation in the identification of the major issues in the topic. After some study of the topic (reading, discussion, viewing a film), the children, guided by the teacher, attempt to formulate the major questions to be studied. Following is an illustration taken from a unit about Japan.

(1) How did the geography of Japan affect the life of the people?
(2) What is the Japanese industry, and why?
(3) What kinds of homes do they build?
(4) What is the history of Japan?
(5) What is the Japanese art and sport?

The conventional school practice is denoted by pupils' search for an answer; it rarely has pupils searching for a question. (count the number of questions raised by children in a typical lesson.) The unit in social studies is one of the few instances, and sometimes the only instance, where raising questions by children is *institutionalized* into the classroom work pattern.

Observing the teaching behavior of the young teachers under discussion, it can be said that the social studies unit is partly developed in terms of the main questions raised by children. The same can*not* be said about the way these novice teachers develop a science or a language arts unit. The latter tends to be more teacher-centered.

The notion that raising a question is often equated with lack of knowledge is only partly correct. One can raise *intelligent questions* only on the basis of some insight into the topic. The Haggadah, the Jewish ritual of the Passover Seder, speaks about the son who is naive, and defines *naive* as "one who does not know to ask." In other words, to ask good questions one must reach a certain level of understanding of the problem.

One of the not uncommon mistakes which novice teachers make is rushing pupils toward identifying the basic problems of the unit without a sufficient background in the problem. In cases such as these children tend to develop a standard set of questions, good for every topic. Raising questions should not be relegated only to the introductory sessions of the unit work. It should be seen as a continuous process. As the work proceeds, questions may be changed and new questions added. (In one classroom I saw a bulletin board devoted solely to questions.)

The value of the cooperative formulation of the major problems inherent in the specific unit is not only the expression of interest or the indication of insight. It is a cooperative attempt to identify long-range objectives.

According to the lesson practice, the pupil achieves the objective at the end of the lesson. Unless he has homework related to the lesson he may be waiting passively for the next lesson when the teacher is going to "unveil" the new objective. The long-range objective in the unit is a goal toward which the learner may move independently, under the guidance of the teacher. In one of the educational films portraying unit work, the first scene describes a class discussion; a few minutes later the door opens and the teacher enters. This class was to a great extent self-directive. It worked in terms of its established and accepted long-range goals. Consider the following questions: (1) What would happen to a typical class if a teacher were late? (2) What could be done to improve self-directiveness in the learning process?

The activation of the learner in the social studies unit is expressed not only by his participation in the setting of the long-range goals, but also in provision for relative *freedom to move toward* the goal. In contrast to the lesson pattern where the learner is moved by a series of questions and assignments and is almost constantly led by the teacher's pace, here the learner has a higher degree of freedom. He can set his own pace in moving ahead. He takes an active part in choosing materials best suited for the study of his problem, such as collecting information from various books.

The progress toward the goal involves much of what teachers call "doing research." Whereas *research* may be too big a word to describe the child's activity, it is an indication of the respect which the educator shows for the learner's independent search for knowledge.

In contrast to the traditional practice of limiting the study to one textbook, the learner is encouraged to consult a variety of textbooks, trade books, encyclopedias, and other resource materials. He can be imaginative with regard to the type of resources he wants to utilize: books, people, records, objects for demonstration. He has a say in the way his completed work will be presented: written essay, use of pictures and graphs, oral report.

The learning process underlying the conception of the social studies unit can be better understood if compared with the learning theory underlying programmed instruction. Both practices reject passive learning and are dedicated to the activation of the learner. However, their conception of activation is very different, and in some respects is even contradictory in nature.

Figuratively speaking, programming visualizes the learner as if he stands in the corner of a room and moves in the shortest direct line toward the other side, not knowing in advance where exactly he is moving. His vision is limited to one step (frame). If he makes a mistake, he is taught the correct step. If he is "right" he is requested to move ahead another step. His route is predetermined. The pace is up to the learner.

The social studies unit visualizes the learner as standing in the corner of the room and deciding on a goal—reaching the other side. Every move he makes is in the light of the final goal he wants to reach. He is free to decide on the nature of his "transportation" (different activities and not only a programmed text). He may get stuck on the way and have to retreat not merely one step, but even back to the starting point. . . .

Whereas both programming and the unit approach are valuable learning practices, the latter would seem to have a richer potential for *creative thinking*. In comparing the logical order of presentation and the psychological order of creation, Dewey [D7:26] says that the difference between them is like

. . . the difference between the notes which an explorer makes in a new country, blazing a trail and finding his way along as best he may, and the finished map that is constructed after the country has been thoroughly explored.

The unit approach resembles "the notes which the explorer makes in a new country," while programming resembles "the finished map."

Social learning

The third impact of progressive education on the social studies program is expressed in the stress on social learning. As part of the attempt of progressive education to *expand* the role of the school to include the attention to the "total development of the child," teachers were urged to be sensitive to children's actions and daily behavior, in addition to observing the amount of knowledge they have in a certain subject matter.

As seen by the proponents of progressive education, the ultimate criterion of knowledge is its expression in actual behavior. There is a cleavage between academic learning and operational values which has to be cemented. Therefore, the personal experience of the learner and his daily human relations are an extremely valuable source for learning which is neglected in traditional education.

These beliefs had a strong impact on the modern school, and especially on the social studies program. The role of the social studies curriculum was expanded to include, in addition to the knowledge of pertinent subject matter and stress on intellectual development, an equal stress on behavioral, interpersonal, and emotional growth.

A stimulating and comprehensive book dedicated to this expansion of the social studies concept is *More Than Social Studies* by Miel and Brogan.[M17] As the title suggests, the authors expand beyond the traditional role of social studies to include emphasis on the development of a healthy self-concept and democratic behavior in personal life.

In a discussion of the social studies program, Kenworthy says that a school which wants to educate mature, sensitive, and competent individuals should recognize that the most important lesson children can learn is self-respect.[K4:1]

Without a healthy self-image children will not be able to identify with others. Unless they value themselves, they will not be able to value others . . . The apathetic ones have already given up the race of life . . . The belligerent ones are already engaged in a lifelong battle against themselves and others.

As an integral part of the stress on the self-image of the learner and on interpersonal relations, a notable change in social studies became evident in the increase of the amount of *group work.* Whereas the social studies unit is not identical with committee work (hypothetically, it is possible for a unit to be developed by the class as a whole and by individual research), in practice some amount of group work is prevalent in the above unit more than in any other area of the curriculum.

In terms of theory, committee work is an expression of two fundamental values underlying the position of progressive education. One was already discussed in the previous section—the activation of the learner. The second is the value of group process for the development of the democratic personality.

Citizenship education calls not only for the intellectual understanding of the law and the structure of government, but also the ability to join in groups to study and resolve immediate social problems; experiences which provide opportunities to practice democratic living in the classroom.

In the past, the conventional practice had been to confine democratic living to school government and other extracurricular activities, and to leave the main school function, namely learning, in the authoritarian domain. One of the most significant contributions of progressive education was to penetrate the main castle of authoritarian teaching and introduce an element of group work.

Committee work is an opportunity for each child to experience a leadership and follower role. The need to resolve an issue or achieve a common task is a factor potentially conducive to high morale. The fact that one has a contribution to make to the group welfare, that one is recognized by the group, tends to generate responsibility and a sense of belongingness. Thus the normal need for self-esteem may find its satisfaction in a committee setup.

The trust which many teachers have in the constructive and educational value of group work is illustrated by the fact that committee work is one of the most common topics selected for research projects on the graduate level. Typical examples are: "The Impact of Group Work on Class Morale," "Helping the Isolate Through Committee Participation," and "Committee Work and Intergroup Cohesion."

Another illustration of the teacher's confidence in the value of group work, and the importance of studying the relationship of the individual child and the group, is the great interest in sociometric techniques. A pioneering work in this area, *Sociometry in Group Relations* by Helen Jennings,[14] is filled with examples of the interrelationship of this approach with group work.

A look at difficulties

The above discussion stressed the role of the social studies unit in the activation of two interrelated agents—the learner and group work. Although the novice teacher values unit work, complaints about difficulties or even dissatisfaction with this process are often expressed. Some concerns are a sense that children waste time; inequitable sharing on the part of children; domineering behavior on the part of a few leaders, and perhaps most important, lack of full knowledge of what the class has mastered and of being unsure of what every child is doing at a given time.

The practice of individualization of instruction, which is a significant aspect of unit work, may result in some lack of unity or cohesiveness of subject matter; a feeling that people are studying in the same room but not working on the same task. In order to overcome this difficulty, both the teacher and the class should continually examine their progress in the light of the generalizations to be developed. The balance between what should be common learning to the class as a whole, and what is individual interest, is an important criterion to be considered by the teacher.

The fact that individual research and committee work are central in unit work does not mean that there is no room for a study of a core of subject matter by the class as a whole. Social studies should be taught on three levels: class, committee, and individual work, the three enriching and interacting with each other.

Committee work is not a panacea for success. As reported by some novice teachers, the excitement over being "democratic" and "experimental" leads them to a "hands off" policy. The impact on children is well-known. It tends to be floundering, domineered by the few aggressive members, and limited in its production.

The impact on the teacher himself is less recognized or discussed. Believing that committee work is the "children's domain," some novice teachers become detached and fail to get involved with the group and with the subject matter—as though the teacher is there to keep order, supply materials, administer, but not to *think with* the children.

In terms of the study of teacher's behavior which is so central in this book, one is confronted here with important dynamics which should be recognized. The novice who is teacher-centered in his behavior may be very involved with his ideas and plans. The positive element in this involvement is the feeling of mastery and its corollary—the communication of solidity to pupils. In the same sense, however, teacher—centeredness can be a product or a cause of a tendency to underestimate the power of children, or not be open to and accommodating the children's sense of direction.

The novice teacher who searches for improved practices and initiates committee work may err in the opposite direction—lack of sufficient planning of subject matter and some neglect of the teacher's formation of his own ideas and perception of the problem. This kind of teacher is too often dependent on what the children are going to produce. He is sometimes detached and may communicate a sense of weakness to pupils.

The problem is how to encourage children's initiative and at the same time maintain the teacher's initiative? How to be in control without being overcontrolling and constricting? How to plan subject matter and at the same time, accommodate the child's sense of planning? Perhaps it is best summed up with the following question: How to encourage children to be strong and at the same time remain a strong teacher?

To guide committee work is a difficult task. Children should be introduced to committee operation gradually. As a beginning, only one committee should be organized. The size of the committee should generally not exceed five children. Committees of young or immature children should be smaller. At the beginning, the progress of the committee should be checked after every meeting, by having the group presenting an oral or written report to the teacher. An assignment should be decided upon at the end of each session.

The teacher should participate as an observer in several of the working sessions and analyze with the committee its way of proceeding both in terms of (1) the process, namely, the relationship among group members, and (2) the content.

The visitor to an elementary classroom on the intermediate level often discovers special charts dealing with the proper leadership behavior of "a good chairman" or "a good committee member." Typical illustrations of the role of the leader are:

> Should try to keep his committee on the topic.
> Should call on different children.
> Should summarize the discussion.

Illustrations of the functions of the group member are:

> Stick to the point.
> Help the group make progress.
> Respect the ideas of others.
> Contribute information.

Facilitating productive relations among committee members is a significant aspect of social learning. It is important that both teacher and children move ahead from the somewhat moralistic presentation of a chart toward an examination of their own group process in actual behavior. The human relationship climate in the small group should be frequently evaluated. One of the main questions to be raised is the extent to which there is *give and take* among the group members about the *content* of the unit. As reported by novice teachers, too many committees serve mainly in the capacity of an administrative function responsible for allocation of roles. The committee becomes a setup for discrete presentations.

Committee work can be analyzed from two positions, although this division may seem somewhat artificial: the nature of human relations, and the nature of the movement toward the task. Looking at the second criterion, some questions need examination: Are the group members preoccupied with the final presentation to the neglect of the content of learning itself?

As reported by novice teachers, committees tend too often to rush prematurely into a discussion of the nature of the *culminating activity*. (Will the presentation be in the form of a television skit or a puppet show?) I am not trying to underestimate the importance of these considerations. They are a source of enthusiasm and involvement. They offer an opportunity for an exprsesion of ingenuity. However, they are only secondary to the main issue—the discussion of the content to be learned.

In some classes the "culminating activity" is evaluated in terms of the quality of the performance. For instance, "Did the children speak in a clear voice? Was the exhibit attractive?"

A dull performance may kill the enthusiasm of even a receptive audience. However, the major emphasis of the evaluation should be on the *intellectual* quality of the presentation. The "performance" is only secondary. The function of the school is to educate thinking people rather than the entertaining and too often superficial master of ceremonies.

A related point is the need to examine the *activity* aspect which is characteristic of group work in social studies. The traditional school stressed reading and recitation. The modern school attempts, in addition, to incorporate activities into the program. It believes in learning by doing. The strong impact of these beliefs on social studies is seen in such activities as scrapbooks and construction.

Especially today when the education of the socially deprived ethnic child has become the central educational problem, the emphasis on a motoric style of learning, on sensory perception, on involving children with doing or role-playing is very valuable.

Despite the importance of "activities," observation of classroom practices suggests that in some cases they are too time-consuming or even wasteful. Whereas the enjoyment and aesthetic values of the activity should be considered, the most important criterion is its contribution to the development of significant concepts.

The traditional school was criticized for its narrow methodology and too great a reliance on book knowledge. It is also possible to err in the opposite direction—doing for the sake of doing. Therefore, the teacher should ask himself the practical question—What do the pupils learn from the activity? For instance, role-playing is a very enjoyable activity. But is the end result of the acting out mainly joy? Does role-playing lead to a better insight into the personality dynamics and the motivation of the characters? Does it lead to a deeper expression of feelings or the ability to think on a higher level of divergency?

Observing classroom teachers employing role-playing and sociodrama, I can report many attempts to delve in depth. An illustration is the experiencing of the conflicts of the settlers in Virginia before deciding to rebel against England. It can be reported also that in some cases the "acting out" leads only to a good laugh!

Similar things can be said about another prevalent activity of committee work—the scrapbook. Were the pictures collected to impress the teacher with a bulky collection, or were they utilized for formulation of issues and concepts? Generally, children find it easier to speak when they illustrate with materials. Therefore, materials such as scrapbooks should be utilized for the development of language facility and concept formation. The materials in most cases are not ends in themselves.

Emphasis on the immediate

The fourth impact of progressive education on social studies to be discussed in this chapter is emphasis on immediate concerns, the present and the functional. The notion underlying this approach is that the most important problems for learning are those concerning the learner in his daily life. Education is criticized as being preoccupied with its own body of knowledge and with the future adult culture, and consequently, as paying relatively little attention to the developmental tasks, immediate concerns, and the daily experiences of the growing child.

These beliefs had strong influences on the social studies program, ranging from stress on the principle of the expanding environment to the stress on firsthand experiences and the concept of the "community school."

The principle of the expanding environment is perhaps the most important criterion guiding the sequence and scope of the *present* social studies program. The learner starts with the "here and now" on the primary grades and gradually moves to the study of problems and cultures more remote in time and location. As Stendler points out,[S18:Ch.9] a typical sequence of the social studies program focuses in kindergarten and grade one on the school and home; in second grade, on the neighborhood; third grade, on the community; fourth grade deals with the state and some foreign cultures; the fifth and sixth grades deal with the U.S.A., and some European backgrounds.

It was not only the emphasis on the expanding environment which became central, but also the stress on the present concerns of the learner. In contrast to programs which moved into the remote in terms of time and location, an attempt was made to focus on the *sociopsychological* present and, to a great extent, on unresolved issues facing the learner.

A landmark in this trend toward the study of sociopsychological issues is the work of Hilda Taba on *intergroup* problems. For instance, her book on *Reading Ladders for Human Relations*,[T1] which became a valuable source for many curricular programs in social studies, deals with themes like the following: patterns of family life; differences between generations; adjustment to migration; economic differences; the problem of growing up, and experiences of acceptance and rejection.

Under the impact of both the stress on social learning and the stress on the immediate, the social studies program became deeply concerned with the study of interpersonal relations. Topics of a mental health nature, such as sibling rivalry, or incidents of aggressive behavior in the playground, became a springboard for discussion. Role-playing or sociodrama were found by many teachers to be useful means in resolving human relations problems and in sensitizing children to social and moral values. The understanding of other people and the development of empathy became major goals. Leading organizations, such as the National Conference of Christians and Jews, embarked on intergroup education. Illustrations of their publications, pertinent to social studies teachers, are: *Role Playing the Problem Story* [S4]; and *Feelings are Facts*.[H6]

The emphasis on the immediate not only led the social studies program toward concern with interpersonal relations, but also served as an impetus to the growth of the concept of the community school. The pioneering, and perhaps best-known work on this topic, is Olsen's *School and Community*,[O2] first published in 1945. He portrays the typical school as an ivory tower situated on an island and in need for closer contact with "the mainland of life." To bridge the gap between the "island," the academic school, and the "mainland," life, Olsen suggests activities such as:

> Intensive use of field trips.
> Use of resource visitors.
> Work experience and service projects.
> Use of interviews.

Whereas the ideal of the community school and its slogan of "youth serves the community" was practical in relatively few situations, mainly small and rural communities, the movement had an impact on the general elementary school by making its social studies program more community-oriented. It encouraged the awareness of the need to study community problems, to utilize community resources, and to become more experiential.

TOWARD CONCEPT FORMATION AND PRODUCTIVE THINKING

In reacting to the incomplete sentence, "The most important thing about social studies is . . ." the novice teachers under discussion stressed group work and human relations. When they reacted to the same item with regard to science, the emphasis was on experimentation and the development of generalizations. It seems that especially in comparison to science the goal of productive thinking does not appear to be as central in the *practice* of the methodology of social studies.

Despite the many constructive contributions of progressive education to the conceptualization of social studies, perhaps more than in any other area of the curriculum this discipline too often operates on level A of knowledge, namely, specificity of information. As Foshay says: [F3:15]

> We have taught places in the name of geography, thus almost losing this vitally important and interesting field to our schools. We have taught facts in the name of history, thus as I say, betraying a basic discipline.

It seems that in too many cases, teaching materials continue to deal with the level of enumeration rather than convergent and

divergent thinking. In a book calling for a strong intellectual orientation in programs for young children, Wann criticizes the elaboration of the obvious.[W1:5]

We develop units of study in which we devote considerable time to
identifying and enumerating the community helpers and landmarks in
the community. On the other hand, when we listen to young children
we find that most of their questions are "how and why" questions indicating a desire for more penetrating understanding than simply being
content with identification of "what is."

Torrance reports two studies relevant to the emphasis on
thinking in social studies teaching. A questionnaire was sent to elementary school teachers in which they were asked to name a subject they taught in social studies, and to list what they considered
to be the three most important objectives of this subject. A classi-
fication of the objectives suggests that around 80% deal with cognition and memory, around 16% with convergent behavior, and
only 1% with divergent thinking.[T4:4-5]

In another study Torrance reports that "even the least effective
mathematics teachers appear to be more concerned about stimulating their pupils to leap the barrier between learning and
thinking," than their social studies counterpart.[T4:6]

The novice teacher is troubled by the relative difficulty of concept formation in social studies: "How do you explain to primary
children the meaning of the Pledge of Allegiance? How do you
reduce this idea into a simple concept?"

They often speak about the "elusiveness" of the social studies
concept (government, ancient times), and compare them with
science concepts. In teaching science the concept, such as vibration, is developed from the concrete to the abstract. It is possible
to sense it, see it, touch it. Even if one does not see with his own
eyes that sound travels or that it travels in all directions, he can
infer it from simple experimentation. The same can be said about
arithmetic. For instance, the concept of multiplication can be introduced through representative materials and developed as a
shortcut to addition. In social studies the relationship between
the concrete and the abstract, the development through firsthand
experience, or the testing of the idea within the four walls of the
classroom is more difficult to attain.

Observing the novice teachers under discussion. I find that in teaching social studies they tend to select concepts which are *too simple* rather than concepts which are too complex. Typical illustrations are the enumeration of the means of transportation or the discussion of the "community helpers." In some cases at least, teaching becomes the repetition of the known rather than moving toward what is not known to the child. For instance, children do know the generally taught information that the firemen fight fire or that policemen direct traffic. They do not know, however, how these "community helpers" are paid, a topic seldom studied.

There is a growing concern within the last few years that the impact of progressive education in the direction of the immediate might be limiting the social studies program. The criterion of the expanding environment in particular is under criticism. Stendler says:[818:277]

It may be logical to start "where the child is" and gradually expand his frontiers of knowledge. But the prevailing opinion among educators as to "where the child is" with respect to concept development has been challenged as unfounded.

The interdependence of the world community is felt much more today than in the past. Every occurrence in a remote land has its echoes in this land. Television brings other people's way of life into the living rooms of every family. The jet and missile age made the world a small community. Therefore, many new programs today are attempting to reorganize the sequence of the home, school, and neighborhood community, and introduce the study of foreign countries and cultures, on the primary school level.[K3]

For instance, a new social studies guide published in California outlines a study in comparative communities as a course for the third grade. It includes: (1) Nomads of the hot, dry lands, and (2) Switzerland. The major questions discussed are:[T9:5]

How do these people provide their basic needs?
What rules govern the family?
How do the people educate their children?
What evidence of change is there?

The publication of literature for children, often being ahead of the school program, has already ventured in the direction of international education by publishing beautifully illustrated books describing life in other cultures. The same can be said about recordings of the music and stories of other lands.

Some new curriculum proposals, in their rejection of what they consider the limiting concept of the criterion of the expanding environment, went to the other extreme. For instance, one organization is in the process of developing a course of study with an anthropological and historical orientation.[E1] Rather than emphasizing the home, school, and neighborhood community on the primary grades, this plan calls for the following: grade 1—a study of the Nestelik Eskimo; grade 2—a comparison between the lives of a Bushman group and a group of Australian aborigines; grade 3—a study of evolution.

Looking at proposals of this nature, it is evident that the post-progressive education era is in the process of challenging the stress on the immediate and the experiential. It points out the negative effect of creating a "provincial" course of study by sticking to the familiar and the immediate. It criticizes the "community school" for having strengthened the utilitarian aspects of the curriculum to the neglect of academic learning. It questions the emphasis on "social learning" as too often leading to superficial study of rules of behavior. Some examples are: introducing friends to each other, saying goodbye to the host after a party, or inviting someone to a party or picnic.

In *Where, When and Why,* a book which is highly critical of the present social studies program and the progressive education influences, Martin Mayer says:[M5:IV]

The mathematicians and scientists have thrown mental health out of their curricula, and the linguists are about to throw it out of the reading program. Let not the social scientists lack the courage to do likewise.

Whereas Mayer's statement may not represent the position of many students of social studies, it does illustrate the dissatisfaction with lack of sufficient depth in social studies teaching. Mayer's contention that social values, interpersonal relations, and mental health, are not formal objectives of the social studies program, should be rejected. However, his appeal for a higher level of intellectual emphasis should definitely be pursued.

A position

The contribution of progressive education to the social studies curriculum cannot be overemphasized. It has revitalized the program. In more than any other aspect of the curriculum, it enhanced the role of the learner as a *"speaker"* and not only as a *"listener."* The process of listening, when overaccentuated, may contribute toward passivity. The process of speaking tends to express a higher level of activation. I have seen listeners fall asleep; I never saw a speaker fall asleep. . . .

Most of the novice teachers being discussed practice in schools populated by socially disadvantaged children of minority groups. In an ongoing study, Adaia Shumsky [S10] postulates that differences in intellectual functioning along social class lines seem to express differences between assertive and passive modes of intellectual approach. The degree to which an individual believes in his capacity to take an active part in shaping his own future may have a direct impact on his academic learning.

It is possible to suggest, though this suggestion needs further experimentation, that a social studies curriculum successful in activating the ethnic child as a learner, will enhance his belief that he can steer his own future. Speaking about the self-concept of the Negro child, James Baldwin says: [B1:39-40]

Negroes in this country . . . are taught early to despise themselves from the moment their eyes open on the world . . . Every effort made by the child's elders to prepare him for a fate from which they cannot protect him causes him secretly in terror, to begin to wait . . .

A social studies program which in both its methodology and in its content ignores the most crucial educational issue—the education of the Negro child—is out of tune with the present realities and needs of American society. Therefore, the emphasis of progressive education on social learning, interpersonal relations, mental health, on the concerns of the learner, and on the immediate and the experiential, is very valid.

Working with white and Negro social studies teachers practicing in Harlem (New York City) I found that the problem of guidance and the use of the firsthand experience of the ethnic child is foremost on their minds. To reject the progressive education principles of social learning or the emphasis on the immediate and experiential, would be to abandon a whole era of educational progress.

A challenging book is *The Fire Next Time* by James Baldwin,[B1] particularly if one thinks about its implications for the social studies program.

In my visit to the Middle East, I had an opportunity to observe schools run by the French organization, Alliance. Spending a day at the school, I had the feeling of being in France. The language, atmosphere, and *content* of study was French. The country in which the school was located was simply ignored, as if it did not exist. This is an extreme example of a school which does not see the socio-psychological problems confronting its population as a rich source for curriculum development.

This position regarding the social studies program does not mean that emphasis on the concerns of the learner—the immediate, experiential, or the community—are the only criteria for curriculum construction. Limiting to the above criteria may mean a *provincial* curriculum. There is a need for a balance, for a curriculum which recognizes the present and the past, the community and the world; a curriculum that starts "where the learner is" and then broadens his horizons. Recent modifications of the social studies program, attempting to integrate the study of the family or the community on the primary level with the study of such institutions in foreign cultures, are very valuable. The examination of the present and the immediate in the light of the past and the foreign is a challenging approach.[K5, T9]

The criticism which states that the social studies program too often lacks depth is also valid. There is a need for a higher level of realism, and particularly for more attention to productive thinking and concept formation.

For instance, an examination of present practices illustrates a tendency to romanticize foreign lands and stress the quaint. Holland is portrayed as a land of windmills and *Klompen*, rather than a land which copes with great problems of irrigation and water control.

There is a growing recognition that a purely descriptive approach to social studies lacks depth. To make social studies a science, there is a need for emphasis on its structure of generalizations. Despite the influences of progressive education, the program is still characterized by covering subject matter, rather than by concept formation. It is this emphasis on the continuity in concept development as the child moves from one grade to another which, I believe, is going to be the main contribution of the coming decade. A beginning in this direction is *A Guide to Content in the Social Studies*,[N2] a report by the National Council for the Social Studies, which suggests fourteen major generalizations as the scope of the program. This suggestion has still to be translated into the language of curriculum practices.

The development of *creative thinking* abilities in social studies needs further exploration. Concepts cannot simply be handed to the learner. The learner must have a hand in discovering them for himself. In contrast to the methodology of science and arithmetic, social studies is only beginning to move in the direction of "discovery." Bruner reports interesting progress in this direction.[B12] He asked a group of fourth graders to locate the major cities of the area on a map containing only physical features and natural resources. The pupils had to explain the rationale underlying their decisions.

The Educational Services Incorporated is in the process of developing social studies materials which will ask the learner to predict what would have happened. For instance, after viewing a brief film on an Eskimo group, the class will have to try to infer the nature of the culture of this group, based on the raw data presented. Then a second film will be presented, and the children will be able to compare their inferences with the documentary film.[E1]

Pioneering work of this nature, promoting creative and productive thinking in social studies, is invaluable. It calls for a teacher who values convergent and divergent thinking; a teacher for whom the social studies material is not mainly an aggregation of facts, but rather an expression of a stream of thought.

As reported in the discussion about Columbus Day, presented in Chapter 4, the teacher who views this event as only factual information tends to merely "cover the ground" in his teaching.

The teacher who experiences for himself a symbolic meaning in this historical event, tends to emphasize interpretation and personal meaning.

Teaching social studies creatively calls for a teacher who himself stands for a position; who has a philosophy. The teacher who is lukewarm about events tends to stick to the repetitive way of teaching.

CONCLUSION

The factors contributing toward a repetitive orientation in social studies are mainly the attempt to stress specificity of information and the teacher's lack of involvement with the values underlying the subject matter.

The factors contributing toward a creative orientation are the teacher's interest in the activation of the learner, integration of subject matter, and concept formation; a teacher who searches for the balance and synthesis between social and academic learning, between the immediate and the remote. And perhaps most important, a creative orientation calls for a teacher to whom subject matter has a personal meaning. Without a position, without strong social commitments, it is impossible to teach social studies creatively.

SELECTED BIBLIOGRAPHY

BALDWIN, James, *The Fire Next Time.* New York: The Dial Press, 1963. An emotional and penetrating analysis of the racial problem. Think about its implications to the social studies curriculum.

HANNA, Lavone and others, *Unit Teaching in the Elementary School.* New York: Holt, Rinehart & Winston, Inc., 1963. A most comprehensive discussion of the unit approach.

KENWORTHY, Leonard, *Introducing Children to the World.* New York: Harper & Row, Publishers, 1956. A valuable discussion of international education.

MICHAELIS, John, *Social Studies for Children in a Democracy*. Englewood Cliffs, N.J.: Prentice-Hall, Inc., 1963. A comprehensive
discussion of the methodology of social studies.

MIEL, Alice, and BROGAN, Peggy, *More than Social Studies*. Englewood Cliffs, N.J.: Prentice-Hall, Inc., 1957. A view of social learning in the elementary school.

9

The Arts: Repetitive or creative?

by Rose Mukerji*

Music, dance, painting, sculpture—in fact all the arts in the curriculum—have a particular advantage for us as we strive for creativity in teaching. The whole weight of centuries is in our favor. We have the support of a whole range of cultural expectations. The very idea of any of the arts brings to mind the creative person, the original product, the imaginative process.

We do not look for the right note in composing a melody, the right color in painting a mountain, the right shape in sculpting an elephant, or the right step in choreographing a dance. Instead we search for a fresh arrangement of notes, a subtle shimmer of color, a curve to suggest the graceful sweep of an elephant's trunk, or a movement theme that is uniquely expressive for a dance of loneliness.

But sophisticated social attitudes and expectations are not enough to guarantee that teachers will, through creative teaching, offer a program in the arts that will encourage the creative self-realization of children. Therefore, this chapter will examine two highly pertinent questions: (1) What holds teachers back from creative teaching in the arts? (2) How can we develop a more creative style in teaching the arts?

* Assistant Professor of Education, Brooklyn College, The City University of New York.

DIFFICULTIES OF CREATIVE TEACHING IN THE ARTS

Although our culture favors creativity in the arts, particularly among the intellectuals of our society, its appreciation is most often lavished on artists who "have arrived," who are "recognized," who are "successful." College students, as part of that segment of society, share this appreciation. Intellectually, they support the values of creativity.

However, when they find themselves as novice teachers in a position to nourish the first sensitive shoots of creativity in children, they face many difficulties. In some instances they are aware of inhibiting factors. They claim that they see very little, if any, creative teaching of the arts in the schools. They find that teachers, under the stress of adult standards, block children's creative expression which does not look "good" to parents or teachers. Sometimes they feel hampered by their own sense of inadequacy in a particular art form.

Other difficulties which they face in trying to develop their style as creative teachers arise from their confusion about the nature of creative teaching in the arts. They are not always able to distinguish between repetitive and creative teaching in music, dance, and art. Nor do they know whether or not it is necessary for them to be creative themselves in order to teach in a manner that will encourage and develop children's creativity.

Sense of inadequacy

Teachers sense a relationship between their own ability in the arts and their capacity for creative teaching in the arts. Some have expressed it in the following ways:

How can I expect any spontaneity from children when I freeze at the thought of having to open my mouth in front of them? You know— I was always a "listener" in music, myself.

I tried out the same idea for rhythmic movement which we did in class the other day. The children loved it and wanted to do more—but I didn't know how to go on, so we stopped. I'm afraid I'm just not creative.

Because teachers feel that there is a connection between their own level of creativity and the act of teaching creatively, it is necessary to explore the questions which they raise. Is it necessary to be creative in an art form in order to teach that art form creatively to children? Is it likely that a teacher who is creative musically will have more success in bringing out musical creativity in his children than one who is not? Will one who is himself creative in dance but not in painting be likely to teach painting creatively? Or is it possible that a teacher who is highly creative in sculpture may inhibit his students' creativity in clay work by his "expertise" so far beyond their abilities?

It all depends on whether he uses his own greater knowledge to foster fluency and variety of children's responses or whether he merely engages in *his own* creative musical process at the expense of the *children's* creative activities.

A teacher who paints may understand the child who endlessly sharpens his colored pencils or who arranges and rearranges the paints and paint brushes before he "settles down to work." Will he be as likely to understand the child who wanders, apparently aimlessly, around the room when his task is to develop a dance idea? It all depends on whether the teacher, knowing that "fooling around" or "pacing back and forth" is part of the creative process, recognizes the many forms it may take. In other words, critical factors in being able to teach creatively in the arts are not only the teacher's own proficiency in the art itself, but also his ability to provide educative experiences of high quality to his children.

Confusion between creative and repetitive teaching

It is not easy for teachers to identify the creative process in teaching painting, dance, woodwork, music, or drama. Much of the difficulty lies in their uncertainty about what makes for creative teaching in these curriculum areas. They frequently confuse repetitive teaching with creative teaching in their observations of teaching practice.

Findings of a study in dance may help to illustrate their confusion. The study makes use of two role-playing demonstrations by the same college instructor. The first one, whom we will identify as Teacher A, illustrates repetitive teaching. The instructor directs the form, the sequence, and the style of each movement pattern. The second one, whom we will identify Teacher C, illustrates creative teaching. The college instructor guides a group of participating teachers in developing their own dances. Even though one theme is common to all the dances, the results show great variety and express uniqueness.

Although Teacher A's content is completely prestructured, many teachers feel there is considerable creativity and freedom because of a certain warmth and enthusiasm in the personal behavior of Teacher A. Some comment:

I like the teacher's attitude—so relaxing. There was no singling out of anyone as clumsy. There was nothing derogatory about anyone. You were free to be yourself.

Children would have as much fun doing it as we did. You didn't know what you were doing. One thing just flowed into another, then suddenly it was a dance. It was very satisfying. Free. It was very creative.

In general, the participants equate their enjoyment of Teacher A with creative teaching. One teacher who had seen children in a highly creative dance program expressed a strong minority opinion, saying:

If I hadn't seen those children in the Maury School (Richmond, Va.) dance, I would have thought this was just great. You could see that teacher A loved what she was doing. And we not only had loads of fun; we felt successful. I would have said this was creative before. But not now. Now, I don't think it is. We were *told* what to do *all* the time.

In discussing the demonstration of Teacher C, who illustrates the creative teaching process, the subjects identify her as a creative teacher. They talk about their own emotional involvement in bringing their dance characters to life. They point out the number of original ideas and the great variety shown in their dance fragments. They speak of the teacher as a resource for helping them express their own ideas more fully.

Some participants, however, still reveal a sense of confusion in analyzing the differences in teaching styles as demonstrated. For example:

But the teaching was not really so different. Both teachers were warm and friendly to the students. Neither one embarrassed us or made us feel stupid whether we're good at dancing or not.

It would seem that teachers who fail to distinguish the elements which characterize repetitive or creative teaching from the personal behavior of the teacher in such matters as friendliness, warmth, enjoyment, and enthusiasm will encounter serious limitations in their efforts to become more creative in their teaching. It is easy—much too easy—to draw stereotypes of teachers. The authoritarian, directive teacher is often expected to be hostile, harsh, and disinterested in his relations with children. This is frequently not the case at all, especially with young teachers.

We can, with justification, expect the authoritarian teacher's style to be repetitive. But it is just as possible that he will show great interest and concern that children shall learn those things which he considers significant and necessary. He can offer real support and security to his students, particularly when they respond well to his values. He may appreciate and respect them as they strive to reach his standards. He will not, however, be teaching creatively, despite an atmosphere of warmth and enthusiasm. We must look beyond the *surface* climate of a classroom to be able to distinguish repetitive teaching from creative teaching.

Unaware of values

In analyzing the difficulties which teachers face in developing a more creative style in teaching the arts, we must pay attention to the problem which arises when teachers are unaware of the distinctive values of creative teaching in the arts. Referring again to the dance study, the following comment will illustrate this problem:

Why do you have to stick to one style? Can't you just shift back and forth between the creative and the other way of teaching depending on how the lesson is going? I don't see why not. It's all the same for the children.

The implication in this statement is that a style of teaching, whether repetitive or creative, makes no difference as to the quality of learning for the child. But this is not so. One has only to see the intensity of committment, the energetic drive, and the glow of accomplishment in children who are learning creatively, to know it is not so.

To conclude, teachers who wish to teach the arts curriculum more creatively face a number of difficulties. They are held back by a sense of personal as well as professional inadequacy. They are sometimes hampered by some confusion regarding the qualities of creative teaching in the arts. The special values of creative learning by children is not clearly understood. They do, however, sense that there is some connection between creative teaching and creative learning. And they are right. Creative teaching permits, facilitates, and encourages creative learning. But it does not guarantee it. Repetitive teaching, on the other hand, inhibits creative learning.

TEACHING MUSIC AND DANCE

Are there some guidelines to help us perceive more clearly the characteristics of creative and repetitive teaching in the arts curricula? Are there guidelines as well to help us determine the appropriate place of repetitive teaching in a program primarily and fundamentally creative in approach?

This section of the chapter will undertake to illumine possible answers to these central questions by examining representative practices in the music and dance curriculum. The discussion will draw heavily on concrete instances intended to illustrate the creative and the repetitive qualities as teachers participate or mediate in children's experiences with music and dance. These instances of teaching will in no sense cover the whole range of the music curriculum, but will, instead, give some view of the diversity of experience which are included in this curriculum area. Hopefully, they will create a few sparks to help teachers toward their own efforts in creative teaching.

First grade: rhythm

In one first grade class the chairs and tables are rearranged to make space for rhythmic activity. This class has a piano and a teacher who can play it. Her lesson will emphasize rhythmic patterns in relation to body movement. She has a plan and has organized the necessary conditions for it. The children form a circle and the line of direction is clearly established. She tells them:

I'm going to play walking music and I want you to walk in time to the music. (Children respond by walking.)

Now I will play skipping music and you will skip until the music stops. (Children respond with varying degrees of skill and accuracy.)

When we skip, we lift our knees very high. Sandy knows how to skip nicely. Show us the right way to skip, Sandy. (Sandy demonstrates.) Fine. Now do it again and see if everybody can skip like Sandy. (Improved response by children.)

The teacher establishes that there is one right way, indicating a move toward repetitive teaching:

Now I will play 16 walks and 16 skips. Follow the music and be sure to change when the music changes. (This activity is repeated a few times until the class does it rather well.)

Now we'll do something even harder. I'm sure you can because you're such good listeners. This part of the class make a smaller circle inside the outside circle and face the opposite way. The inside children are walkers. The outside children are skippers. (Teacher plays same two pieces alternately—sometimes for 16 beats and sometimes for 8 beats. At each change in rhythmic pattern, the teacher gives them the cue to walk or to skip. Then groups exchange activity.)

Because of the teacher's directions, there is no necessity for children to increase their sensitivity to rhythmic changes or to make choices based on musical stimula. Instead of listening to music, children merely take directions from the teacher and follow authority.

Now, everybody come back into the big circle. Since you did that so very well, I'm going to add another part. This is hopping music. Listen. (She plays.)

The teacher expresses approval and moves the activity forward.

Child: It sounds like walking music too.

Teacher: No, this music is just for hopping. We have other music for walking.

Child: But it fits for walking.

The teacher does not allow for redefinition [T4], for seeing something in a way different from the established or intended use. She dispenses with the child's alert comment saying:

That may be, but *this* will be our hopping music.

Over a period of weeks, the teacher continues in much the same way. The children learn to identify and respond to music for galloping, sliding, jumping, swinging, twirling, etc. The teacher feels satisfaction in the evident growth of the children's ability to respond to various rhythmic patterns as related to specific music. She feels a sense of comfort in being able to control the children in an activity which requires so much space and movement. The children have a sense of accomplishment as they progress step by step. The galloping music has become their favorite and they are pleased and excited when the teacher includes it in every rhythm lesson.

One can readily see that teachers might try to emulate such repetitive teaching because of the sense of security it may offer and the feeling of "actually teaching something" which comes from a teacher-directed activity. Because it is easy to see that the children are learning and are enjoying the activity, a teacher can fail to examine the quality of learning and the missed potential for more creative learning inherent in the subject of rhythm in movement.

Another first grade: rhythm

Another first grade teacher approaches the same subject in quite another way. Her children sit in a group on the floor in a cleared area of the room. She too has a plan and has organized the necessary conditions for it. Her lesson is based on developing rhythmic patterns from children's speech. Because the words will come from the children, she has no way of knowing beforehand just what the rhythmic pattern will be. But because rhythm is inherent in speech, she knows that many valuable ideas will come from the children. She leads into a popular subject—food.

Teacher: Who had something to eat that tasted good with his milk?

Child: Cookies and milk.

Teacher: Can you say it slowly over and over again so that we can hear
the rhythm of the words?
(Child begins to chant and teacher suggests, with the lift of her
hand, that others joint the chant, which they do. Teacher joins
also, and, when the rhythm feels solid, she signals a stop with her
hand and voice saying, in time to the rhythm, "and now we stop.")

Encouraging variety within the same frame or theme, the teacher
asks:

Who had something else with milk?

Gerry: Banana and milk. (Procedure similar to that above follows.)

Moving the activity forward, the teacher suggests playing the
rhythm in their hands at the same time. She asks for another
snack with milk.

Maureen: Pretzels and milk.

Teacher: Let's hear it over and over so we can feel the rhythm.
(Maureen chants and others join in, some clapping, some chant-
ing, some doing both.)

Everett: But that's just the same as "cookies and milk."

Teacher: Oh? Do other children think it's the same? (Some "no," some
"yes," some not sure.)

The teacher is careful not to decide the question by her authority.
Sensing this as a highly teachable moment, she recognizes the
problem of the children and leads them to think of solutions in
an open-ended way.

Teacher: How can we find out if the rhythm is the same for "pretzels
and milk" and "cookies and milk?"

Everett: Say them both together. (Half the class chants each phrase
at the same time.)

Teacher: What did you hear? Is the rhythm the same or not? (Some
say the same, some different, about one-fourth not sure.)

Instead of settling the problem herself, the teacher keeps their attention on it, allowing time for better solutions. She also supports them by acknowledging, "It's not easy to be sure about these things."

Everett: It's the words that mix it up. If you did only clapping, you'll see—they're the same. They are!

Teacher: Let's try Everett's idea. (They do. All but three agree with Everett. He smiles with satisfaction.)

It takes time to sharpen our ears to feel ryhthm. (The three negative voters do not appear ill at ease.)

The teacher helps children maintain their integrity. She uses neither her own authority nor the majority opinion of the group to decide that the rhythms are identical. She makes clear by her honest comment that one must come to feel or hear rhythm by oneself in the time that it takes.

Sensing that it is time to move the group forward, the teacher has many choices. In preplanning, she thought of a number of possible directions the lesson might take. She thought that she might lead the group to further short, one-measure, rhythmic patterns by asking for other combinations of favorite foods, clothes, actions, pets, weather. She considered leading their attention to changing tempo by alternating a slow phrase with double-time phrases using the same words.

In actual teaching she leaves herself open, allowing the progress of the children to cue her choice of direction. From the children she judges whether it is wiser to encourage more variations on the same level or to lead into further development on a higher level. In this lesson she chooses a higher level by trying to develop a phrase from the short measure.

Teacher: Can we add more words to "cookies and milk" that will go well together? Let's say it over and over again quietly and listen for some other words.

(All chant quietly: "Cookies and milk, cookies and milk . . .")

Jane: Taste very nice! (Reaction of group shows they are delighted with this.)

Teacher: Let's try this again. Jane, you add your part after two times of "cookies and milk" just as you did before. (If the note values were written out, it would be a four-measure phrase in 2/4 time, as follows:)

Cook—ies and milk,   cook—ies and milk,   taste ver—y nice!

Teacher: What different ways can you show our new long phrase?

The teacher is now encouraging variety and fluency of ideas. Here are some of the combinations which children develop:

(1) One group claps first half of phrase; other group chants second half of phrase.

(2) One group claps first half of phrase; other group makes sounds other than clapping.

(3) One group beats on floor; other group makes mouth sounds.

(4) One group makes sounds on floor; other group shows rhythm by moving their bodies in place on the floor (using arms, shoulders, heads, backs).

(5) One group makes sounds with mouths; other group moves around the room accenting rhythm with feet and body motions.

Watching the children carefully, the teacher looks for teaching clues that are emerging from their activity. She picks up an example of contrasting movement and uses it to illustrate a principle of music:

Something interesting happened over here. The first part of the phrase was smooth movement and the second part was sharp movement. There was a nice contrast in feeling.

Delighted with the children's involvement and exploration of ideas, she motivates them to raise the quality of their movement patterns.

Teacher: Instead of just moving forward, what other directions can you find?
(Some of the floor patterns suddenly become much more interesting and varied, and the designs affect the movement patterns as well.)
How does it feel to go backward?

Janet: Feels funny.

George: Feels like you're going to fall.

Teacher: (enjoying their fun) That's one of the nice things about dancing. If you walk down the street backwards, people might think you very peculiar. But dancing backwards is just as good as any other way if you feel like it.

The teacher helps children find alternatives and establishes a climate in which it is safe to try new things and where there is no one right or best way to react.

The class has a number of sessions on rhythmic patterns using class-made sentences, poetry fragments, song phrases, and original drum rhythms. Soon the teacher feels it is time to further extend the level of experience with rhythm. She plans to focus on personal relations as revealed through rhythmic movement. One day she selects an interesting rhythmic pattern which the children have established. She asks the "musician group" to play the pattern four times without stopping. She asks the "dancing group" to take partners. Then she sets a new problem for the class.

Teacher: Can we tell how people feel about each other just by watching their movements? Partners decide who will move on phrase one, who will move on phrase two, taking turns with all four phrases. Just be sure not to let go each other's hand.
(They try working together a number of times, with the teacher helping them start together with the "musicians.")

Everett: Morris was pulling me! I pushed him back!

Morris: You were mad.

Teacher: We could tell how you felt. Your movement told us even before you said it.

The teacher shows a readiness to accept all relationships, even aggressive ones. She skillfully emphasizes, again, the aim of the lesson—to communicate human relations through movement.

Larry: We have a funny one. Janet made me laugh, so I tried to make her laugh, too.

Teacher: This time, each musician will pick a couple to watch. Let's see how the partners feel toward each other from their movements.

Here are some of the observations:

Sandy: Emmy was the mother. She was nice to Betty like she was her little girl. (Reveals her expectations of mothers.)

Barry: Sam was asking Jenny, and Jenny said, "No." She was mad at him.

Sam: That's right! That's right! She was mean to me!

Norman: They were like playing a game. Like they were friends. Them two.

The teacher had led them to an experience which made possible their response in terms of honest emotional relations between people. Anger, protectiveness, friendliness, fear—all feelings could be encountered in dance and communicated to others. Real emotions and real relationships between people are acknowledged as part of dance. If you were the teacher how would you carry this group forward?

Fifth grade: folk songs

Just as folk songs spring from the roots of a people, so they can help youngsters identify with these people. A fifth grade class has been building their repertoire of American folk songs, tasting the meanings which brought forth the songs. In preparation for an assembly program they choose "So Long"—one of the Dust Bowl Ballads by Woodie Guthrie—and plan to interpret the words of the song in movement as well. They know about erosion and dust storms which carried away precious topsoil in our southwest and with it the hopes of many a farmer and many a sharecropper. They know of the truckloads and carloads of people following Route 66 to California hoping to find work and food. They try to understand what it means to leave land on which they as well as their grandparents have been born. But they are sure of one thing; they are sure that the people had many different feelings about saying goodbye to their homes, friends, and relatives, because each person is different.

Motivation. During an early improvisational period, the children work on the chorus, which says:

So long, it's been good to know you;
So long, it's been good to know you;
So long, it's been good to know you;
Dusty ol' dust is a-gittin my home
And I gotta be driftin' along.

Teacher: Who are some of these characters and how do they feel about leaving?

The class enumerates:

(1) An old grandfather who is afraid to go to Los Angeles because he's always lived on this farm.
(2) His grandson who's dying to get away and see Hollywood.
(3) A young girl who doesn't want to leave her boyfriend.
(4) A young girl who wants to leave her boyfriend. She's tired of him!
(5) A father who has to leave his children behind until he can send for them. He's anxious and excited about going, but worried too. Mixed up, I guess.

Teacher: Interesting to try to show his mixed feelings. We certainly have them often enough about many things. Think of who you are and how you feel about leaving. I'll play the chorus over a few times to get you started, then you can sing the words to yourself as you work out your ideas.

In motivating the group, the teacher helps them bring to the foreground of their thoughts a variety of characters and a variety of emotions that real people feel. She makes it a point to comment on the reality of mixed and contradictory emotions that people have, encouraging the students to tackle such a problem through communicative movement.

Some children get up immediately and begin to improvise as the teacher plays through the chorus a few times. Others sit for a while—thinking? watching? waiting?

The teacher withdraws and watches the children work. She tries to sense when most of them are ready to share their improvisations. At this point she plays the chorus softly, saying that she will play it through once more before they look at the ideas. Being sensitive to the individual differences in children's work tempo, she allows a little time for them to stop their improvisations.

Evaluation. Knowing that her fifth graders are mature enough to comment on each other's work, the teacher also makes clear the purpose of this sharing time. There is no question of good or bad ideas or movements. There is only a matter of having the viewer reflect what the movement says to him about a person and his feelings. The teacher sets the tone by saying, "Let's see what the movement fragments tell us about the person and how he or she feels about saying, 'So long.' "

As children show their ideas individually, others comment on what has been communicated. It is not a matter of guessing correctly but rather of reflecting images that are seen. Frequently one presentation brings quite different reactions from several children, and the reasons for this are explored a bit. Occasionally, after the comments, the dancer tells what he intended.

Integrity of child's intention. Whether in motivating, guiding, or evaluating the music activity, the teacher is conscious of supporting the child's intention in his expression and in maintaining a quality of integrity in their personal relations. The following incidents will point up this awareness.

Jose: I wanted it to be a happy-go-lucky cowboy, but it was hard. The music sounded too sad.

Teacher: Shall I play it at a quicker tempo, more crisp or jazzy?

Jose: Yes, give it a beat!
(Jose now looks satisfied. Some of the other children then tell the teacher how they want the music—fast, medium or slow.)
Miranda: I think I'd rather not have any music at all.
(Her dance has a sense of loneliness in it. One of the boys finds himself humming softly as she dances.)

Miranda: That's better than the piano. Ricco, will you hum the whole thing soft like that—and slow? I'll do it again.

There is magic in that duet. When it ends, the room is filled with eloquent silence. After a while the teacher says softly, "Let's stop for today." There has been a deep encounter with loneliness. It has been accepted and respected as such. This scene would never have happened had the teacher taught her dance, no matter how good the choreography nor how well the students learned it through repetitive teaching.

Fourth grade: social studies and music

Music, as a personally integrative experience, also has a high potential for integrating meanings which emerge from social experience. For this reason, music and dance (as well as other expressive arts) are readily coordinated with social studies, helping to deepen and intensify the knowledge and sensitivity gained about people and their modes of living.

An example of such correlation between social studies and dance occurs in a fourth grade class studying coastal life and fishing culture in northeast United States. The children are coming to understand the extensive interdependence required in a fishing-centered culture. The boys, particularly, are excited by the drama of setting out to sea before dawn, perhaps to battle treacherous storms, and of knowing that the well-being of the whole community depends on their catch.

Planning. As one of their activities, they decide to compose a dance. The whole class, together, decides the major outline of it. There will be two sailings. The first is to show the hardships, dangers, and tragedy of fishing. The second sailing is to show a successful shrimp haul ending with a scene built on the theme of the folk song, "Shrimp Boats."

The "women" are to see the "men" off, carry on their daily chores, and show how they feel when the injured or dead "men" are brought back in the storm. In the second sailing they are to wait excitedly for the successful return and take the men off to the square dance.

The class uses its group process skills, which have been developing as an integral part of their social studies work, to set up six functional committees. Each is to concentrate on a separate part of the task: (1) boys for the storm and tragic return; (2) boys for the successful catch; (3) girls for the send-off and daily chores; (4) girls for the lament; (5) boys and girls for the square dance; (6) music. Later, the work of all six groups will be fused into a unified whole with careful help from the teacher.

Resources. Records for accompaniment are gathered from school and home resources, and from the teacher's personal collection. After much listening, the music committee makes two recommendations which they submit to the class for approval: parts of "La Mer" by Debussy for the storm scene, and the folk song, "Shrimp Boats," to be sung by the women as the men return with the successful catch.

Scheduling. Their scheduled time in the gymnasium is used to work on this project. There is a tremendous sense of energy and vitality as they work—excitedly, smoothly, in fits and starts, arguing, demonstrating, agreeing, disagreeing, laughing, moodily and zestfully. As they put the parts together in a logical continuity, the dance as a whole becomes everybody's dance.

Integrating. All the girls dance all the women roles. All the boys dance all the men roles. There is no such thing as casting. Within the general framework of the dance, of excitement at the host's return, of the calm, steady household chores, each dancer expresses his role somewhat differently each time—keeping the spontaneity alive. Only those parts of the dance which require precision to get across the idea are set and practiced for accuracy. Rowing the boat in unison and hauling the nets fall into this category.

Repetitive teaching. The group decides that the dance should end with a real square dance commonly danced in the northeast United States. The teacher now recognizes a logical place for repetitive teaching. The emphasis now moves to preestablished form, style, and music. The situation requires conformity and consistency in order to perform a dance which, itself, was formed and mellowed in a cultural setting over many long years and generations. The children submit to outside discipline in order to satisfy a decision of their own making.

Empathizing. In addition to guiding, facilitating, and encouraging the growth of this dance, the teacher probes for deeper feelings and meanings during discussions. And she reacts with sensitivity to the children's dancing. Both she and the children respond openly and fearlessly to certain rare moments of creative intensity.

During one session, at the end of the tragic scene in which the women mourn the dead fishermen, there is the usual long pause of stillness while the dancers hold their positions. The mood of one child is incredibly compelling. There is something the little girl knows—in the curve of her throat, the touch of her hand, the look of her eyes—something she knows of loss, perhaps of death. A boy, looking at the teacher in that moment, says "Your eyes are wet." The teacher answers, "Yes." Such is the power of a child's creative dance.

Summary

We have seen the power of creative teaching leading to releasing and integrating experiences for children. We have sampled the potential of creative learning in the music curriculum through rhythmic movement, folk songs, and dances related to social studies content. We have seen children from the first through the upper elementary grades responding with freedom, spontaneity, imagination, and sensitivity. And we have observed their teachers motivating, guiding, encouraging, appreciating, and supporting the children toward creative self-realization.

How else can we nurture this power in children? How can we work with them in other arts to nourish their creativity—and ours as teachers as well?

TEACHING ART

"You Can't Teach Art, Thank Goodness" is the title of a chapter on creativity in the elementary school by Wilt.[W8] In this sensitively written book, the author takes the position that the teacher "deals in skills, knowledge, and attitudes that foster self-realization" through art, but that she "does not show them how or what to draw." [W8:32-33] Does this imply that the child is on his own in his art endeavors? Is there no place for a teacher to help a child express his ideas through art media?

There is a curriculum area called "art" in every school program, and teachers, whether specialists or generalists, are expected to carry the responsibility for its conduct. What do they do? What roles do they play? And what kinds of experiences do children have as the result of these various teacher roles?

Again, as with the music curriculum, depending on the styles of teaching to which they are exposed children will encounter the whole continuum from repetitive to creative experience in art.

Repetitive teaching in art

Repetitive teaching in art ignores the developmental stages of growth in children which directly affect their natural art expression. It violates the deepest purpose of art expression, which is self-realization. Activities which have the power to comment on the meaning of one's life experience, to release and channel one's emotional feelings, to order one's life space, and to involve one passionately in an idea must not be subverted. Yet that is exactly what happens when repetitive teaching in art takes over. More specifically, how does it happen?

Differences in Perception. Children and adults perceive the world differently. In the realm of art the teacher and the young elementary school child look at the world from strikingly different angles. The teacher knows how things look realistically and the part that perspective plays in vision. He is aware of relative sizes of objects, of the important details, and of the usual color of these objects.

The child, on the other hand, passes through a number of phases in his growth, each with differing perception on his part. It is only as he approaches the end of his elementary school stay that he begins to represent his world realistically in art. In accounting for the reason that children's art expression offers a world so different from that of the adult, Lowenfeld states: [L8:259]

. . . the child's creative expression is mainly connected with such subjective experiences as bodily feelings, muscle sensations, and touch impressions . . . The proportions in the child's representation are proportions of value, not the result of aesthetic evaluation.

Thus, differences in perception of people and of the world between elementary school children and mature teachers may lead to attempts to "improve" children's work so that it may conform more nearly to the world as seen by adults.

Prepared Outlines. There is a whole commercial industry devoted to producing repetitive materials for children. We are all too familiar with the workbook and coloring book type of outlined picture where a child may or may not have a choice of colors in filling in forms not his own. On the question of coloring books, Lowenfeld takes an unequivocal stand: [L8:42]

. . . imitative procedures as found in coloring and work books may make the child dependent in this thinking . . . they do not provide emotional relief, because they give the child no opportunity to express his own experience . . . (they) frustrate his own creative ambitions.

Thus, staying within the lines requires a certain amount of physical coordination, but it is in no way related to art, which is an expressive experience.

Prepared Patterns. Student teachers not infrequently are asked to prepare patterns for children's use. They are right to raise the following questions which appear in their logs:

Why should I spend so much time cutting out Indian feathers for my class?

The teacher thinks all those Pilgrim hats (and *I* cut out *every last one* of them) look cute on the children. But why did so many forget to take them home? They always make such a fuss about taking home their paintings.

Many student teachers find a conflict between values of art as individual expression emphasized in their readings and methods courses and the type of "busy work" which withdraws them from contact with children and which only serves to provide "busy work" for children.

Directed Step-By-Step Method. On the other hand, some teachers feel pleased with themselves when they teach an art lesson by the directed, step-by-step method. In an example of such a repetitive process, the teacher selects the topic, the materials to be used, and the forms which are to be constructed. She announces that the class of first grade children will learn how to make trains from paper.

In her motivation, she shows fine photographs of various kinds of cars found in passenger and freight trains, leading to a rather lively discussion with the children. But none of the children's observations are used in making the trains. Although the teacher has provided visual enrichment materials, she has not understood that the value in such materials is to provide an additional reference for children's independent use of that enriched environment. Orderly procedures are used for distributing papers, scissors, and crayons. Following the teacher step by step, children fold the paper, cut it, and draw the required size and shape of windows and doors.

Before precut circles are distributed the teacher shows the class a model passenger car and asks how many wheels they see. The model may prove useful. However, the children are required to perceive as she does! When the answer "four" is given, the teacher says, "But when you look at it sideways, you see only two wheels. We'll use two wheels. Draw spokes like this on your wheels." Here is a situation where the teacher finds a conflict between her preconceived idea of a paper train and the children's perception and knowledge of trains. Her response reflects her conception of the teacher as an authority from whom children learn by directive. One child is heard to mutter "I've seen lots of trains and they had solid wheels," while he makes a few halfhearted strokes on his circles.

In discussing the smokestack, the teacher reviews the various shapes being used on their trains (or should we say her trains?)— the rectangle for the car, windows and doors, circles for the wheels, and a square for the smokestack. It is evident that she is consciously integrating math concepts with her art lesson, and her expression is one of satisfaction.

In this repetitive method of teaching there is no room for children's personal interpretation of trains. There is no room for a child to work at his own tempo. Each has to wait for the next direction to follow. Even the use of effective visual stimuli, of pictures and models, is aborted by the teacher's prior image of the finished product.

The teacher can learn a number of things from this lesson. She learns how to plan with care, how to prepare reference materials such as pictures and models, how to distribute materials, how to set up a demonstration, how to give clear directions, and how to integrate math with paper construction work. But what does she learn about the teacher's role in enhancing the expressive values inherent in art?

A Place For Repetitive Teaching. Is there, then, no place for repetitive teaching in art? I believe there is. But it is relevant to only certain limited aspects of the art experience. Management is one of these. A teacher needs to think through and decide where to store art materials, how children will have access to them, where to replace partly used and unused materials, how to keep work in progress in good condition, how to store finished products, and how to clean up.

Some of these affairs can be decided jointly by the children and the teacher, but the constant reminder and practice of these established routines is hardly creative, nor need it be. It is, in fact, more efficient to handle them in a repetitive manner. Then creative energy can be released for the aesthetic process and product itself.

In addition to management of art activities, there may be occasions when the art process and product itself dictates a repetitive approach. For instance, a group of kindergarten children decide to refurnish their walk-in dollhouse. Many different samples are offered for the wallpaper design. A potato print is finally selected by the group. It is necessary, then, to make a number of potato blocks exactly alike and to agree to the spacing and color of the pattern. The wallpaper can then be made by a committee of eight children. The walls of the dollhouse will have a fair degree of unity.

A similar problem in designing a border for a very large transportation mural is faced by a third grade class. The four children responsible for it agree to use a single design to lend unity to the border. The teacher in this case reminds them of the need for uniformity to accomplish their purpose. In both these instances the teacher's role is to stress conformity and similarity as dictated by the inherent aesthetic needs of the art project and as agreed upon by the group.

CREATIVE TEACHING IN ART

We have seen how repetitive teaching through imposing prepared outlines, or patterns, or step-by-step directed lessons negates the basic self-fulfilling criterion of the art experience for children. We have also seen how repetitive teaching for routine management tasks related to art endeavors can release energy and thought for more significant expression. Finally, we have pointed out certain art activities where repetitive action is required to carry out the intention of the design.

None of these examples touches on that precious quality of art experience which suffuses the person engaged in a creative effort. Nowhere do we sense the impelling force, the intense concentration, the zest, the wholehearted immersion in the self-appointed act of making a visual form where none existed before. How, then, does a teacher construct the conditions which lead children to creative experience in art? Not by repetitive teaching. Not by withdrawal. But by creative teaching.

Creative teaching, like any style of good teaching, requires a teacher to know a good deal about the individual children in his class and about the content of the instructional program. Then he needs to find ways of working that will allow for the sensitive interplay of his knowledge with the specific teaching-learning situation at hand.

Stages of expression in art

Manipulation. By recognizing that children develop through levels or stages in their art work, [L8] a teacher will recognize the importance of providing time and materials for the exploration and manipulation of every new art medium. Scribbling with crayon needs to be repeated with unplanned dabs and strokes of paint, with pounding, squeezing, and rolling of clay, with hammering nails or drilling holes—for their own sake, for the muscular act, not for the idea at all. If children do not experience these activities

before they come to school, it is necessary that they be allowed
to do so.

Representational stage. Gradually these random movements
with paint or crayon take on a rhythmic pattern and circular
forms appear. The clay is broken into bits, later rolled into balls
and "snakes." During the nursery school years these later scribbles
may look no different to the adult, but the change in meaning for
the child is enormous. He now has names for his scribbles—they
become people, events, and places that have importance for him.
His scribbles or coils or balls are now *symbolic*. During the earliest
school years he continues to try to find symbols for what he wishes
to represent.

What characterizes symbolic representation by a child which
is truly his own? Art expressions at this stage are characterized by
the child's reality at the time. They emphasize and exaggerate the
parts which have important meanings for him. The relationships
of size and space are determined by the emotional significance
they have for him. Colors are used without regard to nature's or
man's design. They reveal a child's feelings about lines and hues
which are frequently incomprehensible to untrained adults.

The psychological aspect of teacher guidance during the manipulative and representational stages of art expression raises a
point of caution. As one psychologist states: [D9:11]

Many children lose creative expression in color and form when too great
emphasis is placed upon realistic reproduction of form.

One frequently finds children at this stage drawing the same picture over and over again, day after day. If an adult tries to influence the child to make his picture more realistic by showing him
a more accurate visual model, the "art expression will become a
primitive form of draftsmanship and lose all possibility of creative
expression." [D9:12]

Schematic stage. Usually during the years covered by the second through fourth grades, a child achieves a concept of form to
express his intention—a scheme to represent his active knowledge
of the person, scene, or object he has in mind. Eventually a new
space concept emerges and, instead of painting free-floating fig-

ures and objects, the child begins to tie them down to a base line. Then a thin strip of sky usually binds the picture on the top. It takes quite a while and much effort and experience to develop the changing schema that reflect the changing perception and knowledge of the child.

Realistic stage. Moving into the early realistic stage in art expression, the child attempts to present that which he sees as a realistic visual concept rather than as the earlier emotional and personal meaning of his subject. The stage of visual realism usually emerges in the upper elementary grades.

However, these stages of development in art expression are neither automatic nor inevitable. They come from a child's experiences with art which, *at most*, encourage him, or which, *at least*, permit him to experiment, to make his own selections of ideas and to find his own ways of bringing form and pattern to his feelings and ideas.

As children grow from stage to stage, the sensitive teacher will assess their experiences and make opportunities to extend them. He will help them develop sharper perception and more accurate concepts of the world and people around them. He will reflect their feelings as a way of deepening their understanding of themselves, their emotions, and their behavior as well as those of other people.

With such constantly growing background, the children will have something significant to express through art media. And the teacher will have a reliable base from which to motivate the art activity, to guide its production, and to evaluate its product. It is to these three aspects of teaching art—motivating, moving into action, and evaluating—that we now turn our attention.

Motivation

Creativity in a teacher's style will be revealed, to some degree, in his style of motivation. In reporting motivation techniques in art activities, teachers record the following:

(In a first grade.) What kinds of shapes can you find in your clay? There are so many different shapes.

The teacher recognizes that most of her children are at the manipulative, exploratory stage and she suggests that a variety of shapes are desirable. There is no suggestion to make a realistic object, although some of the children will try to make objects they have in mind.

(In a second grade.) After our trip to the general post office last week, the room was buzzing with plans for our unit. Our project was to make a "movie" with paintings and a story—like the old silent movies. In my motivation, I was conscious of the need for some logical continuity in the story and accuracy as well as interest in the ideas chosen. But I didn't want to impose my ideas of what was most interesting.

The teacher is aware of the value of having children choose their own ideas within the framework of the general subject. She reports this verbatim discussion as motivation:

Teacher: Can you recall some of the things you saw at the general post office that you think would make a good scene in our movie?
Tammy: I liked the package hospital.
Teacher: Yes, I was surprised to see it too. What went on there?
Tammy: All the packages with their insides coming out were getting stuck together again.
Teacher: How could you show what the men were doing?
Tammy: Well, the broken packages were higgledy-piggledy (giggling) on one side. And a shoe sticking out. The fixed ones were all piled up nice. The man had lots and lots of string.
Teacher: You have many good ideas for your picture. All the different shapes for the packages. Some neat and some every which way. That should make a good design. And you have the postal clerks working in your picture.

The teacher helps Tammy visualize the scene with greater detail and points out the possibilities of shapes and people in action. She also shares her own interest in the topic as well as letting the children know that she too learned something new on their trip. She continues:

Teacher: Who has another idea?
Jerry: The machinery.
Teacher: What was it used for?
Jerry: Move the big boxes.

The teacher is now aware that Jerry is thinking of the long series of rollers used for moving boxes of mail. She tries to have a
rather nonverbal Jerry visualize the patterns made by the machinery which caught his interest.

Teacher: Do you mean all those rollers moving the boxes of mail?
(Jerry nods.) Where were the rollers? On the floor? Where?
Jerry: Yes. No. Some way up. Some go zoom inna chute.
Teacher: Jerry, you have a good idea of different places where the
roller machinery goes. It would be exciting if your picture showed
the mail boxes zooming into the chute.

The foregoing excerpts from her log illustrate clearly how the
teacher, through her questioning, helps children realize their purposes through their choice of subjects. In addition, she leads them
to sharpen their mental images. As an important part of her motivation she shows enthusiasm and pleasure in their joint experience. This last factor, personal involvement of the teacher, is the
most significant one in guiding creative development in children.

Caution. There is, however, a temptation to talk out all the
ideas because the teacher feels excited by the responses he finds
in the discussion of a vital joint experience. After half a dozen different ideas, with emphasis on differences, clarity of detail, and
emotional significance of the idea, one needs to cut the talk and
move the children to action.

Moving into action

At this point, the teacher needs to supervise the selection of
materials and the agreed upon working rules as required—but
without nagging. If the organization has been good and the motivation effective, the children will take over. What, then, does the
teacher do?

In replies to the incomplete sentence, "When the children
start working on their art projects I . . . ," a number of student
teachers express feelings of uncertainty, saying:

I don't know *what* to do next.
I feel like a fifth wheel with my cooperating teacher watching me
from her desk.

These replies reflect the feeling of being left out which comes when children are deeply involved with bringing their own form to their own ideas—when children are creating. What can the teacher do in this period?

When children have begun to work, the teacher circulates among them and observes how they are progressing, if their ideas are being carried out, and if they are frustrated by their limitations in ideas or process skills. From these observations he can help children through relevant and selective assistance. Knowing a particular child, the teacher leads him to raise his own standards and offers a desired, but unknown, procedure when it is needed.

Even in a program emphasizing creative teaching and creative learning, there is room for direct demonstration by the teacher. It can properly be used to demonstrate a procedure needed by a child to fulfill his intention in his art expression. Using wire to trim clay and using *slip* (mayonnaise consistency clay) to join parts of animals, people, or objects are typical illustrations. Directions for slow drying of clay work on thin cardboard or paper (to allow for shrinkage) is still another. They are taught by direct domonstration without in any way interfering with the creative process. In this way, procedures can then help children raise their creative expression to a higher level.

Evaluation

In the tangle of views, emotions, and principles which surround the element of evaluation in art, it is not easy for teachers to find a path for themselves. Professional opinions on the subject often support contradictory recommendations. Some of the confusion arises from purely semantic differences. In some cases, evaluation is heavily burdened with an aspect of criticism. In others, evaluation is discussed from the angle of constructive appreciation. It is no wonder, then, that teachers find difficulty in determining what their role should be in the evaluation of children's art.

In a questionnaire on attitude regarding the teacher's role in evaluating children's art, responses from 100 novice teachers, half in early childhood education and half in elementary education, indicate views which may have some relevance to problems in creative teaching in art. A substantial majority, 85%, believe that the teacher should accept favorably all of a child's art, while 12% believe that the favorable acceptance by the teacher should be given only to work which shows real effort by a child. Only 3% are not sure of their views.

In another question dealing with the teacher's policy in displaying children's art work, there is a similar response: large majority support for unconditional display (and implied acceptance) with some indication by the minority that the display of only "good" work will have a positive effect in improving children's art expression.

On both these points of acceptance and display there is only a slight difference between the early childhood and the elementary teachers, with the former showing a slightly higher score of acceptance. However, in the matter of a teacher's criticism of children's art work, there is a greater difference of opinion between these two groups. The early childhood group strongly supports the view that teachers should point out *only* good points in a child's work. The elementary group strongly supports the view that teachers should point out *both* the good and the bad features in a child's work. This difference is quite likely due to the fact that early childhood teachers tend to be more child-oriented, while elementary teachers tend to be more subject-oriented.

Some highly experienced teachers take the view, particularly with regard to young children, that no evaluative comments should ever be made about children's art work. They imply that such comments tend to direct children's attention toward pleasing the authority figure rather than toward their own art expression. Others take the position that evaluation should come only during the working process, when it can constructively influence the child's work. They claim that evaluation *after* completion of a product is unfair because nothing can be done to change what must, then, be considered the best work that the child was capable of at that time. Still another concept regarding evaluation claims that it must come after a product is finished in order to avoid influencing a child's work by adult standards.

General agreement exists among authorities that young children, in the primary grades, should not participate in evaluation of their classmates' products as part of the art program. Some would extend this limitation to include all elementary age children. Others point out the values of having this older group participate in group evaluation sessions under the careful guidance of the teacher, in order to insure protection of the feelings of children and to accomplish the benefits inherent in constructive evaluation of children's art expression. Novice teachers are exposed to these varying points of view in their reading, in their class discussions, and in their field experiences in elementary schools. Naturally, they try to develop a framework for themselves which can guide them in developing their own style of teaching.

In trying to formulate their own behavior, teachers find no difficulty in appreciating children's art when it meets standards which seem appropriate to them. But they are genuinely disturbed in trying to decide how to respond when children's art work is, to them, of questionable quality.

In discussing their classroom experiences with children, teachers reveal their concerns about how to evaluate or react to their art:

After a while it doesn't seem to mean anything when I tell each child his clay piece is "lovely." And I sound like a record with a stuck needle.

How can I honestly comment on those pictures? I don't know what they're all about. But I was told *never* to ask, "What is it?" Why not?

They show concern about their role in helping children make progress in their work, as implied in the following:

Is it right to tell a child to go back and fill up the empty spaces in his painting?

If you hang up any old thing, how does that help children care about good art?

If you never show children how to improve their work, how will they learn?

Novice teachers find it difficult to reconcile the injunction not to interfere with children's creative expression with the idea that teachers are responsible for helping children improve and grow in art, as well as in any other curriculum area making up the educational experience of children.

Climate for creative evaluation. Is there any way to reconcile noninterference with help, while building a climate of honesty with acceptance—a climate of creative evaluation? This is a tall order for a teacher. But it is not impossible. Let us assume that the children are actually doing the best they can in an art activity. When the specific job is done, evaluation can be made either on an individual or a group basis. But the keynote for any evaluation is: *accentuate the positive.*

Principles of art. Through a studied and continuous evaluation by the teacher and eventually, in the upper elementary grades, by the children, emphasis will be placed on examples of work that meet various criteria of art. These principles can and should be stated in language appropriate to the children's age at the same time as the examples are commented upon. Evaluation that is honest, accepting, and positive might sound like this:

Your papier-mâché mask has strong colors which help to bring out the strong lines of those high cheek bones. Bold colors certainly do call attention to important parts.

Your clay piece looks solid with the heavy shape on the bottom. This strong indented part swings beautifully around the base and to the top. Clay has a settling character which is used to good advantage in your piece. The curve is strong and simple. Simple shapes are often very beautiful.

Your mobile moves round and round. This big part on one side balances these small parts on the other side. It's interesting when some things are big and some are little.

The corner where you used your knuckles on the finger paint has a feeling of many things swooping together. When lines move the same way, they can make a rhythm that we like.

The above comments relate principles of art to children's work. They refer to dominant areas, balance in shape, balance in size variation, rhythm, textural contrast, and simplicity. Other comments may be made to call attention to one idea clearly stated, a center of interest, symmetrical and nonsymmetrical balance, balance in color values, contrasts through color, line, or shape, contrast through movement, and originality in use of materials.

All factors will, of course, not be present in every art product. But commenting on any one of them, even if it refers to only one part of the product, has a positive effect in building confidence in the maker. There has been no interference or distortion of a child's intention; there has been a climate of psychological safety and acceptance for children and their work; there has been an effort to increase children's knowledge and appreciation of art principles. There has been creative teaching applied to art evaluation.

Maintaining integrity. But what about the teacher who finds none of these qualities in children's work? This is not infrequent in the work of younger children in kindergarten and first grade, particularly when they are still in the manipulative or symbolic stage. How can a teacher react honestly?

He can react to the *intention* or *process* of the child as he perceives it. First of all, not every piece of work requires a verbal statement. Sometimes just a look or smile or nod will suffice. One may comment that today's colors are different from yesterday's; that you hope he enjoyed making his fingerpainting; that he used many interesting colors. Or, one may ask if he noticed how the color changed when two paints mixed together at one spot.

Particularly when children are at the symbolic stage, one may ask if the child wishes to tell anything about his art expression. If he chooses to reveal anything about it, the adult will then have a cue for an appropriate response. With older children whose work lacks artistic qualities, the teacher may react by saying: "We need to find a way to help you become freer in your designs." Thus, instead of commending inferior work or criticizing negatively, the teacher opens a door to the possibility of improvement for which he, too, assumes some responsibility.

It may be advisable to introduce a new medium that can be manipulated freely while exploring the characteristics of the material. Fingerpainting is particularly useful in this way because it requires little technical skill, responds easily, and can be continuously changed until a more satisfying pattern emerges. Collage work can serve a similar purpose because many arrangements of texture, form, and color can be tried before the pattern is fixed. The teacher can make it a point to offer guidance during the work period as described in a previous section.

When, however, a child's work is clearly regressive or shows lack of involvement, the problem ceases to be rooted in the curriculum area of art. It is now a problem of the child which happens to reveal itself in his behavior during an art activity. Rather than evaluating the child's art product, the teacher must now be concerned wih evaluating the child's behavior in an attempt to understand the causes of the child's low-level functioning.

THE CHALLENGE

Every area of life and, for the child and teacher, every area of the curriculum, is open to creative learning. In principle, schools can do much to further educational experiences that are potentially creative for children, that will lead to personal integration, that will encourage them toward maturity. Yes, schools *can* foster education of this quality. The question is whether school programs, heavily weighted in the direction of repetitive rather than creative learning, are, in fact, crushing the integrating and maturing processes required of them.

One of the strongest indictments of schools on this point comes from a thought-provoking analysis by Lawrence Kubie which relates the educative process to the neurotic process:[K7]

In this tangled interweaving of the processes of learning and the neurotic process, repetition plays a major role. By imperceptible gradations, the repetitive drills of the learning process shade over into the automatic involuntary repetitions of the neurosis . . . (resulting) in an imprisoning of all freely creative preconscious functions.

Instead of intensifying the neurotic process in education as described above, it is necessary to introduce a kind of therapeutic experience which can come only by increasing self-knowledge on the part of the learner. Self-knowledge, of course, is one of the essential ingredients of maturity. Maturity, unquestionably one of the goals of the education enterprise, "requires the capacity to change, to become different, to react in varied and unanticipated ways." [K7:18] These capacities also describe creativity.

Of the many components common to the creative experience, those which most dramatically capture its quality are: (1) the intense encounter and (2) the integrative power of the creative event. In describing persons engaged in a creative experience, one uses words which try to capture the intensity of attention, the high energy level, the acute interest, the absorption, the single-mindedness, the drive, the person oblivious to outside distraction. There is intense excitement—elation. Ideas gush forth; images spring up; plans sing; movements flow freely; paints dance freely; words pour freely. The intuitive and emotional strands take hold. The creative experience is compelling and joyous.

In the creative encounter, one is caught up in the brilliant clarity of the moment. One is whole, unified, core-centered. At the peak of the creative event, one encompasses the dimensions of existence simultaneously—integrated in oneself and in the world.

For the teacher who wishes to taste and eventually to savor the excitement of creative teaching, the curriculum fields of music, dance, and art hold a unique promise. Creativity and the arts are at home with each other. The arts fling open the door to embrace creative teaching for creative learning. They belong. Let twelve year old Abbey speak for us:

Alone To Create

It was like walking into nothing
Whirling into an emptiness of everything
A blank sheet upon which to write.
You were there with everyone—yet no one
No one to discourage; no one to correct;
No one to question your heart.
Alone to dance out limitless joys and sorrows,
Fury and anguish.
Alone to create.

Abbey, age 12

III

The educating agents

10

Relations with children

The data collected in this study suggest that a most important factor determining whether the elementary school teacher will move forward toward creative teaching, or seek the security of the repetitive mode of behavior, is his relations with children. It is the purpose of this chapter to examine these relations with emphasis on their impact on the repetitive-creative conflict experienced by the novice teacher.

THE DEDICATED AND PSYCHOLOGICAL TEACHER

As reported by various investigators,[F4] the most important factor influencing the career choice of prospective teachers is their desire to work with children. They love children and they want to be loved by them. Research [D1] points out that children's reaction is the most significant source of satisfaction or stress in the work of teachers. They are pleased, or even excited, when they see that the children are responding to their presentation and grasp the idea. They are rewarded when children show signs of affection: "We like you"; "You are the best teacher we ever had, please don't leave us."

The significance of the reward of teaching children is clearly seen in the responses of the group to a test composed of incomplete sentences. The following are some illustrations:

It is most rewarding to see . . . children anxious to respond.

. . . children's eyes light up because of something you showed them.

A good teacher wants . . . children to learn well and like her.

The most fascinating thing about teaching is . . . the response you get from children.

Not one of the novice teachers has said: "The most fascinating thing about teaching is . . . the opportunity to develop new ideas and methodology." No one spoke about the reward of teaching as an opportunity to get more knowledge, to be challenged by colleagues, or about possible economic advantages for women. The emphasis was rather on the interaction between the teacher and the child, with specific emphasis on the child as he responds to the teacher as a person. As perceived by this group of beginning teachers, "responding" and "liking" are synonymous terms. It means: "They learn because they like me."

The same primary concern can be seen in the logs written by the teachers. The stress is on the need to serve, give, and love.

Children are children anywhere! Intelligence, the color of one's skin, religion, or sex have never been separated into defined categories. My inner emotions of interest, warmth, love, understanding, and the need to do something valuable for children has always been part of me in preparation for my teaching career.

It is not the kind of youngster you are dealing with which is the determining factor. It is more than this. It is what is in *you* which either builds or shatters the rapport that is most essential when dealing with any child.

It can be said that on the professed verbal level at least, the major characteristic of this group cannot be defined in terms of a social cause or a dedication to a specific discipline of knowledge, but rather in terms of devotion to children. The desire to give to children and be appreciated by children is a dynamic force which tends to motivate the novice teacher to work many hours into the night, to be experimental, and to attempt to be creative.

In their attempt to reach children, the majority of teachers report many successful ventures in individualizing instruction.

Then there is Michael who never had much to look forward to as far as school was concerned. All it took on my part was some extra encouragement in individual work and an interest in him that made him become part of the group. I am all the richer when I see his eyes shine, his face light up, and his hand wave—only too eager to participate in a class lesson.

Their attempts in reaching individual children are often successful, even with deprived lower-class children. The underprivileged child belonging to a minority ethnic group often develops a shell of toughness, aloofness, and noninvolvement. This shell creates a barrier between the child and the education agent of the dominant white and middle-class society.

It is these victims of the clash of cultures and ethnic conflict whom these young teachers attempt to reach (in the psychological sense).

I know these children are underprivileged. I learned that the children are given beatings at home frequently and brutally. They are small and helpless in a big, cold, hard world. I wanted to make these children feel happy and secure. I wanted to ease their suffering as much as I could.

The following incomplete sentences portray a teacher who stresses the importance of understanding lower-class children and their value system:

Classes of children of lower-class origin . . . need extra understanding.

. . . should be taught by the middle-class teacher who must always remember their somewhat different values.

A prevalent response to the same item is that the one who reaches these children is highly rewarded:

Classes of children of lower-class origin . . . admire the teacher greatly, sometimes even more than middle-class children.

. . . can be a rewarding experience to the successful teacher.

The descriptions in the logs of the teachers' experiences reveal that in many cases the individual attention and readiness to accept and provide individualized work help penetrate the ethnic barrier. Under these conditions, the child of a minority group may be ready for the first time to come out of his shell and stretch his hand toward the creation of contact.

Little Debbie (a Negro child), who was always passive and non-demonstrative, kissed me, presented the class letters to me, and said, "I'll miss you when you leave." Pat's enthusiasm in reading was brought to my attention every morning when she would run to me and say: "Don't you want to hear me read today?—I finished another book." She had previously been a nonreader.

This mission to love and give generates not only individualized work with children, but also a sincere attempt to *know* children and understand the dynamics of their behavior.

Both the logs and the incomplete sentences demonstrate that the professional ego ideal of the novice teacher is a psychologically-oriented practitioner who is sensitive to mental health problems. Unstructured logs, where the young teachers are free to discuss topics of interest to them, are full of case studies and anecdotal records which describe the dynamics of children's behavior in the classroom, and which attempt to analyze their home and community background. These writings indicate a strong interest in the psychological analysis of the dynamics underlying the behavior of children with emotional and learning difficulties. The interest is not only in the degree of subject matter proficiency gained, but also in the total emotional and social adjustment of the child.

The professional ego ideal of a psychologically-oriented practitioner sensitive to the needs of children is strongly projected in the incomplete sentences. It can be seen in the following illustrations:

A withdrawn child . . . will often respond to a teacher who has insight into his behavior.

Children who don't learn . . . often have emotional problems.

Children who cling . . . lack security.

The kind of teacher I would most like to be . . . is one who understands and takes a special interest in every individual pupil.

When children don't listen . . . it is time for the teacher to examine her knowledge of the class, her attitude toward the class, and her method of teaching.

It is interesting to note that in responding to an item which deals with the predicted difficulties in the first year on the job, a prevalent reaction is the inability to reach all the children:

The thing I will have to struggle with most in my first year of teaching . . . is the realization that there are some children I'll never be able to reach.

In 1928 Wickman [W5] submitted a list of examples of problem behavior to teachers and psychologists and asked them to classify them from the most to the least serious. It was found that teachers and mental hygienists differed greatly in what they classified as undesirable behavior. The teachers tended to consider violations of classroom order, dishonesties, and immoralities as more serious than recessive and withdrawing personality traits, while the opposite was true of the mental hygienists. The inference of the study is that teachers are more concerned with behavior which interferes with their work than with the nature or degree of maladjustment of the child.

A recent repetition of Wickman's study by Stoffer, [S20] as well as the data collected in the present study with novice teachers, suggests that within the last several decades teachers moved in the direction of becoming more psychologically oriented.

As stated before, the psychologically oriented teacher is eager to work closely with children and is motivated by her affection for them. The promise inherent in this type of motivation has been discussed at length in educational literature by both theorists and practitioners. However, little has been said with regard to the danger involved in it.

The overemphasis on, "I like these children and therefore I want to teach them," also has a negative corollary: "I don't like these children and, therefore, I don't feel like teaching them." They often overlook the possibility that the act of teaching can be done in a less favorable climate of interrelationships. Teaching must continue regardless of subjective negative feelings toward a certain pupil, and regardless of occasional failure to maintain emotional communication with children.

This setting of emotional understanding and affection between learner and teacher as a condition to teaching can also be observed in children. They often set the condition of "liking the teacher" as a prerequisite to learning. Children often talk about wanting to learn from the teacher because they like her, or of being resistant to learning because they dislike her.

While a relationship of animosity and extreme distance is undoubtedly a deterrent to the teaching-learning process, it does not necessarily follow that a child must like a teacher in order to learn from her. Children must learn to continue the process of learning and growth even if the wind blows cold at times. The teacher must go on teaching even when the rewards of emotional closeness and warmth are occasionally absent. It is suspected that children's sensitivity to teachers' feelings for them and their dependency on affection as a condition for learning is probably related to teachers' inability to sometimes keep the functions of love and work somewhat separate in their own attitudes.

Teachers' need to like children and be liked by them is particularly strong with beginning teachers. They need to be more realistic and objective in their goals and attitudes, and recognize that one cannot always like a class or like every single child in the class. The teacher cannot expect to create a personal contact with every pupil or give of her own person incessantly. In spite of this, the teaching process must go on.

In an address to a group of young teachers, Rosenzweig [R4:6] says:

> We must not confuse loving them with teaching them . . . As humans, teachers need love and affection and understanding. As humans, they are subject to the same slings and arrows of misfortune as are other people. As a result some may need the love of children beyond that which is normal . . . You will be loved and respected by your children if you avoid the trap of seeking their love as an end in itself.

THE SLOW LEARNER

Even in the incomplete sentences, one can observe a difference in attitudes in the reaction toward the bright versus the slow learner. Examine the following reactions:

Slow learners . . . need special attention.

. . . have to be studied for possible causes.

. . . are difficult to work with.

The young teacher recognizes the difficulty in working with the slow learner, and notes his special educational needs. However, almost nowhere do the responses to the incomplete sentences indicate that the slow learner is a pleasure or a challenge to the intellectual curiosity and ingenuity of the teacher. In contrast, look at the reactions toward the bright child:

Bright students . . . are a challenge to the teacher.

. . . stimulate my thinking.

. . . are a pleasure to teach.

The novice teachers accept the values of the educational culture which call for study and understanding of the slow learner. However, their "real love" is the academically-minded bright child. It is evident that the slow learner is a source of frustration in the life of the novice.

I noticed in my own college class that when a teacher relates her experience to the group by saying, "I work with a fourth grade; they are slow learners," too often the reaction is short laughter. I stopped many times to ask for the reasons underlying this laughter. After some evasive remarks, many teachers admitted that the laughter was an expression of their identification with the frustrations, or even futility, their colleagues must be experiencing in working with slow learners. They perceive the work with the slow learner as a hindrance to the teaching process. As one group member presented it:

With slow learners, you cannot concentrate on teaching, but rather *flit* around.

Despite their psychological orientation, despite their verbal acceptance of the concept of individual differences, and despite many successful attempts in providing for individual differences, the novice teacher finds it difficult to fully accept those individuals who deviate from the average in their academic ability.

It should be clearly stated that the majority of slow readers (the difficulty bothering teachers most) are not remedial problems. They simply operate in terms of their ability, which is lower than the average norm. However, whether the slowness results from lack of potential, or is a product of cultural deprivation and emotional and psychological difficulties, the fact is that the slow learners compose an important segment of the school population. With the improvement of reading instruction, both slow and bright learners will gain higher "scores." The "average" will be higher. But the statistical reality inherent in the "average" (median) concept is that 50% are always below the norm in the average. Many of these will be regarded as slow learners.

The data collected in this study help us understand why many teachers have difficulty in fully accepting the slow learner as an equal and worthy member of the school community. It seems that the teaching of the slow child is at variance with some of the basic motivation which brings teachers into the profession: the desire to teach, that is, to transmit knowledge. The basic dimension of the teacher's role is to communicate information. The successful fulfillment of this role is easier, and progress is more evident, in working with the bright rather than the slow learner.

The logs show that the involvement of teachers with the transmission of knowledge is only second in its importance to their involvement with children. The incomplete sentences point out that the novice finds it "most rewarding to see children anxious to learn and respond." On the other hand, "The most exasperating aspect of teaching . . . is to teach a lesson and find that no one has gotten anything out of it." It is evident that it is the bright rather than the slow child who more fully satisfies the teacher's need to transmit knowledge. It is the slow child who tends to frustrate this need.

To illustrate, when I went to observe a class of slow learners a young teacher said to me: "They are the slowest group, 5-6. I want you to understand and have *sympathy* . . ." In other words, this teacher does not expect "to shine" in being able to teach much subject matter, and therefore, does not think she will be a "success." She feels defeated and looks for sympathy.

In discussing the bright child in their logs, some teachers mention the resemblance of this type of pupil to their own classroom behavior as students. They see themselves before their own eyes in observing children follow the route toward success that they have followed in earlier years, when they derived their status and sense of success mainly from their academic ability. They ranked in the upper quartile of the student population. They now find it difficult to teach and relate to the lower quartile. With slow learners they often lack "their own kind" and sometimes refer to the slow learners, in their logs, as "those children."

The difficulty of teaching the slow learner, which stems from an emphasis on a standard norm of achievement, the teacher's need for response, for transmitting knowledge, and for relating to his own image, is only accentuated by some realities of the school situation. The young teacher observes that some senior teachers do not adapt the curriculum to the ability of the slow learner, and consequently, observes boredom or even defiance in their classes. He notices that often the established veteran in the school is rewarded by getting the bright class, while the inexperienced newcomer gets the "dumping ground,"—the slow learner. He perceives the administration of the school and the board of education as dogmatic authorities which prescribe the same standard curriculum and norm of achievement to all children. (It should be noted that this perception is often inaccurate.)

An approach

An elaboration of a constructive approach to the teaching of the slow learner calls for the application of some of the basic principles of teaching to this problem.

As said before, most important is the attitude of the teacher. The intangibles of feelings are communicated to the child and deter or facilitate his learning development. The child senses whether the teacher believes that it pays to try, or whether it is useless; whether the teacher feels that it is worth teaching, or the job should be limited to "baby-sitting" and "policing." If the teacher feels the child cannot do it, why should the latter try?

In other words, a prerequisite to constructive work with the slow learner is a realistic acceptance of his academic performance and his ability to perceive and enjoy his relatively slower rate of academic development. The novice teacher who faces difficulties with slow learners should remember that these difficulties are not uncommon and that they do not necessarily imply failure on the part of the teacher. Giving up further attempts to try is inappropriate to this situation. Once a teacher can accept the rate of progress of the slow learner and is no longer defeated by his failure to respond to the teacher's perconceived idea of what progress should be like, she is then prepared to make curriculum adaptations to the level of comprehension of the slow learners in her class.

It has been fairly common practice for teachers to beam the level of classroom instruction at the average learner in the belief that they are thus helping the greatest possible number of children. This method dooms the slow-learning child to failure. The school has to provide every child with the opportunity to experience success and achieve a sense of accomplishment. Success furnishes the motivation for continuous search, exploration, and learning. Continuous failure results in despair—that is, lack of readiness to try. The slow learner will not learn unless he experiences success.

That fact is that even in a homogeneous class, children vary in their ability; some become the relatively "bright," and others— the relatively "slow." The reality of individual differences calls for the abandonment of the adherence to the grade standard theory, and its replacement by an attempt to individualize instruction. The conventional approach to teaching, where the teacher teaches the class as a whole, is gradually giving way to a more balanced approach based on: teaching the class as a whole, teaching small groups, and working with individuals.

The most pronounced expression of the educational belief in the need for adapting the curriculum to the ability of the learner is the movement of individualized reading. The attempt is to help each child, even if he is academically slow, to choose a book of interest to him, to progress at his own speed (without being exposed to class criticism), and to be taught individually in terms of his own learning deficiencies.

Under the optimal conditions of individualized reading, the slow learner does not have to shrink any more when a question is asked, or an assignment is given, as if saying by his physical gesture, "Don't call on me; I am not here." Individualized instruction is rather an attempt to give each child, including the slow learner, the confidence that the classroom is his place, because he can learn.

An integral aspect of the problem of individualizing instruction for the slow learner is the need for adaptation of printed materials. The present basic texts in reading and other subject areas are written on a readability level too difficult for the slow reader. The practice of exposing him to reading matter of lower grades commensurate with his reading skill often results in a reading diet which is too limited, or even "babyish" in terms of his experiential age.

There is a need for more high interest–low reading level materials both in reading and the other subject areas. Much progress in this direction has been made within the last few years with the publication of literature and science books for the beginning reader.

In spite of the insufficient reading materials for the slow reader (especially in the area of social studies), it can be said that in the better school systems the reliance on one text for all children is giving way to a more individualized approach. The latter utilizes a variety of texts and supplementary materials to meet the need of the reading and comprehension ability of each child —bright or slow.

An integral aspect of the problem of adapting the curriculum to the slow learner is the need to utilize a variety of instructional approaches. Traditionally, the major method of instruction was, and to a great extent still is, the recitation based on reading a text. The slow child not endowed with a high reading and verbal ability, or with facility in creating abstract concepts and generalizations, is often left behind when he is required to learn new material by the method of reading-recitation alone.

There is a need for more emphasis on concrete and visual materials; for more emphasis on presenting the subject matter in a functional setting, on doing things in addition to speaking about them. Examples are making map models in order to learn geography, or making toys with dry cell batteries in order to learn about electricity.

The question pertaining to the child's need to do and experiment with things rather than deal with them on the verbal level alone, raises a controversial issue basic to this study: Is an A-centered classroom atmosphere more beneficial to the academic growth of the slow learner, or would the slow learner do better in a C-centered type of classroom? Or, putting it differently: even if one admits the need for more emphasis on a C-oriented curriculum, isn't this approach too dangerous when it comes to the slow learner?

There is a disagreement among the teachers under discussion here about the impact of the *A* versus *C* approaches on the slow learner. Those who support the *A* orientation make the following observations and arguments:

The *A* approach means security and sureness—conditions highly desirable for the slow child. He needs routine and routinized teaching. He needs to be asked specific factual and short-range questions. He cannot play with facts; he can only repeat them. He cannot learn that an arithmetic problem can be solved in different ways, but should rather learn and drill the one most economical way. He cannot initiate a long-range project and work on it independently, but learns through getting instructions and following specific directions. In brief, the slow learner will be lost in a *C*-oriented classroom.

Those teachers who believe in the need for more emphasis on the *C* orientation of creativity and discovery are appalled by the dreary atmosphere of "busy work" that the *A*-centeredness too often generates. They report that in some extreme cases teachers do not plan celebrations, musical events, science fairs, or class bulletins with the slow learner and justify it by their desire "not to break the routines for these children." They observe that school experimentation with new curricular media is delegated primarily to the classes of the bright learners. It is the room of the latter which is well decorated, full of library books, exhibits, and so on, while the walls of the classes of the slow learner are in some cases bare. Some teachers operate under the misconception that work with the slow learner does not call for rich stimulation.

It is interesting to note in this connection that some curricular innovations, such as core curriculum and individualized reading, originally evolved, at least in part, as an attempt to help the slow learner. However, in my observation these curricular practices were adapted and became prevalent in working with the bright, and in contrast are less commonly used in working with the slow.

One of the characteristics of the slow learner's approach to learning is his low level of motivation. The *C* orientation, which emphasizes exploration, self-initiative and use of the subject matter skills in a functional setting, is not only instrumental in fostering a richer person, but is also a great source of motivation for the slow learner.

To conclude, the slow learner needs a good balance of educational activities in terms of the A and C orientations. The A orientation is useful in generating security, success, and opportunity for drill. The C approach is important in releasing initiative, raising level of motivation, and creating more personally meaningful learning. At present, in the practice of teaching slow learners, the balance is extremely skewed in the direction of the A orientation.

As Rosenzweig says in discussing the slow learner:[R5:6]

He is meeting his own time table and is growing according to a schedule dictated by his own physique, as different as they may be. He is not meeting the time table that we wish he would follow or that we have come to expect.

Perhaps the secret of success in working with the slow learner is helping him meet his own time table; not pushing him to achieve the unattainable and not underestimating his potential for growth.

THE AGGRESSIVE CHILD

Whereas novice teachers generally identify with the problems of the "quiet one," they find it more difficult to accept the aggressive child. The latter is often discussed by novice teachers in terms of the irritation and insecurity his behavior arouses in them.

The logs of teachers show that the behavior of the aggressive child is perceived by the novice as a direct threat to her position in the class. It threatens some of the most sensitive and vulnerable areas of functioning—their need to maintain control, and their struggles around the setting of constructive limits.

The behavior of the aggressive child is contagious and must be stopped before it generates total class disruption and a climate of low morale.

Wickman,[W5] in the previously mentioned study, did not realize that teachers *must* differ from psychologists in their evaluation of children's problems. The psychologist may sometimes perceive the hostility directed toward him as a phase of transference, that is, the beginning of growth in therapy. In a classroom situation, it is most difficult to tolerate these expressions of hostility, even if in some cases they constitute a phase of the individual's growth. Aggressive behavior interferes with the accomplishment of the teacher's basic objective—the transmission of knowledge.

Another factor underlying the relative difficulty in relating to the aggressive child is the fact that the group of teachers under discussion is composed of young women. In the role definition assigned to the sexes by our culture, aggression is usually associated with males. Femininity is at variance with direct aggression. (This point accentuates the great need for male teachers to balance the female-centered school.) Illustrations can be brought from some responses to the incomplete sentences:

The best kind of student is . . . the one who pays attention and does his work.

Compared with boys, girls are . . . easier to control.

The kind of boy I like best . . . is the one who is a good student, well-behaved, may be a little mischievous, but never out of hand.

The kind of girl I like best . . . is the one who pays attention and does her work.

. . . is a neat girl who has good manners and pays attention in class.

. . . is the girl who behaves like a little lady.

The picture of the ideal child portrayed in the responses to the above items is well delineated. The adjectives used are relatively limited in number and variety, and point to an emphasis on attentiveness to the teacher, and compliance with work assigned, as the main characteristics of good behavior. The teachers sense that this role is too docile for the boy and, therefore, permit him to be "a little mischievous" sometimes.

Whether the child is earthy and real, whether the child is creative and energetic, whether the learner relates intrinsically to subject matter, whether the student has deep feelings and convictions, does not seem to play a major role in the teacher's thinking. The emphasis is rather on the external manifestations of compliance to the teacher, that is, the eradication of aggressive elements of behavior.

The image of the ideal child has a direct impact on the teaching behavior of the novice teacher; it dictates the norms of behavior which the teacher fosters in the classroom. Two illustrations will be brought out here. In one fourth grade, the following chart hangs on the wall:

Manners

We say thank you.
We say please.
We don't interrupt or tease.
We don't argue.
We don't fuss.
We listen when folks talk to us.

In another fourth grade, a teacher developed a chart enumerating values of good behavior:

I Am a Good Student

1. I raise my hand before I speak.
2. I do not leave my seat without permission.
3. I do not speak out.
4. I walk quietly.
5. I do my work quietly.
6. I am always on time.

The inexperienced and insecure beginning teacher is subverted by his perception of the basic need of his profession—control and compliance, by his desire for oiled and lubricated relations with children, and by his fear of conflict. These dynamics contribute toward a limited conception of what a child should be and, in the long run, contribute toward a narrow conception of what a person should be.

Some novice teachers find it difficult to look objectively at the dynamics underlying the behavior of aggression and anger. D'Evelyn points out that the aggressive child is both fearful and angry. "He is afraid of not being acceptable and he is angry being denied this acceptance." [D6:60] The angry child may want to hurt others as he feels they have hurt him. He strikes out in angry behavior, failing to realize that his behavior gets in the way of being accepted.

The logs reveal that some of the teachers feel so hurt and angry by the actions of the aggressive child that they find it most difficult to attempt to come close to him. Rather than move in the direction of close contact, the reaction of some young teachers is to withdraw into formal relations of group teaching, aloofness, and commanding behavior. A vicious circle is created here. A fearful child who may be craving for acceptance strikes at the teacher, and a fearful teacher who wants to share, withdraws or even strikes back.

A major step in working with the aggressive child is setting firm limits. However, this is only one step. The teacher must communicate to the child the feeling that he is wanted and that he could be accepted as a member of the group. It is easier for the child to accept limits from people who like him, rather than from teachers who enhance, by their withdrawal, his experience of rejection.

Driscoll [D9] suggests that the aggressive child is often impulsive and wants what he wants when he wants it. He may be a child who has had repeated success in satisfying his desires by displays of temper or demandingness. He is not sure that the significant people in his environment have his interest at heart. This child may develop self-control and may gain security when he is guided by a teacher whom he respects and who he feels respects him.

The aggressive child acts out because his inner controls are not developed. It can be said that socially and emotionally he is a slow learner. The recognition of this factor may keep the novice teacher from becoming angry at the aggressive child, or feeling guilty and defeated when he has to repeat the stated limits with little or no apparent or immediate results. Exactly as the slow learner will make more mistakes and need more guidance in subject matter skills, the "behavioral" slow learner, that is, the aggressive child, will tend to err more and may need intensive guidance in the skill of social behavior.

Based on the understanding of the need for a relationship of mutual trust, and the recognition that the aggressive child is a slow learner in the area of social relations, the teacher should look for tangible measures both for dealing with the aggressive incident when it occurs and for preventing its further occurrence.

A variety of techniques can be utilized in dealing with aggressive behavior. They range from ignoring the incident, to humor, verbal appeal or reprimand, or removing a child from the situation. These techniques may be effective provided that underlying the teacher's action is a spirit of desire to help and a belief that the child can be helped.

Another step in handling aggressive behavior is an attempt to prevent it. Basic questions which call for diagnostic thinking and observation are: Why is the child aggressive? Under what conditions do aggressive incidents increase or decrease? To the extent that answers to these questions can be found in social relationships, curricula, or management of the classroom, they can be alleviated by better planning on behalf of the teacher.

To conclude, a comparison of the data collected by the use of the incomplete sentences, and the data found in the logs, suggests that a discrepancy exists between the professional ego ideal and some of the real classroom behavior of this group of young teachers. The professional ego ideal of an understanding and nonpunitive teacher-psychologist does not stand the trial it is subjected to by the aggressive child. This is especially correct when the behavior of the aggressive child is contagious and the whole class becomes a *discipline problem*.

The desire to give to children and to be appreciated by children, the ideal of being an understanding teacher, motivates the novice teacher to work many long hours, to be experimental, and to attempt to be creative. The fear of the aggressive child, or broadly speaking, the fear of discipline problems in the classroom, presents a threat which tends to push the young teacher in a direction which is completely opposed to where she is trying to go. She turns to overstructured teaching and seeks the "safe" A orientation of repetitive teaching.

The relatedness of the novice teacher to the child in terms of attitudes and behavior is a product of the two opposing forces: the desire to love, give, come close to and reach, and the fear of being rejected and having discipline problems. This conflict of being torn between these two poles is revealed in many of the comments they make and questions they raise:

Should we start off very strict and then lighten up? In this way pupils will respect our authority.

Should we win the friendship of pupils first, so that later they will be glad to accept our demands and assignments?

Billy is a difficult child. I work with him individually with some success. Today he sent me a note asking me to be his mother. How *close* should I come to children?

The best advice for the young teacher—at the beginning—is, sit on them.

It is evident that a basic factor which determines whether the novice will move in the direction of the C orientation, or creativity, or the A overemphasis on specificity and routinized teaching, is the resolution of the conflict of discipline.

DISCIPLINE

The nightmare of a driver is maneuvering on a slippery, icy road; the nightmare of the teacher is maintaining discipline. This is especially true of those who are just entering the profession— novice teachers. Chats in the college corridor or formal discussions with the college instructor and senior teachers often boil down to one basic question: "Can I control my students?"

The teachers under discussion here have grown up and lived in relatively sheltered middle-class environments. They experienced some rude awakenings through teaching in lower-class communities. The contact, and sometimes even the clash, with these children became a source of strain and challenge to them, and the attainment of good discipline became the major criterion of success and adequacy in teaching. The criterion of discipline characterizes the responses to the incomplete sentences:

It is often easy to lose sight of . . . your main objectives because of discipline problems.

The most exasperating aspect of teaching . . . is to lose control of the class.

The thing I'll have to struggle with most in my first year of teaching . . . is to have complete control in the classroom.

The most valuable thing I learned from my cooperating teacher . . . is her approach to discipline.

It is easiest to teach when . . . the class is quiet.

Compared with boys, girls . . . are easier to control.

As seen from these typical illustrations, the criterion of discipline is the major category of response and the most frequent one. It overshadows the novice's interest in other basic values of education—understanding children, transmitting knowledge, developing thinking. As the incomplete sentences show, the preoccupation with discipline is often a deterrent to experimentation:

When given freedom, children . . . tend to respond positively. However, this freedom must be guided so that bedlam does not result.

Changing classroom routines . . . may lead to trouble, in some cases even chaos.

Introducing new ideas while being a student teacher in a class . . . will often upset the routines and is therefore dangerous.

The literature on the topic of discipline discusses different levels of interpretation of the meaning of discipline, from the more punitive and authoritarian approaches to the more self-directive and democratic practices.[14] However, when the novice teacher speaks about discipline, his interest is not only in how he should approach children, but also in the impact of this approach on himself as a person.

When beginning teachers freely open up and discuss their perceptions and experiences with discipline, the discussion tends to be charged with fear and anxiety. The cause of this particular emotional response does not have to do with methodology or logic; it stems from a much deeper level. It involves what the participants feel is a major threat to their self-concepts. The teacher is fully aware that when the class is not responding or is unruly, his feelings of adequacy as a teacher and a person are damaged. He feels hurt, depressed, and antagonistic. His bitterness and disillusionment may cause him to have one or more of the following thoughts:

What I have learned is of no use. It does not work.

It is academic and theoretical and would not work in my neighborhood.

The only thing these children understand is punishment.

You must develop routines and never break them.

Don't smile and don't try to be friendly in the first few weeks.

Novice teachers are confused about the nature of discipline. This confusion affects their cognitive awareness of disciplinary incidents, their actual behavior in the classroom, and their self-concepts as teachers. Young teachers are under the strong impact of a teacher education culture which fosters the image of the ideal teacher. They identify with the ego-ideal and aspire to reach it; that is, they want to become friendly, permissive, warm teachers who have excellent relations with children. The need to live up to this roseate expectation becomes a source of strain and confusion, some of the manifestations of which are evasion of, and inconsistency in, the treatment of disciplinary incidents. It is important in working with beginning teachers to help them explore their attitudes and expectations with regard to discipline and to help them understand the impact of disciplinary incidents on their teaching behavior.

Teachers look at discipline

The following analysis draws, to a great extent, on a report of a discussion by a group of novice teachers on the subject of their attitude toward discipline.[89]

At the beginning of the session a cartoon was shown to the group.[B5] The picture portrays three young children and a teacher. Two of the children are covered with paint. The third one says to the teacher, "But I *had* to paint him green, Miss Johnson —I used all the purple on Sally." [B5:3]

The class was instructed to react in writing to the following questions (one sentence for each): (1) How do the people involved feel, think, or what do they say, in the picture? (2) When Sally goes home, what will be her parents' reaction?

After completing the written reactions, the class discussed the cartoon. They discussed the fact that the cartoon was a projective technique, that the picture was open to interpretation, and that different persons might see different things in it. In other words, the reactions the teachers had to the cartoon were expressions of their own attitudes and perceptions. The realization of the deep ramifications of their own ideas of the meaning of the cartoon created an atmosphere of suspense and interest in the nature of the responses.

Reactions to Question One. Illustrations of the reactions to question one, which were read and put on the blackboard, follow:

The children express themselves, and the teacher observes with interest.

The teacher realizes that the action of the boy was just a childish misunderstanding of the use of art materials.

The three children feel fine. It is the teacher who is amazed.

The children in the picture appear to be uninhibited in the class of a permissive teacher.

The children who were painted do not seem to feel that any wrong has been done. The teacher knows it was a misunderstanding.

The child needs to explain his position to the teacher. The teacher will try to help him understand why this action is wrong, if she considers it wrong.

The group carefully studied the responses to the first question and found that they were dealing with two different attitudes toward the situation: the child's and the teacher's. The child expresses enjoyment in an uninhibited, naive way. The teacher expresses understanding and permissiveness and is surprised but definitely not angry.

It is interesting that no one regarded the boy's behavior as a disciplinary violation. It would seem that the need which the novice teachers had to idealize teaching and children interfered with their ability to diagnose unruly behavior.

Reactions to Question Two. Illustrations of the reactions to the second question are as follows:

They probably scold her for allowing the other child to spill the paint.

The parents will be angry because she is dirty.

They will initially react in a shocked manner.

They will blame her and afterwards condemn the teacher.

The class realized that their ideas of the prevalent perception of the parents were in great contrast to that of the teacher. The parent was seen as reacting with anger and punitiveness to the same incident to which the teacher reacted with "understanding."

Although the group was fully aware of the extreme contrast in their perceptions of the two adult figures, they found it relatively easy to suggest explanations, such as:

Parents lack understanding of children.

Teachers are much more objective.

Why cannot the parents understand that the poor child had an accident and spilled the paints?

Although nothing in the cartoon implied an accident, this perception was dictated by the strong need of the teachers to see the child as naive and the parents as lacking psychological understanding.

Reactions to Question Three. Attempting to make the incident described in the cartoon more real to the group of teachers, the instructor asked them to react in writing to a third question: "If you were the teacher in the cartoon situation, what would be your reactions?"

I would not know whether to laugh or scold the child.
Shock, then amusement, then anger.

I would find this answer amusing, but the thought of cleaning up and of the parents' reaction would change that.

What! Are you crazy?

In looking at these responses, the group recognized an important shift in their perception of teacher-child relations. The nature of this shift and why it occurred were the topics of the next discussion.

The answers to question three indicate that the teachers were no longer the totally permissive leaders indicated by their responses to the first two questions. The action of the child is not seen any more as "self expression," or "uninhibited" enjoyment, but rather as conduct often annoying and disturbing to the teacher. In other words, the teachers are starting to see the cartoon situation from a frame of reference which is much closer to their perceptions of the parents' reactions to question two. Questions one and three seem to elicit two different concepts of teaching because the questions are interpreted very differently by the novice teachers. Question one deals with the way teachers *should* act; question three deals with the way teachers *will* act. In the language of one of the teachers:

A teacher is expected to be idealistic. She is always supposed to be loving and permissive, to accept children for what they are. This ideal teacher we saw in question one. However, when you are in the situation yourself, it is different. You cannot avoid, at least sometimes, being angry or disciplining your class.

The difference between the ideal and the real teacher led to a lively discussion. It centered primarily on two points: the guilt which inability to live up to the ideal arouses in the beginning teacher and the inconsistency and arrest in leadership power which are corollaries of this guilt. Preservice education fosters in the young teacher idealistic attitudes of great positive force. It generates enthusiasm, thoughtfulness, readiness to experiment, and warmth. It is a shield against stagnation, apathy, and routine teaching.

However, this idealization has the negative effect of creating an illusion of what the teaching relations are. The novice teacher perceives those relations as a flow of love and affection, whereby a creative, warm, and permissive teacher enchants his students and has their complete attention. For instance, in responding to question one, no one perceived the act of pouring paint on two friends and the expression, "I had to paint him green . . . I used all the purple on Sally," as a disciplinary problem. The illusion the novice teacher has is that the master teacher, being sensitive to the felt needs and interests of children, never has friction and does not have to resort to authority. In their response to question two, the group's expectations of the parents' reaction to a disciplinary violation was rationalized as authoritarian behavior and lack of understanding.

The teachers realized that their illusions interfered with their ability to diagnose a classroom situation and to identify a child who had severe problems in accepting limits. They were preoccupied with what they thought the "educational culture" considered as good education and creative practices. In their preoccupation, they forgot to listen to their own personal judgment of what is right and what is wrong.

The disciplinary attitude

Young teachers operate under the pressure of a need to become "ideal teachers." The group was quick to realize that the expression of this need is not limited to confusions in perceptions of a teaching situation on a projective test, but is also expressed in teaching behavior. In the language of two of the teachers:

I lost control of the class. Nothing helped. I was very angry and I broke the ruler on the desk. They became quiet, but I felt like a heel.

I wanted to be their friend, to be nice, not authoritarian. After a rich experience I asked: "Now children, do you want to write a story?" They yelled "No!" and became wild.

Both anecdotes deal with the difficulty the novice teachers have had in asserting authority. In other words, in the teacher's mind assertion of authority is made synonomous with authoritarianism.

Underlying the guilt and self-deprecation experienced by the teacher in the first anecdote is the variance between the image of the ideal teacher who has "nice" relations with children and the bitter reality of having to assert her authority. Perhaps if the novice teacher were sure of her right to *demand* "discipline," the class relations would not have deteriorated. Perhaps if the novice teacher were sure of her right to be angry, her anger would not have exploded to the point of breaking a ruler.

In the second incident, it seems that on the surface the young teacher wanted to be democratic and let children make choices. However, the children sensed that underlying the informal, friendly, and democratic behavior was a reluctance and fear to assert authority.

In their anxiety to copy the image of the ideal teacher, the teachers fail to realize that there are two types of friendly relations with children, one stemming from strength and the other stemming from weakness and a need for "chumminess." The first fosters healthy relations, but the latter leads to unruly behavior.

The conflicts expressed by the beginner in attempting to establish leadership with children is clearly seen in the following paragraphs taken from a log:

When I talk to children and play with them, I enjoy them very much and I think they like me. However, I cannot seem to use this personal relationship as effectively in front of the class while teaching. Teaching demands more than the teacher being friendly. The teacher's role demands strength. A teacher must exert leadership without becoming cold and excluding the personal element.

I know these things intellectually but not really emotionally! Somehow I am very disinclined to use the power inherent in the teacher's role. . . How can you combine leadership and friendship? Is it possible?

The beginning teacher may need to develop a more realistic expectation of the problems involved in relating to children. The ego-ideal of a democratic, warm, informal, and permissive teacher is an oversimplification of the picture. As Ruth Cunningham points out, teachers who observers agree are most effective, use the widest range of patterns of leadership—adult rule to group-centered management. It is an oversimplification to assume that any teacher is always democratic in his approach to children, or that it is always desirable to be so. The teacher has a right to assert her authority, to demand respect, attention, and accomplishment.

Young teachers, in discussing the most bothersome problem —discipline—raise many "how-to-do-it" questions, such as:

Should I punish?
Should I send children to the principal?
Should I stop talking when the class is noisy?
Should I laugh with my children?
Are routines necessary?

The novice teacher, as most practitioners, is an action-oriented person. He looks for quick "action" solutions to a problem situation. The action approach to problem solution is deeply rooted in human behavior. Confronted with anxiety over speaking in public, one is told to memorize his lecture or to take a refreshing shower, rather than explore the dynamics underlying his anxiety. The common expression is, "What am I going to do about it?" rather than, "How am I going to understand it?"

No attempt is made here to imply that the action-oriented questions with regard to discipline are of no importance. Every activity in the classroom has its discipline ramifications: level of interest, and comprehension, physical surroundings, balance of activities, and teacher's voice. A comprehensive discussion of discipline must lead one to a discussion of teaching. *Discipline* in the broadest sense means teaching.

However, despite the importance of the actions concerning disciplinary incidents taken by teachers, these are only secondary in terms of their impact on children. The most important factor is the *attitude or expectation* of the teacher. To understand this point, an attempt will be made to examine the behavior of two teachers coping with the same task.

Two novice teachers invite their pupils to come close to a tank of water and observe a science experiment. One teacher does it in a routinized way: "Tiptoe, the first row, now the second row," and so on. The second teacher says: "Come over and watch the experiment." The common belief of teachers is that the first orderly teacher will not run into disciplinary problems, while the second one may lead to chaos. This belief is only partially correct.

The first teacher, by routinizing children, may have communicated the notion that she expected good behavior, but she may also have communicated a lack of trust in them. Furthermore, she may have partially stifled the children's spontaneous enthusiasm and curiosity in watching an experiment. This teacher, with young, docile children, may have "good discipline," that is, obedience, but she may be asking the children to pay a rather high price for it.

The behavior of the second teacher may be interpreted in two different and opposing ways: The first interpretation may be that he lacks foresight into the problem involved in pupils crowding around a tank of water to watch an experiment. The teacher lacks experience, is insecure, and perhaps is even so drained by the demanding task of developing the subject matter that he lacks the power to attend to class management. This teacher will probably run into disciplinary problems. He does not communicate the expectations of good discipline.

The second interpretation is very different. This teacher has a sense of power and confidence. He does not have to protect himself by the formal relations and the sense of distance created by routinizing children. He does not have to hide behind the shield of the overprotective leader who manipulates children to "tiptoe" by excessive use of praise: "Look at my sweet children, they behave like real grownups."

This teacher in his total personality communicates to children a businesslike atmosphere of important learning which is in the making, and should not be interfered with. He does not arrest the sponaneity or the thinking generated by the science experiment. He trusts children by permitting them a high degree of freedom of movement and action. However, behind his trust and informality is a sense of a person who definitely will not tolerate nonsense, who "means business." It is highly probable that this teacher will be successful in fostering an atmosphere of positive discipline.

Diagnostic thinking

In discussing discipline, the novice is prone to be preoccupied with the efficacy of various types of punishment, and to consider insufficiently the ways of working with pupils which may render punishment necessary to a lesser degree. Positive and constructive teaching is a prerequisite to good classroom management and discipline.

Studying the attitudes of teachers toward behavior problems, Stendler [818] compared the opinions of teachers on handling behavior problems with those of specialists in mental hygiene. The results show that the approach of studying the child in order to find the cause of his difficulty, as well as planning a course of action which fits his particular needs, was chosen by only fifteen percent of the teachers. This approach was chosen by all of the mental hygienists as the best solution to behavioral problems.

The comparison of the opinions of psychologists with those of teachers on ways of handling misbehavior tends to imply an equation of the role definition of both parties. This may be an erroneous equation. Very often, perhaps most of the time, teachers have to deal directly with the unruly behavior without studying or even looking into the specific causes. Studying the causes and developing a remedial plan of action is generally the second step. When problems occur, teachers need to treat the symptoms directly and immediately, but they must also give continuous thought to the analysis of causative factors, and deal with these causes as well. The primary concern should not only be with stopgap measures, but mainly with *diagnostic thinking* [R1] which determines the causes and develops plans for preventing further undesirable behavior.

The teachers under discussion were asked to report their observations of discipline problems in the classroom. An analysis of the reports shows that the observation consisted primarily of two elements: violations by children and the teacher's reaction to them. Missing was an attempt to search for the cause of the violation and explain the teacher's reaction in terms of this cause.

The neophyte is interested primarily in the teacher's immediate reaction and whether it does the trick of restoring obedience. He looks at the variety of possible responses and wonders which one is most helpful: ignoring the incident, removing the violator, treating him with humor, or sarcasm; appealing to group morale, punishment, etc. He looks for a definite criterion to help in deciding on the specific disciplinary measure.

When the novice teachers were sensitized to the fact that they were preoccupied with stopgap techniques rather than with remedial plans based on diagnostic thinking, they suggested several factors to explain their behavior: (1) The "head-on collision" between a teacher and an unruly class produces anxiety. It is the threat of the immediate reaction to this "collision" which registers primarily in the novice's mind. (2) After the disturbance is stopped, the classroom looks quiet and there is no need for further action. (3) In many cases, it is difficult to establish cause-and-effect relations and develop new plans which differ from the present patterns.

Movement toward a diagnostic thinking approach to disciplinary incidents was reported by the beginning teachers in a discussion, out of which some illustrations will be presented here.

One illustration deals with a complaint about restlessness in a nonEnglish-speaking first grade. Examination revealed that the class was generally passive and compliant, but became disruptive during oral discussion. The children's power of oral expression was limited and their voices were low. It was heard only by the teacher who used to stand close to the child who was speaking, but was barely heard and followed by other children. It would seem that in this class oral discussion should primarily have been conducted in small groups where the children would feel freer to express themselves, follow, and relate to each other.

A second illustration will be taken from the experience of a teacher with a bright class. This group started with an exciting discussion of a topic, but gradually reached the point of disintegration. Some students continued the discussion, while others started to look at their notes, books, etc.

It seems that some outspoken members of this group did not know the difference between discussing and being argumentative. The teacher, being excited about the fact that her class was dealing with controversy, failed to notice early enough that the discussion was turning into bickering. Work with these bright children on the function of debating, such as a discussion of major points versus trivialities, alleviated the problem.

The last illustration of diagnostic thinking is related to the common complaint that children who complete their work early become noisy and disruptive. When the novice teacher examined this question, she discovered that those children who completed their work then had to wait patiently while their papers were checked by the teacher. There were no provisions in this class for children to move on their own from one activity to another. Every step had to be dictated by the teacher. The teacher decided that the class needed training in self-directed activities.

Diagnostic thinking of classroom problems is a second habit for many experienced teachers. However, it has to be developed in the case of the novice. The latter is preoccupied with his lesson plan, his own security, or his need to get a response, and is not sufficiently tuned to the changing moods or attention span of the children. It takes him longer to recognize the signs of restlessness or even disruption, and to sense the need for shifting from one activity to another. He finds it more difficult to foresee difficulties and plan ahead.

The beginning teacher may find that continuous work on the following questions is helpful in promoting a diagnostic thinking approach to discipline problems: (1) What are the high points and low points of your teaching day in terms of discipline problems? (2) What are the factors responsible for the low versus the high points? (3) What could be done to prevent the low points?

Conclusion

In an article entitled "Better Curriculum—Better Discipline," Van Til [V1] observes that the number of discipline incidents in the classroom is related to the kind of job a teacher does in planning, motivating, and presenting the lesson. An intellectually stimulating curriculum and instruction based on knowledge of, and sensitivity to, the reactions of children will reduce the occurrence of discipline problems in the classroom.

There is no foolproof protection system which insures against discipline problems. Hymes [H14] points out correctly that learning discipline is as complex a task for children as learning spelling or reading. We do expect pupils to make mistakes in those subject matter areas. We do expect teachers to have to make corrections—that is, to teach. We do expect individual differences in children's rate of learning. The same can be said about learning discipline. Even under the most optimal conditions, the learner will make mistakes and need guidance. Individual differences among children will mean different rates of learning and different problems in teaching.

Different classroom activities call for different "disciplinary reactions" on behalf of children. When the teacher speaks to the class, children are expected to listen quietly. However, when the teacher asks children to look at the eye of their neighbor and discuss the major structure of the eye, it would be unrealistic not to expect some giggling. It would be erroneous to see this normal behavior as a violation. A quiet class is not always a positive objective.

The data collected in this study shows that, as perceived by the novice teacher, the fear of discipline problems is a major deterrent in creating a healthier balance between the A, B, and C ways of teaching. In explaining the discrepancy between their professional ego-ideal and their actual teaching behavior—"discipline" is first on the list.

Research shows that frustration is negatively related to creativity and experimentation. Lewin [L3] found that the impact of frustration on young children is a decrease in the originality in their use of materials and toys. My own work [87] with new immigrants illustrates that the acculturation tensions make the immigrant cling to the known symbols of the past and make him reluctant to try new modes of living. The same can be said about the impact of discipline problems on the beginning teacher.

Injured and harassed by a disciplinary crisis, the novice teacher becomes professionally, and sometimes personally, rigid. This rigidity is expressed in a reverse pattern: from a loving to a punitive attitude; from democratic to authoritarian behavior; and, perhaps most important, from an experimental approach of readiness and eagerness for new ideas to a dogmatic, disillusioned attitude that what counts is only fear, routine, and "busy work."

Curriculum improvement is dependent primarily on the growth of teachers, that is, on their enthusiasm and readiness to pioneer and experiment. If, too early in their careers, "occupational sclerosis" occurs in many of the novice teachers, the goal of a richer educational program will be very difficult to reach.

RELATING TO THE MINORITY GROUP
AND SOCIALLY DEPRIVED*

Well, I got assigned to a special service school. I was afraid I would. I don't know what I will do now. A teacher should be willing to teach any children, I guess. But, to be frank, I don't want to be there, and I know I should not feel this way. I want to teach, and I want to be in a school where children are interested in learning. Let's face it, in this school most of them won't be. I'll have to spend most of my time in discipline.

* The discussion in pages 277-283 is a digest of a study written by Dr. Watkins of Brooklyn College.[W2]

This novice teacher is white. She has grown up in a white world, and, in recent years, a world of middle-class comfort and affluence. She is teaching in a school located in a "black ghetto" dotted with families of recent newcomers from Puerto Rico. Both this teacher and her pupils live in New York City (it could be almost any large city), but they live in separate worlds—each wary and unsure of the other.

The fact that these separate worlds exist disturbs not only civil rights groups. It disturbs many, if not all, of the beginning teachers under discussion. They feel that the behavior, abilities, and cultural background of Negro, Puerto Rican, and other minority group children are inimical to the process of education as they understand it, and as they are prepared to participate in it as teachers. When one probes below the surface, as the discussion will attempt to do in this section, one finds that it is not that these teachers dislike minority group children. Rather, they fear that they will be unable to handle this assignment adequately, that they will *fail* when they enter this different world of, let us say, the Negroes or Puerto Ricans.

The dichotomy between what teachers will like and what they expect to find in such situations becomes vivid when one examines the images these young teachers have of the ethnic, or deprived child, and compares these with their images of white middle-class children.

Images of minority groups

As viewed by some novice teachers, many Negroes and Puerto Ricans are poor people living in filthy slums. Essentially, they are regarded as "lower-class." For example, to the incomplete sentence, "If I teach in a school that is mostly Negro, my future . . ." a typical response was "will be quite different than if I teach in a middle-class school."

They see the lower-class as holding values contrary to the middle-class culture; as a group which permits aggression and sexual promiscuity in their life style. These people are perceived as feeling inferior and angry at the world and becoming easily discouraged. The parents are seen as problems to the school, to the city, and to their children.

Most of these children are quite poor and come from bad backgrounds. Their main problem is that they do not always receive the affection needed for healthy development.

The pattern is seen as broken families; children unwanted or born out of wedlock; absent fathers, or a series of "uncles" present on a weekly basis. Here are parents who neglect their children either out of disinterest or because they are too ignorant or too overburdened to help. Supervision, love, and affection toward children are seen as characteristically lacking. In short, the family situation of such groups is viewed as a negative influence on the lives of the children.

The school may not be able to solve their problems. Their environment may exert a greater influence on their lives and destroy what the school is trying to create.

The beginning teacher tends to view the ethnic child as basically unmotivated to learn and continue his education.

What happens to most Negro (minority) children is that . . . they become disinterested.

. . . they give up.

. . . they become bitter.

They are viewed as children who attend school because they are forced to go, and who drop out as soon as possible. Their school behavior is characterized by expressed hostility or withdrawal. They are considered to have academic problems as well, as they "are retarded in language development," "lag behind in achievement," and "neglect homework."

Despite the similarities in the way both Negro and white minority children are viewed, there are two differences which seem significant. Whereas both groups may be seen as retarded in language development and academic achievement, when it comes to the Puerto Rican pupil, for example, his retardation is often explained in terms of his parents and his own "language barrier." If the child speaks English at all when he enters school it is probably in a "halting and insecure fashion." To quote from an interview:

What happens to most Puerto Rican children is that they go to school and learn English but lose it at home . . . Puerto Rican parents should not speak Spanish at home if they have some knowledge of English.

Once this language conflict is resolved, according to those questioned, the Puerto Rican children will catch up and reach the achievement level of the rest of the school children, and "become very much like children in better neighborhoods."

Thus, for the Puerto Rican children there seems to be a reason that they are behind; the classroom teacher can thus do something about the situation. But how to account for the achievement lag of Negro children? Here the young teachers are not sure. They point to "prejudice," "poverty," and the "apathy of Negroes themselves," and they have no solution.

If our behavior toward others is related to our images of them, then this assumed difference between Negro and deprived white children will tend to cause teachers to expect more from the latter. This is given further support when we look at a second difference in the views toward minority children held by novice teachers. They are more hopeful about the future of the white minority child. Again one asks, "Why?"

The latter are likely to be poor because "they are recent newcomers to the city." Right now they are at the bottom. But they will move up, just like past immigrant groups have in the United States.

By becoming Americanized these people will gain in social status too. They will gradually become accepted as Americans, and their economic status will rise. . .

Each new group of immigrants has had the same problems and they seem to have survived nicely.

The young teachers are relatively hopeful about the future of the white minority group. As to the prospects for their Negro pupils, their views are much less optimistic, and they feel that as teachers there is not much they can do. The accuracy of their perceptions is not the focus of discussion in this section. What is important here is that the newcomer to the teaching profession is likely to approach Negro children negatively relative to the goals of education. It is probable that this in turn will have an effect on the actual school achievement of all minority group children. It is difficult to achieve when the "significant person" does not believe that one is capable of achieving. It is difficult both for the child and his teacher.

Images of middle-class children

To the young teachers under discussion, white children are generally middle-class. They "usually come to school in a neat manner" and are "generally happy." They enjoy competition and want to get ahead. To control their competitive drive, middle-class children have internalized an acute "sense of right and wrong" to which the teacher can appeal. They want "to be liked by other children and adults." Consequently, "they feel that it is important to please the teacher."

As seen by the young teachers, middle-class families are intact, cooperative units with each member interested in the welfare of others. In marked contrast to the comments about minority group families, not one reference was made to broken families or divorce. The parents are seen as persons who "take care of their children's basic physical and emotional needs." They want to see their children "do well and get ahead." Father, mother, and children participate in a wide variety of cultural activities, such as going to places of local and historical interest. The children are provided with opportunities to participate in music and dance experiences.

With respect to school the middle-class father told his son that . . . this is the road to success.

. . . it is the most important thing in life.

In contrast, look at the following typical responses:

With respect to school, the Negro father told his son that . . . it doesn't matter.

. . . don't let anyone hit you.

Most of those questioned referred to the stress placed on long-range goals and success by the middle-class parent. This was noted as a major reason why middle-class children are motivated and stimulated to do well in school.

In terms of academic standing, I would expect the middle-class child to have more background knowledge in areas of reading, arithmetic, and general information. Thus, more time could be devoted to teaching the curriculum, without first having to teach those things you feel they should have known upon entering your class.

The idealized teaching position

It is interesting to examine the images of lower-class minority children as opposed to white middle-class children in the light of the novices' idealized image of a teaching position. Typical responses to the incomplete sentence "In picking my job, the most important thing is . . . ," are:

getting emotional satisfaction and intellectual stimulation.

the inner satisfaction it will bring.

that I be good at the job and enjoy it.

Though they consider a helpful administration, a cooperative staff, and adequate supplies as necessary, these teachers assume that the enjoyment related to successful teaching is ultimately a matter between the children and the teacher in a classroom. The one characteristic most frequently used to describe a good teacher is "understands her children." To this was often added "and treats them as individuals." A good teacher is a firm and fair disciplinarian who "controls the children" with relative ease. She "stimulates children to want to learn, and they do."

Novice teachers have definite ideas of what they want their pupils to be in the "idealized position." To the incomplete sentence, "Teachers like children who," the responses included one or more of three categories—conforming behavior, achievement, and effort. For instance, "Teachers like children who . . . show respect, behave properly, work hard, possess freedom in their thinking, want to and do learn." The best thing would be to have the kind of teaching situation in which the chances for success, as defined by the young teacher, are very good.

As the previous section illustrated, the major threat of teaching is discipline. Compliant behavior on the part of children is uppermost in teachers' minds. In addition, concern with "motivation" and "getting children to be interested and learn" were frequently referred to along with discipline. The typical response to "The worst thing that could happen to me as a teacher" is "to lose control of the class, to have the children fail to learn, and to be disliked." Consequently, teachers would like to avoid teaching in those schools where they believe they are more likely to meet the problems of discipline, disinterest, and deficiencies in learning abilities. The novice's tendency to prefer a position in a school in a "good neighborhood" is related to the images he holds of lower-class Negro and other economically deprived children.

According to the views of the young teachers, these pupils need mostly understanding and discipline. The academic function is not seen as the first and primary objectives.

In a school composed of first generation Puerto Rican children, the teacher's job will of necessity be rougher. She cannot expect to impart as much knowledge, facts, and know-how as a teacher of white students, but she can teach them skills necessary for the type of lives they are leading, and will as adults lead. . . On a nonacademic level, she can help the child more than anyone else can.

In contrast, the perceptions of a good education for the white child call on the teacher to "teach the lesson" and push the students on to "reach their potential capacity." Thus, the best school is one that emphasizes intellectual development and "instruction geared to academic achievement."

The majority of the beginning teachers view the school that is predominently Negro, for example, as "difficult," "tough," and "a challenge." It is stimulating and rewarding if one succeeds, miserable if one fails. And the chances of failure appear greater than success. As one teacher put it:

I believe that if a young teacher were given her choice of a teaching position, she would choose an all white school. She is probably an average girl with average ideas toward teaching, and she doesn't feel like being a martyr.

In brief, the images of what the young teachers want in the ideal teaching-learning situation, correspond almost precisely to what they think a white, middle-class school is. What they believe a school in a deprived neighborhood is going to be, is in sharp contrast to their idealized teaching position.

The problem of intellectual functioning

It is possible to suggest that the observations of the young teachers under discussion suffer from some lack of accuracy and overgeneralization. For instance, the census data show a wide range of income, education, occupation, and social class levels that exist among Puerto Ricans and Negroes in New York City, and among the white population as well. It is not correct to look at a total ethnic group as culturally deprived, or at a total non-ethnic group as middle-class. The same can be said about the educational level of aspiration of lower-cost parents. As suggested by Weiner and Murray, [W3] many in this group want their children to go to college. Only for them, in contrast to the middle-class parents, college is a wish rather than a reality.

To stamp the Negro or Puerto Rican child with the adjective "problem learner" is a dangerous overgeneralization. The teacher may fail to study the child as an *individual,* and may rather evaluate him, in terms of the teacher's perception of the pupil's group origin, as one who is not teachable. One of the main reasons Negro parents want school integration is their feeling that "If white children are in class with my children at least I know the teacher will try to teach." The emphasis of the beginning teacher on "understanding" and "guidance" is very valuable. However, his lack of emphasis, when it comes to these pupils of minority groups, on academic learning has the detrimental implications of a non-teachable situation. This is very dangerous both for the progress of the learner and the progress of the teacher.

Despite these reservations, and even criticism concerning some of the images and values held by the novice teacher, it is correct to agree with his observation that in coming to teach some segments of the Negro or other ethnic minority population, the young teacher is faced with a very difficult and taxing educational problem. Any attempt to gloss over the difficulty or to look at the large number of socially deprived children through the rose-colored lenses of the romantic, is an evasion of the truth. The first step toward successful teaching of the disadvantaged is facing the issue of deprivation and its learning implications.

In a recent book, *The Other America*,[H3] Harrington speaks about the existence of two nations in this country: one is the known, visible, affluent society and the second is the "invisible land of poverty" characterized by hopelessness, broken families, slum living and ignorance. Very large segments of the ethnic minority groups are members of "the second America." In addition, the deprived Negro child is not only a product of a lower-class culture, but also carries the scars of discrimination, segregation, and the slave tradition of broken families.

Much attention has been given within the last decade to the learning problems of children from deprived backgrounds, especially of Negro children. It has been demonstrated that socially deprived children are at great disadvantage in coping with school expectations, in handling verbal material, and in their readiness for beginning reading.[M18] Studies show that differences in social class are related to variations in the capacity to conceptualize, in verbal facility, in achievement motivation, and in styles of learning.[P5,R3]

In an ongoing study, Adaia Shumsky suggests that differences in intellectual functioning along social-class lines seem to express difference between assertive and passive modes of intellectual approach, which in turn seem to reflect a whole way of life, an approach to the future, and the degree to which an individual believes in his capacity to take an active part in shaping his own life chances. She writes: [S10:1-2]

The socially depressed, and especially the Negro group, for reasons inherent in external obstacles as well as internal difficulties, is repeatedly confronted with the fixedness of its situation and the lack of opportunities for mobility change. Energy is being expended into the attainment of day by day survival needs rather than in attempting to acquire long range abstract goals. Planning ahead, striving for self fulfillment, taking action to improve one's way of life become meaningless. It is only in that segment of society which rewards striving by offering a change in one's life chances, that attitudes of positive assertiveness, social optimism and a reliance on the self as a source of power can develop.

Where a generally passive and resigned orientation toward change is found, a tendency to approach *intellectual tasks* in a passive manner may also be found. Where an individual's orientation centers around the solution of immediate survival needs, long range constructionism in abstract problem solving may be weak.

Where future opportunities include only a very limited number of prescribed possibilities, a certain lack of resourcefulness and fluidity in thinking may also be found. And conversely, where general optimism, a sense of individual mastery and assertiveness are found in relation to one's social situation, a similar assertiveness in intellectual functioning is expected to occur.

In brief, the reported social class differences in intellectual functioning (abstract thinking versus specificity, verbal versus manipulative style of approach, etc.) seem to fall into one category of intellectual behavior. They seem to bespeak a difference in the degree of intellectual assertiveness as opposed to intellectual passivity; a tendency to respond by pulling ideas together, making applications, drawing generalizations and moving beyond the obvious, an assertive approach, as opposed to a tendency to think in terms of the most obvious, immediate and concrete, the passive approach.

The role of the teacher

The deprivation of lower-class children in general calls for a simultaneous frontal attack on the total social situation. However, here the discussion is limited to the role of the teacher, in whose hands society has entrusted the advancement of the intellectual functioning of children.

The Higher Horizon Project in New York City is one of the best-known demonstrations that the school can make progress in helping the socially deprived pupil. The principle underlying the program is an intensive cultural enrichment, individual guidance, and parent involvement. As Riessman says in his evaluation of the program: [R3:103]

It has belief that the non-favored children can learn, and so they do. It has hope that tired, fear-ridden teachers can become devoted and energetic, and they do.

The title of the project, "Higher Horizons," symbolizes the secret of its relative success. In other words, it is not the enrichment itself which can change the pattern of resignation and apathy, and its corollary—limited intellectual functioning—but rather, the ideology of faith. Any attempt to copy the curricular and administrative approach of the project, without adopting its basic ideology of faith in the power of the deprived to move ahead intellectually and socially, will not achieve similar results.

There are many complex problems in teaching the deprived child which call for further research and experimentation. Should the primary grade be transitional to formal instruction? Under what conditions will integration achieve its optimal results? What is the model of a teaching behavior best suited for disadvantaged pupils? [P5]

There is a serious discussion in educational literature about the need for more emphasis on motor-oriented teaching, on starting with concrete approaches to problem-solving, on the use of role-playing and the utilization of teaching machines.[R3] The development of a methodology best suited for the promotion of verbal, ideational, and abstract learning in the deprived child is only in its beginning stages.

Despite the great importance of the problem of methodology, it is secondary to the major issue, the inculcation of an ideology of faith; the sense that the young student and the young teacher are an *avant-garde*. Intellectual functioning is related to self-concept!

The repetitive-creative continuum discussed in this book has definite implications to the ideology of faith and the learning problem of the disadvantaged child. Model A illustrates the constricting teacher who manipulates children with disarming sweetness, who focuses on narrow skills and repetitive behavior. Model C illustrates a climate of trust in the power of the learner to move ahead. His is not a sentimental and laissez-faire attitude, but rather a realistic and a *demanding* approach.

It is evident that under the banner of a crash program for the deprived and his need for an anchor of security, many attempts will be made, by well-meaning educators and laymen, to enhance the A orientation in his education. The implications may be seen in a recent questioning of the Commissioner of Education concerning whether money appropriated for the teaching of reading was "misused" for the teaching of novels and poetry.

The specific methodology for the socially deprived is still under exploration. At this stage it can be suggested that an enriched curriculum, emphasis on movement from the concrete to the abstract, a climate of learning which gives the learner faith in his own power, and mainly an *ideology of an avant-garde,* is the approach to the education of the socially deprived.

SELECTED BIBLIOGRAPHY

HARRINGTON, Michael, *The Other America.* New York: The Macmillan Company, 1962. An analysis of poverty in the United States.

PASSOW, Harry (Editor), *Education in Depressed Areas.* New York: Teachers College, Bureau of Publications, Columbia University, 1963. A series of articles written by leading researchers.

REDL, Fritz, and WATTENBERG, William, *Mental Hygiene in Teaching.* New York: Harcourt, Brace & World, Inc., 1951. A comprehensive textbook.

RIESSMAN, Frank, *The Culturally Deprived Child.* New York: Harper & Row, Publishers, 1962. An original discussion filled with insight.

11

The student-teaching experience

While participating in college courses, observing the cooperating teacher, and reading educational literature, the student teacher asks a fundamental question: "What does all this mean in terms of my teaching?" Along with the teacher education process, the novice is actively searching for his identity as a teacher, for his own style of teaching. Is he going to be permissive or demanding, critical or supporting? Is he going to emphasize factual information, convergent, or divergent thinking? Is he going to emphasis individual and committee work, or the "frontal approach" of teaching the class as a whole?

The impact of the practicum on this search for style is very significant. In expressing their own evaluation, student teachers consider the practicum as the most important single experience in their preparation for teaching. To the incomplete sentence, "The student teaching experience," typical reactions were:

———— is the most meaningful learning I have ever had.
———— is the first time I understood the problem of education.
———— is my opportunity to try my wings.
———— is the entrance to the world of the teacher.

While there is no research to compare the relative impact of the cooperating teacher on the novice's search for a style of teaching, it is a common observation that it is significant. Because of her advantage in working with trainees in an action type program, her influence is perhaps greater than that of the college teacher.

Discussions with cooperating teachers show that they themselves believe in their strong educational influence. They credit the theory of learning through doing for their success in molding, or at least affecting, the novice's way of teaching. They believe that their direct contact with children, their deep understanding of the practical aspects of implementing educational theory, makes their teaching realistic and, therefore, most meaningful.

It is the purpose of this chapter to examine the student-teaching experience (with emphasis on the relationship with the cooperating teacher) in terms of its impact on the quality of the novice's teaching behavior; to explore how the practicum in the school can either encourage creativity in teaching behavior or reinforce repetitive patterns of teaching.

An attempt will be made to look at the main aspects of the practicum and identify the factors which deter or promote the search for a creative way of teaching.

The need for experience

Most teacher training institutions provide their students with a teaching practicum experience consisting of observation and practice teaching under supervision. Variations exist in the length of the student-teaching experience, ranging from part of a semester to a whole year. The time may be divided between spending several weeks in one class and then moving to another, or it may be spent fully in one grade.

The practicum may be taken concurrently with method courses, or precede or follow such courses. It may be assigned to the junior or senior year in college. Regardless of such variations, the practice of student teaching is invariably required of all prospective teachers.

The emphasis on the student-teaching practicum is an integral part of the belief in the importance of experience. In the area of teacher education, as well as in the education of children, there is a growing awareness that the objectives of a modern teacher cannot be realized only through a program based primarily on a textbook and verbal approach. Words are highly abstract and may sometimes become empty symbols unless given meaningful content by direct contact with real situations.

The equation of word mastery with practical application is often erroneous, particularly in the area of teacher training. For example, most prospective teachers study and write papers about the motivation of lower-class children. But they often find it difficult to translate this academic learning into the language of classroom behavior. It may be shown in their continuous emphasis on a curriculum centered on middle-class experiences and a complete lack of consideration of the lower-class way of living.

It seems that this level of "academic knowledge" of lower-class problems, which can be well formulated in papers, is difficult to apply. It may not equip the novice with sufficient resources in facing the reality of teaching. In a situation of this type, student teachers report that the learned subject matter is not always meaningful to them. In some cases they even express the feeling that they merely learn catchwords and slogans. The emotional corollary of this superficial understanding of educational concepts is defeating. It is a feeling of a relative lack of competency and strength in coming to translate them into the language of teaching behavior.

The role of *experience* is to cement the cleavage between the academic theory of education and the student teacher; to penetrate the shell of "verbal understanding" and to move toward deeper knowledge which is alive in the daily work of teachers. The role of experience is to move educational knowledge toward its deepest and most meaningful level—the level of behavior.

Operating on the assumption that a verbal approach to teacher education is not sufficiently effective, forward-looking departments of teacher education are trying to provide their students with a wide variety of firsthand experiences. In an article describing the teacher education program at Brooklyn College, New York, Dietz[D8] illustrates that field work and direct experience are an integral part of almost every undergraduate course. An educational clinic and an early childhood center are in operation at the college to provide opportunities for observation. Introductory classes in education visit housing projects, community agencies, and schools. Each student in the human development course participates in group work activities in a community agency. Seniors combine study of teaching methods with actual practice teaching in the school. New proposals are continuously introduced in colleges to increase the number and duration of direct experiences in education.

Whereas the promise of direct and varied experiences is fully recognized, there is, on the other hand, a tendency to believe that experience alone will serve as a panacea for the problems of teacher education. The assumption that firsthand experience in the social world will automatically lead to the formation of correct concepts or the acquisition of improved skills is oversimplified and, therefore, questionable. Is it correct to assume that extensive visits to a slum area will be conducive to a more sympathetic understanding of lower-class children? Will a trip abroad reduce ethnocentricity? Will the observation of an experienced teacher help the novice be a more creative teacher?

Whether firsthand experiences will serve as a deterrent or impetus for a better balance between repetitive and creating teaching depends primarily on two factors: (1) the quality of the experience, and (2) what the learner sees in the experience.

As reported by student teachers, the climate of the classroom has a direct impact on them. Experiencing a classroom in which freedom and creativity prevail will tend to enhance these values in the novice, while the experience of repetitive teaching may only intensify his need for control. It seems that what is often underemphasized in providing for direct teaching practice is the problem of the *quality* of the experience.

The second point raises a question with regard to the way the novice perceives the experience: is he confusing creative and repetitive teaching; confusing democratic behavior with a smooth-running operation, self-direction with quiet, or scientific thinking with factual information? There is a need for a *guided* firsthand educational experience to help the novice generalize the deeper and broader implications of the student-teaching practicum.

Both the quality of the student-teaching experience and the nature of the needed guidance is, to a great extent, dependent on the cooperating teacher.

RELATING TO THE COOPERATING TEACHER

The promise

Educational literature calls the cooperating teachers key figures in teacher education programs.[821] Most student teachers, in first meeting the cooperating teacher in action, feel that they have finally met the reality of teaching. They have a feeling of coming closer to a better grasp of teaching.

In comparing the college instructor with the cooperating teacher, the student teachers tend to identify with the latter. The cooperating teacher represents the reference group to which the trainee aspires: "Looking at her I see myself in the same situation. When I take over, I play her role." This cannot be said about the college instructor.

The cooperating teacher illustrates in her behavior, in a comprehensive and concrete way, the total professional role that has to be learned in its most real and natural setting. While the college instructor illustrates verbally, the cooperating teacher instructs in action. Attempts to demonstrate the effectiveness of a curricular innovation in a college course are perceived by some prospective teachers as unrealistic laboratory experimentation.

Was it designed for an ideal situation? Most of us here don't have the accommodations or the necessary materials.

It is almost like the unrealistic education film they (the college instructors) show of a teacher working with a committee of six pupils. You wonder what the other thirty are doing.

Generally words cannot communicate the clarity of a picture. But perhaps more important, the learner may feel skeptical in listening to words. He is more receptive when observing a curricular innovation which "works" in a field situation.

Such comments on the part of student teachers may be interpreted as a reflection of a concrete and practical approach to knowledge. Frequently this interpretation is correct. However, just as frequently these attitudes reflect the gaps felt by students between principles of education and the knowledge of how to handle children. These practical attitudes can be interpreted as a healthy search for meaningful knowledge.

In the college class the student is a member of a large group. His relations to the instructor are affected by the size of the group and the formal regulations of the course. The problem to be discussed is generally decided by the instructor, or cooperatively, by various class members. The student has a relatively passive position in the teaching-learning relations.

The relationship between the student teacher and the cooperating teacher is potentially more personal and reciprocal. It is a relationship between two people with the common bond of having to work with the same group of children. The common task brings them closer as people and, to some extent, reduces the status barrier.

Having a student teacher may require a great investment in terms of time and energy on the part of the cooperating teacher. However, the cooperating teacher not only gives; she also receives. The student teacher is not only an observer or one who asks time-consuming questions; he also cooperates by helping with the various teaching responsibilities.

For instance, while the cooperating teacher works with one group in reading, the student teacher may work with another. In a modern teaching situation where a balance between teaching the whole class, group, and individual work is constantly sought, an assistant ready to take over one of the groups or to work with a slow child is most advantageous. As reported by student teachers, their first direct involvement in the class work is generally in helping a slow learner.

The cooperating teacher is appreciative of the trainee who contributes to the class welfare, helps in record keeping, in checking papers and tests. This appreciation is seen in statements like the following:

I remember Mary Brown whom I had two years ago. She was most cooperative and helpful. I still have the relief map she did with my group.

The most common criterion of evaluation used by cooperating teachers is whether the student teacher is "helpful and cooperative."

The student teacher not only helps in teaching but also exchanges roles—takes over the class. This experience is a source of closeness between the cooperating teacher and the novice. The latter is influenced by the experienced teacher's way of teaching and often even imitates her. The cooperating teacher herself often has a strong sense of identification with the student teacher. She may experience nostalgic feelings about her own student-teaching experience. ("I remember the first lesson I ever taught.") She enjoys the sense of achievement in attributing the student teacher's accomplishments to her own teaching.

Working with a student teacher is not only a source of emotional satisfaction, but also a source of intellectual stimulation. In spite of his lack of experience the novice, as some cooperating teachers put it, is their link with college—the source of new ideas. The student teacher is fresh with discussions of the latest trends in education innovations. Being less threatening than any other status leader (principals, consultants, or college professors) the novice can introduce new ideas that may intellectually challenge the cooperating teacher.

The need to stop and explain her practices to the inquisitive novice is an opportunity for the senior teacher to look for their deeper meaning and examine the rationale of her practices. As some cooperating teachers see it, they don't relate any more only to the relatively immature minds of children, but are also challenged by the adult mind of a student teacher.

The fact that the practicum can be a satisfying and educational experience for both novice and senior teacher does not mean that there are no problems involved in these relations.

The difficulty in being observed

One study on the problem of cooperating teaching [A5] suggests that the training of student teachers is somewhat less than the sheer joy pictured by public relations personnel at the college. The fact is that, in addition to the normal class load, the cooperating teacher has to guide the student teacher in practice teaching, to be acquainted with rules and regulations, to assist in securing and organizing materials, to schedule conferences, and so on. All this, suggests the above study, lays a demanding and time-consuming burden on the teacher. As difficult as this burden may be, it would seem that the most taxing aspect of this role stems not so much from the tangible elements of time, energy, and effort, but primarily from the intangible undercurrents of bringing a stranger into the intricacies of teacher-class relations. Putting it somewhat extremely, bringing in a student teacher may sometimes mean opening one's home to a stranger.

A student teacher who enters a classroom may normally go in with the expectation of observing techniques of teaching and learning the skills. He may view the cooperating teacher primarily as a source of ideas and methodology.

Cooperating teachers, however, are more than mere audio-visual machines which demonstrate techniques. They are people. The most significant thing they invest in teaching is their personality. Teaching is primarily an expression of intimate relations between an adult and a group of children.

In another study I described some of the personal and emotional dynamics which may underlie a teacher's relatedness to his classroom.[86] While the following example does not deal directly with the problem of cooperating teacher, it illustrates the emotional climate into which a student teacher has to be integrated. It is presented here to help the novice understand and appreciate what perhaps is the main difficulty of being a cooperating teacher —being exposed, in an important aspect of one's personal relations, to a stranger.

In an interview discussing motivation underlying teaching, a teacher said: [86:74]

I came from a marginal Italian group. Father had social ascendant tendencies and Mother was the traditional Italian. My mother marshaled all her forces and invested them in her children. My father wanted to be a teacher but could not make the grade. We were very poor. I knew the difference between my clothes and those of the other children. I felt angry. The teacher used to bang my head against the wall when I did not do my homework.

Very early I felt the effects of discrimination. I was looked down upon for being Italian. Teachers used to say, "You are so nice, you don't look Italian at all." I changed my Italian accent. I cut myself from the family.

I had a very personal interest in those who were rejected. The underdog always had my sympathy . . . I hate to see children as outgroups. I always see myself in these situations and the "I" is very important. It is the kid who was hurt, who got the raw deal, who has got the short end of the stick in whom I am interested.

Teaching a group of children is more than a livelihood, imparting subject matter, or developing attitudes. Teaching is often a way by which one attempts to find himself as a person; a way one lives in a home and builds his home—in the psychological sense of the word *home*. Into these intricate relations between a person and the meaning of his "home" a newcomer is admitted, not for a lecture or a short course, but rather to become a continuous observer and somewhat a partner.

Bringing in a student teacher is difficult because teaching is more than a skill; it is a personal process. Teaching consists to a great extent of intuitive, subjective, and spontaneous reactions. Many of the techniques used by teachers may never be verbally explained to others because they result from subtle and unrealized communication between the teacher and her students. It is as if an inner sense of timing, an inner sensitivity, exists within the teacher which helps her move and respond to the needs and behavior of children.

The teacher uses her self as a tool in the teaching process. Teaching is an art which develops out of using one's own self; out of learning more about others by way of understanding one's own reactions to others.

It seems that in some cases the fact that teaching is primarily a personal relationship serves to establish a strong bond between the experienced and the novice teacher. Perhaps these are the cooperating teachers which the student teachers describe by expressions such as the following:

Help us beyond the call of duty.
Take us under their wings.
Want us to be almost their daughters.
Enjoy tremendously when we are successful.

On the other hand, in at least some cases, the newcomer is damper to the cooperating teacher's spontaneity and sense of personal fulfillment. Perhaps these are the cooperating teachers of whom some perceptive student teachers report their indirect rejecting remarks or rejective actions:

You were absent today and we had a wonderful lesson. Why do we have some of our best work when you are not here?

Any time I (the student teacher) develop relations with some children she runs over and takes them from me. Is she jealous?

This discussion is no attempt to justify comments of this nature. It only attempts to explain and understand them.

Lack of role definition

Another difficulty underlying the relationship between the novice and the cooperating teacher is the lack of a sufficient delineation of their mutual roles. Both parties are not entirely sure of their rights and responsibilities and do not know what to expect from each other.

Compare the relations of the student teacher and the cooperating teacher with those of the college instructor. The latter are pretty well defined. It is expected that the instructor will set the course requirement, such as assigning readings, papers, or administering tests. It is expected that the instructor will examine the students' oral and written work, criticize and grade it. It is expected that the student teacher will participate in college discussions, introduce ideas, question, and sometimes even disagree with the instructor's position.

When it comes to the relationship with the cooperating teacher, the roles of each party are not clear. There is definitely disagreement in answering questions such as the following: Should the cooperating teacher assign homework or leave it up to the student teacher? Should the cooperating teacher criticize or only answer the questions raised by the trainee? Should the student teacher suggest curricular innovations or disagree with the practices of the senior teacher? Or should his role be limited to accepting things with no questioning?

This confusion about role definition and expectation can be seen in the following excerpts from an interview:

At first our relationship was one of mutual confusion. She (the cooperating teacher) didn't know what to expect of me and I didn't know what to expect of her. I spent most of my time in the back of the room watching her teach. This ridiculous situation persisted until I asked my teacher if she thought I was ready to teach a lesson. After this our relations improved. The teacher was willing to give her opinions and criticisms of my lessons. She no longer felt guilty about asking me to teach and I was no longer afraid to ask if I could give a lesson.

An examination of the logs of student teachers shows that the lack of clarity in role expectations is a source of stress and, most important, a major deterrent to learning. The data also suggest that those student teachers who, on their own initiative or in collaboration with the cooperating teacher and college instructor, were able to reach mutual understanding in the role expectation, utilized the practicum experience more productively.

The status problem

In a college course a group of student teachers was asked to report one incident which occurred in their classrooms. Examination of the responses showed that the most frequent category was the relations of the cooperating teacher to children. The second frequent category was the impact of the cooperating teacher's attitude on the *status* of the student teacher. It is evident that the latter is sensitive—and even, perhaps, oversensitive—to the status problem.

Being preoccupied with the fear of lack of control over pupils, being driven by the need to be respected, one of the novice's first questions is: "Am I going to be introduced to the children as a student or a teacher?" Being introduced as a student is perceived as a threat to their status. The introduction as a teacher is an invitation for an attitude of equality.

The lack of clarity about their status is illustrated by the following two extreme incidents: One student teacher lined up with the children on the first morning and walked in the line into the classroom. This is an extreme expression of the feeling that one is a student rather than a teacher.

The second extreme is the incident of a student teacher who, in presenting herself to the cooperating teacher, reprimanded the class: "I would like you to be quiet and respectful when I am introduced to you for the first time." This is an extreme manifestation of anxiety over the respected status of a teacher.

The majority of the logs discuss the first introduction to the class in terms of the status threat. However, the status problem is not limited to the first initiation. The trainees want the cooperating teachers to treat them with equal respect, especially in front of children; to support in disciplinary situations so that their word will be the rule; to avoid criticizing or correcting them in front of children.

They see interruptions as lowering of status.

I told the class a story and then asked them to develop their own ending. Several children did not want to write and I insisted that they should do it. As we were arguing, the cooperating teacher returned and without consulting me said, "O.K. boys and girls, stop what you are doing and let's do some arithmetic." The children looked at me with laughter in their eyes.

They praise the cooperating teacher who helps them learn to assert themselves.

One day when teacher Z was administering a citywide test to other classes and I was on my own, I had great difficulty in getting the class to the room quietly. I scolded, I asked for a straight line, etc., but all to no avail. I finally gave up and led the mob (for it was a mob) to the room. At the door teacher Z greeted me and told me that if I did not positively assert myself now I would never be able to gain control of this class. She tactfully whispered instructions to me and left me to myself at the front.

They complain about the cooperating teacher who builds her own status by means of competition rather than mutual respect and support.

Speaking to cooperating teachers, Milner says:[M18:9]

It is important that the children look upon the student as another teacher coming to work with them. Play down the idea that he is a "student." Talking about him as the "student teacher" says to the children that he's not really a teacher. It can give them the feeling that he is just a little inferior, that after all you are still going to be the boss.

It is particularly in the upper grades of the elementary school that children will realize that the student teacher is only second in command and is in the process of learning a profession. It is thus somewhat naive to attempt to hide the fact that the newcomer is a student teacher.

It is more realistic for the children to learn that every organization has a power hierarchy. In the school structure it is usually: the principal, the assistant principal, the teacher, the student teacher. Each one of these people has a right to assert his leadership within the limits of the setup. It may also be helpful for children to see a young person in an apprenticeship position, as many of them live in a culture which is detached from the experience of work.

The student teacher may give homework to children, provided it has been previously approved by the cooperating teacher. Of course he may finish a lesson, assuming the time limit was agreed on in advance. Much of the misunderstanding derives from lack of communication and lack of cooperative planning of the various tasks to be accomplished in a specific day.

The vision of the student teacher is sometimes limited only to the specific activity he has to conduct, such as an art lesson. He may take too much time developing this activity, not being aware of the other pressures, such as preparation for a citywide test. An interruption of the art activity may be perceived by the novice as a threat to his status, while objectively it may be necessary in order that time is provided to clean the room before departing for the day.

I would like to suggest that many student teachers are too sensitive to status problems. They may forget that the main objective of the practicum is learning to teach rather than building status. Unwittingly they often seem ready to sacrifice their education for the sake of security.

In the college situation the prospective teacher is a student— a well-delineated role. In the field he is a student teacher—a student to the cooperating teacher and a teacher to the children at the same time. The involvement in both roles is a source of difficulty to the student teacher. In his preoccupation with playing the teacher's role, the novice may overlook his function as the one whose main objective is to learn and thereby make mistakes, get help, and try again.

Another difficulty underlying the status problem is lack of

sufficient communication between the two parties involved. Student teachers report that to the extent that they are able to establish communication with the cooperating teacher, their feeling about their status in the classroom improves tremendously.

Here are a few points which a teacher and a student teacher may want to discuss in order to improve their communication.

Should the student teacher participate while the cooperating teacher is teaching the class as a whole, and vice-versa?

How, where, and when should comments about ways of improvement be made?

To what extent can the student teacher participate, or act independently, in disciplining children or giving homework?

How long should a specific activity last?

How closely should the student follow the teacher's routines and to what extent is the novice permitted to introduce new routines?

How closely should the trainee follow the mentor's way of teaching and to what extent should he experiment with his own ideas?

Conclusion

Relating to the cooperating teacher is a most challenging experience in terms of its promise and its threat. Hypothetically, this is one of the best opportunities to learn. It potentially offers individual tutoring from a mentor; provides firsthand experiences with the totality of the teacher's behavior, ideas, and attitudes; opens the way for intellectual discussion of problems emerging on the job; and offers an opportunity to try one's own wings under sympathetic individual guidance.

The threats are inherent in the "emotional traps" in these relationships. On the part of the cooperating teacher they may be due to the strain involved in having additional responsibility, the burden of constantly being watched by a "stranger," and the resulting tendency to be, in some cases, somewhat resentful of this "stranger." Difficulties may also stem out of a tendency on the part of the cooperating teacher to become overly involved and protective toward the student teacher, and to act overmotherly.

On the part of the student teacher, the tensions may stem

from the fear of getting criticism, lack of role definition, status consciousness, and overcritical or competitive attitudes.

In the light of these challenges inherent in the student-teaching experience, and especially in the relationship with the co-operating teacher, the discussion will attempt to examine the main stages in the student-teaching practicum: *observation, assisting teaching, and independent teaching.*

OBSERVATION: A PASSIVE OR ACTIVE PROCESS?

The first function of the student teacher in his field practicum is to observe the class operation. In terms of the amount of time spent in the classroom, observation is the most time-consuming activity. Even when the novice starts to move toward other aspects of his training, such as assisting teaching and independent teaching, he still spends many of his practicum hours in observation. Observation remains a continuous process through all stages of student teaching, although it may change in terms of time emphasis.

PURPOSES AND PROBLEMS

The function

The main purpose of the activity termed here *observation,* is to help the student integrate the theory of education and its practice. As the discussion will show, when this purpose is fully understood and is kept in focus, observation becomes an enriching experience. When the above main purpose is overlooked, observation may become a drudgery.

Student teachers generally look forward to the experience of observation as they recognize the difference between knowledge from attendance at lectures, and that derived from observations of live illustrations. And indeed, one of the most valuable aspects of the observation experience is that the novice makes progress in learning to think in the analytic language of a situation, rather than solely in the synthetic language of a generalization. The ideas of unit planning, motivation, committee work, or creative writing become more meaningful by being spelled out. He makes progress in visualizing many specific situations of various aspects of teaching, which results in increased clarity, confidence, and a growing readiness to teach.

An educational idea observed in operation in a classroom, such as individualized reading, is convincing. The observer watches the matrix of all the factors (including interruptions by the public address system) as they impinge on each other, and begins to believe that "it can be done." The convincing aspect of the observation experience is illustrated by the fact that the novice tends to use it as "evidence" that a certain curricular innovation is operational. In brief, observation can be a most potentially meaningful experience in the education of the prospective teacher.

A passive or an active process?

As reported by student teachers, the seemingly simple practice of observation varies tremendously in different field situations. For instance, on one extreme is the trainee who sits and watches for weeks, and on the other end is the one who in the first hour is plunged into taking the class over while the cooperating teacher leaves the class. The majority of student teachers fall between these extremes. They spend some time in observation and are gradually initiated into teaching.

Complaining about a prolonged stage of observation, a student teacher says:

Long periods of observation are a waste of time. You see the same thing again and again. You feel as useful as a fifth wheel. You don't feel that you are an integral part of the group.

Other trainees speak about feeling "like a piece of furniture," or complain that they "do only one thing—sit." They wish that the teacher would permit them to take a more active role in classroom affairs.

Complaints about prolonged periods of observation are sometimes valid and will be discussed in another section. The point discussed here is that for too many student teachers, observation implies a passive process. The *active* aspect of observation is not sufficiently understood.

An examination of the logs written by student teachers, shows that there is hardly a person who does not report his observation of the field situation. Some reports are comprehensive and rich; others are sketchy or even poor. They describe, agree and disagree, compare with previous experience and with a theory of education. Some students, on the other hand, go through the motions of observing in a relatively passive way. They see things and accept them for what they are.

The basic difference between the active and the passive observers (if one can divide the group into these two distinct categories) is the *motivation*—that is, what they want to get out of the experience. Excerpts from the log of two trainees, located in the same school, and dealing with the same observation, illustrate this point.

Today was the turn of my teacher to supervise the children as they walk into the classrooms. I went with her to see how it works. She told me that generally the children line up in the yard, but on that particular day they gathered in the auditorium because of bad weather. When we reached the place it was bedlam. The teacher used her whistle and the miracle happened. The children lined up and were quietly led by monitors to their rooms.

While this observation is primarily descriptive, it brings out a very definite frame of reference: "It is my function to know how it is done, so tomorrow I'll be able to do it in the same way." The above observer expresses her admiration to an approach which "works," and the ability to change noisy disorder into quiet order.

The anecdote reflects the type of approach which concentrates on *imitating* the tested practices of his elders. There is no search for examining the above practices in terms of basic principles of education.

The importance of knowing the school practices cannot be overemphasized. It is important to know how children get into their respective classrooms in the morning, the procedures for leaving for lunch, fire drill, etc. An efficient organization on the school and classroom level facilitates learning. Without the ability to establish order, and without knowledge of the school policies, it will hardly be possible for the novice to make progress.

However, critical questions can be raised with regard to such observed practices as the one described above, which may lead the novice beyond the level of merely knowing the school practices without searching for their theoretical rationale.

An excerpt from a log, describing the same situation, will illustrate this point.

When the weather is cold, they wait in the auditorium and line up there. I went to see it today and I felt lost. I wonder how the children feel in this big, noisy crowd. Are these policies consistent with the professed objective of being attentive to individual children? Why cannot a child in coming to school walk directly into the classroom on his own, and be greeted as an individual by the teacher?"

The ability of this student teacher to observe is not limited by the sole need to know practices which work, or to the admiration of a senior teacher who is able to control a poor situation. Her thinking is diagnostic. She looks for the *why* and not only the *what*. She is interested in what happens to children, not only in saving her own skin.

This ability to examine the observed classroom analytically and critically in terms of educational principles we will term an *active experience*. While observation for the sake of imitation is relatively passive, the "active observer" can go on and on for days and weeks observing the same classroom operation without feeling bored. What keeps him going is not only what he observes, but also his personal interpretations and thoughts which interact with the observation. In contrast, the "passive observer" learns the practices quickly. Then he develops the feeling that he sees more and more of the same known thing. He does not *react*, he only absorbs.

Whether the novice will develop a constructive educational orientation which is personally meaningful and whether he will develop experimental attitudes in his practice teaching will depend to a great extent on his ability to experience *actively* the observed field situation.

The focus of observation: teacher and child

An analysis of student teachers' logs shows that the focus of their observation is on the teaching behavior of the teacher; it is on what the teacher does or does not do with only secondary attention given to the child's learning and personal behavior. The discussion will first look at the primary focus of the novice's observation—the teacher, and then examine the need for more emphasis on the child.

The fact that the center is the teacher's behavior is easily understood and to a great extent positive in nature. The reference group of the trainee is the cooperating teacher. As stated by an interviewee:

I observe the cooperating teacher and see myself in this situation. It is I who is faced with all these responsibilities. It is I who has to decide what to do next.

The prospective teacher is interested in all the details of the operation of his future role, and therefore it serves as the main focus of his observation.

It is a common practice among college instructors to request students to keep a student-teaching log. Reading these logs, one finds that the emphasis is on what various observed "actions" of the senior teacher mean to the novice. To illustrate: observing the planning of a trip, a student teacher speaks about the trip as a rich source of social and academic learnings. Observing the punishment of an aggressive child, a novice speaks about the importance of prevention. Observing the administration of a reading readiness test, the observer discusses the strength and limitation of the test approach and compares it with the teacher's own evaluation.

The strength of this emphasis of a discussion based on the observed occurrence was previously called the *active experience*. However, a critical discussion of their observations, valuable as it may be, suffers from the limitation of being dependent on the type of occurred incidents, and may therefore tend to be unsystematic or lacking in comprehensiveness. It may fail to expose the student teacher to the totality of the teacher's role.

It would be most useful to the novice to read some of the descriptions of the teacher's role presented by educational literature, and then to examine the observed behavior from the frame of reference of the respective theoretical formulation. It would add depth and meaning to his observations.

The following are some illustrations of these theoretical formulations.

Wiles, in *Teaching For Better Schools*,[W7] suggests that the main functions of the teacher are: improving the self-concept of children; promoting group development; making provisions for individual differences; stimulating intellectual growth; developing self-directiveness, and exerting leadership in school and community.

Redl and Wattenberg,[R1] discussing the psychological role of the teacher, suggest his function as being: a representative of society who transmits its values; a judge who evaluates pupils; a source of knowledge; a guide in the learning process; referee among children; detective of violations; limiter of anxiety; ego supporter; group leader; parent surrogate; target for hostility feelings; individual friend and confidant; object of affection.

Cunningham [C6] identified five general patterns between teacher and pupils (1) Adult rule, child obedience; (2) The planless "catch as catch can" pattern; (3) Emphasis upon individual attention and initiative, but group interaction is curtailed; (4) Adult-directed group planning, where group interaction is within the boundaries set by the teacher; (5) Group self-management with emphasis on group planning.

A teacher does not use one style of leadership exclusively. It will be educative for the novice to see how teachers alternate between patterns of leadership, or stress the aspect of the teacher's role most appropriate to the specific situation or most paramount in their operational values.

This study itself suggests a theoretical formulation of a continuum of three approaches to teaching: (1) The *A* orientation emphasizes the identification and recall of specific facts. It is very structured, organized, and sometimes even rigid. It is in essence a controlled movement toward a predetermined goal which allows little freedom to the learner and his interests. (2) The *B* orientation emphasizes productive thinking of the convergent type. It stresses the development of the gestalt and is characterized by allowing a higher degree of freedom than the *A*-centeredness. (3) The *C* orientation works toward creativity, emphasizing personal interpretation, movement from the known to the unknown, divergent thinking, and utilization of children's interests.

On the basis of one of these theoretical formulations of the teacher's role, the novice can examine the observed classroom operation in a more systematic, comprehensive, and penetrating way, while he is also observing specific "incidents" and techniques.

As suggested previously, student teachers seem to focus their observation primarily on the role of the teacher in the teaching situation, paying only secondary or even little attention to the child. This type of focus may present a limitation, as it may lead to a preoccupation with knowledge transmitted by the teacher. It may obscure the type of experiences leading to a more analytic approach, which is the process of learning, with the child the center of the learning process. It centers mainly on the question of whether the subject matter has been communicated by the teacher without sufficient consideration of the child's process of arrival and learning.

To understand this concept of "process of arrival" or "children's learning," one should observe points like the following:

Compare a bright and a slow first grader computing $4 + 3 = 7$. Both of them reach a correct answer. Do they differ in their process of arriving at the correct answer?

Ask a group of children to read a story. What was the nature of their difficulty in comprehension? Was the difficulty in the skill of reading, in lack of attention to details, or in lack of ability to generalize?

Let children watch a turtle for a few minutes and then raise any number of questions they want. What can you learn about specific children from their questions?

Observe a group of children drawing a mural. What can you learn about their relationships?

Listen to a group of fourth graders discussing antisocial behavior, such as stealing. Are they punitive or constructive in their discussion? Do they have some feeling for the violator? Are similar variations in interpretation reflected in the actual social behavior of children in the group?

Similar preoccupation with teacher-centeredness is also seen in the student teachers' observations of the climate of *human relationship* in the classroom. Student teachers recognize, and rightfully so, the supporting value of warmth, the stimulation of "fun" in learning, the importance of *nice* relations, or the satisfaction in giving correct answers. However, the classroom climate is perceived primarily as the quality of the reaction to the teacher's instructions. When the reaction is overtly cooperative or if the subject matter is easily digested, then the lesson is successful. When the teacher is inventive in her techniques and children learn about magnets as they play a fishing game, then the observing student teacher speaks about an atmosphere of "fun" in learning.

What is needed is a deeper conception of human relationship than "being nice." This conception is based primarily on respect for children's ability to be self-directive; to raise questions and not only answer the teacher's questions; to develop their own projects and not only to work on the teacher's assignment; to participate in planning of objectives and units, and not only "be motivated" by the teacher.

This study is not written from a child-centered point of view. It is the overemphasis on the teaching process without sufficient understanding of the role of learning and the learner that is being criticized here. The novice's sincere interest in observing how the teacher teaches should be balanced by a similar emphasis in observing the process of children's learning; the degree of their self-directiveness and the nature of their interests.

A central point underlying this study is the belief that the prospective teacher should learn to perceive the principles of education in operation. For example, unless the novice learns to see the development of democratic behavior in the classroom as conveyed through the way the teacher asks questions, gives answers, and makes assignments, the concept of democratic behavior may be empty of content. The simplest possible experiences with classroom living are at the foundation of real understanding of the values of education.

In attempting to apply this principle to the phase of observation, the student teacher may proceed by two main processes:

(1) Observing the specifics of a classroom situation and only afterwards drawing generalizations, and (2) Deciding on a problem or hypothesis for investigation (such as, are there more incidents of cooperation than competition in the classroom?), and observing with this specific question in mind.

Anecdotal records

The first process of observation is an inductive approach leading from the specific details to the generalization. In practice it means taking anecdotal records of classroom situations and evaluating them for their meaning.

In the book *Helping Teachers Understand Children* [P7] it is stressed that it is necessary for a teacher to practice more scientific methods of recording children's actions. The author suggests that in order to do this, the teacher should record only what actually happens, and keep his interpretations out of the report. The children should speak for themselves, in direct quotations, if possible. The interpretation or evaluation should wait at least until a number of anecdotes have been gathered.

My experience with the group of student teachers under discussion only partly agrees with the above stress on separation between anecdotes and interpretation. It is correct that the novice lacks ability to be specific in taking anecdotal records. He rushes too quickly to the use of adjectives, such as "she was interesting," or "the children did not understand the lesson."

There is not a sufficient emphasis on specific descriptions. What did she do to be interesting? What exactly could the children not understand? Answering these questions will add depth and meaning to the observation.

At the same time, however, it is difficult to accept the common emphasis on the abrupt differentiation between description and interpretation, and their postponement to a later stage. Some of the interpretations made on the spur of the moment capture the classroom mood in a way that is not possible by a straightforward description.

While the writing of detailed and specific descriptions should be encouraged, interpretive comments should not be discouraged.

The latter are the observer's attempt to clarify to himself his own emerging concepts and attitudes in relation to the specific situation he is describing.

The following excerpts from a log written by a student teacher will illustrate the strength of this integrative approach to anecdotal records.

The teacher reads a poem "My Shadow," by Stevenson, describing its relation to the child. The class, composed of Puerto-Rican children, listens carefully. Do they comprehend? The poem is enjoyable but I don't sense any reaction in their faces.

The teacher asks: "What does the poem say?" There is dead silence. The teacher calls on a bright girl: "Angela, what does the poem say?" No reply. It seems that the image of the poem did not arouse much in the children. They did not see the play between the shadow and the child.

The teacher calls Angela to come and stand in front of the projector (Why is it always this charming girl?). She starts the projector. The girl's shadow is seen on the wall. I sense that the class stops being passive. The teacher shuts the projector—no shadow; opens—the shadow appears again. Angela moves toward the wall away from the projector and the shadow becomes smaller. She moves back towards the projector, the shadow becomes bigger.

The class is excited. They want to speak, participate, and try things with light and shadows. The teacher finds it relatively easy to draw simple generalizations: The shadow of an object is made by the interruption of light that falls on it. If you move the object closer to the light the shadow becomes taller. If you move it further away the shadow becomes smaller.

The teacher reads the poem "My Shadow" again. The children enjoy it. They laugh and make comments on the same material they ignored in the beginning of the lesson.

It seems that the verbal approach of reading a poem was not meaningful enough. It might give the feeling that these children never paid attention to shadows and have nothing to offer. It is only the concrete manipulation and experimentation that helped the group sense that there is a problem here, and that they have personal experiences with the problem."

In brief, anecdotal records are useful in the process of observation when they emphasize both the specifics of the situation and the emerging educational generalizations.

Observing with a problem in mind

A second approach to observation is deciding on a problem for investigation, and observing with this problem in mind. For instance:

What is the pattern of discussion in the classroom?

Who are the leaders and how do they express their leadership?

What kind of questions does the teacher raise, or what kind of assignments does she give? Are they based primarily on the *A, B,* or *C* orientation?

A fruitful way of focusing the observation on a special problem is preparing an observation guide. Its main function is not a mechanical help for recording, but rather a way of sharpening thinking on the nature of the problems to be observed.

A group of student teachers was asked to present a problem that they would like to observe in the classroom. Illustrations of some typical problems raised by them are:

How does the teacher handle the problem of discipline?

In working with slow learners, it is profitable to see how a teacher helps one child. What happens when there are 25-30 slow readers?

How do children take an active part in a lesson with a teacher who is permissive?

How does the teacher motivate children, capture their interest, and keep them attentive?

In these questions, the student teachers approach observation with *general* questions: What are the relations? How are children motivated? These questions indicate an identification of a broad problem and show a desire for answers. However, they do not indicate an understanding of the operational nature of the problem to be observed.

When the novice wants to observe the promotion of mental health in the classroom, or to find out which children manifest a high or low degree of independence, he will find it helpful to define operationally the components of the problem to be observed.

Teachers who practice better methods of analyzing and defining the problem to be observed gain in terms of actual teaching and the ability to appraise teaching. And on the other hand, teachers who approach this job without thinking through the problem to be observed may find that their observations are shallow and lacking in depth.

Look at the investment of thinking which two observers put in their approach to the observation of the same problem. One observer raised the general question: "Was the science lesson I observed today taught on a repetitive or creative level?" The second observer in evaluating the same experience developed the following *observation guide*:

(1) The teacher a) emphasizes facts only.
                b) develops generalizations.
                c) also stresses application.

(2) a) gives step-by-step instruction to test an experiment.
    b) suggests a hypothesis and guides children to develop an experiment he has in mind.
    c) encourages children to develop hypothesis to test by various experiments and accepts ideas to be tested that he had not planned on.

(3) a) presents an object, such as a flower or a picture, and raises specific questions to guide the group's observations.
    b) presents an object and raises a basic question which emphasizes function, relations, or causation, to guide the group's observation.
    c) presents an object, provides the group with time to observe, raise questions or make reactions, and only then structures discussion.

(4) a) asks children to copy the experiment from the blackboard.
    b) asks children to write down the experiment in their own words.
    c) asks children to express criticism of the experiment, question the results, suggest other experiments, or possible use.

While this observation guide may not be comprehensive, it definitely indicates a higher level of thinking on the problem than the general question of whether the science activities in a specific lesson were repetitive or creative. One observer limited his function to raising a question, the second, to studying the problem and developing more facets of it.

In contrast to anecdotal records, the use of observation guides by student teachers is very rare and should be encouraged. Research studies in curriculum problems, teacher's behavior, classroom climate, etc., often utilize observation checklists or rating scales which can be adapted for the use of the novice.

The function of the cooperating teacher

One factor determining the quality of the observation is of course the perceptiveness of the student teacher, his ability to see theory in action, and his ability to look for the meaning of action in theory. Another factor determining the quality of this experience is the nature of the communication with the cooperating teacher.

Student teachers report various practices in this area, ranging from passivity and lack of involvement to active guidance. The passive cooperating teacher is sometimes one who has never accepted the student teacher imposed on her by the administration. In most cases, however, she is the one who is not sure of her role definition and does not want to impose herself on her guest, but rather waits for the student teacher to raise questions. To the student she may appear aloof and cold.

There are many more complaints on the passivity of the cooperating teacher at the beginning of the observation stage than at the end. As the ice between the two adults gradually thaws and a relationship is established, both parties start to play a more active role: the cooperating teacher in guiding the observation, and the student teacher in raising questions or making comments.

It should be emphasized that the majority of cooperating teachers enjoy their role of guiding the student teacher. They feel it is a source of intellectual stimulation and emotional satisfaction. The novice, on the other hand, finds the briefing about the purpose of the lesson and its relation to the total unit most helpful. He is appreciative of the cooperating teacher who stops in the middle of the lesson to make comments about the ongoing activity, a change of plans, or difficulties encountered by specific children. He feels at home with the cooperating teacher who encourages him to raise questions and share observations.

The student teachers who do not get guidance of this nature report that sometimes they have the feeling of sitting in the dark, moving (or more correctly, being moved) step-by-step together with the pupils. Their field of perception and vision becomes very limited. They may find it difficult to relate the specific questions which the teacher raises to the broader goals of education. In some cases, the end result of this limited vision is the feeling of uselessness.

To repeat again, the stage of observation is an enriching experience to the extent that there is give and take between the mentor and the student teacher, and to the extent that the latter is able to generalize the meaning of the observation.

ASSISTING TEACHING

Somewhat artificially, and only for the purpose of organizing the discussion, the analysis of the student-teaching practicum is divided here into two main stages: observation and actual teaching. These two are not entirely sequential experiences, but rather overlapping. With the movement toward actual practice teaching, the activity of observation is reduced only in terms of the relative amount of time devoted to it, but it continues to be an important aspect of the practicum to its last day.

Many student teachers feel that the movement from observation to actual teaching is too slow. This feeling stems partly from an underestimation of the importance of observation as a preparation for teaching, and an eagerness to rush and try the real taste of teaching.

It is evident that the active student teacher, the one who shows interest, the one who makes suggestions, has a better chance of getting the green light from the cooperating teacher than the trainee who "only sits." His first step in this direction is generally cooperating in or assisting teaching.

The terms *cooperating in teaching* or *assisting teaching*, refer to teaching situations in which the *cooperating and the student teacher share responsibility* in working with the class. Typical illustrations are: the cooperating teacher illustrates arithmetic problems on the blackboard and the student teacher helps check whether the children worked them out correctly in their notebooks; or, each one of the two teachers may work with a separate group during reading.

Especially in the modern elementary school which stresses the need for individualized instruction, there are many opportunities for an assistant teacher to perform a useful function, as a major deterrent to individualized instruction is the burden of class size. Many dedicated teachers ask: "How can I devote time to one individual? What will the other thirty do? Waste time in busy work?" It should be recognized that from the point of view of the individualization of instruction, the availability of a student teacher to assist is a major contribution.

As reported by student teachers, they move from observation to teaching by assisting. Generally they start by helping an individual who is usually academically slow, and gradually move toward working with a small group of slow learners. This initiation has many advantages. An interviewee says:

I find it easier to relate to a small group than to the class as a whole. I am not handicapped by the fear of being on the stage before the class as a whole. The children themselves find it easier to relate and contribute. It is easier for me to know whether the children learned, or to find out about the nature of their mistakes. I am encouraged by being accepted by the group. I feel it prepares me for the more strenuous task of teaching the whole class.

The advantages of the phase of assisting teaching are obvious, and do not call for elaboration. They are primarily related to the personal face-to-face relations which the novice develops with the learners.

There are some difficulties characteristic of the assisting phase. An interviewee says:

I enjoy this type of work. I know that I benefit from it. But it is only being a helper. I am not on my own, responsible for the preparation of the total program for the whole class.

The assisting work is generally denoted by some degree of dependency of the student teacher and by limited *planning* on his part of the work that has to be done. He is too much like a worker who "fills in" because he happens to be there, rather than the one who plans ahead and organizes a systematic program of working with a slow learner.

As reported by student teachers, their own *preparation* for assisting is small in comparison to their preparation when they have to take over the class as a whole. It often results from the notion that the novice's role is only to fall in line and join, rather than participate in, the preparation and planning of the work.

To vitalize the assistance phase of the novice's experience, it is helpful to raise questions like the following:

Is the student teacher aware of the total program, and does he see his own contribution as part of this totality?

Does the novice plan and prepare for his activity? Does he know in advance what the nature of the activity may be, how much time is alloted for it, etc.?

Is there a systematic program and continuity in the novice's assistance work, or is it only sporadic?

Is there guidance of the novice's work, such as cooperative planning of the activity and an evaluation of his learning gains?

It is this last point of the evaluation of what has been learned which should be central in the assisting teaching of the novice. While student teachers generally find that the assisting phase is helpful in terms of their own training, a few wonder at times whether the purpose underlying the assisting work is the education of the novice to become a teacher, or the service to the cooperating teacher and the school. In some extreme cases they ask: "Are we cheap labor?"

The type of work required of the student teacher at this phase may seem somewhat remotely related to teaching a class, but carries as much significance in their training as other functions of the student-teaching experience. There are menial jobs constituting just plain good housekeeping that have to be done in school. Adjusting shades, taking care of the light and heat in the room, straightening chairs, checking supplies, all are part of the duties of a teacher. The trainee has to be aware of all these chores that have to be done, and must carry his share of the responsibility. There are many records to be kept and special forms that one has to be acquainted with. Standardized and teacher-made tests have to be administered and scored. Bulletin boards have to be planned, materials prepared, and worksheets mimeographed. All these are part of the teaching assignment and the student teacher has to practice them.

When is a student teacher *misused* so that instead of being a learner he becomes a teacher's aid? Milner answers this question when he warns cooperating teachers: [M18:19]

But watch out! Don't turn all the work over to him and then forget about it. It is easy to slip into the habit of thinking: a student teacher? Good. I'll give him some of the jobs to do that I dislike so much . . . He's got to find out that teaching isn't all fun.

When the assistance phase of the practicum is skewed day after day in the direction of clerical responsibilities and record-keeping, then the student teacher becomes a *convenient service man rather than a learner*. The cooperating teacher may find it helpful to differentiate in her own mind between situations helpful to the student teacher and situations which seem to exploit him, by using one major criterion: What does the prospective teacher learn from the activity? To test this criterion consider the following illustration.

In two different schools the practicing student teachers were asked to administer a reading readiness test to the first graders and then to score the results. In one school their function was limited to testing and scoring alone. In the second school they had, in addition, an orientation by the assistant principal on the nature of the tests, and a discussion with each cooperating teacher on the meaning of the results and their application to the classroom work.

The student teachers practicing in the first school found their experience "an imposition," while those in the second school found their test work "a rewarding teaching experience."

To conclude, in his rush toward independent teaching (teaching the whole class) the novice tends to attach little significance to assisting teaching. He looks at it primarily as a "temporary stage" leading to the final goal, failing to comprehend the full learning potential within the experience itself.

Assisting teaching offers an opportunity to learn to teach within the optimal conditions of a small setup and to enable the student teacher to gain intimate contact with individual children as learners. Teaching is not limited to the function of giving a lesson to the whole class. It has many functions and assignments. Mistakenly they are sometimes seen as secondary or even insignificant. Assisting is an opportunity to practice, one by one, the variety of the role components of the teaching position and understand their function.

It may be useful for the student teacher to discuss with the cooperating teacher the diversity of her role responsibilities and then ask himself: "Did I try each one of these elements?" In many cases, the novice will find that some aspects were overlooked.

Some teacher's responsibilities which have to be checked are:

Examine textbooks for readability.
Arrange the closet.
Keep health records.
Arrange the bulletin board.
Give a diagnostic test to a child.
Prepare work sheets.
Supervise playground.
Supervise lunchtime.
Prepare a test.
Prepare art materials.
Evaluate and check written work.
Arrange rollbook.
Work with children's cumulative records.
Plan a science corner.
Give remedial help to a child.
Organize the class library.

It is the responsibility of both the student teacher and the cooperating teacher to try to make the assisting phase a learning experience. The prevalent practice of "exploiting student teachers" should definitely be denounced.

INDEPENDENT TEACHING

As perceived by student teachers, the summit of the practicum experience is that of teaching independently, without assistance from the cooperating teacher; the novice teaches a lesson or more, and the cooperating teacher observes. To the incomplete sentesce, "I wish my cooperating teacher . . .," prevalent answers are "would give me more opportunities to teach on my own;" "would permit me to take over more often."

How does the movement from assisting to independent teaching occur? Who initiates this movement? When does it occur? How does one go about planning a lesson? What are some of the difficulties involved? What kind of help can they expect? How much independent teaching should they have? These are some of the questions with which the student teachers are concerned at this stage of the practicum experience.

To the question, "Who initiated your first independent teaching?" the majority of the group under discussion replied, "the student teacher." Only a small group reported that the cooperating teacher took the initiative on this point.

To the question, "When did you teach independently for the first time?" the answers ranged from "the first week" to "the sixth week," with the majority converging on the third week.*

To the question, "How much independent teaching do you do?" the answers ranged from "very rarely" to "daily."

This brief survey indicates that there is no definite pattern of initiation or practice of independent teaching. The practices vary and are determined primarily by the nature of the communication and the mutual understanding between the cooperating and the student teachers.

Evidence of readiness

There are more complaints about cooperating teachers who are slow in letting the student teacher take over than about cooperating teachers who rush the trainee in this direction. It seems that the movement from assisting to independent teaching is relatively more difficult than the movement from observation to assisting teaching. The latter movement is often natural and does not call for a "formal agreement" between the two adults. For instance, in noticing a child who has problems in arithmetic, or

---

* The group under discussion had four practicum experiences—six weeks in each class.

the classroom teacher checking written work, the novice may step over and assist. In contrast, the student teacher cannot step over and *teach* the class. It must follow a formal decision with the co-operating teacher.

The novice who is eager to try his wings and be in charge, therefore, often fails to examine some of the factors which interfere with the attainment of his objective. In order to tap the perceptions of the difficulties involved in the movement from assisting to independent teaching, a group of student teachers was asked to role-play an informal chat among cooperating teachers discussing their feelings about the trainees. The following are illustrations of the comments made.

The student teacher interferes with the class routines. It took a long time to have them well trained and I would not like to have to start again.

It must be confusing to children and I must be sure first that the student teacher follows my methods.

No one can do the job as well. I am under time pressure. The course of study must be covered and with these children it is not an easy job. I know I'll have to go over and teach the same subject matter again.

The general tone of the above comments is a critical attitude toward the cooperating teacher. Many student teachers seem to feel that the senior teacher is reluctant to let them assume more responsibility with the class. But what they seem to overlook is the fact that the cooperating teacher has responsibilities both to her class and to the trainee. She has to protect the rights and further the education of both parties. In terms of her first responsibility, she cannot let her class become guinea pigs for the floundering of a student teacher. She feels that education is a serious business and time should not be wasted. Furthermore, the zeal for learning should not be dulled by the floundering of a novice.

In terms of her second responsibility, the education of a prospective teacher, she cannot follow the hands-off policy or sink or swim. She must be sure that the novice will swim. Mistakes and difficulties are to be expected, as they are a normal part of learning. But there is a basic difference between mistakes and a complete failure stemming from lack of readiness.

As the logs show, the student teacher himself is critical of the cooperating teacher who "plunges" him too early into "taking over" and then "takes a walk." It is this cooperating teacher (fortunately rare) who is perceived as one who misuses the trainee as "cheap labor" rather than someone who is there to guide the learner.

The main criterion to be followed in moving from assisting to independent teaching is the *readiness* of the student teacher. Providing evidence of being ready is mainly the responsibility of the student teacher, which shows up in his behavior and attitude toward the student-teaching practicum.

In my visits to schools I find that the cooperating teacher is highly complimentary of the student teacher who has initiative.

Come and see the science corner Miss Martin prepared with the group.

She has so many ideas. The children immediately take to her.

They value most cooperation and initiative to help. They question the ability, or at least the readiness, of the one who is passive.

I cannot tell you much about this student. She just sits. I'll have to wait.

She did not come out yet. Perhaps she needs to take her time.

The fact is that the same cooperating teacher will permit one trainee to start independent teaching early and another trainee to start only late in the semester. The decision depends on her perception of the readiness shown by the specific student teacher. It will be useful for the novice to examine his own participation in the practicum, in terms of the criterion of showing evidence of readiness. The following are illustrations of points to be checked.

Systematic work with an individual or a group.

Initiative in organizing a special project.

Discussions with the cooperating teacher of learning problems of specific children.

Knowledge of the course of study, textbooks, and other materials used in the classroom.

Participation in planning of the unit under study.

Familiarity with the class routines and management.

The problem of planning

Student teachers generally know in advance when they are going to teach the class and, therefore, have time to prepare and plan. However, some student teachers report that they are called on to teach without having an opportunity to prepare in advance. ("The teacher was called out and I had to take over.")

Following are some of the practices, student teachers report, which are followed when there is a lack of advance planning.

I continue with her work.

She leaves an assignment on the blackboard.

She tells them to practice their spelling and I supervise it.

She gives me instructions of the pages to be covered.

Not being prepared, the student teacher tends to cling to the textbook or the assignment on the blackboard. He tends to become a supervisor of busy work rather than the one who develops creative ideas.

Portrayed by these responses is an apprentice whose whole entity is following and copying the cooperating teacher. His sense of teaching does not come from reliance on his own resources. He fails to experience the excitement of discovering his own power and becoming independent. He rather imitates. Children may be quick to sense that little new can be expected from this novice.

The importance of comprehensive planning of the independent teaching activities cannot be overemphasized. It is an opportunity for the novice to think through his own interpretation of the subject matter to be taught—a main characteristic of creative teaching.

Student teachers vary in the nature and amount of their planning for independent teaching. They range from those who write lesson plans to those who preplan only by reading materials (teacher guides, books, etc.) with the expectation that the structure of the lesson will develop spontaneously once the teacher is confronted with the group.

The lack of systematic planning is defended by some student teachers on such bases as:

Emphasis on spontaneity.

I don't want to be rigid. I must develop the lesson in terms of their responses.

Only when I am faced with children can I create.

In reality lack of systematic planning as a means of promoting spontaneity is often used as an excuse for the novice who finds it difficult to foresee the expected lesson. Planning a lesson means developing a "play" which predicts the development of the theme through the interacting between the teacher and the children. Writing this "play," or thinking it through, enhances the novice's ability of "being" in the lesson and "feeling" the expected interaction.

The novice who is versed in his plan tends to feel secure during the lesson. He knows what he wants to say and where he wants to go. He feels that he is able to be in control. It is often the person who plans well who is also more able to be open to the ideas, questions, and suggestions of children, and encourage them to come into his plans.

The novice who does not plan sufficiently tends to be occupied with the anxiety of what will happen next. His ability to listen to children is undermined. To avoid floundering and relieve anxiety he tends to rely on one method and adapt it to my situation. Rather than being spontaneous, his teaching tends to become trite.

My observation has indicated that there is a positive correlation between comprehensive planning and successful teaching; between superficial planning and trite teaching.

It should be realized, however, that comprehensive planning alone is no assurance of successful teaching. For instance, some student teachers, in their first steps of independent teaching, tend to consult their lesson plan and read from their notes. In reading notes they stop listening to themselves, to the interaction between themselves and children, and rely solely on the external crutch of the preplanned program. It seems that to some extent at least their planning remains in the notes and does not become an integral part of their ideas; it is as if their teaching is borrowed from the notes rather than created. This practice often expresses the alienation of the student teacher from his teaching, a behavior which violates the creative emphasis on personal meaning.

Some student teachers feel that they must follow the lesson plan to the dot and, consequently, fail to bring in and utilize what evolves in the classroom. Discussions with these student teachers reveal that there are many factors which explain this behavior.

One factor is a misconception of the role of the lesson plan, which is often seen as something they must implement smoothly and meticulously rather than as a tentative structure which has to accommodate the unpredictable in the classroom. In their operational values they are teacher-centered, believing that their sense of order and sequence is the best one and, therefore, should not be modified.

Another factor is the security in the known plan and the fear of the unknown changes. Following the lesson plan generates the satisfaction of knowing where one goes. The difficulty in shifting is that it calls for readjustments and new decisions with regard to the direction. The insecure beginner may be threatened by these unknowns. Student teachers reiterate, in interviews, that while being observed by an authority they tend to be more reluctant to modify plans than when they are on their own. The main issue is to develop a plan which helps the teacher live the lesson and free him at the same time to be open to the ideas and plans of children. At the beginning it is desirable to develop this plan in detailed writing, gradually moving to a general outline with increased teaching experience.

The lesson plan

One of the main questions disturbing the novice is how to plan a lesson. It is difficult to answer this question, since in the last analysis a lesson is a *culmination of the teacher's understanding of education.* A comprehensive answer calls for a discussion of the basic principles of education as they affect the teacher's work. The discussion here will be limited only to some of the main steps through which the novice tends to move in organization his ideas into a lesson plan.

The teacher's objective. A main point of emphasis is the goal, or as some call it, the objective of the lesson. The goal is the main theme of the study under which the subject matter and the activities are organized.

Examining lesson plans and observing lessons in operation, one comes to realize that there is no other aspect of lesson planning which is more confusing to the novice than the function of the teacher's goal in a lesson. In order to get more insight into this function the discussion will attempt to demonstrate ways in which lesson goals are developed. An interviewee says:

The general unit for my class in social studies is transportation. I decided to work on this topic. I asked myself, what is an important understanding in this area which can be dealt with in one session? I decided to choose the main factors underlying the transportation jam.

In this illustration, the objective of the lesson was determined in the light of the broader goals of the transportation unit.

A general notion of the subject matter may sometimes lead to the identification of a goal. For instance, the teacher examines the subject matter on magnets and decides on an objective for one lesson—the function of the magnet as a compass.

Again, one sees here that the objective of the lesson is a product of the broader goals of the unit. In this specific case a broad unit was the use of magnets. The objective of the lesson —the function of the magnet as a compass—is an attempt to spell out one aspect of the broader goal.

As part of teaching about life in other countries, the novice may want to teach the well-known story, "The River," by Pearl Buck. He examines the subject matter (the story) first and only then develops the objective: compare the values and way of life of the Chinese girl portrayed with the life of the children in his class.

The social climate in the classroom, and the needs and interests of children, can play a main role in identification of lesson goals. In a school participating in the open enrollment setup in New York City (a provision whereby parents may register their children in schools outside of their neighborhood), a teacher noticed social distance between the children who were bused in and those who lived in the school district. She decided to teach about similarities and differences between people.

The lesson's goal can be a development of a question raised by children in a previous session, or a task children wanted to accomplish. This is especially common in classes where cooperative planning is encouraged. For instance, as part of a study of the turtle, a point was made that it was cold-blooded. Some children raised questions with regard to the function of this characteristic in the life of animals. It was decided to take up this topic in a special lesson.

As seen in these illustrations, the goal for a lesson serves two important functions. It is a way of looking at the specific lesson in the light of the broader context of the classroom curriculum, and it is a guide for determining the specific subject matter to be taught in a lesson.

Examining the work of the novice, one finds that in some cases the above functions are not understood and, consequently, the goal for a lesson is either not formulated at all or is stated in vague terms. Interviews with student teachers suggest two main explanations of this lack of emphasis on goal formulation. Some student teachers feel that the goal is an "epectation" dictated by the professed values and norms of the educational culture and, primarily, by the college instructor. They feel that goal formulation is part of "theory," and that it does not have a direct and practical impact on the lesson.

Another factor which explains this lack of emphasis on the lesson's goal is the difficulty in identifying the main theme of the lesson. The lesson is perceived primarily as an aggregation of facts and details—the A orientation without the ability to see the uniting idea—that is, the B of the C orientation. It is this kind of practitioner who tends to pay lip service to goal formulation and who formulates his lesson goals in vague terms: "to understand the story," "to understand the problems facing Washington," or "to study about Holland." No attempt is made by him to *clarify* the meaning of the story to the teacher, the problems facing Washington, or the concepts which may be developed through learning about Dutch life.

A lesson goal does not necessarily aim only at the development of the understanding of specific subject matter. Another type of lesson goal deals with the development of desirable attitudes or ways of behavior, such as scientific thinking, imagination, cooperative work, self-directiveness, or curiosity.

These attitudinal goals determine the approach or the methodology of the lesson. Referring back to teachers *A*, *B*, and *C*, they all approach the same subject matter in such different ways primarily because *A* believes in specificity and recall, *B* believes in convergent thinking, and *C* believes in creativity. The science teacher who believes in scientific thinking will emphasize experimentation and observation. The one who is not oriented in this direction will limit presentation to reading and discussion.

As may be seen from these illustrations, the development of lesson goals, in terms of subject matter and attitudes, is not a simple objective process. Looking at the same subject matter and relating to the same children, teachers may come out with somewhat different objectives. What may seem the same topic, such as transportation, is taught by one teacher with a goal emphasizing means of transportation, by another emphasizing that the world is small, and by another as a search for development of a better system. Whether he is conscious of it or not, the objective of the lesson is the product of the teacher's educational philosophy.

The subject matter. Another important point for consideration in lesson planning is the specific subject matter to be taught. The goal is only a statement of the main theme or the "title," it is not specific and comprehensive in terms of content. To illustrate, in stating the objective of teaching the number 7 to a first grade class, the problem is the scope and the sequence of the subject matter to be developed. There are many things that can be taught about number 7: counting, identifying, grouping, addition, subtraction. Each one of the above concepts includes many subcategories. Deciding on the scope of the subject matter means that the teacher should tentatively decide which concepts are going to be taught in a specific lesson. A related question to be decided is the sequence of the concepts, that is, the order of their development. This order is especially important in arithmetic (addition and subtraction of number 7 will come after the teaching of the grouping concept, and not vice-versa).

The same topic in science (electricity), or in social studies (the American Revolution), can be taught on the elementary school or on the university level. The teacher should decide on the depth and comprehensiveness of the subject matter to be taught in order that it will be adapted to the mentality and interests of a specific group of children.

As the discussion suggests, in developing the subject matter the novice should keep in mind two main considerations. The first is, to what extent is there a direct relationship between the teacher's goal and the specific subject matter? Will the lesson on the American revolution attain the goal of understanding the main factors which caused the historical event? Or will it be used in the context of helping children develop a better understanding of the African revolution?

An examination of lesson plans and observations of lessons taught in the classroom show that the relation between the goal and the subject matter is an important point which calls for a great improvement. There are far too many lessons in which the forest cannot be seen because of the many trees—too many lessons in which the subject matter taught does not lead to the crystallization of the main idea—the objective. In some cases the feeling is that the novice jotted down an objective only because he is expected to, and did not think through its structuring impact on the lesson.

A second consideration to be kept in mind is the suitability of the subject matter to children. There are teachers who want to teach *social studies* to children and there are others who want to teach *children* social studies. It is the latter who generally do a more meaningful job of subject matter development. It is not enough to be involved with the structure of the subject matter and simplify it for children but it is as important to have insight into the process of concept formation in children.

At present, our knowledge of the structure of subject matter is more advanced than our understanding of the processes of concept formation, making the adaptation of the second criterion —teaching *children* subject matter—difficult.

A third point to be thought through in lesson planning is *ways of presentation.* Under this point fall the significant problems of *motivation,* development of the *children's objective, methods and materials, summary,* and *assignment.*

Motivation. The actual presentation of a lesson has to start in a way that suggests to the learner that meaningful problems are here to be mastered, and must evoke in him a desire to master them. Teachers generally call this starting point "motivation." (This is a somewhat oversimplified term because, in the long run, everything that is done in a lesson, and not only the starting point, has a motivational value.)

There is a variety of ways of creating motivation in a lesson. In my observation, student teachers are ingenious in this area. They usually relate the lesson to an experience the children have had. For instance, they discuss the visit of the fireman and then raise the question, "But really, how does he extinguish fire? Can we try to extinguish fire here in the classroom?" Or they relate the lesson to the unit under discussion; they may summarize the class study of communication up to the development of the radio, and then raise the question of the limitation of radio in terms of the visual images. From here they move to the discussion of television, which answers this problem.

A strong "motivation" technique is to emphasize a contradiction or to identify points of confusion due to insufficient knowledge. An illustration of emphasis on *contradiction* is examining, through magazines, the present friendly Anglo-American relations and then raising the question, "So why were they at war during Washington's time?" An illustration of motivation through emphasis on the recognition of *insufficient knowledge* is working on arithmetic problems where division is seen only as partitioning, and then discovering, through introducing a new problem, that division also has another function—measurement division.

The above illustrations show that the success of the beginning of the lesson as a motivating factor for learning stems from the fact that it identifies a problem for the learners and there-

fore sets the children's objective for the lesson. To the extent
that the children are aware of an existing *difficulty* (How does
the fireman extinguish fire? What is the difference between the
two paintings?) they are motivated to work on the lesson's objective.

The assumption underlying the above discussion is that children are curious and that they have a healthy appetite for learning. The cooperative search for the identification of a *difficulty*
will arouse this appetite and create motivation for learning. Lack
of understanding of the value of identification of a difficulty as
a motivation for learning may result in the use of "pseudo-moti-
vation." Here is an illustration:

> Children, what did you have for breakfast today?
> Eggs.
> I mean, what did you drink?
> Milk.
> What else?
> Juice.
> Yes.
> Water.

In this illustration, by no means atypical, the relation between the objective—study about water—and the "motivation" is
based only on *associative thinking*. The fact that a specific child
was drinking water for breakfast does not suggest an identification
of a difficulty that has to be resolved. The strength of a "motiva-
tion-discussion" of this nature is limited, as it will arouse only
those who are anxious to please the teacher.

The children's perception of the objective. The beginning of
the lesson called *motivation* is culminated by a statement which
combines the teacher's goal and the objective as perceived by
the pupils. Many teachers like to accentuate the children's objective of the lesson by putting it on the blackboard or asking
children to explain, in their own words, "What do we want to do
today?" The reason for this emphasis is the realization that being
aware of and accepting the objective will enable children to
develop the subject matter in a more meaningful way and see
its unity. The children's objective is *their perception* of the ques-

tion which the lesson has to answer; their perception of the direction toward which they have to move in order to develop a new concept.

For instance, as part of the discussion of Manhattan, children relate experiences about its congestion. The motivation leads to a formulation of an objective for the lesson. "Let us suppose that Manhattan does not have any transportation. What kind of transportation system can we devise for this borough?" In the light of this objective, the children examine a sketch of the area (bridges and roads not identified) and start to develop a plan. Whether they work on the connection of Manhattan with New Jersey or the fact that the city is no longer than wider, they always do it in terms of their awareness of the objective—a transportation system.

In contrast, when children are not aware of the lesson's objective, they will be slow, or even fail, to see the unity of the subject matter. They will discuss the bridges and wait until the teacher moves them to the discussion of the subways. In terms of the process of thinking and self-direction, these pupils will not be searching actively for a solution to the total problem. The quality of the children's thinking is dependent on the teacher's ability to formulate and elicit a meaningful objective.

Examination of lesson plans written by student teachers, and observation of their teaching, show a conspicuous lack of emphasis on the aspect of the children's objective. It may be partly due to the great involvement on the part of the novice in the lesson and its goal, taking for granted that the goal is as obvious to children as it is to him. Or, it may be partly due to an unconscious expression of the teacher's need to control. It is as if they feel that it is sufficient that the leader knows the goal and, therefore, should expect his followers to do what they are told—namely, move step by step as instructed and wait at the end of one step for the leader's instructions concerning movement to the next.

Going back to the previous illustration about transportation in Manhattan, the controlling teacher who spoon-feeds the children discusses the topic in the following terms:

This is good, today we'll study about water.
Now, let's look at the Lincoln tunnel. Where is it?

In Manhattan.
What does it connect?
New York and New Jersey.
How is it similar to the Washington bridge?
Both connect New York and New Jersey.
How is it different?
One is a bridge, the second is a tunnel.
Very good, children, now let's see, is there anything else south of
     the Lincoln tunnel which connects with New Jersey?
The Holland Tunnel.
Very good. Where is the Holland Tunnel?

This orderliness, specificity, and the step-by-step advancement are subtle ways of controlling the class. There is no movement unless the teacher moves because there is no total goal in terms of which children can initiate their own steps.

Imagine that a cooperative statement of an objective for the above lesson was formulated, such as, "to devise a transportation system which connects Manhattan with other places." The end result would tend to be an element of *freedom* for children to suggest various means of transportation, to move on their own from one subtopic to another.

It is evidence that guiding the students to formulate the lesson's objective tends to emphasize the common task facing the group, raises a meaningful goal to be achieved, and encourages freedom and initiative to think and participate. The cooperative identification of the lesson's objective is an attempt to alleviate a major difficulty inherent in lesson planning—the *involvement* of children in learning.

Underlying the lesson approach is a problem of leadership. It is the leader, the teacher, who invests time, thought, and energy in the preparation of the lesson. He reads books, develops materials, devises a plan. It is the leader who is involved and is interested in the plan. The problem is how to make children involve themselves in the same questions with which the teacher is involved; how to make pupils realize that the idea selected for its importance in the teacher's perception can also become important to them.

The answer to the problem of leadership may lie in a lesson plan which makes use of a cooperative search for the identification of the difficulty and the cooperative formulation of an objective. It is the function of the motivation discussion and the sharing on the part of children in the development of an objective, to help the learner get involved in the goal of the specific area of learning. Without these elements of lesson planning learning may tend to become a passive process of imposition.

Once the children's objective is formulated, the class has to move to work on the common task. Two important and interrelated points to be planned are the methods and materials to be used in presenting the subject matter.

Methods and Materials. Elementary education has moved a long way from the traditional practices emphasizing lecturing and the assign-study-recite-test method. The lecture approach, rarely used in the elementary school, does not emphasize the active role of the learner, since it puts him primarily in the position of an absorber. The second method, more commonly used in the elementary school, makes use of the teacher assignment of reading or exercises, followed by testing of the reproduced assignment. Here, too, the frame of reference is the predetermined subject matter in the text, rather than the involvement of the learner in the delineation of a problem and the cooperative formulation of an objective for learning.

The novice is generally aware of the need for a methodology which attempts to bring out the pupil and encourage him to *participate;* participation is a value very close to the heart of student teachers. Consequently, the most common method used by them in presenting subject matter is the *teacher-led discussion.*

In comparison with the lecture or the assign-study-recite-test method, the emphasis on discussion with its goal of participation is very valid. However, as suggested previously in this study, the novice's conception of leading a discussion is often limited. The pattern is too often on teacher-child-teacher-child conversation with lack of sufficient emphasis on the pattern of teacher-child-child-child-teacher discussion where children interact among themselves.

The novice's teacher-centeredness in leading a discussion is a product of the A emphasis in his operation values and his great need for control and security. It is usually true that those student teachers who are able to operate on the *B* and *C* level are more successful in making the method of discussion an experience of interaction among children.

Similar observations can be made concerning the use of the method of *experimentation* commonly employed by the student teacher. Its strength lies in the emphasis on scientific and productive thinking, whereas its limitation, when used by the novice primarily as demonstration and directed observation, becomes a learning situation which deemphasizes experimentation by children or use of the learner's free observation for science learning. Again it is evident that the novice tends to be teacher-centered in his approach to the method of experimentation and observation.

There is a variety of methods that can be utilized in lesson planning: discussion, experimentation, reading, construction, committee work. The novice is confronted with making a choice of the most appropriate method for his specific lesson. Is he going to begin with experimentation and later move to discussion, or vice-versa? Is he going to teach the class as a whole or suggest individual and group work? Does he want to begin by teaching the class as a whole and later move to group work, or do it the other way around?

Similar questions can be raised with regard to the problem of materials. There is a variety of materials used in the school, such as books, audio visual equipment, or science instruments. Which is to be used in the specific lesson and how is it going to be employed?

Generally it can be said that one important difference between successful teachers and poor teachers is the variety of methods and materials they employ. The novice, being industrious and dedicated, is very aware of the importance of utilizing a variety of methods and materials. Much credit for this should go to the cooperating teachers who, generally, do not tend to limit their work to the traditional reading-recitation or to the use of a single textbook for all children. In many classrooms the basal readers were replaced, or at least supplemented, by a class library. Variety in methods, as well as variety in materials, can be seen in many classrooms today. Such experience is positive in its impact on the novice's ability to plan. He stresses the use of concrete and representative material and makes use of a variety of teaching materials and techniques.

Both in his lesson plan and in the implementation of that plan the student teachers show one recurring difficulty—namely, the lack of a good sense of timing and of the ability to shift from one method or material to another. In some cases the novice tends to be slow in moving from one approach to another and sometimes fails to sense that even a group eager to learn will gradually lose interest if a discussion, for instance, is too lengthy. A shift in the method of presentation from class discussion to experiments conducted in small groups, or a shift to writing, may generate new life and interest in learning.

In other cases, the novice tends to shift from one type of activity to another too rapidly. In his too early shifting or the over-reliance on the rich variety of methods and materials, one may overlook the fact that the material has to be *used* in order to be effective. An illustration of overrushed planning and teaching is the student teacher who reads a story to his class about the circus and, without pausing for any discussion or reaction to the story, moves to present the main characters arranged as cut-outs on a flannel board. The novice may be impressed by the variety of the materials—story, cut-outs, flannel board—but a closer examination shows that they were not utilized to bring out learning.

Another illustration of misuse of materials is a lesson in individualized reading where children "sell books." The emphasis is on the visual materials (wheels and covers) made by children rather than on the characters of the story and what they stand for. In other words, the danger is that the concrete materials will become the focus rather than the generalizations and the ideas that they have to help develop.

Through the presentation of new subject matter by the use of various methods and materials, one fundamental criterion has to be kept in mind—the goal of the lesson. As suggested earlier, the subject matter goal determining the specific knowledge to be presented and the attitude or skill goals determine the *method* of presentation.

With regard to the latter, if the goal is scientific thinking, then the method of presentation should not be the A orientation of repetition and recall. If the goal is skills in cooperative work, then the method should not be teacher-centered but rather based on the practice of, and the sensitivity to, the experience of group work.

Only too often do intangible objectives, such as creativity, critical thinking, or cooperative work, express superficial professed values to which one pays lip service. It is with the implementation of such values through the method and materials aspect of the lesson that the spirit of the objective is translated into the language of behavior.

Summary. The culmination of the presentation is to develop a summary or to draw conclusions for the lesson. The function of the summary is to synthesize the learning reached in the light of the stated objective. A common practice in summarizing the lesson is asking children to restate the objective ("What were we looking for?") and then state the answer ("What did we find out?").

The aspect of summary is generally well stated in the lesson plans of student teachers in the form of generalizations or evaluation of the learned subject matter. However, when it comes to practice, under the time pressure of other obligations, the summary is often pushed aside. Children in many cases move from one lesson (social studies) to another (arithmetic) not because they have reached some closure in their intellectual endeavor, but rather because external circumstances caused it.

Summarizing is an important aspect of the lesson and should not be rushed. The children themselves should reiterate the objective of the lesson and in *their own words* should draw the generalizations. Known is the poor practice of telling children "what we have learned today" and then asking them to repeat it (recite it) or copy it in their own notes. Summarizing should be approached as an expression of productive thinking, of putting things together, of applying and creating, rather than as a process of repetition and specificity.

Summarizing is not necessarily an oral process. It is possible to summarize through other media, such as writing or dramatization. For instance, when the science experiment is over the pupils may describe the problem, procedure, and findings in writing.

Summarizing does not necessarily mean drawing generalizations; it can also be a process which emphasizes application or divergent thinking. For instance, as a culmination of a lesson discussing punctuation, the children apply their learning by punctuating a composition. Or, as a culmination of reading and discussing a story, the pupils move from the known to the unknown by adding a part or a scene to show their personal interpretation of the dynamics involved.

It is an effective practice to have a brief discussion of the work which still *has to be done* on the specific topic as part of the summary aspect. For instance, after summarizing, the teacher says:

> Now we understand the function of the roots in helping the plant grow. What did we say the other parts were?
>
> Stem, leaves.
>
> Next time we'll look into the function of the leaves and compare it with the roots.

The student teacher is often interested only in a single lesson. For the regular teacher, and especially for the pupils, a lesson does not exist in isolation but is rather a part of a larger unit. The emphasis on the unfinished business, that is, on things that have to be done next time as a result and a continuation of the learning gained today, is conducive to the development of unit in subject matter. The child is helped to see the total picture.

There is also a psychological aspect of motivation and involvement in suggesting the direction for the next lesson. The field vision of the learner is not limited to one lesson alone. He does not have to wait in the dark until the teacher next day unwraps an unknown package to reveal a new objective. In other words, one function of the discussion of "what we will do next time" is to activate the learner.

The Assignment. To better understand the concept of activation, the following discussion will center on what is generally the last part of the lesson plan—the assignment.

One known and important function of the assignment is for

the learner to review the material presented in the lesson. This can be done at home or at a special work time at school. The former is generally referred to as *homework* and the latter as *seat work*. Typical examples of assignments may be drill on arithmetic exercises or review of readings in social studies and then answering questions on the topic. The commercial publications are very prolific in this area and have produced the workbook whose main function is review.

However, looking at the function of the assignment primarily in terms of review is very limiting. Too often is the emphasis only on the repetitive A orientation. Whether one calls the assignment *drill,* or a nicer word *practice,* or a still nicer word, *review,* one cannot avoid the feeling that too much of it results in what teachers call "busy work."

Limiting the assignment only to one function—review—is an underestimation of the importance of encouraging the learner to go ahead on his own with the subject matter. It stems from a philosophy which perceives the child as a helpless creature who can only absorb rather than create; a philosophy which believes that the only important knowledge is communicated by the teacher, underestimating that discovered by the learner. It is a position which perceives the responsibility to move ahead, to initiate further learning as the prerogative of the leader only. The child has to follow the leader, and review.

A second function of the assignment is to give the pupils an opportunity to go beyond the review, to react to the subject matter learned in the lesson, apply it, and create something new on their own. The following are some illustrations of this more creative approach to the assignment task.

In a science lesson a class studies the topic "air takes space." They see that a napkin put in the end of a glass turned over in water does not become wet. The water does not fill the whole glass as the napkin is protected by a barrier of air. As an assignment the children have to develop other experiments or suggest other observations which show that air takes space.

In a bright sixth grade class the lesson deals with Lincoln's life. The assignment is: "Imagine Lincoln is alive today. What would he do or say?" Such an attempt to relate the two eras stimulates the pupils to write about topics like the following: "President

Lincoln meets President Johnson," "Lincoln visits Harlem," or "My tour with Abe Lincoln."

After an individualized reading session the class is asked to prepare for "selling" their respective readings to the other pupils. The emphasis is on accentuating the learner's interpretation of one feature of his reading, such as a character or a scene. The children are free to utilize writing, oral expression, dramatization, construction, or any other media.

Studying about "The United States—A Country of Immigrants," a meaningful assignment may be: "Make direct contact with an immigrant and find out his reasons for coming to America."

The above examples illustrate a somewhat deemphasized role of the assignment as review and emphasize the need to encourage children to create new learnings independently. Most of the examples also illustrate the encouragement of the learner to look forward toward the new lesson and share with the teacher the responsibility of preparing for it.

The review function of the assignment means that the pupil is past-oriented; what will happen next is not his concern. The creation and application function of the assignment means that the learner is future-oriented, that he is aware of (the former tends not to be even aware), and involved in, the coming lesson. The development of the next lesson is at least partly dependent on the quality of his preparation and contribution.

There are not many more important principles in education than activating the learner in sharing in the responsibility for the progress of his learning. There are few principles which are so often violated by teachers. Perceiving the role of the assignment not only as review but also as creation of new learning, extending the field vision of the learner and encouraging him to share in the responsibility for the next lesson, is a step toward the education of the active learner.

Conclusions. As suggested earlier, a lesson plan is a culmination of the teaching philosophy of the teacher. The discussion here was limited to the main steps a teacher may move through in organizing his ideas into a lesson.

In the reality of actual teaching, the lesson steps presented here in a sequential fashion may not proceed in this order at all. The researcher following the steps of research design often finds out that he has to reformulate the problem or add a hypothesis at the advanced step of data analysis. Similarly, the teacher following the steps of lesson planning may often find that he begins the lesson with the children's objective or that he has to change his own goal in midstream.

The structure of a lesson presented here is an attempt to help the novice plan. Followed rigidly, it becomes a routinized procedure which stops the teacher from being open to the children's suggestions and sense of direction. As stated in the discussion of model *C* (the creative teacher), a major problem of planning is to develop a flexible structure which is a foundation for the learner's own structure.

Despite the usefulness of the lesson plan described here, one should be aware of its major limitation—planning is limited to one lesson; the horizons of the learner and his involvement with a specific objective are limited to a short-range goal. Productive and creative thinking call for *long-range* planning in the light of a *long-range* goal. Therefore, to the extent that it is possible the pupils should be sensitized to the broader context of the lesson, that is—the unit. (For a discussion of this topic the reader is referred back to the chapter on social studies.)

Practicing the teacher's total role

In the course of student teaching the number of lessons taken over by the student teacher gradually increases and becomes a daily arrangement. At the beginning he teaches only individual and discrete lessons, but later he becomes responsible for an area of instruction, such as arithmetic or science, or for a unit of instruction, such as weather, clothing, or transportation. Toward the end of the practicum the novice may take on the responsibility for a full day or even several successive days of teaching. While in the beginning student teaching consists primarily of observation and occasional teaching, toward the end the balance changes toward more emphasis on assisting and independent teaching. In the last month or weeks of student teaching, observation should play a very minor role.

The importance of being responsible for a large area of instruction, in terms of subject matter and duration, cannot be over-emphasized. As the vision of the novice tends to be narrow, he looks at one lesson, one practice or problem, as separate entities. He tends to be present-oriented without taking into account what has happened to the group in the past or what their plans may be for the future.

A lesson does not exist in a vacuum. Teaching is much more than the preparation and the implementatios of discrete lessons. To the extent that the novice can be responsible for large blocks of time and large areas of study, he may come closer to experiencing the total role of the teacher and thus come to broaden his vision of the meaning of teaching. It is perhaps impossible, under student teaching conditions (as many student teachers point out), to realize the full role of a teacher. Even if the senior teacher is not in the classroom, the student teacher operates in terms of the former's power. Despite this reality, the objective should be to come as close as possible to the goal of the total role.

One factor which explains the importance of practicing the total teacher's role rather than discrete lessons is the emphasis of modern education on the value of the *unity* of subject matter. This trend toward unity stems from a criticism of traditional education as being too fragmentary and compartmentalized. Experimentation with curriculum patterns within the last era, the movement from the subject matter to the correlated curriculum, the innovation of the broad field and the core curriculum can probably be seen as an expression of the trend to search for unity in subject matter.

When a student teacher plans or teaches a single lesson and fails to see its relation to the total unit, he ignores this emphasis on unity. This type of student teacher may teach, for instance, about the nest in a single lesson and fail to put it in the broader context of the life of the birds, or the problems of adjustment to the environment. He will tend to fail to see the need for integration into broad units or major ideas and concepts, and thus have limited success in developing a high level of thinking.

The emphasis of modern education on unity of subject matter goes hand in hand with the emphasis on the increased role of the learner. A preoccupation with discrete lessons leads, sometimes unwittingly, to a deemphasis on the above function. This point needs elaboration.

The previous section, describing steps in lesson planning, limits the role of the learner to the participation in planning and developing of one lesson. It does not emphasize the role of the learner in the cooperative planning of the unit as a whole. The novice who looks at teaching as a series of discrete lessons gets the wrong impression that "motivation" and "the children's objective" are something to be limited to a separate lesson. They fail to see the dynamic force in terms of motivation and comprehension of learning, of involving pupils in long-range planning of the total unit.

Teaching, when approached as a series of discrete lessons, may not only ignore the significance of emphasizing continuity in learning, but also may present the danger of overlooking the role of *balance* in the curriculum. A student teacher may tend to be interested in the success or the quality of one lesson, not realizing that the quality of his lesson is at least partly dependent on its relation to other aspects of teaching and its balance with other activites of the day.

Taking over the class for the whole day is an opportunity to examine practical, though sometimes overlooked, questions such as the following:

Is there a balance between sedentary activities and moving? Our schools no longer have a recsss period at the end of each period as was practiced in the traditional school. When does the child then have an opportunity to move around? Is he expected to sit for three successive hours?

Is there a balance between teaching the class as a whole, working with groups or with individuals? Whereas this balance may be better achieved in the present school than in the traditional setup, is there, nevertheless, in a specific classroom, an overemphasis on one of the above organizational patterns?

Is there a balance between intellectual discussion and other activities, in moving from a discussion of current events to a discussion of literature? Would it be better to balance the overemphasis on class discussion by introducing reading in literature?

Is there a balance between difficult learning activities and easier ones, and attention to their proper sequence? It may not be the best practice to start the day, as too many teachers do, with "red tape" activities or with spelling. Both do not call for the investment of a high degree of intellectual energy. It is better to start with a class discussion of a subject area.

These are only illustrations of the problem of the day balance. The student eacher who looks at teaching as a lesson plan may fail to become sensitive to this problem. Teaching a unit, and especially teaching the class for several days, may be even more demanding and educative in terms of the balance criterion. Here are illustrations of questions to be examined in this circumstance:

Is there a balance between committee presentations and teacher-directed discussion or between individual interests and common learning for the whole class in unit teaching? For some teachers a unit utilizes individual interests and committee presentations; for others the term *unit* is only a "respectful title"; under its disguise they can continue with traditional instruction.

Is there a balance between emphasis on various subject areas? In the self-contained classroom, where planning is mainly in the hand of the teacher, there is a common tendency to emphasize an area in which the teacher feels strong and to underemphasize or even neglect subjects in which one is not very competent. (As reported by student teachers, the amount of time spent on science is too often limited.)

Is there a balance between the A, B and C orientations in teaching? As suggested in this study, there is room for more emphasis on the development of convergent thinking and creativity.

In brief, a practicum limited to the planning and teaching of discrete lessons tends to be denoted by a narrow vision of the broader dimensions of teaching.

As reported by student teachers, the topic of the unit to be taught is generally determined by the cooperating teacher. For instance, she advises the trainee whether the class is going to study the water supply of New York City, housing, or the westward migration. The choice of the subject of instruction is generally up to the student teacher and is often made in terms of the special competency of the student teacher. The choice of subject area is often made by the student teacher in terms of his observation of the limitation of the senior teacher in a certain area.

("Children seldom have science. I thought I would help by teaching this subject.")

Competency in a certain area and desire to contribute to the class are good guides for the first selection of a unit or subject for instruction. However, in the long run, they may lead to a situation where the trainee limits his practice to one area and fails to experience the total role of the teacher.

An analysis of the practices of the group under discussion reveals that they differed to a great extent in their success in attaining the goal of playing the *total* role of the teacher. They differed in terms of the number of lessons taught, variety of subject areas engaged in, or extent of independent teaching by the end of the practicum.

The analysis of the practices in which the novice is engaged suggests a positive correlation between good quality of teaching and the intensive experience of the total role of the teacher. It is the resourceful and involved student teacher who continuously explores the various aspects of the teacher's role and attempts to practice them. It is the insecure or detached teacher who withdraws, sits back, and limits his participation.

The findings of this study suggest that, despite the fact that the cooperating teacher is the decision-maker with regard to the classroom management, in the long run it is primarily up to the initiative of the student teacher whether he will practice the total role of the teacher or whether his practicum will be a limited experience.

ROLE TAKING: IMITATIVE OR CREATIVE?

Prior to the actual experience of student teaching, the prospective teacher reads, writes, and thinks about the role of the teacher. Now for the first time he is taking the role himself as an observer of classroom practices, as an assistant, and as an independent teacher. What is the impact of role-taking on the student teacher? Examination of the group's reactions reveal both positive trends and unresolved difficulties.

A prevalent reaction to the practicum is a deeper awareness of the dimensions of the teaching problem. An interviewee says:

Only when you teach do you really understand what it is all about. You are faced with the problem. You must think and act . . . In observing the classroom teacher I tend to take it for granted that what she is doing is the right thing. I don't have to make choices. I follow her actions and get the false impression that the problem is simple.

Another student teacher brought the following example to illustrate the point that in teaching one finds out that the problem is more complex than expected.

I was working on developing an experience chart with the children. The title was: "The Circus Comes To Town." I am critical of the teacher who asks children to contribute and then uses her own ideas, or selects only what she had in mind. So I decided to put down the children's statements as they were given and add only the name of the contributor. The kids got a kick out of it, but I found out that not being selective, the story lacked continuity. So we had to do what I didn't plan on—rewrite the story.

As seen in this example, role-taking means that the behavioral role is generally more complex than its *predicted* intellectual formulation. Therefore role-taking, such as delegating responsibilties to children, evaluating compositions, or starting committee work, leads to better insight into the broader dimensions of the problem.

Role-taking is perceived by the student teacher as a most important educational experience, and by many subjects as *the* most important one. The confrontation with the need for "action" is a dynamic force which promotes further learning. The conventional emphasis on "first learn then act," is changed into a new pattern of continuous interaction between learning and action: learning → action → learning → action, and so on. The surge of interest in learning is identified by the student teachers themselves, and also can be seen by the increased amount of non-assigned educational literature they read on their own. The search for knowledge deepens when a new dimension is added, namely the search for knowledge on how to behave as a teacher.

Another positive impact of role-taking is a gradual increase in the feeling of competency. Teaching is partly a skill (in the broad sense of the word) and therefore has to be practiced. There is much skill to be mastered and many practices to become acquainted with. The novice speaks about an improved sense of timing, better ability in leading a discussion, growing sensitivity to the individual differences, with a corresponding ability to adapt the content to these differences, growth in realistic planning, and a richer development of a repertoire in terms of content and techniques. As some student teachers put it: "I start to feel like a ham."

In terms of relating to children, the positive impact is seen through a better awareness of their needs, and a more realistic expectation of the leadership problem. They learn that relating to children is more than being permissive or authoritarian. Teaching is a complex role which calls for different patterns of behavior in different situations.

Role-taking, along with its positive impact, raises a question in the mind of the student teacher: *the expression of his individuality as a teacher.* The difficult and unresolved problem is whether the novice's teaching behavior is going to be only an imitation of the senior teacher, or is also going to be an expression of the student teacher's own exploration and experimentation.

Excerpts from interviews illustrate the problems involved in searching for self-expression.

Naturally you respect the classroom teacher for achieving what you have yet to attempt to achieve. Along with this respect goes a feeling that her way is the right way since it is getting results.

In theory, and even in your mind, you believe there are many different ways of approaching a problem. However, in reality, when faced with a difficult situation you are more likely to resort to the tried and tested than to attempt a new approach to a situation. It is here that I believe a cooperating teacher has the greatest influence on her student teacher.

The student teacher is appreciative of the functional model of teaching demonstrated by the cooperating teacher, but he also questions whether he is free to find himself. Despite the feeling of progress, there is nevertheless an expression of the apprehension that something is lost in the process, or perhaps unrealized in the student-teacher experience—namely, the expression of individuality as a teacher.

Her relations with the children, her personality, her manner all have an effect on your teaching. Almost unconsciously you pick up her way of teaching which you have been observing for six weeks . . . It becomes difficult to fully express your personality in someone else's classroom.

This student teacher feels that in some respects he is being molded rather than growing, that he becomes primarily an imitator rather than a creator. What is the basis for these not uncommon feelings? Is there something inherent in the climate of the student-teaching practicum or in the consultative behavior of the senior teacher which contributes toward a feeling of limited freedom? Or does the problem lie less within the objective reality and more in the subjective and selective perception of the novice?

The data collected in this study does not suggest a conclusive answer to this question. It only permits some speculation. Look at the following responses to the incomplete sentence "Introducing new ideas while being a student teacher in a class . . ."

> a challenge.
> a fascinating and rewarding experience.
> rewarding, but also frightening.
> may lead to trouble. The teacher may resent you.
> may be resented by the class.

Introducing new ideas is seen both as a challenge and a threat. The main source of the threat is perceived primarily in the attitude of the cooperating teacher and in the reactions of the children.

Similar results can be seen in the responses to the incomplete sentence "changing classroom routines . . ." Positive reactions approve the idea as contributing toward flexibility and innovations. Negative reactions warn that introducing change in routines:

> is very difficult as children do not believe there is any way other than their teacher's.

> is a source of confusion.

> may upset the children and the teacher.

In discussing changing classroom routines, a common expression used by the student teacher is, "breaking the classroom routines." In the metaphoric language of the novice, routines are perceived as so solid and rigid that if bent only a little they will tend to *break*. No wonder that, with these perceptions of the classroom climate, he student teacher feels the lack of freedom, often needed freedom for his own exploration and experimentation.

The question should be raised again whether in the objective reality the classroom climate is denoted by more freedom to experiment than the student teacher is willing to recognize and make use of? Whether in reality the cooperating teacher is much more permissive than the student teacher cares to admit?

A group of student teachers was asked at the end of the practicum to discuss as a panel the following topic: "My advice to the young generation of teachers." The *first* point on the agenda was routines, and a major part of the presentation dealt with the need to *routinize* the class. A typical expression used was the advice to "clamp down" on the class in the first weeks of the year. One extreme expression used was, "the first job you have to do is to tame them down." (The dictionary defines *tame* as "to reduce from a wild to a domestic state.") The point was made that:

These children are confused in so many other areas of life, that the school should become the secure force in their life. It is the good training of a routinized classroom atmosphere which makes the school a source of security.

This study does not question the point that the development of routines should be an integral part of the teacher's job. It does question, however, the exaggerated proportion given to the role of routines in the thinking of the novice. It is almost as if success in teaching is magically related to success in structuring classroom routines.

The perception of the classroom as a routine-oriented institution which does not tolerate modifications interferes with the novice's ability to develop his individuality. This, however, does not necessarily mean that his perception is always correct in terms of objective reality, as the needs of the student teacher affect their perception. Those who are less open and imaginative as people, those who crave for protection and security, those who need the exactness of the model, those who are satisfied with the status quo, tend to perceive routines as the center of their work. Those who are tolerant to ambiguity, those who are actively trying to realize themselves as educators, tend to perceive routine in its proper perspective.

The former group in their student teaching tends to be preoccupied with the imitation of the model. The second group attempts to develop a teaching behavior based both on imitation and on one's own exploration. Some student teachers have power to try their own way even under rigid classroom conditions, while trainees may remain fixated in the imitation stage, even under optimal conditions and a free climate. "Freedom to try" is primarily a subjective phenomenon!

Another factor which affects the novice's sense of "freedom to experiment" is his consultative relations with the cooperating teacher. The impact of the latter is expressed mainly in two ways: (1) demonstration and (2) consultation.

The prerequisite to growth is experimentation, and the prerequisite to experimentation is freedom to explore. To the extent that the objective reality of the "demonstration" is characterized by behavior which permits freedom to children, the student teacher is more likely to encourage freedom in his teaching. If the climate is generally experimental, then the novice may be encouraged to develop ideas and try them in action. To the extent that the model demonstrated is characterized by overemphasis on controlled behavior, it will interfere with the student teacher's desire to explore.

Demonstration is a recognized function of the cooperating teacher. This is her unique contribution to the guidance of student teachers. It somewhat overshadows her second guidance function —consultation. As reported by student teachers, when consultation is stressed in their relations with the senior teacher they feel encouraged to try ideas. When emphasis on consultation is limited, the tendency is to feel that there is no room for trying. As one novice put it:

I get best results when I do what she does. But deep in my heart I am confused on whether all that she does is right and on what I really have to do.

It seems that consultation is conducive to encouraging experimentation in the student teacher in two main ways: (1) It brings the senior and the novice close together as people, and therefore generates a sense of security and freedom in the latter. (2) Consultation is an attempt to look at the dynamics of teaching. The specific pattern of teaching is not accepted as "this is the way to do it," but is rather generalized in terms of its underlying principles. In other words, thinking through educational practices is conducive to experimentation.

As perceived by student teachers, the main strength of the cooperating teacher is in the first function of demonstration, rather than in her second role of consultation. To the incomplete sentence "I wish my cooperating teacher . . . ," a typical response is "would criticize my work more often." To the incomplete sentence the "cooperating teacher criticizes mainly . . . ," the overwhelming majority responds:

> She does not.
> She never criticizes but simply says thank you.

It seems that many cooperating teachers themselves perceive their main contribution as demonstration and tend to deemphasize consultation. In a conference a cooperating teacher said to me:

> I work very intensively with my student teacher. While she is teaching, I take *your role* and jot down detailed notes to be discussed later in a conference.

In the perception of this dedicated cooperating teacher, the intensive examination of the teaching behavior of the novice is not within the exact boundaries of her role, but rather is more characteristic of the consultation role of the college instructor.

When the novice is faced with the experience of a forceful model of teaching behavior (the senior teacher) without sufficient systematic and deliberate attempt to help him analyze the dynamics and explore other possible directions, he is faced with the two alternatives: (1) to copy the pervasive and concrete teaching behavior, the "sure-proof," "the one which works," or (2) to mobilize his resources and in addition to learning from the model, adapt it with his own personal interpretation.

Under the insecure condition of being a beginner and a guest in a classroom, with the not uncommon and often mistaken perception that the strength of the classroom climate is primarily the routines, the tendency of too many beginners is to emphasize the imitator-repetitor role of the learner, and to "postpone" the role of pursuing the expression of their individuality in teaching.

The emphasis given to the importance of the expression of individuality in student teaching can be challenged. The question can be raised: Isn't the primary function of the student teacher to learn the existing practices? Is exploration a proper objective for the novice who still has to do the ground work before he is ready to spread his wings? It can be argued that individuality should not be a major objective of student teaching, but is rather an aspect of independent and full-time teaching.

This position is at variance with the major tenet of this study —the emphasis on creativity in learning. To use Mackinnon's terminology,[M1] the student teacher should learn both by "sense perception" and "intuitive perception." The first is stress on things as they are; on ties to the model. The second is an alertness to the as yet not realized and to be explored practices; on ideational movement from an original stimulus.

The emphasis on sense and intuitive perception are not sequential tasks of learning, but are rather simultaneous processes. One is not a prerequisite to the other, but rather feeds and enriches the other. In terms of elementary school practices, it is not fully correct to assume that the teaching of reading skills is a prerequisite to the teaching of literature and poetry. They should be taught simultaneously. In terms of student teaching, both learning through sense and intuitive perception—that is, imitation of the model and exploration—are the task of the novice.

When these two processes are seen as sequential tasks, the second task may never be realized. The end result may be the type of teacher of whom it is said: "She teaches for twenty years, but has only one year of experience."

To experience a sense of freedom to try, to actively search for improved ways of working, is a challenging, but a threatening task. The challenge and threat involved can be understood in terms of the broader theory of motivation underlying this study. As Maslow suggests in his article on "Defense and Growth":[M3:37-38]

Every human being has both sets of forces within him. One set clings to safety . . . hanging on to the past . . . afraid to take chances, afraid to jeopardize what he already has, afraid of independence,

freedom, separation. The other set of forces impels him forward toward . . . uniqueness of self, toward full functioning of all his capacities . . . safety has both anxieties and delights; growth has both
anxieties and delights.

It seems that it is not at all difficult to relieve, at times, the
anxiety over lack of growth. The mechanism used frequently is
that of externalizing the source of the trouble and blaming it on
factors outside oneself. In another investigation, exploring the attitudes of *experienced* teachers toward experimentation, I got
reactions like the following:[86:203]

Attempting to do anything new brings down the wrath of the system
on your head.

Our fear is a direct product of a dogmatic board of education. Democracy in education is for the children. Little free thinking is allowed to
teachers.

The prevalent reaction of the experienced teachers was perception of the external threat of the *authority figures*—principal,
board of education, etc.—concerning experimentation. It was the
rare response which dealt with the experience of the *internal*
threat.

It is my observation that both experienced and novice teachers tend to have more freedom to experiment than they are willing to make use of. Student teachers often admit that when they
make a suggestion for a new approach to the cooperating teacher,
she generally reacts: "It is interesting; why don't you go ahead
and try it?"

It is of utmost significance to start on the level of student
teaching to avoid overemphasis on repetitive teaching; to see
the practice of exploration and the search for the expression of
individuality as an integral part of the definition of the teacher's
role.

SELECTED BIBLIOGRAPHY

BROWN, Thomas, and BANICH, Serafina, *Student Teaching in an Elementary School.* New York: Harper & Row, Publishers, 1962. A systematic discussion of the major problems involved.

MILNER, Ernst, *You and Your Student Teacher.* New York: Teachers College, Bureau of Publications, Columbia University 1961. A warm and insight-filled presentation.

STRATEMEYER, Florence, and LINDSEY, Margaret, *Working with Student Teachers.* New York: Teachers College, Bureau of Publications, Columbia University, 1958. A most comprehensive discussion. Written for cooperating teachers.

WIGGINS, Sam, *The Student Teacher in Action.* Boston: Allyn and Bacon, Inc., 1957. A functional discussion written for student teachers.

12

The student and the department of education

As students, the young teachers under discussion are majors in the department of education. While the first two years of their college careers are spent studying general education in the liberal arts and science departments, the last two are spent majoring in education, concentrating in a subject area along with elective courses. Every effort is made to see that the major in education will develop a concentration in an additional area. The subject areas chosen most prevalently by majors in Elementary Education are sociology, psychology, and english; mathematics and science are chosen less frequently. Altogether, about one fourth of the student's course work is devoted to education; the other three fourths are devoted to general education, concentration, and elective courses.

The preparation of elementary school teachers is, in essence, a cooperative responsibility of the college as a whole. The assumption underlying this program is that the student has to be educated in the best tradition of the liberal arts and sciences. It is the function of the department of education to build its professional preparation on the basis of the above scholarly traditions; to examine the social foundations of our culture, human growth and development, and the structure of subject matter as these factors affect the learning process. Another important function of the department of education is to provide firsthand experiences

356

for its students in order to strengthen their theoretical understanding and prepare them for the practice of teaching.

The purpose of this chapter is to examine the impact of education, as an area of specialization, on the novice teachers in
terms of the main theme of this study—repetitive versus creative
teaching. Does education inculcate in its majors a professional
ego-ideal of a creative teacher? Does it prepare the novice with
the theoretical and practical skill for coping with the problem of
creative teaching? Does it foster a sound professional self-image
in the young teacher which provides him with the emotional and
intellectual resources necessary to be experimental?

THE IDEAL AND THE REAL

In the process of preparing to become teachers, the student
teachers live in a certain education culture and introject its ideals.
They care about the role of education. They care immensely about
their relationship with children and aspire to establish a warm
relationship based on mutual respect and affection. They are most
critical of rote learning, harsh treatment of children, rigidity, and
boredom. They are critical of the waste of time, overemphasis
on "busy work," and monotony which exists in too many classes.
The student teachers identify with the slogans of the education
culture, the importance of being democratic, the development of
self-direction, thinking, creativity, the emphasis on the education
of the whole child, and provisions for individual differences. They
internalize this sense of mission and are determined to be giving
and creative.

The pressure to change

The impact of the ideals of the education culture is successful
primarily in affecting change in the official system of values of
the new teachers—the level of verbal expression. It does not necessarily have the same impact of change on their conduct as teachers. A discrepancy often develops between their professional and
operational values, between the theoretical ideals and their actual
teaching behavior. It seems that the process of reeducating the

young teachers—helping them change from a traditional conception of knowledge to which they were exposed as children, to a modern orientation—is only partly successful. Lewin says: [L4:28]

Re-education is frequently in danger of reaching only the official system of values, the level of verbal expression and not of conduct; it may result in merely heightening the discrepancy between the super-ego (the way I ought to feel) and thus gives the individual a bad conscience.

In the case of the teachers under discussion, the experiencing of a discrepancy between the ideal and the real leads to a feeling of ambivalence which is expressed on the one hand in identification with the department of education and in skepticism on the other. These ambivalent attitudes may be seen in their reactions to the incomplete sentences dealing with ideals of education. On the one hand they introject the values of education.

A good teacher wants children to . . . think for themselves and depend less on her . . . grow intellectually, emotionally and socially.

When children don't listen . . . the teacher should examine the causes.

Children who steal . . . should be understood.

When children use bad language . . . talk to them privately.

In contrast to the above positive and constructive reactions, examine the following responses to the incomplete sentence "Educational ideals . . ."

are ridiculous.

go out of the window in the classroom.

are often unattainable.

are only theory and not practical.

On the same battery of incomplete sentences, a teacher may harbor diametrically opposed attitudes toward education, simultaneously identifying and rejecting them. One factor underlying this ambivalence is the difficulty in moving from theory to practice, from professed to operational values. Discussing the courses taken in college, an interviewee says:

I took two courses—one in 17th-Century English Literature and the second, a course in education. I found that the English course was stimulating . . . With regard to the ed. course, I could not see its implications for my work in the classroom.

Examining this not atypical excerpt from an interview, it is easy to recognize that the novice teacher approaches the two courses with different criteria in mind. Reacting to an English course, the college student asks, "Do I understand it?" Whereas, in participating in a discussion on education, he asks, "What does it mean in terms of my teaching behavior?" From education courses the student expects broader knowledge—behavioral as well as intellectual. While it may be relatively easy to meet the student's quest for intellectual knowledge, it may be rather difficult to meet his needs in terms of translating ideas into his practical teaching behavior.

Teacher education is based to some extent on the erroneous equation of word mastery with practical application. Contradiction between ways of talking and ways of behaving is something all of us have observed in ourselves and in others. However, being able to talk about better teaching or recalling accurately the wise statements of others is not assurance at all for better teaching. New teachers, also, very often experience a discrepancy between their facility with words and educational ideas, and their ability to behave (that is, teach) according to these ideas.

One of the most difficult problems in teacher education is that of making subject matter more meaningful to teachers. How can studying about learning influence the behavior of the teacher? How can the shell of verbal understanding be penetrated so that teachers can move toward the deeper knowledge which is alive in daily work?

Despite an awareness of this problem by teacher-educators, and despite much progress toward its resolution, many novice teachers still experience "lack of integration" or "a sense of discrepancy." In some extreme cases, they feel that their understanding of the educational subject matter is "too glib," or is "not personally meaningful."

Teacher-training programs are perceived by teachers as a call to change; change not only in terms of how they think, speak, or write, but also how they behave with, and relate to, their pupils. The same function of education courses is also perceived by the instructor who often uses "action expressions," such as the following:

"You have to . . .

"The function of the classroom teacher is . . .

"In working with children one should . . .

Both the instructor and student of education perceive the study of education as a stimulus for growth in teaching behavior; as an agent which attempts to shatter the familiar, safe way of teaching and thus attempts to move from overaccentuation of recall and identification of facts toward convergent and divergent thinking; from teacher domination toward emphasis on the child's curiosity and initiative; from routinized child behavior to self-discipline; from a narrow to a functional conception of knowledge; from a preoccupation with expected norms toward sensitivity and respect for individual differences. In brief, education courses are a call to change from the safe boundaries of the known to the laden potentialities of the unknown.

Change on the behavioral, rather than merely on the verbal level, is most difficult to achieve. When pressed to do it one may feel threatened or even resentful. Lippit [L7:7] points out that new ideas in the physical sciences are rather quickly absorbed by a competitive market. In the human sciences, however, because of our emotional involvement in the present way of behavior and the difficulty in visualizing the tangible results of new practices, we often tend to resist change.

Corey [C3] suggests that research generalizations which are applicable to the production of instructional materials, school buildings, and other material innovations, are accepted faster than research generalizations which have implications for teacher-pupil relations. The first type of generalization deals with the physical aspects of teaching and is, therefore, absorbed without too much difficulty or threat. The second type of generalization, however, deals with the personal and human elements of teaching, of which the teacher as a person is an integral part. In trying to adapt to such generalizations the novice often finds himself threatened and resistant.

Modern education courses challenge some of the basic assumptions underlying the meaning of knowledge and teaching held by teachers, and thus, inevitably, pose a source of some confusion and even threat to them. To further illustrate this point, look at the criticism of some common assumptions of educational theory presented by Earl Kelley in his book, *Education for What is Real.*[K1:15-22]

1. Knowledge is not something that can be handed down by authority.
2. Subject matter taken on authority is not necessarily educative.
3. The best way to teach is not through the setting out of subject matter in unassociative fragments.
4. Education is not preparatory to life, but rather life itself.
5. Education should stress cooperative processes. The teacher is not the only one to establish the goals of learning, and positive discipline is related to the cooperative planning of objectives.
6. The process of reaching an answer to an academic problem is as important as the product.
7. Evaluation is a cooperative teacher-pupil function.

The young teacher is challenged by the stimulation and daring of such ideas. When he continually evaluates the progress of his behavioral learning in terms of the "ideals," he may often find that he cannot measure up to such ideal practices as stressing cooperative planning and evaluation. He feels confused, and in some cases, even defeated.

The conflict which novice teachers often experience when they face the discrepancy between educational ideals and what they consider practical, can be seen in the following illustration. After a visit to an experimental school, a group of teachers was asked to jot down a brief reaction. Positive responses were:

an ideal situation.

everything a teacher could wish for.

. . . like a movie picture coming true to life.

Negative responses were:

Far different from my experience . . . Many things seemed unreal and artificial.

I do not think that I would like to be a teacher in such a school, despite its many attractions.

> There is no feeling of unity or belonging. I think children should
> have their own seats and tables; a place to call their own.

The teachers in this visit had, on the one hand, a feeling of an
ideal situation; on the other, a sense of unreality. The perceived
expectation that they, too, should move in their own teaching toward the ideal symbolized by the visit, seemed not only attractive, but also (to some students) impossible.

In reaction to the same school visit, one teacher said:

> We think of ourselves as being idealistic, but it is a surface kind of
> idealism. We may gripe, discuss, but not risk our own positions. The
> young teachers are extremely idealistic in the beginning, but as time
> goes on their idealism is drowned in conformity . . . It is like having
> a fancy dress, but it is always in the closet. You are a little better be-
> cause you have ideals, even if you do nothing about them . . . Very
> few of us are fighters for principles.

While one may agree with the observation that the novice
teachers are not "fighters for principles" in which they believe,
the above observation does not give sufficient consideration to the
difficulties involved in initiating educational change and the threat
associated with it. In contrast, look at the following excerpt from
an interview dealing with the same problem—the reaction to
educational ideas as a source of pressure:

> The educational textbook I am reading now starts with a cartoon. It
> shows bedlam in a classroom and raises the question, "Why did it
> happen?" The implications of the cartoon are very direct: "You did
> not practice the principles of education and therefore something is
> *wrong with you.*" Why is it always the fault of the teacher for failing
> to understand education and teach children? Is it possible that the
> teacher is faced with problems which are impossible to overcome in a
> particular school setting? It is often society which is the "failure,"
> rather than the teacher.

This teacher is down-to-earth in his perception of education
as a call to change. He perceives education as pressure to live up
to expectations, which, if not met, lead to a sense of failure.

The ambivalent attitudes toward educational ideals are primarily a product of the novice's difficulty in comprehending the
depth of their meaning and the difficulty in translating them into
the language of teaching behavior. The perception which the nov-

ice has of the existence of some discontinuity between the education and the public school cultures only accentuates the feeling of ambivalence toward education courses and theory.

College versus elementary school

In discussing the discrepancy between their professional ego ideals and their practices—the creative orientation in teaching, and their actual overemphasis on repetitive teaching—the most prevalent explanations given by the novice teachers are the fear of discipline problems, and their experience in the elementary school which frequently consists of an encounter with what they perceive as conservative teachers.

To the question, "How are you different from your cooperating teacher?", the novice tends to see himself as closer to the educational ideals of individuality and creativity than the cooperating teacher. The young teacher would like to see movement toward a higher level of creativity. At the same time, however, the elementary school practicum raises some doubt in the mind of the trainee as to whether education theory can be translated into the reality of classroom living. In some extreme cases the novice expresses the feeling that educational theory consists of professed values to which one has to pay lip service, but does not have to practice. An interviewee expresses the feeling in a symbolic way:

I see Education as a king and queen seated on a throne, dressed in beautiful clothes, but they have no servants to work for them.

The impact of the cooperating teacher on the novice's attitude toward education can be seen from the responses to the incomplete sentence: "In comparison with what I have learned at college, the cooperating teacher . . ."

says teaching methods look good solely in books.

says that theory must be forgotten as soon as you leave the college steps.

is more practical and is concerned with reality.

is completely different. She does not seem to go by the book.

says they are good methods but could not be carried out in the classroom.

puts into practice what, at the college, had been only theory.

Hypothetically, the field practicum should be a laboratory where the novice experiences the theory of education learned at the college. It should be an opportunity for a deeper understanding of education on both the intellectual and behavioral levels. It is evident that in the experience of the young teacher there is a certain feeling of discontinuity between education (theory), and the elementary school (practice).

Being unable to experience the full implementation of educational ideals in a field situation, the novice tends to feel unsure that he has a clear picture of the behavioral meaning of these principles. Sometimes he feels that what he learns is mainly slogans or catchwords (*integration, democratic, cooperative planning*) which do not have sufficient guides for action.

In the past, the attempt to bridge theory and practice was achieved through the development of campus model schools which implemented the modern theories and illustrated their application to the student teacher. However, in spite of the fact that the campus schools were successful in terms of their educational climate and often became laboratories of experimentation, their value as demonstration centers became limited.

The campus model school drew primarily on children from the professional community, which made their pupil population highly unrepresentative. They became unrealistic laboratories which no longer represented the reality of the field situation; a situation which made the transfer of learning to a more typical school difficult and limited.

The majority of student teachers today have their practicum within the public school system. In contrast to the campus school it is a more typical illustration of the future field situation in terms of its pupil population and facilities. It is also a laboratory for some interesting and sound experimentation, such as individualized reading and team teaching. However, in spite of great progress in experimentation in the public schools, they are not primarily centers for pioneering in education, nor is the staff selected in terms of its ability to guide student teachers.

Perhaps some degree of ambivalence toward educational theory is inevitable. It is a natural by-product of the discrepancy between the ideal and the real. However, in order to limit this ambivalence and develop a more personally meaningful background in education, the novice must experience the values of educational theory in operation.

There is a need for demonstration centers which resemble a typical public school in terms of the composition of their population and their facilities, and which are as "idealistic" as the campus school used to be in terms of their spirit of experimentation and the quality of their personnel.

As suggested previously, the cooperating teacher is selected primarily because of her demonstrative rather than her consultative abilities. There is a need for special certification for cooperating teachers based on further study of educational theory and methodology, and study and training in *consultation.*

Only when the instructor in education and the cooperating teacher come closer together in their educational orientation, will the discrepancy between the "ideal" and the "real" be decreased and the education of the novice be further improved.

MAJORING IN EDUCATION

In addition to the discrepancy between the ideal and the real, there seems to be another factor contributing to the ambivalent attitudes of prospective and new teachers toward education courses. This factor deals with the teacher's attitude toward being an education major in a liberal arts college.

The education major

The data collected in this study show that the novice teacher has, on the one hand, positive feelings of pride and self-realization, and on the other, negative feelings of self-depreciation with regard to majoring in education.

Look at the following negative reactions to the incomplete sentence, "Education majors in comparison to other college students . . ."

are often looked down on.

are regarded as lowly.

are not as hard workers.

are having an easier time.

In the perception of the young teacher, the college is denoted by a status hierarchy where the education major ranks low. This does not mean that the teacher is unequivocally critical about education as a major field of study. To the incomplete sentence, "If I had to choose my major all over again . . .", the answer, with few exceptions, was: "I'd choose education." To the incomplete sentence, "If I had to choose my career all over again . . .", the response, with few exceptions, was: "I would choose teaching." While it is possible to prepare for teaching in the elementary school by majoring in another field, most teachers prefer to major in education possibly because they are aware of the *unique* contributions for future teachers of this field, although they may be troubled by some of its features.

One of the major sources of tension in the life of young teachers on campus is that they sense a conflict and constant comparison between the "ed. major" and the "liberal arts major." To quote from an interview: "God forbid if you are an ed. major and you take history. They look down on you."

Rather than looking at education and liberal arts courses as they really are—partners which aim at a common goal—the emphasis is on the conflict and self-depreciating attitudes. The interview data show that it is rather the exceptional teacher who rejects the negative comparisons and raises the stimulating questions: "Why is a course on the Greek culture considered more liberalizing than a discussion of comparative education?" Or, "Why is a science laboratory of a higher status than a student-teaching practicum?" The majority of young teachers tend to accept the status hierarchy as an objective fact.

There are many factors underlying this conflict between the education major and the liberal arts major. Majoring in education means going into teaching and is, perhaps, being viewed by society with certain of the prejudices that led George Bernard Shaw to quip: "Those who can, do; those who can't, teach." As

Margaret Mead points out,[M11] even the two national groups known for their scholarly traditions, the Chinese and the Jews, portray the teacher in a negative light in their own folklore.

With few exceptions the education majors are women, and many in our society still hold the intellectual ability of women somewhat in question. To quote from interviews which illustrate the status hierarchy as related to the sex of the student and his profession:

They say to us in a belittling voice, "You are going to college, so you are an ed. major . . . The boy is the doctor and the girl is the teacher.

If the boy has 140 I.Q., he wants the girl to have 137. And this is what the girl wants, too.

The pressures on education

There are some characteristics in the development of the schools of education themselves which are related to this status controversy. Historically, the teacher-training institutions aimed only at the preparation of teachers and emphasized primarily methods of teaching rather than theory and research in education. They were separate teaching-training institutions and developed with relatively little contact with the intellectual climate of the university. These institutions were criticized mainly because they did not stress classical education and overemphasized "How-to-do-it" courses.[81]

While this criticism was generally valid with regard to the teacher-training institution of the past, it is questionable whether or not it is pertinent to the present, when the majority of students majoring in education are integral parts of a university as a whole. As suggested previously, these students usually take only one quarter of their program in education, and do so mainly in the last two years of their undergraduate program; otherwise, they are primarily students of liberal arts and science. Therefore, the intellectual development of the students majoring in education at present is a product of their academic training as much as it is a product of their professional education.

Whether or not education courses place too great an emphasis on methodology is a controversial issue. The history of education can be described as a story of an institution which had been pulled by opposite poles: the academic departments which call for an accentuation of the theoretical orientation of the education offerings, and the field practitioners (teachers and administrators) who demand more emphasis on the practical methods courses.

For some people in the first (academic) group, the word *methods* means a low-quality course; in some cases they even demand that these courses not be an integral part of the university curriculum, but rather, be delegated to the public-school program of inservice training. This attitude toward methods courses as lacking in academic status is illustrated by the anecdote about a college committee which rejected a new course entitled "methods in research." According to the purely academic orientation the function of a university is to develop the mind; it is primarily intellectual; learning should be pursued for the sake of learning rather than for vocational purposes. ("Don't make the Torah an axe to chop with" is the rabbinical saying.) This viewpoint suggests that, to the extent that professional education may be tolerated under university auspices, it should deemphasize its practical orientation—its methods.

The second pole pulling the education field is the field practitioners. In their view, the primary role of education courses is to train teachers who will be able and ready to cope with the realities of the field problems. They want the program to be realistic and practical, to emphasize methods of teaching and ways of handling discipline problems.

They feel strongly that education as a discipline should not isolate itself in the proverbial ivory tower of the university, become philosophical, theoretical, or past-oriented. They want not only to train teachers, but to also be open to the realities of the present burning educational problems and lead in their resolution. They want the discipline to be community-centered!

The strong feelings which school people have about the direction of education can be illustrated by the fact that in a recent meeting of school principals, they discussed the undergraduate training of teachers at college and proposed to eliminate the study of the history of education in favor of emphasizing methodology of school subjects.

The data collected in this study suggest that the young teachers themselves definitely side with the school personnel, rather than with the academic professors. Methods and practical applications are perceived as the most valuable courses; theory is rejected as lacking reality and guide for action.

The method course in education . . . is the most valuable course I have taken both in theory and practice.

. . . is a practical way of learning.

. . . is most helpful in terms of school problems.

Or:

Courses in education . . . are most valuable when they have practical applications.

. . . are too general and theoretical, with the exception of student teaching.

It would seem that both the academic professors and, at the other end of the pole, the field practitioner, in their attempt to influence education, approach the problem of the education of teachers from a one-sided, and therefore limited, frame of reference. Those academic professors who criticize education instructors for being interested in practice and methods, fail to realize that the ultimate criterion of the meaningfulness of educational knowledge to the teacher is the way he can experience it in the classroom. The ultimate test of knowledge is the teacher's ability to bring the principles of education alive. Unless the teacher learns to encourage the development of children's creativity in the way he asks questions, gives answers, and makes assignments, the concept of creativity will only be a phantasm—empty and without content. The simplest practical experience of classroom living is the foundation of real understanding of the values of educational theory.

Says Martin Mayer (not a professional educator) in his book, *The Schools*: [M4:473]

What future teachers need . . . is the course which attempts to explore the profound aspects of the deceptively simple material they are going to teach, which analyzes case by case the types of difficulty that children find in approaching such material, which suggests tools and techniques and methods of presentation that may help children overcome the difficulties.

Overemphasis on methods tends to characterize the field practitioners. Being faced with on-the-job problems which disturb the teachers in their daily work, their impatient reaction is, "Give me a solution." Attempts to analyze the theoretical dynamics underlying the problem are often perceived as stalling techniques, useless, or at best, as being of secondary importance. The orientation is often of a "What-am-I-going-to-do-about-it?" nature, rather than, "How am I going to understand it?" They are too often impatient with theory. They want action!

The tendency of those teachers who overemphasize "action" and deemphasize "theory" is to look for a gimmick, a prescription, or a rule of thumb as an answer to curricular problems. These are the teachers who may go through the motions of introducing committee work, for instance, without changing their autocratic attitudes; teachers who change their report cards from a system of grades to a descriptive letter without gaining insight into the development of the total personality of the child; teachers who shift from discrete subject matter to a core curriculum, with the result that the only "progress" that can be observed is a change in the length of the session. In other words, these are teachers who change the external form rather than the content and the spirit.

Curriculum improvement is not a sequence of additions, revisions, and production of new materials. These new aids prove to be ineffective unless they are based on a change in the conception of education in the minds of the teachers who are going to adopt them. In spite of the fact that curriculum revisions may *look* concrete, they are of little value unless teachers delve into the theoretical considerations underlying them.

When theory is not understood, curriculum innovations tend to be applied mechanically. Within the past several decades the American educational system has gone through a number of colorful eras. There was the "What-do-you-want-to-do-and-talk-about-today?" period; the "self-expression" and "Let's-do-it-in-a-group" eras, and so on. Each of these approaches to the improvement of education had *depth and value* which tended to be run into the ground because of lack of sufficient attempts to delve into the meaning of the new innovations.

The attempts to create a dichotomy between theory and practice in education constitute a narrow, and therefore misleading, conception of the problem. Unfortunately, this dichotomy is even expressed in the department of education itself, where courses are too often departmentalized into the theoretical and the practical. In the theoretical courses the tendency of some college instructors is to get too far away from the realities of field situations. In the practical courses some instructors, under pressure to teach "how-to-do-it," become insensitive to, and overlook, the more far-reaching aspects of classroom problems. On the graduate level, one sometimes hears suggestions of dividing the program in two parts: in-service education ("how-to-do-it" courses), and courses leading to the master's degree (theoretical courses).

The above trends, illustrating the dichotomy between theory and practice, are at variance with the position of *integration* suggested in this study. Education is a behavorial science. In many respects it is a call for change from dealing with the known to exploring the unknown. The teacher reacts to the challenge of teaching in terms of his understanding of the expected change, in terms of his attitude toward the change, and in terms of his ability to adapt his behavior in accordance with the desired change.

The concept of integration of theory and practice suggests that a most crucial aspect of teaching and learning has to do with the teacher's self-awareness and ability to understand and cope with his own problems. Kelley writes, in *The Workshop Way of Learning*: [K2:6]

The unsolved problems of the teacher's life and work [should] become the point of attack. The solution of these problems . . . will lead to others more remote, and, at least theoretically, will spread out indefinitely.

A sound curriculum is determined by vigorous testing of theory in practice; the collection of evidence from practice upon which to modify theory. Any attempt to differentiate between "theory" and "practice" generally leads to a glib understanding of theory or to a mechanistic approach to practice.

The opinions of the education majors

To repeat, the awareness of conflict between education and liberal arts courses, and the confusion of whether education is a theoretical or a practical discipline, are points of stress for the young teacher. Sensing the pressure emanating from the academic demands and expectations, while being faced with the demanding task of having to deal in their daily teaching with various areas of subject matter, a small minority of teachers wonder if "Perhaps having more liberal arts and science rather than education courses will help me better prepare for my job."

However, the overwhelming majority of teachers believe that while more liberal arts and science courses may be desirable, they are not substitutes for the teaching of education.

To suggest that the improvement of the quality of teaching is a function of increased information acquired by teachers, is only partly true. The amount of knowledge available to a teacher is not necessarily related to the success with which it is communicated to children. The prospective teacher who studies only the subject matter but does not study ways of teaching may often become merely an imparter of information, and may fail to consider individual differences; may lack perception of the nuances of the learning process, or he may fail to inculcate a spirit of inquiry in children.

A study by Travers and Rabinowitz [7] illustrates that greater emphasis on liberal arts does not necessarily improve the novice's conception of modern educational practices. It points out, however, that stress on education courses promotes this goal. The subjects of the study were education students in two colleges that varied greatly in their educational orientation. In one college the program consisted mainly of liberal arts. Students had very limited contact with the public school until they began practice teaching. The other college provided courses in professional education along with opportunities to observe pilot schools from the beginning of their college training.

In the same study, students from two colleges were asked to give portrayals of teachers. The seniors from the first college were much less likely to draw pictures in which teacher control was relaxed, than were those from the education-centered college; they tended to portray a more restricted, teacher-dominated classroom climate.

Education attempts to go beyond the conception of the teacher as a technician who transmits knowledge acquired in academic courses. The aspired goal is to train a kind of teacher who elicits, and reinforces, the intellectual curiosity of the child; a teacher who does not only repeat, but also creates.

The young teachers themselves perceive the education courses as somewhat different in approach and emphasis, as compared to the academic courses. They view this difference with both positive and negative attitudes. These attitudes are reflected in the following responses to the incomplete sentence, "Education courses in comparison with others given in the college . . ."

are what you make out of them; not assigned, as in others.

are more personal.

permit more self-expression. What you think counts.

permit you to do a lot with yourself, if you want to.

have a much more homey atmosphere. You feel you belong.

expose you to people who care who you are.

are taught by teachers who know the students' names.

do not make you feel like a number or a machine.

are sometimes snap courses.

are easy A's.

raise your college average.

are too much talk with no definite direction.

The positive responses view education as characterized by freedom, self-expression, personal relations, and a sense of belonging. The negative comments blame education for verbalism, a non-demanding atmosphere, and easy grading.

Progressive education has had a strong impact on the American education professor, perhaps a greater impact than it has had on the elementary school practitioner. He has moved a long way from his European ancestor—the detached, impersonal, subject-centered professor—in the direction of being more person-oriented. He is interested in the total professional development of the prospective teacher, that is, both in his intellectual and personal development. He wants to practice in his own teaching that which he preaches to others.

The most pronounced expression of the person orientation of the education professor is the movement of *group dynamics*. Despite the fact that the majority of education instructors do not follow its teachings, many are influenced by its orientation. One of the major tenets of the group dynamics position is the observation that in the interest of achieving the *task*, the *person* is often neglected; his desires are not recognized and his position may be ignored. An attitude scale was developed to differentiate between "person" and "task" orientation. In training for leadership and group work the accent was on concern for individual participation ("Did everyone have an opportunity to contribute?"); on sensitivity to human relations ("I sense some tensions in the air."); on permissiveness ("How free are we to speak?"), and on group evaluation ("Let's see if we are doing what we want to do.").

Similarly, many education instructors feel that preoccupation with subject matter and standards of achievement may result in some rigidity. The student, his needs, and his abilities, may be ignored; the emphasis may often be placed on knowledge itself, rather than on its impact on the student as a person; a tendency may develop to overpower the student with a barrage of ideas, and to underestimate the student's own perception of the problem.

The novice teacher appreciates the personal approach of the education instructor—his stress on the development of a professional image and on the promotion of individuality. He feels that he is given an opportunity to grow as a person.

The young teacher feels that the Education instructor offers a high degree of freedom. ("An ed. course is what *you* make of it.") The promise inherent in this approach is—self-direction; the danger for the student is the tendency to waste time and take the easy way out.

It is interesting to note that the ambivalence felt by the young teacher toward the experience of freedom as a *learner*, resembles his conflict with regard to freedom as an aspect of his own teaching behavior. Typical reactions to the incomplete sentence, "When given freedom, children usually . . ." are listed below.

perform at their highest peak.

make the most of it.

run wild.

become unruly due to lack of direction.

react favorably if the freedom is defined.

Both as a teacher and a learner, the major in education perceives freedom as a mixed blessing. In a teacher's role the two extremes of behavior resulting from giving freedom to children are "self-expression" and "running wild." As a learner the two extremes resulting from being given freedom are "self-expression" and "taking the easy way out." Freedom is an essential condition to the process of individuation of the growing person. To achieve it in the life of pupils and teachers, or as suggested by Fromm in *Escape from Freedom* [F5] in the life of a nation, is a very difficult task.

In the perception of many teachers, education courses are not as demanding and do not call for the same investment of work as other courses. The grading policy is typically used as an illustration of the relative lack of sufficient demand exerted by the education instructor. For many novice teachers the feeling that there is some easier policy of grading students in education programs is a factor which reduces the status of a major in education and, consequently, the status of teaching as a profession.

The following are some reactions to the incomplete sentence, "Grades in Education courses . . .":

have a tendency to be higher.

are easy *A*'s.

do not really show your ability as a teacher.

are often not based on how good a student will be as a teacher, but rather, on how well she can take a test.

should be eliminated.

The interesting point is not only that they view grades in education courses negatively, but also, that they touch on some of the difficulties with the instructor of education is faced in giving a grade.

As discussed earlier, the education instructor attempts to look at the student in terms of his professional promise—that is, his intellectual progress, his relatedness to colleagues and children, his dedication to the profession, and so on. He tends to find it difficult to narrow down this evaluation to a grade. The education instructor tends to believe in a guidance approach to students, where consultant-consultee relations are fostered. How does one translate these relations to the language of grades? He tends to speak about subject matter which is personally meaningful; he wants his students to have their hearts in the experience of learning rather than in the external reward of a superior grade.

The instructor of education wants his students to experience learning based on intrinsic motivation in order that they will be able to transfer these experiences to their own teaching behavior. Grades are definitely an extrinsic motivation, and in some cases, both on the college and the elementary school levels, are used as a whip. The education instructor speaks about experimentation, trying new ideas, and moving toward the unknown in teaching behavior. Should the college supervisor give a low grade to a student teacher who, in experimenting with creative teaching, runs into difficulties? Should the same supervisor give a high grade to a trainee who is playing it safe and gives successful repetitive-type lessons?

Both in the perception of many instructors of education and of majors in education, the present grading system is in conflict with the principles of modern education!

THE COLLEGE SUPERVISOR

Student teachers generally feel that being observed by the methods instructor on the job (in this capacity he is generally called the *college supervisor*), is one of the most meaningful experiences in their training. To quote:

It is myself as a person and as a teacher, my ideas, my behavior, my relationship with children, and my knowledge of subject matter which is the center of the observation and the discussion.

As in most personal experiences, the *observation* (as it is generally called by student teachers) can be an impetus for growth in learning, or a source of defeating anxiety. The factor which determines the quality of the observation as a learning experience is the expectations of the student teachers and their relationships with the college supervisor. Whether the observation is perceived as an opportunity to learn, or primarily as an examination, makes a great difference in the educational quality of the experience. The observation is an experience which undoubtedly produces anxiety. Having been asked to report their dreams the night before an observation, some students met me in the morning and said: "I don't have any dreams to report; I didn't sleep all night."

The dreams reported by student teachers reveal a high level of anxiety, such as loss of lesson plans, barriers between themselves and children, lacking the proper clothes, being unable to find a way to the classroom, children becoming giants, or the college supervisor becoming one of the family's relatives.

Instead of giving a lesson on arithmetic, I was talking about coconuts. Instead of seeing observers in the back of the room, they were right up front against the teacher's desk. There was a fence between the children's desk and me and I kept asking—but where are the children?

The following is an excerpt from another dream:

All the children were absolutely huge. I looked dwarfed compared to them. Suddenly I was panicked. The lesson which I thought might be a little too taxing for them now seemed ludicrous . . . I gave my lesson and fortunately the class responded favorably. I felt relaxed and once more the children were small.

Why do the observation lessons produce so much anxiety? The following are some explanations offered by student teachers:

(1) It is a special event built up as a tense experience by the school. Many cooperating teachers warn children to "behave," and even take out one or two behavior problems.

(2) It is a test. In the long run, these observations are the basis for grading. A test and a grade are perceived as a threat.

(3) The individual is in the center performing. Whereas in the college class he is lost in the crowd of examinees, here he is the center of the stage; whereas the college test taps the student's ability to write, here his total personality is tested—thinking, speaking, gestures, etc.

(4) Success is not dependent only on the student teacher himself, but also on the nature of the class reaction; one braces himself to cope with the unexpected. To quote an interviewee: "I wish for the best, but try to be ready for the worst."

(5) The observation is followed by a conference, characterized by an atmosphere of an evaluation, or putting it more bluntly, by criticism. The latter is perceived as threatening.

Those student teachers who perceive the main objective of the observation lesson as an opportunity to learn, tend to experiment with new ideas, be open to criticism, and apply new insights to other lessons. Those student teachers who perceive the observation lesson primarily as an examination tend to be interested less in the detailed analysis of their teaching behavior and more in whether they were rated "good" or "bad." They tend to play it safe and blame the cooperating teacher for their own lack of experimentation. They tend to be defensive in the conference and show relatively little evidence of progress.

Similar difficulties occur at the conference. In contrast to the novice's relationship with the cooperating teacher, the conference with the college supervisor is characterized by criticism. Is the criticism going to be perceived by the novice as constructive or destructive? When the threat experienced is acute, the student teacher tends to be consumed by anxiety, and feel defensive. He tends to brush off the analysis of his lesson:

Impractical ideas . . .

You can't do much with this class, anyway.

I did what my teacher wants; these are really not my ideas.

To make the conference an educative experience where teaching behavior is examined without creating a sense of futility, or without evading the issues, is the responsibility of both the college supervisor and the beginning teacher. It cannot be achieved without the fullest cooperation of both parties.

In the role of evaluating teaching behavior, the supervisor may find himself involved in a number of pitfalls and emotional traps. He may identify with his consultees; their success is his success, and their failure is his failure. He may become annoyed and overcritical about the quality of the teaching of the slow student teacher, and get overexcited about the success of the one who is quick to learn.

To criticize is to face the novice teacher with reality; it may also mean causing pain and perhaps behaving in an unpopular manner. To avoid causing pain by resorting to deliberate praise as a means of sweetening the bitter pill of negative criticism, is one of the faulty methods used in some cases. Handing out two points of praise, two points of criticism, and again, a point of praise, is one way of evaluating which often blurs the truth.

For the young teachers the observation lesson and the conference are a tremendous intellectual and emotional investment. They want criticism. They sense when the truth is blurred. They may even come and say: "I feel that you didn't say everything you wanted to say. May I have an additional conference?"

Teachers appreciate criticism when it is given in a matter-of-fact manner, without annoyance or defensiveness. They want to sense that the supervisor does not like a specific teacher more, or less, because of the quality of his work. The latter does not become "good" by doing an excellent job, or "bad" by doing a poor job. These are attitudes which are easy to understand logically, but are very difficult to develop emotionally.

Student teachers tend to recognize the attitude and behavior of the college supervisor as fundamental in the conference relations. They are not sufficiently aware of their own attitudes playing a major role in these relationships. Of cricial importance are their expectations of the status leader. Does the young teacher wish primarily to be "patted on the head" by his elder, or does he want primarily to learn? When one accepts the latter as the major function of the conference, then the identification of weaknesses is not perceived mainly as an indication of failure, but rather as a diagnosis of new tasks and learnings to be mastered. The meaningfulness of these new goals to the novice is a product of their origin— the analysis of his teaching behavior.

The anxiety of the conferee over the nature of the evaluation tends to contribute toward dependent relations. A situation may arise where the novice does not even attempt to analyze the observed lesson on his own as a partner in the conference, but rather passively waits for the "verdict" of the "answer man"—the college supervisor.

The constructive conference is the one where both parties are active in the search for the meaning of the experience, where an atmosphere of working together exists. An important criterion of progress in conferences is the growing ability of the student teacher to take an active role in the analysis of problems and in the setting of goals for improvement.

In my experience, an approach conducive to the activation of the student teacher is to make both the observation and the conference a group experience; the novice is observed by three or four of his colleagues, in addition to the supervisor; all of them then participate in the conference. It is possible in this setting to encourage teamwork and consequently to also decrease the dependency on the college instructor.

Since the principal, supervisor, and college instructor are usually perceived by the teacher as status leaders, a suggestion on their part may imply criticism or even threat. The richest source available for the teacher is his neighbor in the next classroom. Those novice teachers who are able to cooperate as a group tend to have high morale, improve their teaching, and learn the promise of future teamwork.

Student teachers report that the time and thinking applied to the observation lesson is greater than any other lesson. The question is how to move beyond the point of preoccupation with one lesson toward a discussion of the future teaching of the novice. The conference is the place to start movement in the latter direction, and to look at the lesson as a segment of the total work by raising, cooperatively, questions like the following:

What were the activities which led to this lesson?

What are the other approaches a teacher may take to the same problems?

Is there a balance in his approach? For instance, in teaching reading does he overemphasize skill and underemphasize literature?

What are the specific recommendations to be tested by student teachers which result from the discussion in the conference?

The identification of difficulties made in the conference should not be brushed off by the conferee as "I do not wash my dishes in my own kitchen, and therefore, can do nothing about it." In order that the observation will have a direct impact on the teaching behavior of the teacher, curricular plans must be developed cooperatively, tested in practice, and reported to the college supervisor. For instance, if the identified limitation in the novice's work happens to be overcontrolling behavior, or failure to emphasize children's questions, constructive suggestions should be planned in these areas, and should be tested and evaluated.

In brief, every effort has to be made to alleviate the anxiety associated with the observation and the conference. The emphasis should be on gaining insight and on the charting of directions for an improved way of teaching. This goal cannot be attained by the college supervisor alone. He must have the full and active cooperation of the novice teacher.

THE EDUCATION OF THE TEACHER: CONCLUSION

The controversy of education versus liberal arts, with the heat it generates on the national arena, has negative as well as constructive implications. On the negative side, the conflict contributes toward the development of a status hierarchy in colleges, and is damaging to the self-concept of the prospective or graduate teacher as a creative professional person.

On the constructive side, the controversy accentuates the need for realizing that the preparation of teachers is not solely, or even primarily, the domain of education; it is rather the responsibility of the college as a whole. Both parties have to look for ways of improving their own operation and the mutual coordination of their operation.

The value of a strong liberal arts background lies not only in the knowledge which it imparts, but also in the liberalizing spirit of inquiry which is its hallmark. In order to improve the preparation of teachers, it is the degree of achievement of the latter objective which needs continuous examination and improvement.

The science departments should look for ways of encouraging elementary school teachers to choose science as their field of specialization. At present, the number of elementary school teachers concentrating on science is very limited. The reasons are mainly two: (1) Being primarily a female group, these teachers are aware that their culture generally regards science as a "masculine" subject matter. As an interviewee put it, "My friends say to me, 'You are such a pretty girl. Why do you study physics?' " (2) In general, science departments have not taken an active role in recruiting elementary school teachers. Traditionally, they have been primarily interested in their own majors.

On the positive side, it can be reported that these attitudes are in the process of reexamination and change. Both the education and the other college departments are looking for ways to improve the coordination of their work. There is less emphasis on which students are in which departments, and more on the task of meeting the specific needs of the student. The education of the teacher is in the process of becomisg the responsibility of the college as a whole.

The Conant report[C2] on "The Education of American Teachers," written primarily from the administrative point of view, calls for more freedom for colleges in developing their own programs and for more emphasis on the role of the school practicum. The report fails to emphasize the interaction between theory and practice. It tends to underestimate the role of theory, and therefore constitutes, in some respects, an oversimplification of the problems involved in teacher education.

This chapter suggests that in contrast to most other departments, the success of the education department is determined not only by its ability to communicate concepts on the intellectual level, but also by its impact on the *operational* values of teachers. Intellectual and operational learning of values is not the same; the latter is much more difficult to achieve. It is only a training program based on the fundamental concept of the integration of theory and practice which can cope with the complex task of preparing teachers.

SELECTED BIBLIOGRAPHY

Conant, James, *The Education of American Teachers*. New York: McGraw-Hill Book Company, 1963. A stimulating discussion in terms of its administrative provisions.

Sarason, Seymour, Davidson, Kenneth, and Blatt, Burton, *The Preparation of Teachers*. New York: John Wiley & Sons, Inc., 1962. An insightful psychological discussion.

Epilogue: Toward the ever flowing stream

The postprogressive education era, in which we live today, resembles an unnamed child. Its namelessness suggests that the present school of thought differs from progressive education, but that its own entity and sense of direction is yet to be formed. Despite such lack of crystallization, it is possible to postulate that the major difference between the present and past educational movements is their conception of *knowledge*.

Progressive education, the most imaginative and idealistic educational movement this country has ever experienced, approached knowledge from two somewhat distinct frames of reference which reflected its own polarization. One wing sought the answer primarily in terms of the meaning of knowledge to the individual learner. For instance, in developing the "project method," Kilpatrick spoke about purposeful activities, intrinsic motivation, and the role of the learner in planning and organizing the subject matter. A second wing approached knowledge primarily from the frame of reference of the social objectives. They daringly stressed the role of the school in changing the social order and in improving the democratic way of life.[V1]

While different in their approach, the common denominator between the two wings of progressive education was that they did not stress knowledge for its own sake. In reviewing the educational scene within the last era, Foshay says: [F3:6]

384

The theory on which I was behaving now seems to me to be true, but inadequate. Hindsight says that it was flawed from the beginning by a failure to acknowledge a third element necessary for the making of intelligent curriculum decisions.

I learned . . . that curriculum decisions should be based on the knowledge of the child and of society . . . This was inadequate . . . What was left out of it was the nature of organized knowledge. As professional educators, we have taken organized knowledge—the disciplines out of which man's knowledge is made—for granted.

The major contribution of the postprogressive education era is its addition of the third element. Perhaps when it finally becomes an entity with a name of its own, the title will focus on the meaning of knowledge.

This volume deals with the meaning of the knowledge imparted on the elementary school level. It suggests that the decision with regard to the nature of the expected knowledge is crucial; that in essence, it affects the total educational climate in the classroom. In other words, it demonstrates the direct relationship between the *nature of knowledge* in school, and the quality of the *teacher's behavior.*

Applying Anderson's definition of closed and open systems of education to the discussion of the repetitive-creative continuum, one could say that models *A* and *B* constitute a closed system, while model *C* constitutes an open system of education.

The basic emphasis of the closed system in education is the transmission of a body of knowledge, facts, and generalizations. The problems of study have fixed answers. The answers are in the back of the book, are agreed upon by the culture, and are in the teacher's head. The closed system of education—that is, the transmission of factual information and the development of convergent thinking, is essential as it constitutes the basic learning of skills and agreed norms of behavior. In many respects it constitutes the static culture. However, if teaching stops with the closed system of education (and as evidence presented indicates, it too often does stop there), it may result in a younger generation of people who know how to rediscover what someone else thinks is right or wrong. Such people believe that excellent performance is identical with conforming to external norms. They are productive in the narrow sense of following patterns established by others.

Anderson's definition of the open system of education resembles the present discussion of creative teaching. It is a stimulating system of relationships which encourages originality, experimentation, and self-direction. It does not bow to the pressures of the conventional course of study and it is not bound to the dictum of "covering" specified subject matter. The open system of education encourages the individual to listen to and experience himself, and to develop his own personal interpretation of subject matter.

To live creatively is to live truthfully. It is to live truthfully as one himself sees the truth. To live namely according to the truth as anyone but himself sees the truth is not creativity, but conformity. [A2:4]

The observer who spends some time in school, listens to teachers questioning pupils, examines assignments, tests, workbooks, and teacher guides, cannot avoid the observation that too often elementary school teaching is A-oriented. This critique of the school curriculum is presented most eloquently by Foshay in his presidential address to an educational convention. [F3:15]

We pedagogues have brought up a whole population that doesn't know the difference between grammar and composition because we taught the one in the name of the other. Similarly we have taught prosody in the name of poetry, thus killing poetry in our culture. We have taught places in the name of geography, thus almost losing this vitally important and interesting field to our schools. We have taught facts in the name of history, thus as I say, betraying a basic discipline. We have taught computation in the name of mathematics, and the facts and principles in the name of laboratory sciences.

The problem confronting the educator is how to change the lack of balance at school—how to move from overaccentuation of specificity, retention, and repetition, to a balanced curriculum which gives equal stress to application, interpretation, and creativity.

Looking at the imbalance of the elementary school curriculum, one cannot avoid raising the following questions: Why is the curriculum—that is, the actual daily experience going on at school, repetitive-oriented? Why is it difficult to move ahead on the continuum from a repetitive toward a more creative emphasis on knowledge and teaching? Why is the magnetic pole of repetition much stronger in actual school practice than the magnetic pole of creativity? And is it correct that the latter has no power of attraction at all?

Analyzing the repetitive-creative conflict experienced by novice teachers, the discussion suggests that the improvement of the curriculum is more subtle than revising statements written down on paper, or changing the course of study. Real improvement means bringing about changes in people, in their aspirations, beliefs, in their perceptions, knowledge, and skill. The teacher's conception of the learning experiences which should operate in the school, his relatedness to knowledge, his sense of realization and security in a way of teaching, provide the key to the nature of the curriculum.

It would be fallacious to overlook the most important factor in curriculum development—the *classroom teacher*. An educational idea is alive mainly if it is practiced—that is, becomes a teaching behavior.

In one century, education moved from the moralism and adult centeredness of McGuffey and his readers to the child-centeredness of one wing of progressive education. Today, the post progressive education era is moving toward a balance by stressing excellence in intellectual potency. Dewey criticized the rigidity and formalistic nature of the curriculum and stressed the importance of firsthand experience.[D7] Today, the question is how to utilize experiences and activity as a springboard to a higher level of abstraction; how to move from empiricism to constructionism.[B11]

New technological innovations and organizational patterns, such as teaching machines and team teaching, are at present under discussion. It is too early to reach a conclusion with regard to the merit of these innovations. It can only be said that they are certainly secondary to the major issue of curriculum improvement—the teacher's perception of his teaching role, or his relatedness to the repetitive-creative conflict.

Rabban Johanan Ben Zakkai had five disciples. Metaphorically speaking, two of them are the center of discussion in this book.

Rabbi Eliezer Ben Hyrcanus—a plastered cistern which loses not a drop . . .
Rabbi Eleazar Ben Arak—ever flowing stream . . .
Plastered cistern: He never forgot a thing he learned.

> Ever flowing stream: In his learning he could even add to the
> traditions he received and knew how to deduce one thing
> from another . . .

The "plastered cistern which loses not a drop" represents a mode of thinking characterized by retention of the known; a person who stresses the expected and the ordinary. The "ever flowing stream" symbolizes movement toward the unknown—creativity, inventiveness, and originality.

Both modes of thinking are crucial for the development of a learner, a teacher, or a culture. It is mainly because the first mode is emphasized and the second is neglected that this book is dedicated to the promotion of a teaching behavior aiming at the "ever flowing stream."

BIBLIOGRAPHY

A1 ALMY, C. Millie, *Children's Experiences Prior to First Grade and Success in Beginning Reading.* New York: Teachers College, Bureau of Publications, Columbia University, 1949.

A2 ANDERSON, Harold, "Creativity and Education." *College and University Bulletin,* Vol. 13 (May 1961), No. 14.

A3 ————, *Creativity and Its Cultivation.* New York: Harper & Row, Publishers, 1959.

A4 AUSTIN, Mary, *The First R.* New York: The Macmillan Company, 1963.

A5 ————, *The Torch Lighters.* Cambridge: Harvard University Press, 1961.

A6 AXLINE, Virginia, *Play Therapy.* Boston: Houghton Mifflin Company, 1947.

B1 BALDWIN, James, *The Fire Next Time.* New York: The Dial Press, Inc., 1963.

B2 BARRON, Frank, "The Psychology of Imagination." *Scientific American,* Vol. 199 (September 1958), No. 3.

B3 BARTLETT, Frederic, *Thinking.* New York: Basic Books, Inc., Publishers, 1958.

B4 BIBER, Barbara, *Premature Structuring as a Deterrent to Creativity.* New York: Bank Street College of Education, 1959.

B5 ———— (Editor), *Cartoon Situations.* New York: Bank Street College of Education, 1954.

B6 BLOOM, Benjamin (Editor), *Taxonomy of Educational Objectives.* New York: Longmans, Green & Co., Inc., 1956.

B7 BLOUGH, O. Glenn, and SCHWARTZ, Julius, *Elementary School Science and How to Teach It.* New York: Holt, Rinehart & Winston, Inc., 1964.

B8 BOHEM, Lenore, "Exploring Children's Thinking." *The Elementary School Journal,* Vol. 61 (1961), No. 7.

B9 BROWN, Thomas and BANICH, Serafina, *Student Teaching in an Elementary School.* New York: Harper & Row, Publishers, 1962.

[B10] BRUNER, Jerome S., "Learning and Thinking." *Harvard Education Review*, Vol. 29 (1959).

[B11] ———, *On Knowing*. Cambridge: Harvard University Press, 1962.

[B12] ———, *The Process of Education*. Cambridge: Harvard University Press, 1960.

[B13] ———, GOODNOW, Jacqueline, and AUSTIN, George, *A Study of Thinking*. New York: John Wiley & Sons, Inc., 1956.

[B14] BURROWS, Alvina, *They All Want to Write*. Englewood Cliffs, N.J.: Prentice-Hall, Inc., 1952.

[B15] BURTON, William H., "Education and Social Class in the United States." *Harvard Education Review*, Vol. 23 (Fall, 1953), No. 4.

[B16] ———, *The Guidance of Learning Activities*. New York: Appleton-Century-Crofts, 1962.

[C1] CLARK, John R. and EADS, Laura K., *Guiding Arithmetic Learning*. New York: World Book Company, 1954.

[C2] CONANT, James, *The Education of American Teachers*. New York: McGraw-Hill Book Company, 1963.

[C3] COREY, Stephen M., *Action Research to Improve School Practices*. New York: Teachers College, Bureau of Publications, Columbia University, 1953.

[C4] CREMIN, Laurence, *The Transformation of the School*. New York: Alfred A. Knopf, Inc., 1961.

[C5] CUMMINGS, Howard H. (Editor), *Science and the Social Studies*. Washington, D.C.: National Council for the Social Studies, 1957.

[C6] CUNNINGHAM, Ruth, *Understanding Group Behavior of Boys and Girls*. New York: Teachers College, Bureau of Publications, Columbia University, 1951.

[D1] DAVIDSON, Helen, *Satisfying and Stressful Experiences of Student Teachers*. New York: Office of Education Research, The City College, 1960. Mimeographed.

[D2] DAVIS, Allison, *Social Class Influences upon Learning*. Cambridge: Harvard University Press, 1951.

[D3] DEANS, Edwina, *Elementary School Mathematics: New Directions*. Washington, D.C.: U.S. Department of Health, Education, and Welfare, 1963.

[D4] DEUTSCH, Martin, *Minority Group Class Status as Related to Social and Personality Factors in Scholastic Achievement*. Society for Applied Anthropology, Monograph No. 2 (1960).

[D5] ———, "The Disadvantaged Child and the Learning Process," in Passow, A. Harry, *Education in Depressed Areas*. New York: Teachers College, Bureau of Publications, Columbia University, 1962.

D6 D'EVELYN, E. Katherine, *Meeting Children's Emotional Needs*. Englewood Cliffs, N.J.: Prentice-Hall, Inc., 1959.

D7 DEWEY, John, *The Child and the Curriculum*. Chicago: University of Chicago Press, 1902.

D8 DIETZ, Elizabeth, "Vitalizing Teacher Education." *The Journal of Teacher Education*, Vol. XI (March 1960), No. 1.

D9 DRISCOLL, Gertrude, *How to Study the Behavior of Children*. New York: Teachers College, Bureau of Publications, Columbia University, 1941.

D10 DUKER, Sam, "Basics in Critical Listening." *The English Journal*, November, 1962, pp. 565-7.

D11 ———, *Classroom Educational Environment*. New York: Office of Educational Research, Brooklyn College, 1962. Mimeographed.

D12 DUNFEE, Maxine, and GREENLEE, Julian, *Elementary School Science: Research, Theory and Practice*. Washington, D.C.: ASCD, 1957.

E1 Educational Services Incorporated, *Social Studies Program*. Watertown, Massachusetts: 1964. Mimeographed.

F1 FLEMING, S. Robert (Editor), *Curriculum for Today's Boys and Girls*. Columbus, Ohio: Charles E. Merril Books, Inc., 1963.

F2 FLESCH, Rudolph, *Why Johnny Can't Read*. New York: Harper & Row, Publishers, 1955.

F3 FOSHAY, Arthur, *A Modest Proposal for the Improvement of Education*. New York: Teachers College, Bureau of Publications, Columbia University, March, 1961. Mimeographed.

F4 Fox, Raymond, "Factors Influencing the Career Choice of Prospective Teachers." *The Journal of Teacher Education*, December 1961.

F5 FROMM, Erich, *Escape from Freedom*. New York: Hold, Rinehart & Winston, Inc., 1941.

G1 GAGE, N. L., *Handbook of Research on Teaching*. Chicago: Rand McNally & Co., 1962.

G2 GETZELS, Jacob, and JACKSON, Philip, "A Study of Giftedness," in *The Gifted Student*. U.S. Office of Education, Cooperative Research Monograph OE-35016 (1960).

G3 ———, *Creativity and Intelligence*. New York: John Wiley & Sons, Inc., 1962.

G4 GOLDBERG, Miriam, *Adapting Teacher Style to Pupil Differences*. New York: Teachers College, Columbia University, March, 1963. Mimeographed.

G5 GOLDIN, Judah, *The Living Talmud*. New York: New American Library of World Literature, Inc., 1957.

[G6] GRAY, S. William (Editor), *Before We Read.* Chicago: Scott, Foresman & Company, 1951.

[G7] ———, *The New Friends and Neighbors.* Chicago: Scott, Foresman & Company, 1952.

[G8] GUILFORD, J. P., *A Revised Structure of Intellect.* Los Angeles: Reports from the Psychological Laboratory, No. 19, University of Southern California, April 1957.

[H1] HANNA, Lavone, POTTER, Gladys, and HAGAMAN, Neva, *Unit Teaching in the Elementary School.* New York: Holt, Rinehart, & Winston, Inc., 1963.

[H2] HARGRAVE, Rowena, *Building Reading Skills.* Wichita, Kansas: Mc-Cormick-Mathers Publishing Company, Inc., 1960.

[H3] HARRINGTON, Michael, *The Other America.* New York: The Macmillan Company, 1962.

[H4] HARRIS, Albert (Editor), *Readings on Reading Instruction.* New York: David McKay Co., Inc., 1963.

[H5] HAVIGHURST, Robert, and NEUGARTEN, Bernice, *Society and Education.* Boston: Allyn and Bacon, Inc., 1957.

[H6] HEATON, Margaret, *Feelings Are Facts.* New York: National Conference of Christians and Jews, 1952.

[H7] HEIL, M. Louis, POWELL, Marion, and KEIFER, Irwin, *Characteristics of Teacher Behavior Related to the Achievement of Children in Several Elementary Grades.* New York: Brooklyn College, 1960.

[H8] HENDRIX, Gertrude, "Learning by Discovery." *The Mathematics Teacher,* Vol. 54 (May, 1961).

[H9] HILDRETH, Gertrude, "Learning to Read with McGuffey." *Elementary School Journal,* LXII (April, 1962).

[H10] HILGARD, Ernest, *Theories of Learning.* New York: Appleton-Century-Crofts, 1948.

[H11] HOFFMAN, Banesh, "The Tyranny of Multiple-Choice Tests." *Harper's Magazine,* March, 1961.

[H12] HUGHES, Marie, *Assessment of the Quality of Teaching in Elementary Schools.* Salt Lake City, Utah: University of Utah Press, 1959.

[H13] HUNTER, Elizabeth, and AMIDON, Edmund, *Student Teaching: Cases and Comments.* New York: Holt, Rinehart & Winston, Inc., 1964.

[H14] HYMES, James, *Discipline.* New York: Teachers College, Bureau of Publications, Columbia University, 1962.

[J1] JAHODA, Marie, *Research Methods in Social Relations.* New York: The Dryden Press, 1951.

[J2] JAROLIMEK, John, *Social Studies in Elementary Education.* New York: The Macmillan Company, 1963.

J3 JEFFERSON, Blanche, *Teaching Art to Children.* Boston: Allyn and Bacon, Inc., 1959.

J4 JENNING, Helen Hall, *Sociometry in Group Relations.* Washington, D.C.: American Council on Education, 1959.

J5 JERSILD, Arthur T., *When Teachers Face Themselves.* New York: Teachers College, Bureau of Publications, Columbia University, 1955.

K1 KELLEY, Earl, *Education for What is Real.* New York: Harper & Row, Publishers, 1947.

K2 ———, *The Workshop Way of Learning.* New York: Harper & Row, Publishers, 1951.

K3 KENWORTHY, Leonard, "Ferment in the Social Studies." *Phi Delta Kappan,* October, 1962.

K4 ———, *Helping Boys and Girls to Understand Themselves and Others.* New York: Brooklyn College, 1964. Mimeographed.

K5 ———, *Introducing Children to the World.* New York: Harper and Brothers, 1956.

K6 KIEL, Norman, "The Myth of Fun." *The Journal of Educational Sociology.* September, 1961.

K7 KUBIE, Laurence S., "Education and the Process of Maturation," in *Today's Children are Tomorrow's World.* New York: Bank Street College of Education, 1957.

K8 ———, *Neurotic Disturbance and the Creative Process.* Lawrence, Kans.: University of Kansas Press, 1958.

K9 KUEHNE, Elizabeth, *Predicting Weather.* Rochester, New York: Graflex, Inc., 1963.

L1 LANSDOWN, Brenda, "Creating Mathematics." *Mathematics Teachers Journal,* Vol. X June 1960, No. 3.

L2 ———, "Orbiting a Science Program." *Science Education,* March, 1962.

L3 LEWIN, Kurt, "Field Theory and Learning." Forty-first Yearbook, Part II, National Society for the Study of Education, 1942.

L4 ———, "Principles of Re-Education" in Benne, Kenneth, *Human Relations in Curriculum Change.* New York: The Dryden Press, 1951.

L5 LEWIN, Kurt, and LIPPIT, Ronald, "Patterns of Aggressive Behavior in Experimentally Created Social Climates." *Journal of Social Psychology,* May, 1939.

L6 LINDQUIST, E. F., and HIERONYMUS, A. N., *Iowa Tests of Basic Skills.* Grades 3-9, Form 1. Boston: Houghton Mifflin Company, 1955.

L7 LIPPIT, Ronald, *Training in Community Relations.* New York: Harper and Brothers, 1949.

L8 LOWENFELD, Victor, *Creative and Mental Growth*. New York: The Macmillan Company, 1957.

M1 MACKINNON, D. W., "Identifying and Developing Creativity." Berkeley: University of California Press, May, 1959. Mimeographed.

M2 MAIMONIDES, Moses, *Guide for the Perplexed*. New York: Dover Publications, Inc., 1956.

M3 MASLOW, A. H., "Defense and Growth." *Merril Palmer Quarterly*, 3:37-38, (1956).

M4 MAYER, Martin, *The Schools*. New York: Doubleday & Company, Inc., 1963.

M5 ———, *Where, When and Why*. New York: Harper & Row, Publishers, 1963.

M6 McCRACKEN, Glenn, and WALCUT, Charles, *Basic Reading*. Philadelphia: J. B. Lippincott Co., 1962.

M7 McGUFFEY, William Holmes, *McGuffey's Fifth Eclectic Reader*. 1879 Edition. New York: New American Library of World Literature, Inc., 1962.

M8 McKEE, Paul, *The Teaching of Reading in the Elementary School*. Boston: Houghton Mifflin Company, 1948.

M9 ——— (Editor), *Getting Ready*. Boston: Houghton Mifflin Company, 1949.

M10 ——— (Editor), *Tip and Big Book*. Boston: Houghton Mifflin Company, 1949.

M11 MEAD, Margaret, *The Schools in American Culture*. Cambridge: Harvard University Press, 1951.

M12 MEARNS, Hughes, *Creative Power*. New York: Dover Publications, Inc., 1958.

M13 MICHAELIS, John, *Social Studies for Children in a Democracy*. Englewood Cliffs, N.J.: Prentice-Hall, Inc., 1963.

M14 MIEL, Alice, *Changing the Curriculum*. New York: Appleton-Century-Crofts, 1946.

M15 ——— (Editor), *Creativity in Teaching*. Belmont, Calif., Wadsworth Publishing Co., Inc., 1961.

M16 ——— (Editor), *Individualized Reading Practices*. New York: Teachers College, Bureau of Publications, Columbia University, 1958.

M17 MIEL, Alice, and BROGAN, Peggy, *More Than Social Studies: A View of Social Learning in the Elementary School*. New Jersey: Englewood Cliffs, N.J.: Prentice-Hall, Inc., 1957.

M18 MILNER, Ernst, *You and Your Student Teacher*. New York: Teachers College, Bureau of Publications, Columbia University, 1961.

M9 MILNER, Esther, "A Study of the Relationships Between Reading Readiness in Grade 1 School Children and Patterns of Parent-Child Interaction." *Child Development*, Vol. 22, 1951.

M20 MORSE, Arthur, *Schools of Tomorrow Today*. New York: Doubleday & Company, Inc., 1960.

N1 NASS, Martin, "Characteristics of a Psychotherapeutically Oriented Group for Beginning Teachers." *Mental Hygiene*, Vol. 43 (October, 1959), No. 4.

N2 National Council for the Social Studies, *A Guide to Contents in the Social Studies*. Washington, D.C.: National Education Association, 1957.

N3 NAVARRA, J. Gabriel, and ZAFFORONI, Joseph, *Science Today for the Elementary School Teacher*. New York: Harper & Row, Publishers, 1963.

N4 NELSON, Henry B. (Editor), *Rethinking Science Education*. Part I. National Society for the Study of Education, 1960.

O1 O'DONNEL, Mabel, *Guidebook for Runaway Home*. Basic Sixth Reader, The Alice and Jerry Basic Reading Program. Illinois: Harper & Row, Publishers, 1957.

O2 OLSEN, G. Edward, *School and Community*. Englewood Cliffs, N.J.: Prentice-Hall, Inc., 1945.

P1 PACKARD, Vance, *The Waste Makers*. New York: Pocket Books, Inc., 1963.

P2 PAGE, David, *Arithmetic With Frames*. Urbana, Ill.: The University of Illinois Arithmetic Project, 1957.

P3 PARKER, Don, *Teacher's Handbook, S.R.A.* Chicago: Science Research Associates, Inc., 1958.

P4 PASSOW, Harry (Editor), *Curriculum Crossroads*. New York: Teachers College, Bureau of Publications, Columbia University, 1962.

P5 ——— (Editor), *Education in Depressed Areas*. New York: Teachers College, Bureau of Publications, Columbia University, 1963.

P6 PITMAN, James, *I.T.A. Bulletin*. Spring 1963. New York: Pitman Publishing Corp.

P7 PRESCOTT, Daniel, *Helping Teachers Understand Children*. Washington, D.C.: American Council on Education, 1945.

P8 PUGH, Griffith, *Guide to Research Writing*. Boston: Houghton Mifflin Company, 1963.

R1 REDL, Fritz, and WATTENBERG, William, *Mental Hygiene in Teaching*. New York: Harcourt, Brace & World, Inc., 1951.

R2 RIESMAN, David, *The Lonely Crowd*. New York: Doubleday & Company, Inc., 1953.

R3 RIESSMAN, Frank, *The Culturally Deprived Child*. New York: Harper & Row, Publishers, 1962.

R4 ROSENZWEIG, E. Louis, *On Teachers and Teaching*. New York: Brooklyn College, January, 1964. Mimeographed.

R5 ———— *The Slow Learner*. New York: Brooklyn College, March, 1964. Mimeographed.

R6 ROUCEK, Joseph, *The Difficult Child*. New York: Philosophical Library, 1964.

R7 RUSSEL, David, *Children Learn to Read*. Boston: Ginn & Company, 1961.

R8 ————, *Children's Thinking*. Boston: Ginn & Company, 1956.

S1 SARASON, Seymour, DAVIDSON, Kenneth, and BLATT, Burton, *The Preparation of Teachers*. New York: John Wiley & Sons, Inc., 1962.

S2 SCHACHTEL, Ernest, *Metamorphosis*. New York: Basic Books, Inc., Publishers, 1959.

S3 SCOTT, Cecil W., and others (Editors), *Great Debate: Our Schools in Crisis*. Englewood Cliffs, N. J.: Prentice-Hall, Inc., 1959.

S4 SHAFTEL, George and Fannie, *Role Playing the Problem Story*. New York: National Conference of Christians and Jews, 1952.

S5 SHEEHY, D. Emma, *Children Discover Music and Dance*. New York: Holt, Rinehart & Winston, Inc., 1959.

S6 SHUMSKY, Abraham, *The Action Research Way of Learning*. New York: Teachers College, Bureau of Publications, Columbia University, 1958.

S7 ————, *The Clash of Cultures in Israel*. New York: Teachers College, Bureau of Publications, Columbia University, 1955.

S8 ————, "The Personal Significance of an Action Research Problem to Teachers." *The Journal of Teacher Education*, June, 1958.

S9 SHUMSKY, Abraham, and MURRAY, Walter, "Student Teachers Explore Discipline." *The Journal of Teacher Education*, December, 1961.

S10 SHUMSKY, Adaia, *Social Orientation and Intellectual Approach*. New York: The Great Neck School System, 1964. Mimeographed.

S11 SMITH, Nila, *Reading Instruction for Today's Children*. Englewood Cliffs, N.J.: Prentice-Hall, Inc., 1963.

S12 ———— (Editor), *Beyond the Horizon*. Columbus, Ohio: Charles E. Merril Books, Inc., 1960.

S13 SMITH, Othanel, STANLEY, William, and SHORES, Harlan, *Fundamental of Curriculum Development*. New York: World Book Company, 1950.

s14 SNYGG, D. and COMBS, A. W., *Individual Behavior*. New York: Harper & Row, Publishers, 1949.

s15 SPOONER, George, *Mathematics Enrichment*. New York: Harcourt, Brace & World, Inc., 1962.

s16 ———, *What About Modern Mathematics?* New York: Harcourt, Brace & World, Inc., 1962.

s17 STAHL, Stanley, "Methods in Teaching." *The Journal of Teacher Education*, December, 1961.

s18 STENDLER, Celia, *Teaching in the Elementary School*. New York: Harcourt, Brace & World, Inc., 1958.

s19 STERLING, Edna, *English Is Our Language*. Boston: D. C. Heath & Company, 1957.

s20 STOFFER, G. A., "Behavior Problems of Children as Viewed by Teachers and Mental Hygienists." *Mental Hygiene*, Vol. 36 (1952).

s21 STRATEMEYER, Florence, and LINDSEY, Margaret, *Working with Student Teachers*. New York: Teachers College, Bureau of Publications, Columbia University, 1958.

s22 SUPPES, Patrick, *Sets and Numbers*. New York: The L. W. Singer Company, Inc., 1962.

s23 SUZUKI, D. T., *Zen Buddhism*. New York: Doubleday & Company, Inc., 1956.

T1 TABA, Hilda, *Reading Ladders for Human Relations*. Washington, D. C.: American Council on Education, 1947.

T2 TAYLOR, Calvin, "A Tentative Description of the Creative Individual," in *Human Variability and Learning*. ASCD, 1961.

T3 TERMAN, Lewis, and MERRIL, Maud, *Measuring Intelligence*. Boston: Houghton Mifflin Company, 1937.

T4 TORRANCE, E. Paul, *Education and the Creative Potential*. Minneapolis, Minn.: The University of Minnesota Press, 1963.

T5 ———, *Guiding Creative Talent*. Englewood Cliffs, N.J.: Prentice-Hall, Inc., 1962.

T6 TRACE, Arthur, *What Ivan Knows that Johnny Doesn't*. New York: Random House, Inc., 1961.

T7 TRAVERS, R., and RABINOWITZ, W., *Exploratory Studies in Teacher Personality*. New York: Division of Teacher Education, The City College of New York, 1953.

T8 TROW, William Clark, *Teacher and Technology*. New York: Appleton-Century-Crofts, 1963.

T9 Tulare County Social Studies, *A Study in Comparative Communities*. Tulare County Schools, Visalia, California.

V1 VAN TIL, William, "Better Curriculum—Better Discipline." *N.E.A. Journal*, September, 1956.

V2 ———, "Is Progressive Education Obsolete?" *Saturday Review*, February 17, 1962.

W1 WANN, D. Kenneth, DORN, Miriam, and LIDDLE, Elizabeth, *Fostering Intellectual Development in Young Children*. New York: Teachers College, Bureau of Publications, Columbia University, 1962.

W2 WATKINS, Don, *Prospective Teachers, Minority Group Children, and Teaching*. New York: Brooklyn College, 1964. Mimeographed.

W3 WEINER, Max, and MURRAY, Walter, "Another Look at the Culturally Deprived and Their Level of Aspiration." *The Journal of Educational Sociology*, March, 1963.

W4 WEISS, Robert, and RASSMUSSEN, Glen, "Grading Practices in Undergraduate Education Courses." *Journal of Higher Education*, December, 1959.

W5 WICKMAN, E. K., *Chilidren's Behavior and Teachers' Attitudes*. New York: Commonwealth Fund, 1928.

W6 WIGGINS, Sam P., *The Student Teacher in Action*. Boston: Allyn and Bacon, Inc., 1957.

W7 WILES, Kimball, *Teaching for Better Schools*. Englewood Cliffs, N.J.: Prentice-Hall, Inc., 1959.

W8 WILT, E. Miriam, *Creativity in the Elementary School*. New York: Appleton-Century-Crofts, 1959.

W9 WOOD, Anne Helen, *Science Teaching*. New York: Brooklyn College, 1964. Mimeographed.

INDEX